RETURN TO YESTERDAY

RETURN
TO YESTERDAY

FORD MADOX FORD

LIVERIGHT · NEW YORK

ISBN: 0-87140-563-6 (cloth)
ISBN: 0-87140-080-4 (paper)
Library of Congress Catalog Card Number: 32-26052

LIVERIGHT PAPERBOUND EDITION 1972

1.987654321

Manufactured in the United States of America

CONTENTS

PART ONE
LANDSCAPES AND LETTERS

i. COMPOSTELLA AMERICANA   13

ii. PERSONAE   26

iii. THE OUTER WORLD   40

iv. RE-AGENTS   58

PART TWO
LETTERS AND THE LEFT

i. IN DARKEST LONDON   75

ii. FARTHEST LEFT   92

iii. THE OUTSIDE   115

PART THREE
THE HEART OF THE COUNTRY

i. CABBAGES AND QUEENS   139

ii. PURE LETTERS   167

III. WORKING WITH CONRAD   186

IV. RYE ROAD   202

PART FOUR
THE BL——Y WORLD

I. COMPANIES AND KINGS   221

II. "LET US TAKE A WALK DOWN FLEET STREET!" 235

III. SOME CURES   261

IV. INTO DEPTHS   282

V. GOTHAM   304

PART FIVE
THE LAST OF LONDON

I. REVUES   343

II. REVIEWS   372

CODA   399

PART ONE

LANDSCAPES AND LETTERS

CHAPTER I

COMPOSTELLA AMERICANA

THINKING of Henry James the other day I was led to wonder when I first went to the Antient Town of Rye. Rye is not a Cinque Port but one of the two *antiquiora membra* of the honourable Corporation, the other being Winchelsea. Thirty years ago or so Henry James lived at Rye. I had a house at Winchelsea.

Still thinking and walking up and down in the tall room of a friend in Greenwich Village I looked at a bookshelf, then took out a dullish-backed book at random. At the bottom of a page were the words:

"So you see, darling, there is really no fear, because, as long as I know you care for me and I care for you, nothing can touch me."

I had a singular emotion. I was eighteen when I first read those words. My train was running into Rye station and I had knocked out the ashes of my first pipe of shag tobacco. Shag was the very cheapest, blackest and strongest of tobaccos in England of those days. I was therefore economising. My first book had just been published. I was going courting. My book had earned ten pounds. I desired to be a subaltern in H.B.M.'s Army. The story was Mr. Kipling's "Only a Subaltern." The next station would be Winchelsea, where I was to descend. I had given nine of the ten pounds to my mother. If I was to marry and become a subaltern, I must needs smoke

13

shag. And in a short clay pipe, to give the fullest effect to retrenchment! Briars were then eighteen pence, short clays two for a penny.

That is my oldest literary recollection.

It is one of my most vivid. More plainly than the long curtains of the room in which I am writing, I see now the browning bowl of my pipe, the singularly fine grey ashes, the bright placards as the train runs into the old-fashioned station and the roughness of the paper on which there appeared the words . . .

So you see, darling, there is really no fear . . .

I suppose they are words that we all write one day or another. Perhaps they are the best we ever write.

The fascicle of Kipling stories had a blue-grey paper cover that shewed in black a fierce, whiskered and turbaned *syce* of the Indian Army. I suppose he was a *syce,* for he so comes back to me. At any rate, that cover and that Mohammedan were the most familiar of objects in English homes of that day. You have no idea how exciting it was in those days to be eighteen and to be meditating, writing for the first time *there is really no fear* . . . And to know that those blue-grey booklets were pouring from the press and all England buzzing about them. Alas . . .

The whole of England has never since buzzed over a book or a writer. I daresay it never will. Those were proud times for England!

Years after—fifteen, I daresay—I was going up the narrow cobbled streets that led to the Master's house at the top of the pyramidal town when I met Mr. and Mrs. Kipling hurrying down. They appeared to be perturbed.

Conrad and I had gone in from Winchelsea to Rye to hire a motor-car. We must have sold something. In those days the automobile was a rapturous novelty, and when we had any buckshee money at all it went in hiring cars. It would cost about six pounds to go eighteen miles with seventeen breakdowns and ourselves pushing the car up most inclines.

Conrad had a passion for engineering details that I did not share, and he had gone in search of a car as to which he had heard that it had some mechanical innovation which he desired to inspect. I knocked, therefore, on the door of Lamb House, alone.

Lamb House was a majestic Georgian building of the type that Henry James had gone to England more especially to seek. Its best front gave on the garden. The garden had an immense smooth lawn and was shut in by grey stone walls against which grew perennial flowers. It contained also a massively built white-panelled pavilion. In that, during the summer at least, the Master usually sat and worked.

In Rye Church you could see the remains of a criminal hung in chains. It is that of a murderer, a butcher, who set out to kill a Mr. Lamb and killed a Mr. Greville. Or it may have been the other way round. Rye Town was prouder of its murderer than of its two literary lights—Fletcher and Henry James—but the murderer always seemed to me to have been a clumsy fellow. Lamb House had belonged to the family of the gentleman who was—or wasn't—killed. But Henry James gloated most over the other legend, according to which the house had been occupied by a mistress of George IV. The king, sailing down channel on a battleship, was said to have been rowed ashore to visit the lady in the garden pavilion. I always used to wonder at the prodigious number of caps, gloves, canes and hats that were arranged on a table—or it may have been a great chest—in the hall. How, I used to say to myself, can he need so prodigious a number of head-coverings? And I would wonder what thoughts revolved in his head whilst he selected the cap or the stick of the day. I never myself possessed more than one cloth cap at a time.

When I was admitted into his presence by the astonishingly ornate man-servant, he said:

"A writer who unites—if I may use the phrase—in his own person an enviable popularity to—as I am told—considerable literary gifts and whom I may say I like because he treats me—" and here Mr. James laid his hand over his ear, made the slightest of bows and, rather cruelly rolling his dark and liquid eyes and moving his lower jaw as if he were revolving in his mouth a piquant titbit—Mr. James continued, "because he treats me—if again I may say any such thing—with proper respect." And there would be an immense humorous gasp before the word "respect," " . . . I refer of course to Mr. Kipling . . . has just been to see me. And—such are the rewards of an enviable popularity!—a popularity such as I—or indeed you, my young friend, if you have any ambitions which I sometimes doubt—could ever dream of, far less imagine to ourselves—such are the rewards of an enviable popularity that Mr. Kipling is in the possession of a magnificent one thousand two hundred guinea motor-car. And, in the course of conversation as to characteristics of motor-cars in general and those of the particular one thousand two hundred guinea motor-car in the possession of our friend. . . . But what do I say? . . . Of our cynosure! Mr. Kipling uttered words which have for himself no doubt a particular significance but which to me at least convey almost literally nothing beyond their immediate sound . . . Mr. Kipling said that the motor-car was calculated to make the Englishman . . ." and again came the humorous gasp and the roll of the eyes . . . "was calculated to make the Englishman . . . think." And Mr. James abandoned himself for part of a second to low chuckling. "And," he continued, "the conversation dissolved itself, after digressions on the advantages attendant on the possession of such a vehicle into what I believe are styled golden dreams—such as how the magnificent one thousand two hundred guinea motor-car after having this evening conveyed its master and mistress to Batemans Burwash, of which the proper pronunciation is Burridge, would tomorrow devotedly return here and reaching here at twelve would convey me and my nephew William to Burridge in time to lunch, and having partaken of that repast to return here in time to give tea to my friend Lady Maud Warrender who is honouring that humble meal with her presence tomorrow under my roof. . . . And we were all indulging in—what is it?—delightful anticipations and dilating on the agreeableness of rapid—but not, for fear of the police and consideration for one's personal safety, *too* rapid—speed over country roads and all, if I may use the expression, was gas and gingerbread when . . . There is a loud knocking on the door and—*avec des yeux effarés* . . ." and here Mr. James really did make his prominent and noticeable eyes almost stick out of his head . . . "in rushes the chauffeur. . . . And in short the chauffeur has omitted to lubricate the wheels of the magnificent one thousand two hundred guinea motor-car with the result that its axles have become one piece of molten metal. . . . The consequence is that its master and mistress will return to Burwash, which should be pronounced Burridge, by train and the magnificent one thousand two hundred guinea motor-car will *not* devotedly return here at noon and will *not* in time for lunch convey me and my nephew William to Burwash and will *not* return here in time for me to give tea to my friend Lady Maud Warrender who is honouring that humble meal with her presence tomorrow beneath my roof or if the weather is fine in the garden. . . ."

"Which," concluded the Master, after subdued ho, ho, hos of merriment, "is calculated to make Mr. Kipling think."

"Rye," say the women of Kent, "is the sinkhole of Sussex and Sussex is the sinkhole of England." That is because Rye was once a great mercantile and naval port and Sussex a great maritime county. The men from adjacent Kent, as is the case with men from the hinterlands of Hongkong or San Francisco or Aden or Cardiff, would go into Rye and get among the bad gels, Saturday nights. They also counselled their daughters: "Ye see yon man, 'a cooms from Soossex, 'a sucked in silliness with his mother's milk and's been silly ever since. But never you trust a man from the Sheeres!" The Sheeres are the Shires—all the rest of England—Hampshire, Wiltshire, Devonshire, Buckinghamshire, Shropshire. So it is Kent and Sussex against the Rest, as cricketers say.

It is a great attraction to strangers and foreign settlers

when places have these dominant rivalries. You feel really settled when you can despise a neighbouring city, and James, living at Lamb House, Rye, Sussex, was infinitely a Sussex man when he met that true man of Kent, Joseph Conrad Korzeniowski who lived at Pent Farm, Postling, Kent. In just the same way he was inordinately a Rye man two miles away in Winchelsea. I can still see his sturdy form as arrayed in a peajacket which nobly enhanced his bulk, wearing one of his innumerable cricket caps, emphasising his steps and the cadences of his conversation by digging his cane into the road, he stumped under the arch of the sea-gate up the hill into Winchelsea, lugging behind him on a ten-yard leather lead his highly varnished dachshund, Maximilian. The dog would gyrate round his master. Mr. James would roll his eyes; he would be slightly out of breath. There would be a gentle snifter of rain; he only, for reasons I will later explain, came to Winchelsea in the late autumn and winter. In that great square, round the great half-fallen church, the rain would run in light drifts. He would dig his cane point into the grass between the cobbles and exclaim: "A Winchelsea day, my dear lady. A true Winchelsea day.... This is Winchelsea.... Poor but proud." Waspishly patriotic we would point to the red-roofed pyramid across the marsh and exclaim:

"That's your Rye. It's *pouring* there.... Rye.... Not rich but dirty."

These were the only occasions on which we stood up to the Master. And he never heard. He would scuttle off towards tea, dragged forward by Maximilian who scented the little hot buttered tea-cakes, called "fat rascals."

We would have tea in a frame house. It might have been Canaan, New Hampshire. The house had been built in 1782 by General Prescott, the first Governor-General of Canada.... In exact imitation of a Canadian frame-house, just as the "fat rascals" were exactly like the little hot biscuits you get in farmhouses, now, in Tennessee. The General had been homesick for Canada.

Winchelsea had that North-American feature. It had others. The streets were all rectangular, like those of New York, and the houses in blocks. That was because it had been built all of a piece by Edward III in 1333. He had planned it, ruling squares on a sheet of vellum, after the sea had drowned Old Winchelsea on the flats below. It is exhilarating to stand in the heart of a town and gaze out into the country. I have felt the same exhilaration in both Winchelsea and New York. In New York it is fascinating to be able, on Fifth Avenue, to see, on the one side the Palisades, and on the other, the cross street giving a view of the sky above the East River. In Winchelsea, standing in the heart of the town, you could see on the one hand the green heights of Udimore, on the other, the marsh and the sea, and before your face, where the broad street ended in nothing, the red pyramid of Rye with its flashing weathercock a-top.

In the church were pews built of wood brought back from Plymouth by the *Mayflower*. That is the story. The wood was said to be tulip wood. Certainly it was no local wood, and I found on going to New York and seeing the tulip-wood panels of the offices of the S. S. McClure Co. in East Twenty-third Street that those panels much resembled the wood. That would be in 1906. Someone told me the other day that tulip wood is too soft for interior decorations, but in Sam McClure's office it was very pretty. The softer body of the wood had, I believe, been burnt out, leaving hard, as it were, lace-patterns like the fibres of skeleton leaves. The wood of the pews had the same lacy ridges. It is said that the mariners of the *Mayflower* had brought the timber back from the New England woods as souvenirs. When I lived in Winchelsea, the wood was rapidly going back—to New England, Missouri, Wisconsin, Seattle, Spokane, and Winchelsea, Mass. In addition, a dim-sighted early Victorian rector—the same who had the fourteenth-century stained glass broken out of the windows because it prevented his reading the words of *Lead Kindly Light*—had had most of the pews removed from the chancel to make way for deal missionary-chairs. So between the purblind ecclesiastic and the sharp penknives of the souvenir hunters remembrances of Plymouth were waning in the Antient Town.

There were, however, a number of Plymouth Brothers there. They used to pray for my conversion—from literary pursuits. It was queer, of a Sunday afternoon, to hear oneself prayed for by name.

I cannot now remember whether I met Henry James before Conrad, but I think I did. I remember, at any rate, that I felt much younger when I at last went to see him than I did when Conrad first came to see me. I was in those days of an extreme shyness and the aspect of the Master, bearded as he was then and wearing, as he habitually did in those days, a great ulster and a square felt hat, was not one to dissipate that youthful attribute. I must have been seeing him in the streets of Rye on and off for eighteen months after Mrs. W. K. Clifford had asked me to go and see him. The final pressure put on to do so had by then become considerable.

The adoration for Henry James amongst his relatively few admirers of those days was wonderful—and deserved. And I imagine that his most fervent adorers were the Garnett family, of whom the best known member is today Mr. Edward Garnett, the publisher's reader who first advised a publisher to publish Conrad. In those days it was Dr. Richard Garnett whose reputation as Principal Librarian of the British Museum was world-wide. He had a number of sons and daughters and, for a long time, I was in and out of the Garnetts' house in the Museum courtyard every day and all day long. Their hospitality was as boundless as it was beneficent.

The public opinion, as it were, of the younger Garnetts must have had a great effect in shaping my young mind. In one form or other it made for virtue always—in some members for virtue of an advanced and unconventional type, in others for the virtues that are inseparable from, let us say, the

Anglican communion. The elder Garnetts at any rate had a strong aversion from Catholicism.

Mrs. W. K. Clifford, a by no means unskilful novelist of those days, had put pressure upon me to go and see James. She was, I think, his most intimate friend. He corrected the manuscripts of almost all the books of Mrs. Humphry Ward, an act of great generosity. Of Mrs. Ward he always spoke as "poor dear Mary," with a slightly sardonic intonation. But I remember his saying several times that he had respectful, if he might so call it, affection for Mrs. Clifford. Therefore, when the Master, for reasons of a rather painful disillusionment, decided to leave London almost for good, Mrs. Clifford was greatly concerned for his health and peace of mind. She urged me very frequently to go and see him, so that she might be posted as to his well- or ill-being. I remained too shy.

Then, hearing that James was almost permanently fixed at Rye, the young Garnetts, who knew that I paid frequent visits to the next-door town, began to press me in their turn to call on their cynosure. Their admiration for him was so great that merely to know someone who knew the Master would, it appeared, ease their yearnings. They admired him above all for his virtue. None of his books so much as adumbrated an unworthy sentiment in their composer; every line breathed of comprehension and love for virtue.

For myself, I disliked virtue, particularly when it was pressed between the leaves of a book. I doubt if, at that date, when I was twenty-three or -four, I had read anything of his and the admiration that was wildly showered from Bloomsbury in the direction of Rye made me rather stubbornly determined not to do so for some time. I daresay I was not a very agreeable young man. But unbounded admiration quite frequently renders its object disagreeable to outsiders. Boswell must have alienated quite a number of persons from Johnson, and I have known a great many distinguished figures who would have been better off without surroundings of awed disciples who hushed roomfuls when the genius gave signs of desiring to speak. James suffered a great deal from his surroundings.

My resistance broke down eventually with some suddenness. James, who was always mindful of his health, had written a distressing letter to Mrs. Clifford—about his eyes, I think. Mrs. Clifford had influenza. She sent me three telegrams the same day begging me to go see the Master and report to her. I sent him a note to ask if I could visit him, mentioning that Mrs. Clifford desired it.

I do not imagine that Mr. James had the least idea what I was, and I do not think that, till the end of his days, he regarded me as a serious writer. That in spite of the fact that subsequently during whole winters we met almost daily and he consulted me about his most intimate practical affairs with a touching trustfulness in my *savoir faire* and confidence in my discretion. He was, however, cognisant of my ancestry and of the members of my grandfather's and father's circles. These he much disliked. He thought them Bohemian. I, on the other hand, considered myself as belonging, by right of birth, to the governing classes of the literary and artistic worlds.

I do not mean to say that I talked about my distinguished relatives, connections or family intimates. But I am now conscious that I acted and spoke to others as if my birth permitted me to meet them as equals. Except for the king and my colonel on parade, I do not know that I ever spoke to anyone except on that basis. On the other hand, I never spoke even to a charwoman on any other. I have, however, always had a great respect for age, if accompanied with exceptional powers.

I certainly felt not infrequently something like awe in the presence of James. To anyone not a fool his must be a commanding figure. He had great virility, energy, persistence, dignity and an astonishing keenness of observation. And upon the whole he was the most masterful man I have ever met.

On that first occasion he was bearded, composed and magisterial. He had taken the house of the vicar, furnished, and had brought down his staff of servants from de Vere

Gardens. At lunch he was waited on by his fantastic butler. The fellow had a rubicund face, a bulbous red nose, a considerable paunch and a cutaway. Subsequently he was to become matter for very serious perturbations to his master.

His methods of service were startling. He seemed to produce silver *entrée* dishes from his coat-tails, wave them circularly in the air and arrest them within an inch of your top waistcoat button. At each such presentation James would exclaim with cold distaste: "I have told you not to do that!" and the butler would retire to stand before the considerable array of plate that decorated the sideboard. His method of service was purely automatic. If he thought hard about it he could serve you without flourishes. But if his thoughts were elsewhere, the flourishes would return. He had learnt so to serve at the table of Earl Somebody—Brownlow, I think.

At any rate, James seemed singularly at home where he was. He was well-off for a bachelor of those days, when £400 a year was sufficient for the luxurious support of a man about town. You might have thought that he was in his ancestral home, the home itself one of some elegance in the Chippendale-Sheraton-Gainsborough fashion. He had the air of one of the bearded elder-brother statesmen of the court of Victoria; his speech was slow and deliberate; his sentences hardly at all involved. I did not then gather anything about the state of his eyes.

He was magisterial in the manner of a police-magistrate, civil but determined to receive true answers to his questions. The whole meal was one long questionnaire. He demanded particulars as to my age, means of support, establishment, occupations, tastes in books, food, music, painting, scenery, politics. He sat sideways to me across the corner of the dining table, letting drop question after question. The answers he received with no show at all of either satisfaction or reproof.

After the meal he let himself go in a singularly vivid display of dislike for the persons rather than the works of my family's circle. For my grandfather, Ford Madox Brown, and for my father he expressed a perhaps feigned deference. They were at least staid and sober men, much such as Mr. James affected and believed himself to be. Then he let himself go as to D. G. Rossetti, William Morris, Swinburne, my uncle William Rossetti, Holman Hunt, the painter of the *Light of the World,* Watts-Dunton and all the rest of the Pre-Raphaelite circle. D. G. Rossetti he regarded with a sort of shuddering indignation such as that he devoted, subsequently, to Flaubert —and for much the same reason. When he had called on Rossetti, the painter had received him in his studio, wearing the garment in which he painted, which James took to be a dressing-gown. It was a long coat, without revers, like a clergyman's and had extremely deep vertical pockets. These Rossetti used for the keeping of his paint rags.

For Mr. James the wearing of a dressing-gown implied a moral obloquy that might end—who knows where? And he deduced from the fact that Rossetti received him at tea-time in what he took to be such a garment that he was disgusting in his habits, never took baths and was insupportably lecherous. He repeated George Meredith's account of the masses of greasy ham and bleeding eggs which Rossetti devoured at breakfast.

He mimicked the voice and movements of Swinburne with gusto. He let his voice soar to a real falsetto and jerked his body sideways on his chair extending his hands rigidly towards the floor below his hips. He declared that Swinburne's verse in its flood and noxiousness was only commensurate with the floods of bad chianti and gin that the poet consumed. He refused to believe that Swinburne in those days, under the surveillance of Watts-Dunton, drank no more than two half pints of beer a day. And he particularly refused to believe that Swinburne could swim. Yet Swinburne was one of the strongest salt-water swimmers of his day. One of Maupassant's *contes* tells how Swinburne's head with its features and hair of a Greek god rose from the sea beside the French writer's boat three miles out in the Mediterranean and how it began glorious to converse. And so conversing, Swinburne had swam

beside the boat to the shore. No doubt Maupassant had his
share of a poet's imagination. But Swinburne certainly could
swim. He was also a remarkably expert skater.

My uncle William Rossetti Mr. James considered to be an
unbelievable bore. He had once heard the Secretary to the
Inland Revenue recount how he had seen George Eliot proposed to by Herbert Spencer on the leads of the terrace at
Somerset House.... The Inland Revenue headquarters is
housed in that building and the philosopher and the novelist
were permitted by the authorities there to walk as a special
privilege.

"You would think," Mr. James exclaimed with indignation, his dark eyes really flashing, "that a man would make
something out of a story like *that*: But the way he told it was
like this," and heightening and thinning his tones into a sort
of querulous official organ Mr. James quoted: " 'I have as a
matter of fact frequently meditated on the motives which
induced the Lady's refusal of one so distinguished; and after
mature consideration I have arrived at the conclusion that
although Mr. Spencer with correctness went down upon one
knee and grasped the Lady's hand he completely omitted the
ceremony of removing his high hat, a proceeding which her
sense of the occasion might have demanded....' Is that," Mr.
James concluded, "the way to tell *that* story?"

I did not again see Mr. James, except in Mrs. Clifford's
drawing-room for several years. Then, when I had settled into
residence in General Prescott's frame house, I went to see him
with Conrad, when we went to hire the automobile.

CHAPTER II

PERSONAE

W<small>INCHELSEA</small> stands on a long bluff, in shape like that of Gibraltar. Two miles of marsh separate it from Rye. Once it was sea where the marsh now is; one day it will be so again. When it was sea all the navies of England would ride in that harbour. And the Five Ports and the two Antient Towns provided all the navies of the King of England, as against certain privileges. A Baron of the Cinque Ports can still drive through all toll-gates without payment and sell in all markets toll-free.

In the face of the cliff that Winchelsea turns to Rye there is a spring forming a dip—St. Leonard's Well, or the Wishing Well. The saying is that once you have drunk of those dark waters you will never rest until you drink again. I have seen— indeed I have induced them to it—three Americans, Henry James, Stephen Crane and W. H. Hudson drink there from the hollows of their hands. So did Conrad. They are all dead now.

It was perhaps those waters that induced their frequentations of those two towns. But indeed there were sufficient other inducements. An historic patina covers their buildings more deeply than any others, in England at least. Indeed, I know of no place save for Paris, where memories seem so thick on every stone. The climate, too, is very mild. There is practically no day throughout the year on which a proper man cannot eat his meals under a south wall out of doors. Then, it is near France. On most days you can see the French cliffs. Once, by an effect of mirage, the city of Boulogne was brought so near to Hastings, which is next door to Rye, that the promenaders on the parade of the English town could discern the faces of the tourists inspecting the column of Napoleon on the Boulogne sward over the sea which Napoleon erected to celebrate his invasion of England. That was as near as anything of his which ever got to the coasts of the Five Ports.

At any rate, it is an infectious and holding neighbourhood. Once you go there you are apt there to stay. Or you will see in memory, the old walled towns, the red roofs, the grey stones, the country sweeping back in steps from the Channel to the North Downs, the great stretch of the Romney Marsh running out to Dungeness. In the Middle Ages they used to say: "These be the four quarters of the world: Europe, Asia, Africa and the Romney Marsh." But that was before Columbus committed his indiscretion. Hendrik Hudson drew many of his sailors from the Rye town. A Rye man was the first European to lose his life by an arrow in Manhattan—on the shores of the Hudson, I should imagine, beneath where Grant's grave is.

Gotham sent two men to spend their last years beside the Rother—the one Henry James, the other Stephen Crane. America sent to the Sussex countryside the writer who gave the world the most beautiful book that was ever written about English country. The book was *Nature in Downland*, the writer W. H. Hudson. Hudson was of pure New England blood. When he came to England in 1882 or thereabouts he was, he used to say, the first of his family to have visited that country for two hundred years and more.

At the date of my visit to James with Conrad, he had just been visited by Hudson for the first time. Hudson had been to see Conrad at the Pent, where I had been, and then me at Winchelsea where Conrad was. Hudson was stopping then at New Romney in the Marsh. For some reason or other he had not told us that he was going on to see James. Later he revealed to me that he had sensed that Conrad and I did not like James. He had thought that I might regard him as offending against the laws of hospitality if, immediately after taking a meal at my house, he should call upon a man I disliked. Hudson was at that date making a regular tour of the literary world, as he at other times for sedulous and immobile days would watch the nests of cuckoos or the colonies of rooks in bare trees. I remember once, near Broad Chalke in the great bare downs where he had his hide-hole, standing with him for half an hour at least watching a rookery. It was all alone in the valley that formed a broad bowl in the chalk downs. Its peculiarity was that it stood alone: rooks always affect the society of men and practically never build in the open but in the shadow of great manor houses. Whilst we stood there he told in his slow, low, keen tones the story of a family who, having left one great manor, moved to another. At the second there were no rooks. Within a day there were rooks building in the great elms round the house and the rooks had deserted their nests in the old habitation to follow that family. He told that story as if he believed it. In the case of the rooks we were watching, the manor house had fallen down half a century before. He was interested to observe whether the inhabitants of houseless rookeries behaved exactly like those—in their parliaments, conclaves, penalties and executions—whose nests were near the stables of great, red brick houses. He spent hours watching the rookery at Wilton, then returned to the one at Broad Chalke, and so on for weeks.

At the date of which I am speaking—in the last year of the last century—he had before him the problem of whether or no he himself was a writer. He had always considered himself a naturalist. Now he was conscious that he was regarded as a great writer by a great many writers. He had therefore—just as in the case of the rooks—set out to observe writers, visiting James, Conrad, Crane, round Rye and, I believe, Mr. H. G. Wells, Mr. Kipling and the Poet Laureate—then Sir Alfred Austin, who lived as it were in a patriotically protective ring round that settlement of aliens.

That was, at any rate, the image that it presented. Some years ago my friend Mr. H. G. Wells wrote to the papers to say that for many years he was conscious of a ring of foreign conspirators plotting against British letters at no great distance from his residence, Spade House, Sandgate. I will draw a rough sketch map of that neighbourhood. It shows how judicious were Mr. Wells' views.

For indeed, those four men—three Americans and one Pole—lit in those days in England a beacon that posterity shall not easily let die. You have only got to consider how empty, how lacking a nucleus, English literature would today be if they had never lived, to see how discerning were Mr. Wells' views of that foreign penetration at the most vulnerable point of England's shores.

At that date Henry James was clean-shaven. As clean-shavenness was then comparatively rare he had in his relatively quiet moments the air of a divine; when, which was more frequent, he was animated, he was nearly always humorous and screwed his sensitive lips into amused or sardonic lines. Then he was like a comedian. His skin was dark, his face very clear cut, his brow domed and bare. His eyes were singularly penetrating, dark and a little prominent. On their account he was regarded by the neighbourhood poor as having the qualities of a Wise Man—a sorcerer. My servants used to say: "It always gives me a turn to open the door for Mr. James. His eyes seem to look you through to the very back-bone."

His vitality was amazing. You might put it that he was very seldom still and almost never silent. Occasionally when he desired information and you were giving him what he wanted he would sit gazing at you with his head leaning back against his grandfather's chair. But almost immediately he would be off with comment and elucidation—or with more questions accompanied by gestures, raising of the eyebrows and the humorous twisting of his lips. His peculiarities were carefully thought out by himself. A distinguished man in the fifties must have peculiarities if he has a strong personality.

His conversation used to contain a great many compliments to his interlocutor, male or female. They were the current coin of his conversation, learned in France and having no real significance but the fact that they were agreeable. Every woman from the Lady Maud Warrender on the hill to Meary Walker in the meshes was "dear lady"; every man, "my dear fellow." If you did or produced anything it was always admirable: "Your admirable verses, your admirable still lifes, tea-cakes, knowledge of stock-exchange operations, market gardening." It was agreeable when you were used to it but many people—and most Americans—it bewildered or repelled because of a supposed insincerity. Until you know a person well, it is perhaps not ethically better to say to him or to her *"Muy Hermosa Señora beso los manos de Usted,"* than to employ a universal "buddy" for social contacts. But it is not insincere.

On the other hand, if he liked or were intimate with you, his manner changed at once. You would not lack for censure, criticism or exhortations along with exactly calculated praise. He liked to live with people of leisure who were intellectually no wasters of time. At times he was unreasonably cruel—and that to the point of vindictiveness when his nerves were set on edge. I remember him at a tea party given by one of his most gentle and modest admirers. He was talking to the young man's equally gentle, modest and adoring wife. The young man interrupted him by several times offering him sugar, tea-cakes, cigars. The things that he at last spat out to that young man I will not repeat. He indicted his manners, his hospitality, his dwelling, his work, with a cold fury in voice and eyes.

I was once walking with him and Mr. John Galsworthy along the Rye Road to Winchelsea. His dachshund, Maximilian, ran sheep; so, not to curtail the animal's exercise, the master had provided it with a leash at least ten yards long. Mr. Galsworthy and I walked on each side of James, listening obediently whilst he talked. In order to round off an immense sentence, the great man halted, just under Winchelsea Hill beneath the windows of acquaintances of us all. He planted his stick firmly into the ground and went on and on and on. Maximilian passed between our six legs again and again, threading his leash behind him. Mr. Galsworthy and I stood silent. In any case we must have resembled the Laocoön, but when Maximilian had finished the resemblance must have been overwhelming. The Master finished his reflections, attempted to hurry on, found that impossible. Then we liberated ourselves with difficulty. He turned on me, his eyes fairly blazing, lifting his cane on high and slamming it into the ground:

"H ... !" he exclaimed, "you are painfully young, but at no more than the age to which you have attained, the playing of such tricks is an imbecility! An im ... be ... cility!"

The politeness of Conrad to James and of James to Conrad was of the most impressive kind. Even if they had been addressing each other from the tribune of the Académie Française their phrases could not have been more elaborate or delivered more *ore rotundo*. James always addressed Conrad as *"Mon cher confrère,"* Conrad almost bleated with the peculiar tones that the Marseillaises get into their compliments *"Mon cher maître."* ... Every thirty seconds! When James spoke of me to Conrad, he always said: *"Votre ami, le jeune homme modeste!"* They always spoke French together, James using an admirably pronounced, correct and rather stilted idiom such as prevailed in Paris of the seventies. Conrad spoke with extraordinary speed, fluency and some incomprehensibility, a meridional French with a strong Southern accent as that of garlic in *aioli*. ... I speak French with a strong British accent and much too correctly. When I was a boy my grandfather, who was French by birth and had a strong French tinge to his English, used to say to me: "Fordie, you must speak French with absolute correctness and without slang which would be an affectation, but with the strongest possible English accent, to show that you are an English gentleman." We talked in those days, with those distinctions of language, for many hours on end. Or, rather, I listened whilst they talked.

Conrad had the most unbounded, the most generous and the most understanding admiration for the Master's work but he did not much like James personally. I imagine that was because at bottom James was a New Englander *pur sang*, though he was actually born in the city where I am writing. James, on the other hand, liked neither Conrad nor his work very much, mostly, I imagine, because at bottom Conrad was a Pole, a Roman Catholic and romantic and Slav pessimist. It was hardly to be expected that James should like, say *Lord Jim*, for, though that may less appear to-day, the technique of Conrad's work was then singularly revolutionary. James, on the other hand, never made fun of Conrad in private. Conrad was never for him "poor dear old" as were Flaubert, Mrs. Humphry Ward, Meredith, Hardy or Sir Edmund Gosse. He once expressed to me, as regards Conrad, something like an immense respect for his character and achievements. I cannot remember his exact words, but they were something to the effect that Conrad's works impressed him very disagreeably, but he could find no technical fault or awkwardness about them. So that, since so many men whose judgment he affected regarded Conrad even then as a great master, he must not be taken as uttering any literary censure. . . .

The Conrad of those days was Romance. He was dark, black bearded, passionate in the extreme and at every minute; rather small but very broad shouldered and long in the arm. Speaking English he had so strong a French accent that few who did not know him well could understand him at first. His gestures were profuse and continuous, his politenesses Oriental and at times almost servile. Like James he would address a society lady, if he ever met one, or an old woman in the lane, or his own servants, or the hostler at an inn, or myself, who was for many years little more than his cook, slut and butler in literary matters, or Sir Sidney Colvin, or Sir Edmund Gosse, all with the same profusion of endearing adjectives. On the other hand, his furies would be sudden, violent, blasting and incomprehensible to his victims. At one of my afternoon parties

in London, he objurgated the unfortunate Charles Lewis Hinde
—a thin, slightly stuttering, nervous, dark fellow who was
noted as a critic, mostly of paintings. Hinde in a perfectly
sincere mood had congratulated him because his name was on
all the hoardings in London. Conrad's *Nostromo* was then
being serialised in a journal that gave the fact unusual prominence in its advertisements.

Conrad, on the other hand, despised the journal and himself for letting his work appear in it. His hatred of the publicity was as real as if it were an outrage on the honour of his
family. From the windows of my house his name was visible
on a hoarding that some house-breakers had erected—visible
in letters three feet long. This had driven him nearly mad and
he had really taken the congratulations of Mr. Hinde as gloat-
ing over his bitter poverty. Mr. Hinde had a sardonic manner
and spoke with a rictus; bitter and dreadfully harassing poverty alone had driven Conrad, mercilessly, to consent to that
degradation of his art.

In the event, next day Conrad was very ill with mortifica-
tion and I had to write the part of a serial that remained to
make up the weekly instalment. Our life was like that. That
manuscript of mine is in the hands of a collector in this city.

Otherwise he was the most marvellous *raconteur* in the
world. There was no country he could not make you see when
he talked, from Poland to the palms of Palembang. He suffered
at that time and till towards the end of his life from agonies
of poverty. He was terribly concerned for the material future
of his family to whom he was almost unbelievably attached.
Crane and Hudson he really loved personally. His admiration
for their works was unbounded. When their books came it was
as if he bounded into them like a schoolboy running from the
school door. I do not think he took much real stock in other
writers of English. He would utter elaborate politenesses to
them if he met them.

But you could always tell when he really admired work.
It would manifest itself in two ways. You would be reading

at one end of the room and he at the other. It would be a new book he was reading—or perhaps a Flaubert, a Turgenev or a Maupassant. He would begin to groan and roll about on the couch where he was extended. After a time he would say: "What is the use? I ask you what is the use of writing? When this fellow can write like this. There's no room for us." He would go on groaning. Then he would, after a time, spring up, holding his book. "Listen to this!" he would exclaim in sheer joy, laughing with it as if with his whole body. "By God," he would cry out, "there was never anything like this." And he would read out a phrase of Crane's: "The waves were barbarous and abrupt"; or a short passage of Hudson in which he shows you dandelion globes, when you are lying on your back on Lewes Downs, globes illuminated by the sun against the blue sky, in millions, for miles up into the blue. Or he would close a book by Henry James, sigh deeply and say: "I don't know how the Old Man does it. There's nothing he does not know; there's nothing he can't do. That's what it is when you have been privileged to go about with Turgenev."

Hudson immensely admired Conrad personally. He was very lean, *very* tall, big-boned, long-limbed, grey. He was slow in his motions. You have to be if you are a field naturalist. His head was smallish for his great frame, but as if chiseled by the wind, as rocks are; his cheeks weather-beaten. His eyes were small and keen, usually a little closed as if he were looking up along a strong wind. His voice was very gentle, soft as a rule, sometimes a little high and reedy, his accent neither English nor American, but very scrupulous. He had a little, short, pointed grey hidalgo's beard and a heavy grey moustache. He was all gentleness and infinite patience. I have been with him in circumstances of ill-natured companionship and querulousness in which his patience was unending. He would stroll along, swinging his shoulders, stooping a little, mostly silent, occasionally putting in a word of dissent, to shew that he was paying attention. He suggested, the immensely long fellow, a man holding in his hand a frightened bird, but making his examination with such gentleness that the bird's little heart would soon cease to beat fast. If he stood against an old grey wall in a field, he was so grey that he would be almost invisible from a few yards away unless you looked specially for him.

He knew on the surface little about books. He would say again and again, indignantly: "I am no writer. I am a naturalist." He looked at books from afar. It was perhaps longsightedness but it gave the idea that he was mentally aloof. He would stand up, holding *Heart of Darkness* and say: "Yes, the river's all right. The trees are all right. Yes, not so bad. No doubt he's a master." James personally a little alarmed him. Hudson was used to high society, moving in aloof realms that are usually closed to imaginative writers. They were then open to almost all Americans, because they committed you to nothing socially. The Greys of Falloden loved Hudson because he loved birds. So he would look at James enigmatically, breathing rather uncertainly through his nose. James was a society figure all right—but a little too flamboyant. Like an unusual species of a familiar genus. The early works of James, in their first versions, Hudson liked and he was ready to acknowledge that the Old Man was the master of us all. Old Man means captain on a ship, a colonel in a regiment, a head foreman in a gang of stevedores, a master shepherd on a farm.

Crane was the most beautiful spirit I have ever known. He was small, frail, energetic, at times virulent. He was full of fantasies and fantasticisms. He would fly at and deny every statement before it was out of your mouth. He wore breeches, riding leggings, spurs, a cowboy's shirt and there was always a gun near him in the mediæval building that he inhabited seven miles from Winchelsea. In that ancient edifice he would swat flies with precision and satisfaction with the bead-sight of his gun. He proclaimed all day long that he had no use for corner lots nor battlefields, but he got his death in a corner, on the most momentous of all battlefields for Anglo-Saxons. Brede Manor saw the encampment of Harold before Hastings.

He was an American, pure-blooded, and of ostentatious manners when he wanted to be. He used to declare at one time that he was the son of an uptown New York bishop; at another, that he had been born in the Bowery and there dragged up. At one moment his voice would be harsh, like a raven's, uttering phrases like: "I'm a fly-guy that's wise to the all night push," if he wanted to be taken for a Bowery tough; or "He was a mangy, sheep-stealing coyote," if he desired to be thought of cowboy ancestry. At other times, he would talk rather low in very selected English. That was all boyishness.

But he was honourable, physically brave, infinitely hopeful, generous, charitable to excess, observant beyond belief, morally courageous, of unswerving loyalty, a beautiful poet—and of untiring industry. With his physical frailty, his idealism, his love of freedom and of truth he seemed to me to be like Shelley. His eyes with their long fringes of lashes were almost incredibly beautiful—and as if vengeful. Of his infinite industry he had need.

It was delightful to go to Brede Place because Steevie was there, but nothing was more depressing than to drive down into the hollow. In the Middle Ages they built in bottoms to be near the water, and Brede, though mostly an Elizabethan building, in the form of an E out of compliment to Great Eliza, was twelfth-century in site. The sunlight penetrated, pale, like a blight into that damp depression. The great house was haunted. It had stood empty for half a century, the rendezvous of smugglers. On the green banks played fatherless children—and numberless parasites.

Crane never forgot a friend, even if it were merely a fellow who had passed a wet night with him under an arch. His wife was minded to be a mediæval chatelaine. A barrel of beer and a baron of beef stood waiting in the rear hall for every hobo that might pass that way. The house was a nightmare of misplaced hospitality, of lugubrious dissipation in which Crane himself had no part. Grub Street and Greenwich Village did.

The effect on James of poor Steevie was devastating. Crane rode about the countryside on one of two immense coach-horses that he possessed. On their raw-boned carcases his frail figure looked infinitely tiny and forlorn. At times he would rein up before the Old Man's door and going in would tell the master's titled guests that he was a fly-guy that was wise to all the all-night pushes of the world. The master's titled guests liked it. It was, they thought, characteristic of Americans. If the movies had then existed they would have thought themselves confronted with someone from Hollywood. James winced and found it unbearable.

From Steevie he had stood and would have stood a great deal more. The boy for him was always: "My young compatriot of genius." But he would explain his wincings to English people by: "It's as if ... oh dear lady ... it's as if you should find in a staid drawing-room on Beacon Hill or Washington Square or at an intimate reception at an Embassy at Washington a Cockney—oh, I admit of the greatest genius— but a Cockney, still, a costermonger from Whitechapel. And, oh heavens, received, surrounded and adulated ... by, ah, the choicest, the loveliest, the most sympathetic and, ah, the most ornamented. . . ."

And the joke—or, for the Old Man the tragedy—was that Crane assumed his Bowery cloak for the sole purpose of teasing the Master. In much the same way, taking me for a pre-Raphaelite poet, at the beginning of our friendship, he would be for ever harshly denouncing those who paid special prices for antiquities. To Conrad or to Hudson, on the other hand, he spoke and behaved as a reasoning and perceptive human being.

And indeed the native beauty of his nature penetrated sufficiently to the Old Man himself. I never heard James say anything intimately damaging of Crane, and I do not believe he ever said anything of that sort to other people. But what made the situation really excruciating to James was the raids made by Crane's parasites on Lamb House. No doors could keep them out, nor no butler. They made hideous the still levels of the garden with their cachinnations, they poked the Old Man in the ribs before his servants, caricatured his speeches before his guests and extracted from him loans that were almost never refused. There were times when he would hang about in the country outside Rye Walls rather than make such an encounter.

The final tragedy of poor Steevie did not find him wanting. It was tragedy. The sunlight fell blighted into that hollow, the spectres waved their draped arms of mist, the parasites howled and belched on the banks of Brede. That was horrible. But much more horrible was the sight of Crane at his labours. They took place in a room in the centre bar of the E of the Place, over the arched entry. Here Crane would sit writing, hour after hour and day after day, racked with the anxiety that he would not be able to keep going with his pen alone all that fantastic crew. His writing was tiny; he used great sheets of paper. To see him begin at the top of the sheet with his tiny words was agonising; to see him finish a page filled you with concern. It meant the beginning of one more page, and so till his death. Death came slowly but Brede was a sure death-trap to the tuberculous.

Then James' agonies began. He suffered infinitely for that dying boy. I would walk with him for hours over the marsh trying to divert his thoughts. But he would talk on and on. He was for ever considering devices for Crane's comfort. Once he telegraphed to Wanamaker's for a whole collection of New England delicacies from pumpkin pie to apple butter and sausage meat and clams and soft shell crabs and minced meat and ... everything thinkable, so that the poor lad should know once more and finally those fierce joys. Then new perplexities devastated him. Perhaps the taste of those far off eats might cause Steevie to be homesick and so hasten his end. James wavered backwards and forwards between the alternatives beneath the grey walls of Rye Town. He was not himself for many days after Crane's death.

So the first of those four men to die was the youngest. Taken altogether, they were, those four, all gods for me. They formed, when I was a boy, my sure hope in the eternity of good letters. They do still. Long ago the greatest pride of my life used to be that Crane once wrote of me to a friend (I had presumably upset him by some want of Oriental deference):

"You must not mind Hueffer; that is his way. He patronises me; he patronises Mr. Conrad; he patronises Mr. James. When he goes to Heaven he will patronise God Almighty. But God Almighty will get used to it, for Hueffer is all right!"

And the words are my greatest pride after so many years.

They are now all dead, a fact which seems to me incredible still. For me they were the greatest influence on the literature that has followed after them—that has yet been vouchsafed to that literature. Young writers from Seattle to the Golden Gate and from Maine to Jacksonville, Florida, write as they do because those four men once wrote—and so with old writers in old houses in Greenwich Village. That fourfold tradition will not soon part. To that tradition I will one day return. For the moment I have been trying to make them live again in your eyes.... "It is, above all, to make you see."

Between my first visit to Henry James and my period of intimacy with him, my meetings with Conrad and Crane had taken place. I was then living at Limpsfield, in a region of commons and public woods just across the Kent border in Surrey. A mistaken search after high-thinking took me to Limpsfield; all the while I was there I was humiliated at being in Surrey and not in Kent. Kent is a man's county, with hops, orchards, chalk downs, Men of Kent. You can see France from Kent; from Surrey you can only see the loom of London lights on the sky. It is in a county of commuters, and Limpsfield was a queer place, as outer fringes of suburbs are apt to be. Their inner regions are conventional, crowded and wealthy-ish; their outer rings are sparsely settled and given over to odd people.

Limpsfield was the extra-urban headquarters of the Fabian Society. Its permanent secretary dwelt there, and there meetings sanctioning the marriages of members—in the case of the Committee usually with wealthy American women—were held. Mr. Shaw's marriage was there sanctioned. Other meetings defined the beliefs, rules of conduct and other private details of the lives of the members. Today the Fabian Society is an integral part of the British Government. It was not then. Its members then wore beards, queer, useful or homespun clothes and boots, and talked Gas and Water Socialism. They were the Advanced.

They advanced, however, only by rule. I remember consternation at a meeting in Limpsfield. The Fabians were all happily discussing in polite and not brilliant speeches the nature of the Deity if there was a Deity. It had been going on for a long time. A lady in the audience suddenly rose and exclaimed determinedly:

"What I want to know is: does this Society, or doesn't it, believe in God?"

This brutal manner of address caused deep perturbation in the quiet hall. You could no longer hear the sheep bleating on the common. At last an agitated official rose and exclaimed—bleatingly, too:

"If Mrs. —— will consult Fabian Tract number 677a she will see what Fabians are expected to believe in this matter."

I was once gravely reproved by the Fabians, not as a member of the Society, for I wasn't one. My hat—rather like a Stetson of yesterday—had been blown off on Waterloo Bridge whilst I had been making for the station on its southern side. I bought at the bookstall a cloth cap of the type still worn by golfers and went on my way to Limpsfield. I continued to wear that cap; in those days I did not think about what I wore. I was approached by a deputation of Fabian members. My cap "stuck out" on their countryside. I was requested to abandon it.

These things may seem trivial but they have made England what she is today. Mr. Shaw, Lord Ollivier, Mr. Sidney Webb, all wore beards and homespuns and Stetson hats, and now they govern England. Local residents were requested to imitate them. I don't think I wore a beard in those days, though I did earlier. It was long and rufous, and the late William Archer once mistook me in it for Mr. Shaw. I then abandoned it.

I wrote a poem in those days and was proud of it. It ran:

"Three Sidneys once to Britain's realm were born,
Who the British Museum, the Colonial Office and the
Dictionary of National biography did adorn.
The force of nature being on the ebb
To make a fourth invented Sidney Webb." [1]

The other three were Sir Sidney Colvin, the biographer of R. L. S., Lord, then Mr. Sidney, Ollivier, and Sir Sidney Lee. Mr. Webb is also now a peer.

Anyhow, there on those breezy uplands, amongst the geese, donkeys, goats and sheep of the gorse-covered commons, with a sprinkling of Russian revolutionists and a few stockbrokers, flourished the Advanced.

I was not a member of the Fabian Society, for I never took any stock in politics. I subsequently became one in order to have eleven votes for the election of Mrs. Wells to the Governing Body of that Society. I don't know why subscribing a guinea should give me eleven votes but it apparently did. I don't even remember whether Mrs. Wells was elected. At any rate, my friend Mr. H. G. Wells was at that date engaged in turning the Society inside out. He thought its members had not enough imagination. But I think it takes imagination to see a golfer's cap stick out of a landscape.

I made an impassioned speech in support of Mr. and Mrs. Wells at some meeting or other. I have never been received with such hatred—not even in Springfield, Ohio, where I once made a speech about the War to an audience that turned out to be almost entirely German. I fancy I did more harm than good at that Fabian meeting, employing too much imagination. I must have imagined statistics or something. Anyhow the meeting broke up in disorder and I went to Germany. Mr.

[1] Note—At the time of Lord Passfield's betrayal of the Zionists I wrote another:

"A Jew did once betray our Very Lord—
A record in a world of fire and sword!
Ambitious P—f—d, having power to abuse,
To beat it, has betrayed the very Jews."

Wells was not successful. I lunched one day whilst the struggle was on at the house of the editor of the *Quarterly Review*. Next me was Mrs. Sidney Webb, now Lady Passfield. She addressed but one remark to me. It was:

"Your friend Mr. Wells thinks he will get rid of us from the Fabian Society. He calls us the Old Gang. But he won't. It takes gentlefolk to run a political body in England."

It seemed a queer remark to be made by a Socialist leader.

There is of course something to be said for not sticking out of a countryside, at any rate when it comes to architecture. I have always liked the rather rare white frame houses that are to be seen in England. They are mostly on the sea-shore there. Indeed, I have liked them here till the other day. But I have heard Americans speak of them as tiresome, and wondered at it. I remember being years ago on a trolley-car somewhere between Concord, Massachusetts, and Boston. I gave the trolleyman a rather large tip because he had been helpful with my baggage and amusing about the residents in the frame houses that we passed. He said: "If I had many like you on my trolley I'd soon build a brick house." He said that was a local saying. I hoped that countryside would not unduly prosper. But the other day, being taken on a very protracted automobile excursion through New Jersey, Pennsylvania, West Virginia, Virginia and Tennessee, I found myself thinking that the white frame houses that covered all those countrysides were tiresome. The countrysides, particularly in Tennessee, are of an extreme, simple beauty. You might be in England; (There is insularity for you!) the slopes and declivities running for miles and miles away from the highroads are so cropped by cattle and sheep that they look just like English downs. And great clumps and spinneys of timber standing isolated have for all the world the air of trees in august parklands. There the little, white frame houses "stuck out." After a thousand miles or so of them one wished they would not cut into the slopes and be at discord with the beautiful spinneys.

The Fabians of Limpsfield had thought that out. They

had arrived at the conclusion that houses should be built of local materials so as to weather down into the general hues of the hillsides. They were probably right. At any rate the there-favoured architects in those days used to quarry enormous boulders of the local stone that they mortared undressed together, covering the resulting houses with thatch or slabs of local stone.

I daresay they weathered all right. But I was only a very little time a resident amongst those uplifting uplands. Whilst I was there, the solid, rough houses, like monoliths, were bright yellow, the local stone being like that when first quarried. As it was, they stuck out from the green hillsides.

They confused people. When Crane came to see me in my cottage, he called it a bully old baronial ruin. It was then a fortnight old.

Let us consider for a moment more the surrounding period. It was a warlike era. There were Boer wars, China-Japanese, Russo-Japanese wars. There had been very nearly a war between this country and Great Britain. Mr. Kruger, President of the Transvaal, and Mr. Chamberlain between them manœuvred Great Britain and the Transvaal into what Lord Salisbury called "a sort of war." It occupied the whole strength of the British Army for several years. Mr. Chamberlain, on the other hand, had the credit of having, together with Mr. Olney, extricated Lord Salisbury and President Cleveland from the disagreeable positions into which their obstinate characters had forced their respective countries over Venezuela. Then came the Spanish-American War.

It was a period of riots and reactions, the late nineties, and these clamours were not without their reactions on the tribe of writers. Mr. Kipling, the matchless short-story writer, began to come out as the jingo lyrist. Crane made his appearance in Limpsfield fresh from Cuba. I first saw him when he was delivering a lecture on flag-wagging at the house of the Secretary of the Fabian Society, up the hill. Mr. Cunninghame-Graham, born, like Hudson, in South America, and, like him, bearded à la Henri IV and romantic—oh, but infinitely romantic when you saw him sombreroed and with negligent reins, riding in the Row—Mr. Graham, the magnificent prose writer, rightful King of Scotland, head of the Clan Graham, Socialist member of Parliament, gaolbird and all, came out violently in favour of Spain and, in consequence, with a rare hatred for the inhabitants of this country.

He took it out by, in various ways, infuriating the Master. He called for instance at Lamb House, Rye, and must tell Mr. James that he had had extreme difficulty in getting directed to that stately residence. He said he had asked of various citizens and several policemen. "It would take Mr. Graham," Mr. James said, "to find in Rye a policeman who did not know where *I* lived." And we all felt that Mr. Graham had carried his Hispanic sympathies too far.

Once, driving with Mr. Graham to Roslyn Castle from Edinburgh, I heard a politically minded lady say to him:

"You ought, Mr. Graham, to be the first President of a British Republic."

"I ought, Madam, if I had my rights," he answered sardonically, "to be the King of this country. And what a three weeks that would be!"

Robert I of Scotland married two ladies without going through the ceremony of divorcing the first, something like that! The Stuarts were the offspring of the second marriage, the Grahams of the first and Mr. Graham was the head of the Grahams. He was, all in all, the most brilliant writer of that or of our present day. But he was aristocratically negligent of the fate of the products of his muse and he has remained fittingly little known. Nevertheless, such things as *Beattock for Moffat* or the figure of the Spanish officer, sitting a skeleton in an armchair on the Cuban shore long after the battle of Guantanamo, are pieces of writing that can never die. Thomas Hardy at Dorchester was at that time resenting the outcry against *Tess of the D'urbervilles* and getting ready with *Jude the Obscure* to abandon novel writing. George Meredith at

Box Hill was immensely eminent and writing *Lord Ormont and His Aminta* and *The Amazing Marriage*. Mr. Swinburne was living at Putney with Mr. Watts-Dunton. The Poet Laureate was—I think—Mr. Alfred Austin. But all these Great Ones, like Mr. Kipling, sat apart on their little hills. The English Great Writer is seldom intercommunicative, living in the company, usually, of several devoted females, a lawyer, some scientists and a few parasitic beings, and mingling very little with his kind.

There had been—I am talking of 1898 or thereabouts—a brief moment when England had been a nest of singing birds, and in that moment Mr. James and his attendant Americans had played their part. There had been, that is to say, the Henley gang and the *Yellow Book* group. Henley was a great, rough, tortured figure but a considerable and fine Influence. Without him Stevenson would hardly have bulked as he did; and such writers as Whibley, Wedmore, George Warrington Steevens and Marriott Watson made up with Henley a formidable group. In his *National Observer* Henley serialised Conrad's *The Nigger of the Narcissus* and I have always liked to think that, according to Conrad, it was Henley who recommended the author of the *Nigger* to ask me to collaborate with him. As I shall afterwards point out, that can hardly have been true, but Conrad always maintained that it was.

The "note" of Henley and his gang was on the whole one of physical force and Tory reaction. They revelled in the good brown earth, the linotype machine, motor-cars as promotive of thought, and such things. The *Yellow Book* movement had—as became a largely American movement—much more really a technically literary impulse. The periodical was founded by Henry Harland the author of *The Cardinal's Snuff-box*. Its principal backer was Henry James. It fell with the trial of the miserable Oscar Wilde.

Wilde I can never forgive. You may maintain that he had a right to live his own life and, for the sake of sheer vanity, get himself into Reading Gaol. For there was no reason for his going to prison and the last thing that the British authorities wanted to do was to put him there. On the day of his arrest his solicitor received warning that the warrant would not be issued until after seven P.M., the night train for Paris leaving at 6:50 from Charing Cross. I remember still the feeling of anxiety and excitement of that day. Practically everybody in London knew what was agate.

Wilde went to his solicitor—Mr. Robert Humphreys; I once had him for my lawyer—about eleven in the morning. Humphreys at once began to beg him to go to Paris. Wilde declared that the authorities dared not touch him. He was too eminent and there were too many others implicated. To that he stuck. He was immovable and would listen to no arguments. There came a dramatic moment in the lawyer's office. Wilde began to lament his wasted life. He uttered a tremendous diatribe about his great talents thrown away, his brilliant genius dragged in the mud, his early and glorious aspirations come to nothing. He became almost epic. Then he covered his face and wept. His whole body was shaken by his sobs. Humphreys was extremely moved. He tried to find consolations.

Wilde took his hands down from his face. He winked at Humphreys and exclaimed triumphantly:

"Got you then, old fellow." He added: "Certainly I shall not go to Paris." He was arrested that evening.

I always intensely disliked Wilde, faintly as a writer and intensely as a human being. No doubt, as a youth he was beautiful, frail and illuminated. But when I knew him he was heavy and dull. I only once heard him utter an epigram. He used to come to my grandfather's with some regularity at one time—every Saturday, I should say. My grandfather was then known as the Grandfather of the pre-Raphaelites and Wilde passed as a pre-Raphaelite poet.

He would sit beside the high fireplace and talk very quietly—mostly about public matters: Home Rule for Ireland and the like. My grandfather was a rather down-to-the-ground sort of person, so that Wilde to him talked very much like anyone else and seemed glad to be in a quiet room beside a high fireplace.

Once, at a garden party at the Bishop of London's, I heard a lady ask him if he were going to the dinner of the O. P. Club that evening. The O. P. Club had some grievance against Wilde. It was a dramatic society or something of the sort. Dramatic organisations are excitable and minatory when they disliked anybody. It was a dramatic society that booed and hissed at Henry James when he took his curtain call after *Guy Domville*. But really they were venting their wrath against Sir George Alexander, the actor manager who had that evening for the first time made a charge for programmes. So Wilde would have had a rough-house at the dinner of the O. P. Club. He therefore replied to the lady at the Bishop's party:

"I go to the dinner of the O. P. Club! I should be like a poor lion in a den of savage Daniels."

I saw Wilde several times in Paris and he was a truly miserable spectacle, the butt usually of a posse of merciless students. He possessed and it was almost his only possession— a walking stick of ebony with ivory insertions, the handle representing an elephant. This he loved very much because it had been the gift of some one—Lady Mount Temple, I think. He would be of an evening in one or another disagreeable *bouge* in Montmartre. The students would get about him. It was the days of the apaches. There would be a fellow there called Bibi La Touche or something of the sort. The students would point him out to Wilde and declare that Bibi had taken a fancy to his stick and would murder him on his homeward way if he did not surrender it. Wilde would cry, the tears pouring down his great cheeks. But always he surrendered his stick. The students would return it to his hotel next morning, when he would have forgotten all about it. I, once or perhaps twice, rescued his stick for him and saw him home. It would not be agreeable. He did not have a penny and I had very little more. I would walk him down the miserably lit Montmartrois streets, he completely silent or muttering things that I did not understand. He walked always as if his feet hurt him, leaning forward on his precious cane. When I thought we were near enough to the Quartier for my resources to let me pay a cab— usually in the neighbourhood of the Boulevard de la Madeleine —we would get into one and would at last reach the rue Jacob. This happened I think twice, but the memory is one as if of long-continued discomfort. It was humiliating to dislike so much one so unfortunate. But the feeling of dislike for that shabby and incoherent immensity was unavoidable. It had proved so strong that, the locality taking on an aspect of nightmare, I have only once since visited Montmartre at night in, say, thirty-five years and then found it very disagreeable. Of course, the sight of the young people, like starlings, tormenting that immense owl had a great deal to do with my revulsions.

On one occasion—I should think in the *Chat Noir*—I was with Robert de la Sizéranne and, looking at Wilde who was across the room, he said:

"Vous voyez cet homme là. Il péchait par pur snobisme."

He meant that, even in his offences against constituted society, Wilde was out to *épater les bourgeois*—to scandalise the middle classes. Sizéranne added: *"Cela le faisait chaque fois vomir !"*

That was pretty generally the French view and, on the face of it, I should say it was just. Sizéranne who was then accounted a very sagacious critic of art, mostly pre-Raphaelite, moved in French circles where Wilde had once throned it almost as an Emperor.

The rather idle pursuit of *épaté*-ing the bourgeoisie was very much the fashion amongst the *Yellow Book* group who surrounded Wilde. In order to "touch the Philistine on the raw," as they called it, the Thompsons, Dowsons, Davidsons, Johnsons and the rest found it necessary to introduce an atmosphere of the Latin Quarter in its lighter—or more dismal side—into London haunts. The Latin Quarter is in fact a very grave, silent and austere region. But it has its Bohemian fringes—and a non-Anglo-Saxon population bred to survive such dissipations as are there to be found. Anglo-Saxons are not so bred. They resemble the populations of Central Africa succumbing before the clothing, gin and creeds of white men. That in the bulk. There are, of course, individuals who survive.

The Bodley Head group did not survive. They succumbed in London's Soho haunts—to absinthe, to tuberculosis, to starvation, to reformers or to suicide. But in their day, they were brilliantly before the public, and London was more of a literary centre then than it has ever been before or since.

The book world was then electric. Books were everywhere. Accounts of the personal habits of writers filled the daily papers. Minute volumes of poems in limited editions fetched unheard prices at auction. It was good to be a writer in England. And it is to be remembered that, as far as that particular body was concerned, the rewards were earned. They were skilful and earnest writers. They were an immense improvement on their predecessors. They were genuine men of letters.

I was looking last night at the works of Ernest Dowson. They are faint, like dry-point etchings. Their daringnesses are the common coin of today. But they have the authentic note. When you read them you have a faint flavour of what was good in those days: the tentativeness of thought, the delicacy, the refinement of point of view. In their day they were international and brilliant. I do not think they will ever appear ignoble.

But all that went with the trial of Wilde.

I hardly came at all in contact with either the Henley or the *Yellow Book* group at that date, though later, I just knew Henley, and Messrs. Whibley, Wedmore and Marriott Watson. I thought then that the others were too harshly brilliant for me. So I was astonished to find in the work of Dowson just now, almost New England delicacies—an as it were Bostonian after-taste. And, if you consider what a considerable part was played by Americans of that type in the art worlds of London and Paris, you will be less astonished to find that flavour.

Those were days when James and Howells and Harland and Whistler and Sargent and Abbey, not to mention lesser lights like G. H. Boughton, more popular ones like Bret Harte or immensely great ones like Mark Twain, bulked enormously in politely advanced artistic circles in London.

The *Yellow Book* was, as I have pointed out, an American venture and made for those American virtues of delicacy French technical achievement and New England refinements—thus touching hands with both sides of the Atlantic. And the *Yellow Book* as nearly captured the stronghold of the Established Comfortable that London is, as later—and I hope to show you that—the American movement led by Ezra and called indifferently Vorticism, Futurism, Imagism, so nearly achieved that feat. The condemnation of Wilde wiped out the one, a larger cataclysm the other.

Wilde, then, brought down the *Yellow Book* group and most of the other lyrists of a London that for its year or two had been a nest of singing birds. James and Harland were almost the only survivors. Poets died or fled to other climes, publishers also fled, prosateurs were fished out of the Seine or reformed and the great public said: "Thank heavens, we need not read any more poetry!"

You may think that an exaggeration. So did I at the time. But, just after the papers had announced the conviction and sentence on Wilde, I was going up the steps of the British Museum. On them I met Dr. Garnett, the Keeper of Printed Books, a queer, very tall, lean, untidily bearded Yorkshire figure in its official frock coat and high hat. I gave him the news. He looked for a moment away over the great yard of the Museum, with its pigeons and lamps and little lions on the railings. Then he said:

"Then that means the death of English poetry for fifty years."

I can still hear the high tones of my incredulous laughter.

At the moment he seemed to me an old obstinate crank, though I knew well how immense was his North Country common sense.

Having a passion for cats, Egyptology, palmistry and astrology, the great scholar could assume some of the aspect of deaf obstinacy that distinguishes cats that do not intend to listen to you. He cast the horoscopes of all his friends and reigning sovereigns; he knew the contents of a hundred thousand books and must have stroked as many thousand "pussies" pronouncing the "pus" to rhyme with "bus." He was inseparable from his umbrella with which he once beat off two thieves, when at five in the morning he had gone to Covent Garden to buy the household fruit. He was the author of the most delightful volume of whimsico-classical stories that was ever written and the organiser of the compilers of the catalogue of the British Museum Library—an achievement that should render him immortal if his *Twilight of the Gods* fails to do so. He would say to you that the ancient Egyptians were the only really civilised race, for, when fires occurred in their great buildings, they organised environing cordons, not to put out the fires but to see that no cats re-entered their burning homes.

On this occasion he held his top-hatted head obstinately and deftly on one side and repeated, with half closed eyes:

"That means the death blow to English poetry. It will not be resuscitated for fifty years." ... We have a decade or so to wait for that phœnix. Dr. Garnett was in the right of it....

I never, as I have said, saw much of that brilliant group. I was at that time mainly a horticulturist. I was attempting to promote the growing of corn, tobacco and wine on my own land in England. Hence my early visits to the United States. I may add, as a detail, that I have grown as good Golden Bantam and Country Gentlemen in Kent and Sussex as I have ever seen, grown or planted, in Virginia. But as for wine and tobacco, the Inland Revenue effactually stopped that by enforcing the duty of £50 per acre on all of either sort of crop.

The land which I occupied at Limpsfield was stifled by thistles. I made several experiments in their quick eradication, more particularly by intensive plantations of potatoes, which has become the standard method. Whilst at Limpsfield, I wrote an article on this subject and submitted it to several literary journals. It was sent back.

Crane came to see me whilst I was doing these things in the troglodytic cottage that he mistook for a baronial ruin. He was brought there by Mr. Edward Garnett, the son of the Keeper of Printed Books, who will be as immortal amongst publishers' advisers as was his father amongst cataloguers. I don't think Crane wanted to come and see me because he took me for a pre-Raphaelite poet. But in Limpsfield there was a strong get-together movement in those days and poor Crane had to come and plant a rose tree beside the lintel of the door which was formed of half a mill-wheel.

The rose tree was there a few years ago. You may no doubt have souvenirs. I may add that Conrad and I once planted an orange tree, grown from a pip, under a south wall at the Pent. That also was still growing when I visited the place after Conrad's death. It grew no higher than the rim of the wall, the north wind cutting it back; but the fact should to the incredulous be a testimony to the climatic mildness of that Gulf-Streamed part of the shores of England. For the matter of that, at this November moment of writing, I am looking at an avocado pear tree grown from a pip in a Greenwich Village back yard. May the omen be propitious to its orange-leaf-like foliage!

Crane could use a spade all right. He could, that is to say, lift a heavy, wrought steel, sharp implement and, bringing it down from the full extent of his uplifted arm, smash into the yellow clay between a couple of rocks with accuracy and all his small weight duly in operation. I watched him with the sardonic attention that the inhabitants of Kent and Sussex bestow on all foreigners. One did not credit writers and particularly American journalists with much practical knowledge or skill. I once was visited by a fellow who wrote and talked about camping in the Rockies with the volubility and technical knowledge of a man who had been a lumberer all his life. I was then cutting timber and we gave him an axe. He grasped it by the extreme end of the helve, whirled it round his head as if he were throwing the hammer at the Olympic sports and, letting it glance at the tree-trunk, all but cut his leg off. My foreman turned paler than I have ever seen a man turn and we set that fellow to carrying logs and saw that it was the big ones he carried. I still have not forgiven him the scare he gave us.

But Crane was all right. He could use a spade or an axe; he rode well. And he had, as I have said, an enviable trick with a gun. He would put a piece of sugar on a table and sit still till a fly approached. He held in his hand a Smith and Wesson. When the fly was by the sugar, he would twist the gun round in his wrist. The fly would die, killed by the bead-sight of the revolver. That is much more difficult than it sounds. One may be able to use a gun pretty well, but I never managed to kill a fly with the barrel much less the bead-sight.

I don't know that physical gifts are necessary to the imaginative writer. But I think a certain delicacy in handiwork goes often with accuracy of observation, just as the patience of the field naturalist goes with good prose. Hudson, White of Selborne and Waterton were three of our best prose writers —Hudson the best of all. For myself, I know that the writer whose cadences have most intimately influenced me were those of Thomas Edwardes, the Scottish cobbler-naturalist who could neither read nor write till long after middle-life—and after following birds alongside the sea on the links of Banffshire for years and years.

In the Middle Ages they used to say that the proper man was one who had written a book, built a house, planted a tree and begotten a child. I don't know that Crane ever built a house. He avoided having children because he was afraid of giving them the heritage of tuberculosis. But as a writer of books he was incomparable, and the Limpsfield tree that he planted is alive at this day to testify to his handiwork.

There are few men that I have liked—nay, indeed, revered —more than Crane. He was so frail and so courageous, so preyed upon and so generous, so weighted down by misfortunes and so erect in his carriage. And he was such a beautiful genius.

When I was at the Front, on Kemmel Hill in 1916, I had —I have elsewhere related it but I will here re-adumbrate it since it is almost the most singular tribute that one can pay to a writer—the curious experience of so reading myself into the *Red Badge of Courage*, which is a story of the American Civil War, that, having to put the book down and go out of my tent at dawn, I could not understand why the men I saw about were in khaki and not in the Federal grey. And I can still see the Bride coming to Yellow Sky, the barbarous and abrupt waves that tossed about the Open Boat, the ring of the gun-muzzle in the saloon of the White Mice.... The beautiful genius!

I saw him, as I have said, first at a lecture he was delivering up on the Chart at Limpsfield, and I was much attracted to him then. He was enormously belauded and, on account of the harshness of his voice and his precision of language as a lecturer, I had taken him to be arrogant. The subject of his discourse was flag-wagging, as he called it— Morse signalling by flags. It is not a very inspiring subject, though I remember getting some amusement when, being examined for signalling at Cardiff in 1915, I transmitted to a classically minded fellow-officer the line of Sappho's:

Eramen men ego sethen athi palai pota

The recording colour-sergeant struck the message off his tablets. It was to have been inspected by the examining general and the good sergeant thought that anything in a foreign language must of necessity be obscene.

But I have not even that as a memory of Crane's lecture.

I remember his standing on an improvised platform in a Fabian drawing-room and looking young, pained and dictatorial. I avoided being introduced to him.

It is curious that I should have at first rather disliked all three—Crane, Conrad and James. That must have been because of the nature of the adoration bestowed upon them by their respective groups. I was a young man of a little achievement of my own. I must at that date or before have had larger sales for my books than James and certainly than Conrad, though Crane, of course, with the *Red Badge* was a best seller of fantastic proportions. So it may have been latent jealousy. But I think it was rather a form of dislike for being, as it were, taken by the elbow and thrust into the presence of personages before whom the thrusters orientally prostrated themselves.

And I was not much of a reader in those days. I do not think that I had read any of James or Crane before I met them. Conrad's second book—*An Outcast of the Islands*—I had read in typescript. Mr. Garnett had brought it down to my cottage in Bonnington-in-the-Marsh along with a lot of other manuscripts, and I had read it with a great deal of admiration. But that was rather tempered by the fact that Mr. Garnett laid almost more stress on the anti-colonising force of the book than on its literary qualities. I never took much interest in politics though from my earliest days I always hated the idea that any one man or set of men should have any temporal powers over any other men of different races and religions. So were I a politician, I should be an embittered anti-Imperialist. I have always called myself a Tory, much as Shelley called himself an atheist. It stops political discussions when I find myself amongst the Advanced and, as for the Right, no one of that complexion knew what a Tory was—at any rate then.

I daresay that irritated Mr. Garnett into emphasising the propagandist nature of the *Outcasts*. But I disliked the idea that a man of the gifts shown in the manuscript should prostitute them by putting them to political purposes. Nevertheless, I was so shocked when Mr. Garnett said that his employer was in some doubt as to publishing the book because it could not be expected to pay expenses—I was so shocked that I offered to guarantee the publisher against loss on the book. I had lately come into money left me by an uncle who had been a forty-niner....Yes, I too had my *oncle de l'Amérique*. Indeed I had two. Thus dollars might even in those early days have played their part in Conrad's fortunes and the history of literature. They did not in the event. The book just paid its way. Conrad earned a minute sum by it.

He must have come to see me a year or so later, just after the visit of Crane and I remained rather prejudiced against him. As in the case of Crane, it was Mr. Garnett who brought him to my door. I don't know why. I was no very amiable character in those days and I was temporarily in no mood for meeting men of letters. I had my potatoes and my thistles.

CHAPTER IV

RE-AGENTS

CONRAD came round the corner of the house. I was doing something at the open fireplace in the house-end. He was in advance of Mr. Garnett, who had gone inside, I suppose, to find me. Conrad stood looking at the view. His hands were in the pockets of his reefer-coat, the thumbs sticking out. His black torpedo beard pointed at the horizon. He placed a monocle in his eye. Then he caught sight of me.

I was very untidy in my working clothes. He started back a little. I said "I'm Hueffer." He had taken me for the gardener.

His whole being melted together in enormous politeness. His spine inclined forward; he extended both hands to take mine. He said:

"My dear faller.... Delighted.... *Ench ... anté.*" He added: *"What* conditions to work in.... Your admirable cottage.... Your adorable view...."

It was symbolic that the first remark he should make to me should be about conditions in which to work. Poor fellow! Work was at once his passion and his agony, and no one, till the very end of his life, had much worse conditions. On the last time I saw him, a few weeks before his death, he said to me:

"You see, I have at last now got a real study of my own. I can work here uninterrupted." He was to do so little more!

He was staying at the moment of that visit up on the Chart, to be near Mr. Garnett. He had been living in the rather lugubrious village of Stamford-le-Hope, on the estuary of the Thames, amongst the Essex marshes. His poverty was like a physical pain, but his reputation as a writer was already enormously high. A week after the publication of his first book, he stood absolutely in the front rank of English authors, yet the great public was extraordinarily slow to hear of him. I suppose it did not really do so till the publication of *Chance,* fifteen years after that date. And they were fifteen years of agonised labours and the most fell anxieties, the most desperate expedients. The highest note of his life was his passion for his work, the most dominant one that of being assured of having provided for his family. His tastes were of the least expensive. He was as happy playing dominoes in a city Mecca—a coffee house—over a cup of coffee as in any other situation in the world. He would place on the marble table-top the winning domino of a series, his whole face lighting up with animation and triumph. Yet, since I never won one of innumerable games that I played with him, the triumph could only in the beginning have had any novelty for him.

In those early days he still had a great deal of the master mariner about him. His characteristic attitude was that, with his hands in the pockets of his coat and his beard pointing at the horizon. There was something masterly about him. He strode, with the rolling gait of the quarterdeck, into a room or onto a terrace. He had the air of a Caliph entering a slave-market—as if he could confiscate any of the beautiful slaves or do what he would with the view beneath his eyes. He was an unexampled *raconteur.* If his ambition in writing was, as he said, "above all to make you see," he could in telling stories, in his dusky and affectionate tones and with his singular accent, make you see almost anything in the world. It is to be remembered that he was Polish of very aristocratic ancestry. That was what gave a particular agony to his anxieties for his family's welfare. He sat almost in rags and groaned with the fear that his pen would not be able to provide for his children and grandchildren, great mansions to withstand the snow, elaborately ornamented sleighs, blood horses, innumerable retainers and halls opening out, the one into the other, beyond the eyesight. I never heard him lament the shortage of the present. He was happy with, and even proud of the few poor things that he had. The old mare that he drove, Nancy, had such long ears that she had the air of a mule, but for him she was the most engaging of beasts with the most enlivening characteristics and the speed of a Rolls-Royce amongst quadrupeds. His old harness and his old cart were of the noblest pedigree of such things. He never knew that he was shabby. If he had two odd gloves they would have been manufactured by the best maker Bond Street could shew. But for his son the future must hold a Rolls-Royce all of silver and clothes all from Poole who made for Edward VII.

But indeed he wore his old clothes with the air of a Prince and when he was behind Nancy you thought her the horse of the Cid; he so dominated all views. He had a singularly nice taste in cooking, and in that respect fate was good to him. In the direst times of his poverty, he yet had a table that was better than almost anybody's I have ever known. For with care, two eggs, a little butter, some potherbs and a few scraps you may eat as did Brillat Savarin, and Conrad had a devoted family.

Except for his unexpected, queer, rather stiff appearance, his sudden melting into Oriental mannerisms, and the fact that his first speech was about conditions of work, I do not remember much more of that first visit of a man with whom I was destined to become extremely intimate and whose memory remains the most treasured of my possessions. I remember mostly his smile of satisfaction and enchantment at his son and my daughter as they climbed determinedly on all fours and wrestled like eighteenth-century cherubs on the sloping grass of Mr. Garnett's property which was called the *Cearne*. I must have told him that I was writing a novel about Cuban pirates. That the sequel will shew. But I did not see him again during his visit to Limpsfield and he went away back to Stamford-le-Hope and its marshes.

I was destined to deepen my acquaintance with Crane before I saw Conrad. That, remembering back, comes to me rather as a queerness. I got to know Conrad so well that I seem to have known him all my life. That was because he represented to me Man—humanity as it should be. Crane, on the other hand, was like the angels. He did not seem to have the motives of common clay. Conrad produced with agony and you saw how it was done; Crane hovered over his foolscap sheets using a pen as a white moth uses its proboscis. His work had for me something of the supernatural. He comes back to me always as joyous.

That was perhaps due to his youth and his early death, for in those he was fortunate. But I daresay it was due to the fortuitous circumstances that on several times when I visited him, or he me, he had just had pieces of good fortune.

My first visit to him was at a villa called *Ravensbrook* at Limpsfield, a horrible place in a bottom, damp, and of the most sordidly pretentious type of suburban villa architecture. I was trepanned there.

There was in Limpsfield a very energetic, advanced lady, Scottish, indomitable and the wife of a Fabian official. You would see her boyish figure, in knee breeches and a bonnet with strings, dragging at the reins of a donkey in a governess-cart, up hill, in the mists of the Common and the Chart. There would be two freckled little boys in the cart. They would fight, fall out, scramble in again somehow. They would disappear and come again into view amongst the clumps of gorse, always with the indefatigable lady dragging at the unwilling donkey, bending forward, striding along.

She would be going on her ceaseless errand of getting people together. She was in those days my terror, but she comes back to me in a sudden warmth of affection—her ingenuous face, Scottish brogue, her optimism, length of limb and heather tramp with its springy gait. She was like a daughter of a Duke of Argyle urging her father's tenants to be friendly with the Macgregors.

She appeared one afternoon in my cottage and ordered me to go at once to *Ravensbrook* and teach Mrs. Crane how to make mediæval dresses. I was confused and unwilling. She said that I ought to know how to make mediæval women's clothes because of my pre-Raphaelite origins. One of the members of my family wore what we should now call a *robe de style*, a close-fitting bodice, a very full skirt and a sort of yellow surcoat with dangling pointed sleeves which got into the baby's milk. The lady said that that proved that I knew how to make hennins, cottes, surmantels and the rest. I was alone in the cottage and she managed to convey to me that there was breathless need of my hurrying to Mrs. Crane.

I reached *Ravensbrook* about seven. Mrs. Crane, large, fair and placid, with her attendant dark, thin and vivacious Mrs. Rudy, would no doubt have looked admirable in a *hennin*. But she was puzzled by my appearance. She had never had any idea of abandoning coats and skirts. We worked out that Mrs. Pease had determined that I should get together with the Cranes. Mrs. Pease wanted to see the countryside covered with ladies in mediæval attire.

Mrs. Crane was almost as puzzled by my English-English accent as by my errand and we finally did talk about mediæval dress. It was perhaps the beginning of poor Crane's undoing. For it was, I think, Mrs. Crane's amiable romanticism which led her and poor Crane into various fantasies and ended with their lodging themselves in Brede Place. There, truly, Mrs. Crane wore hanging sleeves, hennins and pointed shoes. Beneath the refectory tables were rushes where the dogs lay and fought for the bones that were dropped to them. I did, of course, know a little more of how the ladies of the Courts of Love garbed themselves than she did.

I remember as a detail that when I said she must cut the stuff for her sleeves on the cross or they would not hang right, she did not understand the words "on the cross" and finally worked out that I meant that she should cut "cater" the material. It pleased me very much to find that fine old Kentish dialect word in common American use. Or perhaps it was merely Southern? Mrs. Crane came from Jacksonville, Florida.

Do you know the story of the truthful curate? He called on a family of his parishioners at tea and every time they said to him "Must you *really* go now?" he replied that it was not absolutely necessary. So he stayed to dinner, and the master of the house had to sleep on the billiard table because the curate was in his bed; and he breakfasted there and sent for his sermon paper and composed his sermon in the master's study and so on for ever. I must have been like that at *Ravensbrook*.

At any rate I was there at half past twelve when Crane came down from Town by the last train and I went to bed in the drawing-room, with the dog on top of me at four in the morning and began again arguing with Crane about writing at a seven o'clock breakfast. Our views on life and letters were not really divergent but Crane would ascribe to me sets of theories and then demolish them with the manner and voice of a Bowery tough hammering an Irish scavenger. He was immensely happy.

Mrs. Crane's alleged reason for making me stay till after midnight had been that Crane, coming down from a momentous interview, would need to talk. Presumably he would want to talk in such Gargantuan gusts that she and Mr. Rudy would be insufficient to sustain his assaults of language.

He certainly talked. He had been up to town to see James B. Pinker, the remarkable literary agent on whose lips hung half the young writers of that day. Pinker certainly deserves a page to himself, for without him you could never have had Conrad, and poor Crane could hardly have lived. He smoothed out, too, furrows in the later paths of Henry James. I had mysterious and obscure rows with him myself. I never understood what they were about. I suppose he was sensitive and I patronising. He lived in an outer suburb, so as to ride to hounds. This he did two or three days a week. He had none of the airs of the stable but he certainly knew something about horses—which is unusual for Scotsmen. At any rate, he once bought for £5 a horse out of a bus yard and immediately afterwards took with it second prize for tandem leaders at Richmond Horse Show. That was no mean feat. The horse would not go in harness or under the saddle and had been kicking a bus to pieces when Pinker had passed the yard. He liked driving tandem and it occurred to him that the animal might stand the light traces and blinkers which are all that go on a leader. And so it did. He gained added satisfaction from the fact that he sold the animal immediately after the show and it ran the new owner's cart against a post and threw him out, breaking his arm.

There used to be a grim gleam in Mr. Pinker's hard eyes, behind his benevolent spectacles when he told that story. I think the first London agent was a man called A. P. Watt who looked like something between a bishop and a butler. As far as England was concerned, he invented the practice of syndicating articles in newspapers that circulated at sufficient distances the one from the other. I remember that he sold articles on music by my father to twelve newspapers at once. But he was very high and mighty to editors and the like. I remember that when I edited the *English Review* I went to ask him for something by one of his clients and he was so patronising that I still feel like a worm when I think of it. He was agent only for the enormously distinguished. Pinker, on the other hand, was little and vivid and had a singular accent. He must have taken the cream off Mr. Watt's business.

I should say that on the whole an agent is of little use to the author who has any business faculties at all, but so many have not. The agent's function is to be a sort of bar loafer who hangs around, finding what publisher, magazine or paper wants what. He may be of use. But few agents will handle the work of young authors who have always been my particular preoccupation. And the agent's interests are not always by any means always at one with the individual author's. He will place a highly paid author in preference to another on his list; he gets more commission. He will place an author who is indebted to him rather than one who isn't. He is then sure of getting his money back. It is not always to his interest to press a dishonest or defaulting publisher to the point of definitely offending them. He has other authors that he will wish to place with that publisher.

All out then, you had better do without an agent unless you are a very big seller. But, to his favorite clients—and they were not always the most prosperous—Pinker was all gold. I never could quite know how I felt towards him. He was so good and helpful and patient with Conrad and Crane and James and so quarrelsome to myself. But on the whole I felt kindly and I very much regretted his death which took place in New York. I remember thinking that New York was no place to go to if it could kill anyone so hard as Pinker.

I dwell thus on him because you could have little real idea of what the literary world I am portraying for you was like unless you imagine that Scotsman as looming always somewhere in the background of lettered thoughts. I remember James, when, as he sometimes did, he consulted me as to his financial affairs, telling me that for years he had sold all the rights of his books to one individual publisher—for £200 a time. So he had long given up looking at writing as even a very thin stick. And he had had financial misfortunes and the future looked like a gloomy vista of pinched discomfort. "And then suddenly," said Mr. James, "along came a little man called ... Pinker." And Pinker offered enormous prices for this, and great sums for that, and to place things here, and serialise them in the *Illustrated London News* and syndicate them from Beersheba to Spokane.... And he jumped about and kept his promises. And all was gas and gingerbread! ... Pinker would allow him to build his gazebo in the

garden and take apartments in Chelsea and buy "bits" of
China. Similarly he would let Conrad go to Bruges or Poland
and Crane to Brede Place. For always, when you proposed
to buy or travel or have a new mare, you first interviewed the
little man in spectacles at the bottom of Arundel Street.
"A rundel Street" you would say to the hansom cabman who
took you to learn your fate. "You mean Ar*un*del Street," he
would answer contemptuously. And in a quarter of an hour
or so you would know whether you could have the wish of
your heart or must go back to your cottage and live on potatoes and cheese for another quarter. Pinker would take quite
long odds in backing you. Conrad must have been many thousands of pounds in debt to him before *Chance* really brought
him before the public eye. On the other hand, the little man
could softly and inexorably turn down anyone in whom he did
not believe.

On that Oxted night—for *Ravensbrook* is just outside
Limpsfield and just inside Oxted—Crane was coming down
from having seen Pinker.

It had been a crucial moment in his career and I imagine
that Mrs. Crane had been anxious that I should stay with her
and her friend simply because they could not bear themselves
in the suspense. Crane was then—was, as you might say, still
—the immensely successful author of the *Red Badge*. But it is
the second and third books that have anxious passages. And
Crane had not been very successful with them as far as the
public were concerned. His adventure as a journalist in the
Spanish-American War had not been a great success journalis-
tically. Out of his sheer imagination he had created the most
wonderful, real and vivid book about war that had ever been
written. It was argued that, if then he saw a real war, with
the shells flying and the flags wagging and the troops advanc-
ing at the double, he must do something superhuman in the
way of journalism. He didn't.

He wrote as always beautifully and such by-products of
the war as the stories in the *Open Boat* are among the master-

pieces of all literature. But he had not been good at getting
his dispatches through; he had not been in at the best deaths.
He had endured great hardships, some dangers, some sick-
nesses; he had worn himself to a threadpaper, without gaining
much success as a journalist. What was almost worse, he had
acquired a thirst for the sort of thing. When the Turco-Greek
War came he beat about London from office to office, like a
butterfly against a window pane. He was trying to get sent to
Greece. The desire seemed to burn him up.

But at the moment of which I am speaking, his troubles
had been mainly financial. The Cranes had run seriously into
debt at Oxted. They were at the moment almost short of food.
The meal of which I had partaken with Mrs. Crane had certainly been exiguous. When Crane did arrive his arms were full
of parcels containing mostly delicatessen with a bottle or two
of claret. The local tradesmen had cut off supplies. In any case
Ravensbrook was an unreasonably expensive establishment to
run. Poor Steevie was certainly not fortunate in those who
chose his English residences for him. *Ravensbrook* would well
have suited a rich stock-broker.

What was almost worst, poor Crane's conscience and artistic imagination made him take his creditor's case against
himself. Most people see dunning tradesmen as fiends. Crane
saw them as starving fathers of families. He would say: "Do
you suppose Simpson, the butcher, will be bankrupted if I
don't pay him?" Or: "Oving, the saddlemaker's children are
said to be going without shoes. Damn it! I owe him £50 for
harness." So, as two of my visits—on one of which I was with
difficulty admitted because I was taken for a bailiff—as, then,
two of my visits coincided with the arrival of considerable relief, he associated me with pleasant things.

He came back, nervous, distracted, loaded—and elf-like.
Before he spoke to me, he had to have a whispered colloquy
with Mrs. Crane in the doorway. They leaned one against each
door-post. He had his hat tilted over his eyes. I was holding

the parcels in the dark hallway. He said a low phrase. Then there were explosions of joy.

Pinker had guaranteed him £20 per thousand words. For everything that he wrote: £20 per thousand, is $10 per hundred, is ten cents per 1, words. You just sat down and wrote anything. But it is not merely dollars and cents. It is miles travelled. You could go to Ispahan, to Yokohama. You wrote for ten hours at fifteen words a minute and there was £180—900 dollars. And in those days dollars were dollars, not nickels. You could go to Australia and back the other way for ten hours' writing! ... And writing without tears. Without a crease of the brow. Without anxiety at the back of the mind. He had brought a new collar for Flannel. Flannel was the unimaginable dog. Conrad had been given its brother called Sponge. It had, however, been re-christened Escamillo after the character in *Carmen*. How romantic Conrad was! Crane, in the doorway, drew the new collar from his pocket.

I have never seen such gladness as there was on that Oxted night. They were very simple people really. All great authors are. If you are not simple, you are not observant. If you are not observant, you can not write. But you must observe simply. The first characteristic of great writing is a certain humility.

For me, Crane came nearer the otherworldly than any other human being I have encountered. He was what Trelawney made us believe Shelley to have been. But he observed the littler things of life. He was the poet.

He kept it exaggeratedly beneath the surface. Outwardly he was harsh and defiant; his small, tense figure and his professional speech were those of the Man of Action of dime drama. He loved to suggest that he could draw his gun quicker than your brain could telegraph to your hand to approach your hip. He meant by that to shew that he was not a poet.

But he was. I will venture to say that no more poetic vision of humanity in our late Armageddon was ever written than *The Red Badge of Courage*—and that was written twenty years before our Armageddon burst upon us. And it was written about a war that ended sixty-five years ago. Yet it was amazingly vivid even in 1917. I am not at the moment writing about Literature; I am trying to re-constitute for you men that I loved...long since in ages past. Still Literature will come creeping in. I wish I could re-read *The Open Boat* but I have no copy and it appears to be out of print. It is astonishing that any book of Stephen Crane's should be out of print and that one should not be able to find a copy. It is lamentable!

He was astonishingly glad that night at Oxted. Oxted is an exceptionally banal suburb of London; but the night was dark and it was hidden. In the darkness the joy shone out of him as heat glows sometimes through opaque substances. He could get away from Oxted! Crane hated his villa.

With the falling from his shoulders of that intolerable burden he desired, as Mrs. Crane had foreseen, to talk. He talked. He kept me there, listening, half through the night, nearly until breakfast time. He had the most amazing eyes. They were large, like a horse's. They frowned usually with the gaze of one looking very intently. But they shone astonishingly at times. When he became excited the studied New York argot disappeared or nearly so. He then talked a rather classical English. That night he planned his glorious future.

It was not merely that he planned to travel. He planned to travel the world over, flinging coins from the purse of Fortunatus that be-spectacled and benevolent Pinker had put into his hands. But he was to render that world when he had roamed all over it. He talked therefore about his technique. That was unusual with him.

I do not flatter myself that it was to me that he talked. That night he would have talked in the same way to Conrad's dog, Escamillo. I had for him the aspect of a pre-Raphaelite or æsthetic poet and he seemed to make me responsible for the poems of D. G. Rossetti and the gilded prose of Mr. Richard Le Gallienne. He began by telling me that I could not write and never should know how to write. Then he went on to tell me how writing should be done, pausing to denounce me and my family only when his mind paused for context. Then he told me what he was going to do.

He was going to write a great series of heroic poems in vers libre. He wrote only one, *The Black Riders*. He hated both formal metre and rhyme. He had never seen a word of my poetry, but at one time he shouted at me: "You ruin... ruin... ruin all your work by the extra words you drag in to fill up metres and the digressions in sense you make to get in rhymes."

The dawn came up on these harangues. Then, as I have said, I slept on the sofa with either Soap, Flannel, or possibly Sponge on top of me. I eventually went back up the long steep hill to the Chart rather sadly. Actually the domestic troubles of the neighbourhood made me leave Limpsfield that day and I did not see the place again for more than twenty years. Then I went to see Crane's rose. It was flourishing, being a monthly rose, though there was actually snow on the cropped turf between the clumps of gorse.

I moved back to the Pent which I had let to an artist, then of some fame. His name being also Crane he had painted a bird of that species on the front door which gave on to the stockyard beyond a narrow strip of terrace and lawn. He had also painted numbers on all the room doors. There were thirteen. His family used to take baths on the lawn which worried and astonished the stockmen and shepherds in the yard below. When they left there remained behind them an extraordinary number of gloves. In every drawer of the bedrooms there were old, soiled and crumpled gloves. I have remained wondering to this day what they can have been wanting with so many. Is there a *maladie de gants,* as there is said to be of boots? At any rate, we used them all to manure the roots of a vine that covered the front of the house. Leather is the best of all manures for vines and also for figs. Indeed, if you want to plant a fig tree, you should plant it with its roots in an old leather portmanteau. You will have wonderful figs.

That autumn I had a letter from Conrad asking that he might be allowed to collaborate with me in the novel about pirates that I was writing. He said that he wrote English with great difficulty because he thought his more unspoken thoughts in Polish and his carefully spoken ones in French. These last he translated into English when he wished to write. Henley had suggested that he might gain fluency if he collaborated with some good English stylist. Conrad said that Henley had said that I was the finest stylist then writing English. That cannot have been true because, as I have said, Henley later told me that he had never heard of my existence. But Conrad liked to please as much as Henley liked to knock the nonsense out of you.

PART TWO

LETTERS AND THE LEFT

CHAPTER I

IN DARKEST LONDON

ONE of the greatest pleasures of my life—and it was accorded me at Limpsfield—comes back to me with the remembrance of sunshine, open doors and windows, climbing roses—and Prince Kropotkin. Mild, blond, spectacled, gentle spoken, the great scientist inspired me with singular affection. We wrangled by the hour together on the steps of the troglodyte cottage, the Princess being always watchfully near at hand. I cannot imagine about what we can have wrangled. It was rabbits, I think. Kropotkin immensely admired the rabbit. It was for him the symbol of perdurability—and mass production. It stood out against selection. Defenseless and adapted for nothing in particular, it had outlived the pterodactyl, the Hyrcanian tiger and the lion of Numidia. The coneys, in short, were a feeble people, yet had their homes in the everlasting rocks.

I don't know what I had to say against that. I obviously found something or the arguments could not have taken place. What I did say must obviously have had *some* sense, or he would not have returned to argue with me. He did that very often. It was perhaps because he was never allowed quite to finish an argument. His heart was weak; suddenly the Princess would descend upon him when he had just thought out something really crushing but before he had had time to formulate it. She would drape his plaid about him, he would be led off, spitting fiery sentences at me over his shoulder.

I knew nothing in those days about science. I know nothing now and it seems probable that I shall remain in a similar state of ignorance till I die. I have always entertained the most vivid distrust for the scientific mind. All the scientists I have known have seemed to me to be extraordinarily untrustworthy. I was once, at a public dinner in London, placed next to Professor Metchnikoff. He was at that time one of the most eminent scientists in the world. I was placed next to him because I was the only guest who could speak French. He was mild and gentle, his voice and accent resembled those of his compatriot, Kropotkin. His specialty was the great bowel. All the ills of life, all illnesses, poverties and distress were to be cured and life itself infinitely prolonged by proper attention to the great bowel. It was the rabbit of Kropotkin. You were to eat nothing but lettuce and milk. At any rate, you were to eat nothing that you would possibly want to eat.

On this occasion the beaming savant was reckless. He pointed to his plate and said:

"Tiens: je vais faire la noce.... I am going on the spree."

His plate contained a steamed sole. Save for blotting paper, there is nothing so without taste.

Having eaten it, he began to talk. He talked of the fowls of the air. As with Kropotkin, the coney of the rocks, so for Metchnikoff was the bird of heaven. Either because they have no great bowel or because, having it, they take great care of it, birds, according to Metchnikoff attain unheard of ages. Ravens, he said, lived to be a thousand, vultures are practically immortal. And as for peacocks . . . He was in ecstasies over the white peacocks he had just seen at Warwick Castle. Lady Warwick said they had been given to her by Disraeli who had them through his grandfather who had them from Hamburg where they had already attained the age of two hundred. . . .

I suggested to my smiling and triumphant neighbour that Disraeli was one of the most romantic liars of his generation and Lady Warwick was one of the most romantic . . . oh, figures of the court of Edward VII. But these facts conveyed nothing to the professor. In his subsequent volume on the great bowel, the white peacocks of Warwick occupied prominent positions.

When I was a child I had a Barbary ringdove called Jack. For a dove he was very combative. If you put your finger in his cage he would peck it. That is rare with doves.

He was fourteen when my grandmother gave him to me. She bred them and he was her favourite male bird, so she knew his age. I had him till I in turn was fourteen and he twenty-two. I gave him then to my nurse. At her house in Walthamstow he lived several years more. Then he laid an egg and shortly afterwards died. He must have been nearly thirty then.

When he laid the egg, he having been an indomitable male, my mother told me his story. He had first died at the age of seven, which is the average age of ringdoves. My mother, knowing that my grandmother would be grieved at the loss, had replaced him without telling her mother. She had twice done the same thing for me. My nurse being very old, her daughter had once done as much for her. So altogether it had taken five Jacks, the last at least being a lady, to reach the unprecedented age of thirty. A good deal of science is like that—lovingkindness supported by credulity. So too is religion, perhaps. Kropotkin desired the good of humanity, so he had his transfigured rabbit. Metchnikoff desired to multiply the sum of human good health, hence his belief in the white peacocks.

My old nurse Atterbury was married to a descendant of the great Atterbury of Rochester; her daughter to one of the great Racine's. Thus even in the lower part of the house I lived among resounding names whilst the great of those days—at least in the arts—thundered and declaimed upstairs.

M. Racine, the cook's husband, had been a member of the Commune in 1870. He was a striking, very tall man, with an immense hooked nose that leaned to one side and blank, black, flashing eyes. I used to listen to his declamations against

MacMahon and Gambetta with a great deal of edification. He must have been the first politician of the extreme Left that I ever listened to, but about the same time I must have had my first lessons in French literature from a M. Andrieux *fils*. He was another Communard. He comes back to me as the most elegant man I ever knew. His little moustaches were most comically waxed and he had the enviable gift of being able to make two cigarettes at once. The crook to the right of M. Racine's nose I always put down to the Versaillaise troops, figuring that they had done it with an immense paper clip. Thus I early developed a hatred for tyrants and a love for lost causes and exiles that still, I hope, distinguish me. Poland, Alsace-Lorraine, Ireland and even the Jews exiled from their own country—those were the names of romance of my childhood. They so remain for me.

My nurse, Mrs. Atterbury, had one singularity; she had come in contact with more murders and deaths by violence than any person I ever met—at any rate until 1914. In consequence, I imagine, my childhood was haunted by imaginary horrors and was most miserable. I can still see the shadows of wolves if I lie awake in bed with a fire in the room. And indeed I had the fixed belief for years that except for myself the world was peopled with devils. I used to peep through the cracks of doors to see the people within in their natural forms.

Mrs. Atterbury had been in the great railway accident near Doncaster where innumerable persons were burned to death; she had seen seven people run over and killed and her milder conversations abounded in details of deaths by drowning. I don't think she was present at the sinking of the *Princess Alice* but she talked about it as if she had been. Her normal conversations ran:

"When I lived with me yuncle Power in the Minories time of the Crimea wower, me yuncle let 'is top front to a master saddler. 'N' wen wower broke out the master saddler 'e worked niteanday, niteanday fer sevin weeks without stop er stay. 'N' 'e took 'is saddles to the Wower Orfis 'n' drawed 'is pay. All in gowlden sovrins in a Gledstun beg. 'N' wen 'e got 'ome 'e cut 'is froat on the top front landin' 'n' the blood 'n' the gowld run down the staircase together like the awtificial cascades in Battersea Pawk."..."The blood 'n' the gowld!" she would repeat and catch my wrist in her skinny fingers.

She was a witness—or an almost-witness of one of the Jack-the-Ripper murders in Whitechapel. She certainly came on the body of one of the victims and claimed to have seen a man vanish into the fog. I never actually heard the details of that. My mother, worried by the advent of a questioning police sergeant and the hysterics of the household below stairs, forbade the old lady to tell us children about it. But her impressive and mysterious absence in her best black bonnet and jet beaded cloak, and the whispers of the household made me fully aware that she was giving evidence at the Inkwedge. For long afterwards heaven knew what horrors were not concealed for me in the pools of shadow beneath the lamp posts. In solitary streets her footsteps echoing and a smudge of fog in the gaslight!

The last time I saw the old lady she was sitting—as she did day in day out for years—in the window of a parlour that occupied the apex of a corner lot in an outer suburb. She could look right up and down two long streets.

She greeted me with great vivacity. The day before there had been a tremendous thunderstorm. The streets up which she looked had been almost obscured by falling water. She said to me:

"I calls out to Lizzie.... Good gracious me! That man! 'E's struck dead!... 'N' 'e *was!*" she added triumphantly.

I fancy the physical gloom of London adds to the heaviness of my memory of those days. A city whose streets are illuminated only by the flicker of rare street lamps seems almost darker than one not lit at all. And the corners of rooms are always filled with shadows when the sole illuminant is a dim oil lamp or a bluish gas flame. And in London it was always winter. I remember, at any rate, no spring.

Above the darkness brooded the Hard Times. I am talking now of the early nineties. It is difficult to think how people lived then. In cold, in darkness, lacking sufficient clothes or sufficient food. With the aid of gin perhaps, or beer when you could cadge a pint. Charles Booth in his *Life and Labour of the Poor in London* states that ninety per cent of the population of London in those days depended for its *menus plaisirs*— its glimpses of light, of pleasure, its beanfeasts, its pints at the pubs—on windfalls. A working man got the price of a pint of beer for dexterously holding a lady's skirt off the wheel as she stepped out of a carriage. He would get as much for hailing a cab on a wet night. A charwoman got an old dress given her and sold it in a rag and bone shop for the price of a quartern of gin. Cooks had their perquisites—their "perks." Old women with "puffity pockets" beneath their skirts slunk up and down area railings. When they went up, the pockets would contain pounds of dripping: mutton fat, half plum cakes, remains of joints of beef. With the price of them the cook would get a new hat and some tobacco for her father in the workhouse. You lived in slums in Seven Dials, Whitechapel, Notting Dale. You burned the stair rails and banisters, the door jambs, the window frames for fuel. The rest of the world was no better. In Paris half the population was insufficiently fed; on sunny days the most horrible, half-nude creatures sunned themselves on the benches of the Champs Elysées. In Berlin the greater part of the population never thought of tasting meat. In St. Petersburg the condition of the poor would not bear thinking of. When you did witness it, you went mad or divested yourself of all your goods. Kropotkin had done that and was only one of scores of princes and great landowners. "The poor," the middle class householder said, "are always with us. These are the words of Jesus Christ." So he put on several mufflers, buried his purse in an inner pocket and buttoned up his overcoat to the chin, the better to avoid the temptation to give a starving woman a ha'penny. I remember taking the young daughter of my father's most intimate friend who was Queen Victoria's Master of Music, on the River Blythe in a canoe. I talked to her about the conditions of the poor. Next day her mother Lady Cusins said to me:

"Fordie, you are a dear boy. Sir George and I like you very much. But I must ask you not to talk to dear Beatrice ... about Things!" *Punch* itself was once almost suppressed. It printed a drawing of Charles Read's, showing two miserable women of the "Unfortunate Class" soaked by rain and shivering under one of the Adelphi arches. One of them says to the other: "Dearie.... 'Ow long 'ave *you* been gay!" "Gay," of course, signified "unfortunate." The consternation in Victorian London was terrific. *Punch* had spoken about Things. It never has again.

The natural corollary of these pressures was ... Anarchism, Fabianism, dynamitings, Nihilism. I saw a good deal of the inner workings of these.

I never took any stock in politics. But political movements have always interested me. I have only once voted. It is one of my most passionate convictions that no one individual can be sufficiently intelligent to be entrusted with the fortune or life of any other individual. Far less can he be morally capable of influencing to the extent merely of a single vote the destinies of millions of his fellows. I, at any rate, never could feel myself so entitled. I don't believe a creative artist can have any intellect; he is an observer and a recorder. He may have passions but he must mistrust them.

My own predilections have always been towards the Right. I like pomp, banners, divine rights, unreasonable ceremonies and ceremoniousness. It seems to me that when the world was a matter of small communities each under an arbitrary but responsible head then the world was at its best. If your community did not prosper you decapitated your chief. Till then he was possessed of divine rights. Presumably you cannot better the feudal system.

So I was always a sentimental Tory. But inasmuch as the Tories stood in the way of Home Rule for Ireland, I never voted or wrote for that Party. The Liberals of the nineties, on the other hand, were mostly great employers of labour. Their aim was to have always fringes of pauperised and parasitic working people so that wages might be kept low. It was perhaps an unconscious aim. My Tory view was that every workman should first be assumed of four hundred a year. Let the employer of labour assure that before he started his factory—or clear out. So, though the Liberals supported Irish Home Rule I could not support them.

The literary man in England is usually predestined to the Left. Ranking socially with the governess and the butler—a little above it if he prospers, a little below if he is poor, he cannot, *qua* writer, be a gentleman. In consequence he tries to achieve importance outside his art. The Tory Party was always the stupid party. And proud of it! In the nineties it let Henley starve and cold-shouldered Mallock. The Left, on the other hand, for ever stretches out its arms towards intellect. In consequence the English intelligentsia are almost invariably of the Left—Liberals, Fabians, Communists, Nonconformists or worse. The Liberals once offered me myself a constituency. ...Clackmannon and Kinross, a scattered and bleak district to work in politically!

It has from my earliest days been my fate to be regarded as a brand to be snatched from the burning by the Left. From my earliest days in darkest London! I never quite knew why. I suppose it was because as a boy I was of a family influential in the arts and letters. At any rate, whether it was the Rossettis or the Garnetts of the Left or straight Labour, Fabian, or Morris Socialist agitators, I was seldom, between the ages of twenty or thirty, without someone putting Left pressure upon me. I was for ever being shouldered off to meetings of Hammersmith Socialists at William Morris' house,

to meetings of Marxists at the Avelings, of Anarchists in Hyde
Park, of Parliamentary Labour leaders at the Holbourn Res-
taurant or to those of Pro-Boer agitators in Piccadilly Circus.
In that way I saw some pretty fights. I saw the Anarchists
break up a Morris Socialist meeting at Kelmscott House, the
Morris Socialists break up an Anarchist assembly in Hyde
Park and a tremendous set-to between Morris Socialists and
Fabians in a North Kent suburb—the Crays, I think, or
Eltham. In addition, being profoundly impressed by the use-
lessness to England of the British Empire and with the
savage nature of the Dopper Boers and wishing solely that
South Africa might be returned to its real owners, the natives,
and Kruger and Mr. Chamberlain hung on the same gallows,
I was once chased for three quarters of a mile along New
Oxford Street by a howling mob of patriots. That was during
the South-African War. On the other hand, I once saw Mr.
George Bernard Shaw brought to a clean stop in the middle
of a Socialist speech. Few people can have seen the like.

My cousins, the young Rossettis, did that.

They were Anarchists. Today they are almost infinitely
respectable. But when the hot blood roared in the young
nineties what were the young intelligentsia to do? The young
philistines joined the Skeleton Army and brought bladders of
ink or flour with which to disfigure young women of the Sal-
vationists. The Salvation Army was then young and marked
out for persecution. I remember Mr. Edward Garnett, then
too young and gallant. He constituted an anti-Skeleton Army
and, purchasing an enormous cudgel, went down to protect
the Salvationist lasses at Brighton. But if you did not do that
and were young and hot-blooded, militant Anarchism was your
logical occupation.

The young Rossettis, then, were Anarchists. They fostered
the Red Revolution with their pocket moneys; they harangued
meetings with childish voices; they ran a printing press and
an Anarchist journal called *The Torch* in the basement of
William Rossetti's house—which belonged to his wife, my Aunt

Lucy. The Torch press printed two literary curiosities at least. A pamphlet by Mr. George Bernard Shaw called *Why I Am an Anarchist* and my own first poem.

In our families, as children, we were trained to be geniuses under the powerful shadow of pre-Raphaelism. I think I have told all that before but I can't find the passage. I still remember, however, the painfulness of the process and the conviction that whilst my young cousins undoubtedly were geniuses I at least was a philistine. *They* wrote Greek dramas at the ages of five, nine and fourteen. I read penny dreadfuls in the coal cellar to avoid my father's eyes. And one of the acutest agonies of my childhood, after I was past the age of fearing the shadows at night was being pressed into acting in those dramas. The Rossettis' large back drawing-room in Endsleigh Gardens was converted into a stage....

It is astonishing how memories come back. When I write "Endsleigh Gardens" suddenly the name "Borschitzky" comes up before me. That is because I used to have violin lessons from the queer, tragic Borschitzky whose dismal adventure caused Euston Square to be re-christened. He came home late at night and found his landlady murdered in the kitchen. Being nearly blind he fell over the body, got himself covered with blood and as a foreigner and a musician was at once arrested by the intelligent police. He was of course acquitted but the trial caused so much sensation as the "Euston Square murder" that the respectable inhabitants petitioned to have the name of the square changed and it became Endsleigh Gardens. (Do you know how the inhabitants of Rugeley tried to get the name of their city changed? An atrocious series of murders were there committed by a man called Palmer, the reports of the Rugeley murders shaking all England. The inhabitants sent a deputation to the Home Secretary—Lord John Russell, I think. Lord John listened to them with attention and then suggested critically that they might call Rugeley after the Opposition Minister—Palmerston. They didn't.)

Poor Borschitzky was a small, bald man with an immense

nose who wore his greyish hair brushed stiffly forward into peaks, and his Gladstone collars came forward into peaks equally stiff. He was usually dressed in an immensely long frock coat that nearly hid his tiny legs and enormous feet. He spoke the most extravagantly pidgin English I have ever imagined and told the longest and most extraordinary stories.

His stories went like this:

"Zair voss a Gris-chun met a Chew. 'E sez to 'im: 'You uckly Chew I haf ad a mos' 'orible tream. It voss a mos' 'orible tream. I tream I co to dhe Chewish Evven an it voss a mos' 'orible place. Ze spidoons voss all filzy an ze daples coffred viz creese and dher voss no sand on de floor and de praziers voss dhick wiz rust. O it voss a mos' 'orible place and it voss fooll fooll fooll of 'orible uckly Chews spiddin on ze floor and shmoking; shmoking filthy filthy paipes.'

" 'Dad voss vairy curious,' sez ze Chew. 'I allso haf a tream. I tream I co to dhe Gris-chun Evven. O, and it voss a mos' loffely place. De spidoons voss of prass zat shone laike colld and dhe sand on der floor laike silber. Ond de daples voss viter ass a snotrift ond de praziers voss silber ond de dobacco poxes oll retty do be smoaked; O it voss a mos' loffly place. Loffly; loffly! ontly... zer vos nowun in it!' "

Towards the end of his life great troubles fell on poor Borschitzky. His mainstay had for years been the preparatory school to which I was sent. All his other pupils fell away; no orchestra would any longer employ him or play his compositions. Then his old friends, the owners of the school, died. They had supported him for years in spite of his peculiarities. The new owners of the school dismissed him. Then he had nothing and was perhaps seventy-two. He packed up his never-played compositions in several bundles and took them to the British Museum Library. Doctor Garnett told him kindly that the Museum only accepted the compositions of the dead. He went to the Post Office at the corner of Endsleigh Gardens, mailed the parcel to the Museum and then back to his room. He tidied it very thoroughly and destroyed a number of papers. Then he went out and by the railings of the Square before his windows he cut his throat. If he had done it indoors it would have caused his landlady a great deal of trouble and have made a horrid mess for her to clean up.

But still, when in continental cathedrals I hear the boom of the serpent and the sharp tap of the cantor as he starts the choir in its plain song, I see the form of poor old Borschitzky with his bow held over his beloved fiddle and the school choir with its mouths all open before him. He taps magisterially three times with his bow, his side-locks stick forward, his coat tails hanging down to his enormous boots. "Van! Doo! Dree...Pom-Pom," he shouts and off we all go on his rendering of the words that accompany the Ninth Symphony. God send him an old leather cushion stuffed with straw for his hard chair in his Chewish Evven...and send to all old, worn-out artists to be as considerate in their final distress.

Those were grim enough times for artists—the eighties and early nineties. I don't know that they are any better now. There was a blind poet called Philip Bourke Marston. He was not a very striking poet, but because he was blind he occupied a position of some note amongst the minor pre-Raphaelite group. He was bearded like an elder statesman of those days and, with his down-glancing eyes, was of noble appearance. Members of the group used to take it in turns to read to him in his gloomy room in the Euston Road. One day another poet of much greater reputation came in. He threw a fit of delirium tremens and imagined himself a Bengal tiger; he fell upon poor Marston and mauled him rather severely, the blind man being unable to defend himself at all. William Sharp came in and found them struggling on the floor. He pulled off the dipsomaniac who immediately burst a blood vessel, his blood pouring all over both Marston and Fiona Macleod. Sharp ran around to the nearby hospital to fetch a doctor. The physician in charge immediately cried out that Sharp must be arrested for murder. He was drunk. In the meantime, the dipsomaniac bled to death and Marston nearly went out of his mind.... Yes, grim times in that city of dreadful night!

I don't know if you know how many material comforts were lacking in the civilisation of those days. I was told by one of the frequent hostesses of Mr. Gladstone that that statesman and his wife always took to bed with them a hot water bottle filled with beef tea. They drank the fluid in the night. At six in the morning Mr. Gladstone had a grilled chicken leg and an egg beaten up in sherry brought to his bedside. At eight he ate a great breakfast.

But all the statesmen I have known were hearty feeders. I remember being privileged to wait on a Lord Chancellor at lunch at his Club. A young relative of mine to whom I acted as guardian had just become a Ward of Court and my financial adviser had strongly recommended against investments in Consols which stood then at 113. His Lordship disposed of the affairs of his wards at any odd moments outside the law courts.

The meal that he consumed was unthinkable, considering that it was lunch. He began with a tumbler of sherry and half of the upper side of an enormous *Turbot au Gratin*. (Brillat Savarin says that the perfect lunch consists of a small slice of *Turbot au Gratin*, a glass of sherry and a slice of thin bread and butter.) Then he had two immense beef-steaks, the greater part of an apple-pie, at least a quarter of a pound of Stilton and some grilled herring roes on toast. With the turbot after the sherry, he drank a bottle of hock; with the steak a bottle of Burgundy; with the cheese and savoury two dock glasses of port and he topped it all with a small glass of very good *fine*. His conversation was of a singular joviality on the side of salaciousness.

Immediately afterwards he delivered in the House of Lords a judgment in a peerage case—of extraordinary acumen, clearness of language and memory of details. And he was in his place in the Lords till far into the night, a full-dress sitting. I don't know what he had for dinner.

I have always thought that these extraordinary assimilative powers of statesmen were necessitated by the great fatigue incident on their calling. A man like a Prime Minister or a Chancellor of the Exchequer must burn up in the forced draughts of his career at least twice as much fuel as anyone leading a retired or a contemplative life. At any rate they gorge—and live to the ages of Methuselahs.

It is probably that, too, that makes them so extraordinarily touchy and ready to accuse their opponents of drinking. At any rate, all the Prime Ministers and most of the Members of the Cabinet who occupied seats in my time were automatically accused by the Opposition of drinking. On the face of it that would be impossible. You cannot drink habitually to intoxication and attend to innumerable details in an atmosphere of lunacy and at the same time live to great old age— any more than you can write good prose for long if you are habitually drunk.

Political acrimonies of the nineties were astonishing in England. They resembled those of the United States today— or was it yesterday? Here in New York, during a late Presidential election, I was told by a lady for whose veracity I would vouch before the Recording Angel that she was invited to a meeting of one great Party. It was a private ladies' meeting in Grand Concourse, New York City, say. The principal speaker alleged that, by oath, the Knights of Columbus were obliged to disembowel every Protestant woman they should meet who was with child. One of the Presidential candidates was a Roman Catholic. No one at the meeting uttered a word of doubt. My informant herself had no doubts. She asked me naïvely, as being a Roman Catholic, whether the allegation was not true. In the event, the Roman Catholic candidate was not elected.

Similar but less extensive mendacities distinguished the Gladstonian era of politics. I remember going to a tea party at the house of the lady who afterwards told me of Mr. and Mrs. Gladstone's beef tea. Mrs. Gladstone came in with the tapes of her bodice hanging down on her bustle. No one dared inform her of it. The incident created an extraordinary sensation in London and was widely used as an argument against Home Rule by the Tories. The argument was this: The Grand Old Man spent so much money in houses of ill fame that, firstly, his wife could not afford a proper lady's maid and, secondly, his behaviour drove Mrs. Gladstone mad, so that she ran about with her clothing in disarray. Actually Mrs. Gladstone was provided with a perfectly adequate and devoted staff of servants. But as old age came on she disliked standing still whilst her maid adjusted the armour of proof, the whalebones, the hooks and eyes, bustles and jet caparisons that finished the lady's—and the charwoman's—uniform of that day. So whenever she could escape from her maid's hands she would.

The legends that the Tories invented as to Mr. Gladstone's incontinence were extraordinary—and they died hard. It is only a few years since a scabrous memoir writer revived some of them and was suppressed. As a matter of fact, both the Grand Old Man and his wife interested themselves in re-claiming the "fallen" amongst females—a Victorian pursuit that, if it was as odious as most Victorian moral activities, might still be said to leave its practitioners on the side of the angels.

And indeed I have always regarded with extreme suspicion allegations of, let us say, unconventionalities against political Front Benchers. The Cabinet Ministers I have known were usually followed by detectives—for their own good. And they had a healthy fear of blackmail.

In any case, opposing Front Ranks in England balance things out. Great General Staffs of armies intrenched against each other in the late war considered it merely good manners not to shell each other's Headquarters. Similarly Ministers seldom put in motion machinery for the personal discredit of

opponents of equal rank. They allow their party organisations
to settle with each other what eccentricity shall balance against
what usualness. A Tory leader being alleged to be the father
of the children of several peers was given an unopposed seat
in a Northern constituency. Against that the Tories promised
not to oppose an Irish leader who had occasioned considerable
private scandal by leaving his wife rather cynically. When
a Liberal Minister, having an exaggerated appreciation of my
writing, offered to put me up for a Scotch seat I pointed out
that I was a Roman Catholic and an author. He said, "Oh,
that is all right. I have arranged that the Tories shall put up
against you a Jew with a practically criminal record in the
Stock Exchange. That will give you quite a sporting chance."
He, that is to say, wanted my pen for the support of his party,
the other side wanted the Jewish gentleman's questionably
earned money for their party chest.

That, of course, was in later days; politics in England
had become a more tranquil and cynical affair of jobbery
between ins and outs. A young man of a little ability and
inclination for discipline might be certain after several years
of docile voting for his party of a Junior Lordship of the
Treasury if his party remained in, or a comfortable consulate
general in a Scandinavian Kingdom or a South American Republic, if they fell. But in the early nineties all life was
bitter. The political pendulum was about to swing violently
towards the right. The artistic activities symbolised by the
physical force schools of Henley or Mr. Rudyard Kipling
were to find, in the world, their counterparts in outrages,
wars, rumours of wars, pogroms, repressions.

If the Ins and the Outs of the Front Benchers reviled
each other and even fought on the floor of the House of Commons, the extreme Left was not slow to learn from its betters.
The extreme Left of that day is the governing class of the
moment of writing, not only in England but over vast sur-
faces of the globe. The wheels of Parliament formerly nearly
stopped when Mr. Keir Hardie appeared on the floor of the

House in a cloth cap. He was the forerunner of Labour in power. The Left nearly burst itself with rage, when Lord Salisbury cynically called Mr. Dadabhi Naraoji, Liberal Member for Holborn, a "blackman." Today Mr. Naraoji's compatriots have fairly mastered the British Raj. It has been a curious process and one has perhaps been privileged to have witnessed during one lifetime so tremendous a world revolution. I would rather be twenty again than have that privilege.

CHAPTER II

FARTHEST LEFT

I CAN'T be twenty again, and I have little hope of witnessing the revolutions that the next three decades shall bring to this sphere. There remains then the dubious pleasure of remembering analytically the process of revolution that has gone on in the thirty years or so that have elapsed since I was twenty. I repeat—I must have said it a thousand times already —that I have never taken any part in party politics. I have always doubted my ability to interfere in the lot of my fellow-beings. So that if my one vote or voice could turn an election anywhere in the world I would employ neither, ever.

But I have always taken a passionate interest in politics everywhere and have never missed a chance of witnessing political activities. I have been to councils of the Primrose League and of the Anarchist Party, to Democratic Congresses and the meetings of anti-Dreyfusards, of Irish Sinn Feiners, and of German National Liberals. I have known quite well, at one time or another, two or three Cabinet Ministers, French or English, two or three Nihilist leaders, two or three Tzarist high officials. I have spoken to, or rather I have been questioned by, two reigning and one dethroned sovereign. I have lunched with two Tory Prime Ministers in private, with at least one President of a Great Republic and two or three Presidential candidates, as well as with at least one high Soviet official and one or two officials of the Kerensky régime in

Russia. I have in fact rolled my hump, as the French say, in whatever kind of political *parages* I could attain to. But from none of these contacts did I ever receive any infection. I have always—but so platonically!—preferred the idea of a Duke as Prime Minister to that of a Labour leader. Until you see them, Dukes seem more picturesque. On the other hand, Mr. Ramsay MacDonald is more picturesque than any Duke I have ever seen; so, for me, he may be Prime Minister as long as he wishes. I did once travel three thousand miles in order to vote in a British election. But that was to vote for a Suffragette candidate of I don't know what political complexion. I suppose he was a Tory, for the Liberals were then in power and engaged in refusing the vote to women. They were also, led by the Rt. Hon. David Lloyd George, engaged in assaulting as many women as they could with prudence lay hands on. So I hope no woman has ever, or ever will, voted for Dai Bach. But I don't know what his politics are now. Perhaps he is a Cwmric Home Ruler. I once saw Mr. George nearly out of his mind because the proprietor of a Winchester hotel had written a letter to the *Hampshire Sentinel* or some such paper. The hotel keeper said:

"The Chancellor of the Exchequer with three ladies in a car stopped at my hotel last Wednesday. The ladies made liberal use of my cloak rooms. They drove off saying that they were going to Salisbury Plain and would return to lunch. They did not. Neither did the ladies tip the cloak room attendant."

Now you might tell Mr. George to his face that he was ruining his country and he would be agreeably amused. Or you might tell him that he was a bad man to handle the land question because he doesn't know that pheasants do not eat mangold wurzels. He will still laugh, if a little on the other side of his face. For, once in an impassioned speech about the wickedness of landlords, he drew a moving picture of a small farmer ruined by the depredations of the landlord's pampered pheasants among his poor root-crops. But the flagitious suggestion that he traveled with the sort of ladies who didn't tip freely—that drove him almost out of his mind! He proposed to use all his powers as Chancellor of the Exchequer to ruin all the landlords of the Three Kingdoms; he threatened to commit the Winchester host to the Clock Tower; he proposed to have him cudgelled by the Liberal Party's Anti-Suffragette Volunteer Police. Eventually, at the suggestion of C. F. G. Masterman, then Chancellor of the Duchy of Lancashire, the matter was settled by sending the Winchester landlord a guinea for his cloak-room attendants. And I have no doubt the landlord, flattered by the autograph from a prominent statesman, for ever after that proclaimed what a grand gentleman Mr. George was. Perhaps he even voted Liberal.

But nothing ever said against Mr. George at his worst ever came anywhere near like the allegations hurled against Mr. Gladstone. I remember hearing a dear old lady, Miss Boyd of Penkill, who was not without artistic intelligence and the habit of the great world, definitely assert that the Grand Old Man was in the pay of the Pope and personally officiated at Black Masses. She said she had that on the authority of a Dean of the Anglican Church. I daresay she had.

I had a personal prejudice against Mr. Gladstone. He resigned finally on the day when my first book of poems was published. So, although the *Pall Mall Gazette* gave that work a two column review, it passed unnoticed. The tumult of that awful fall obscured all other events in England!

The privileged classes of the day were no doubt right in hating him. A renegade from their ranks, he, more than any man, knew the weak places in their armour. With each successive ministry he became more and more destructive to them. Indeed, looking at the course of English politics since his first Home Rule Bill, it becomes evident that the tremendous landslide of English politics towards the Left and against imperialism was almost entirely due to the tradition that he imposed on his followers. The Liberal Prime Ministers who followed him were almost all pale replicas of his figure. They had of course personalities of their own. Lord Rosebery was a jocular and sporting peer; Sir Henry Campbell Bannerman was of the type of the genial and successful shopkeeper; Lord Asquith was a cold Scots lawyer; Mr. George the most sanguine of small country attorneys and the most impassioned of special pleaders. But, be their voices what they might, their plow hands were the hands of Gladstone. It was his furrow that they prolonged. Nay, you might say the same of Mr. Bonar Law, Mr. Baldwin or the present Prime Minister, who, in his day, and from his own angle hated Mr. Gladstone as much as anyone else. I remember—at the time when Labour was at its most violent over the great dock strike—having tea along with Mr. MacDonald at the house of some Manx people. Mr. MacDonald was not then, as far as I can remember, on the executive list of any labour organisation. The members of the extreme Left party whom I then best knew regarded him with considerable suspicion as never having been a manual labourer. To me he seemed too good to be true.

He was *too* eloquent, *too* handsome, *too* genial, *too* ready to identify himself with the interest of everyone present. To the writer, he was the writer *pur sang*, to the sculptor, a sculptor. And, the majority of the company being from the Isle of Man, he was astoundingly a Manxman whilst to the one or two Scotch he was incredibly Scottish. I believe his Manx contacts were very limited. But our host was a Manxman who had been a member of the House of Keys—the Island Parliament. Mr. MacDonald, however, knew more about the procedure of that House than our host and far more of the island's topography and history. More even about Deemsters! I can still see his dark eyes and his white teeth flash as he talked about one particular Deemster whose feats are chronicled in one of Mr.—or is it Sir?—Hall Caine's books. Mr. MacDonald made him vastly more amusing than Mr. Caine.

Few people, seen not often, and very long ago, have so impressed me. For me Mr. MacDonald remains *the* journalist. The journalist must be able at the shortest notice and with the scantiest of knowledge to identify himself with anybody or anything. This Mr. MacDonald could do.

I don't know whether he was a highly successful writer for the Press. Perhaps he was too good a hater. I remember his genialities well—but still better his rancours. The Labour leaders I knew best at that day were Mr. Tom Mann and Mr. Ben Tillet. I happened to mention the opinions of one of them to Mr. MacDonald. I have seldom been so violently spoken to. The good journalist became at once the black hater. I was held personally responsible for the opinions of Mr. Mann or Mr. Tillet—whichever it was I had quoted. I did not hold those opinions, so I was not perturbed. The rest of the company was. Mrs. MacDonald intervened. She comes back to me as a very charming and modest woman. She certainly had great influence with her husband.

Mr. MacDonald then turned his attention to the Left in general. I don't know who were then his friends. He did not mention any. His eyes and teeth had flashed geniality before. Now they were like those of a fox at bay. There were no just men of Labour. They were all obtuse, venial, traitors, time servers. From Sir Charles Dilke to Ravachol! I gathered that something had that day gone wrong in Labour councils. But the phials of real wrath were opened on the memory of Mr. Gladstone.

That was not unreasonable. Gladstone had monopolised the energies of the Left. He had completely ignored Labour. It is astounding to consider that the minute index of John Morley's *Life of Gladstone* contains no reference to British Labour. But so it is. For the Liberals of Mr. Gladstone's prime the working man at his best was a devoted chapel-goer who might, say, read the *Penny Cyclopædia*, but must touch his head to his employer. At his worst, he was a drunkard who beat his wife, raced whippets and could be left to the Tory Beer Lords.

For Mr. MacDonald these views were anathema. But the

really extreme Left, he said, was almost worse. The one side tracked the working men, the other turned him into a bogey. Mr. MacDonald stood in the middle. He wanted a Parliamentary Labour Party whose councils should be composed of educated, black-coated, well-behaved, walking delegates. That type which was to become common enough later and to win, in the person of Mr. John Burns, to Cabinet honours, and in that of Mr. MacDonald to the Premiership—that type was little known in the days of which I am talking. Labour leaders then were violent or fanatical. Their names brought pallor to the cheeks of sewing circles and the crimson of rage to those of Dames of the Primrose League.

Mr. MacDonald must have been almost the first of the suaver type. It used to be said by the more violent that he obtained his election to the Council of the Labour Party by mistake. There was another J. R. MacDonald, said to be of the loud-voiced, horny-handed type, and the Trades Unionists when they voted for the present Prime Minister were said to have thought the other was the candidate. I daresay that the story is not true. I daresay no political stories to anyone's disadvantage are true. But I certainly met another MacDonald in those days and he was bewilderedly indignant over the election of his namesake.

I came myself in contact with Labour through a Manchester-enriched working-man-philanthropist called Charles Rowley, a queer, scarlet-bearded, gnome-like little man with an immense voice. He had been a journeyman frame-maker but his business had grown. He had a manner of bewildering jocularity, most of his witticisms being uttered in a nearly incomprehensible Lancashire accent and concerning themselves with unknown Manchester worthies or scoundrels. But he did a great deal of good with his money in the poorer outskirts of Manchester. He had founded in Ancoats a Brotherhood and there he provided the poorest cotton operatives—who are mostly avid for education—with a great deal of very good classical music, lectures by distinguished figures and exhibitions of pre-Raphaelite works of art. On account of his connection with Manchester, perhaps also with frame-making, Rowley became in later days very intimate with my grandfather and the two old gentlemen did what they could to throw me into the arms of the Left. They did not succeed very well.

It might be as well here to define what I mean by the Left.

In the nineties in England—as indeed in the United States, France, Germany, Spain and Italy, and subterraneously in Russia—advanced politicians fell into sharply graded divisions. There were Anarchists, Socialists, Radicals, Labour politicians, Liberals and Whigs. In addition, the Irish had Fenians, and the Russians Nihilists. These last were by that date mostly Terrorists. All the major divisions hated the one the other with extraordinary violence. They in turn were divided up. There were philosophic Anarchists like Prince Kropotkin or Mr. Bernard Shaw, physical force Anarchists who were mostly men crazed by witnessing the sufferings of their fellows— like Ravachol, Vaillant or the imbecile boy whom the Tzarist *agents provocateurs* persuaded to attempt to blow up Greenwich Observatory. Of course there were also actual criminals and criminal lunatics.

The philosophic Anarchists were strongest in London, where the police left them unlisted. There was also a small group round Réclus, the mathematician, in Paris. I think there were few in Chicago or New York and in Russia, Italy or Spain.

The physical force Anarchists were mostly active in Chicago, Paris, Rome, Naples and Barcelona. Their presence in London was usually transitory. They found refuge there when the pursuit of their native police forces grew too hot. The London police left them alone. They committed practically no outrages in that city. The outrages in London and the north of England were mostly committed by Fenians. Their idea was to terrorise England into granting freedom to Ireland. They dynamited, successfully or unsuccessfully, underground railways, theatres, the Houses of Parliament and docks. They murdered officials, landlords' agents, tenants who paid their rents or refused to subscribe to the *Clan-na-Gael* in Ireland. They had many sympathisers in the United States. They not infrequently crossed the American border to commit outrages or foment insurrections in Canada.

The physical force Nihilists were, like the Fenians, political terrorists. They assassinated Tzars, members of the Imperial family; generals, superior officials. They hoped thus to terrorise their rulers into granting political concessions or into abdication. They were mostly members of the middle classes, highly educated and of great physical energy. They included many women of the heroic type. The constitutional Nihilists took in the great majority of the Russian educated classes, nearly all professional men and a great many officials and army officers and a great majority of university students. Poverty in Russia of that day was at its most horrible. There were a great many of both Terrorist and Constitutional Nihilists in London then, some in Paris, a good many in Geneva and some even in New York, Boston and Chicago. In each city the Imperial detectives, spies, secret police and *agents provocateurs* much outnumbered the revolutionists. The police of every country except England worked hand in glove with the Tzarist organisations. A large proportion of the Tzarist agents took wages from both sides.

The Socialists of those days divided themselves in the purely sentimental groups like those headed by William Morris, the poet at Hammersmith or Charles Rowley's Ancoats Brotherhood. Their economic ideas were vague, but they desired to see people happy, dancing around maypoles and reaping plentiful wheat harvests with sickles. The Socialist movement in America was largely produced by Henry George's book, *Progress and Poverty*. This had its economic themes based on State ownership of the land, but practical or sentimental communion had long been a favourite exercise of the American intelligentsia from the earliest days of the Brook

Farm Experiment to Shaker and other religious Communistic brotherhoods.

Towards the nineties the Socialist movement took an energetic spring forward in the direction of economics. This was principally the work of the disciples of Karl Marx. In the United States Marxism speedily swallowed up the movement that had grounded itself in Henry George's doctrine. In France it gained little or no ground. In England it made a little stir. A Marxian group founded itself around Dr. Aveling who had married Elinor Marx. Her suicide rather broke up the group. But, all out, in those days Socialism was a middle-class, sentimental movement. Its exponents were mostly rich men or those, either by inheritance or marriage, who were in easy circumstances. It received support from young intelligentsia and persons not quite of the ruling classes who were dissatisfied with the way the actual ruling classes managed affairs. Later in the nineties the Fabian Society—the exponents of what they called "gas and water Socialism"—took the hegemony out of the hands of the William Morris, or Aesthetic, group. They were extraordinarily doctrinaire and rather grotesque personally. But they have made remarkably good. In Germany, where Socialism was not politically powerful, the movement had a terrorist Left Wing. Cohen, the half-brother of my grand-parents' adopted daughter, Mathilde Blind, attempted to murder Bismarck, and this attempt and other activities of the German Reds seems to have made a powerful impression in the minds of the German ruling classes.

Labour divided itself into Revolutionists, Trade Unionists, the Parliamentary Labour Party and Labour leaders with some economic doctrines. The Revolutionists desired any kind of Social Revolution, with lots of fun, looting, the burning of Government buildings and the paralysis of all authority. Trade Unionists aimed at the raising of wages by means of strikes, the Parliamentary Wing hoped to better the conditions of Industrialism by legislative action.

The Radicals were the active wing of the Liberal Party.

They usually attained to office by subverting their leaders or changing their coats. I have it on the authority of Mr. Frederick Harrison, the Positivist Pope of those days, that about 1882 Mr. Chamberlain and Sir Charles Dilke came to him to ask him if the times were not ripe for the declaration of the First British Republic, with Mr. Chamberlain as President. Later Mr. Chamberlain became Mr. Gladstone's Judas much as Mr. Lloyd George became Mr. Asquith's.

The Liberals shaded off into Whigs, the Whigs into Peers, but, as the Gladstonians became more radical, these grew scarce. One of the most comic dilemmas that Mr. Gladstone had to face at the beginning of his last Ministry was to find a Peer to meet the Prince of Wales at dinner. A new Ministry had to give the Prince of Wales a dinner. The Prince of Wales had to be received by a Peer. There was no Peer in the Ministry. I don't know whom he got. I suppose Rosebery. Hartington had abandoned him along with Chamberlain. Nobody, however, called *him* Judas. I suppose it was taken to be natural that a great Whig landowner could no longer stay with the Liberal Party. They had a wing whose shibboleth was "Three Acres and a Cow," the land to be taken from the owners and divided up, so that every man in England should have a house, three acres of land and a cow of his own. It would have been a great pity for the cow!

It was a symptom of the day that the great Whig Lords, the Russells, Cavendishes and the rest who had traditionally belonged to the Left ever since the days of Cromwell should have at last gone over. Liberal Peers since that day have, like Mr. Sidney Webb, invariably been the temporary expedients of the Minister in power. Their sons have equally invariably become Tories. The Liberal complexion was practically unknown in France and the United States. It was fairly strong in Germany, and strong, if of necessity concealed, in Russia. I am talking of countries that I have known fairly well. The Revolutionary Directorate that men in St. Petersburg after Bloody Sunday was composed almost exclusively of lawyers, doctors, merchants, army officers and fairly high State officials. They debated forms of government along English Liberal lines. They found that their interests differed and were so long about the debate that the Tzar and his Ministers ventured back and resumed power. The Revolutionists had not yet settled on a form of government. Similarly the Kerensky Government of 1917 was an affair of very mild Liberals and was swept out of power by a far grimmer impulse before it had really constituted itself. I had a relative who was a member of both these Liberal bodies, and I knew several of the Kerensky Ministers. They were intolerable theorists and used to drive me crazy with their interminable professions of political virtue.

My personal contacts with nearly all schools of Left thought were very numerous during the earlier nineties. A good many were accidental. Of Liberal Front Benchers I saw several during my grandfather's lifetime. They were the Manchester School and he was painting his frescoes in Manchester Town Hall from 1882 till his death—a matter of twelve years. They were much disliked by the Manchester Town Council who were mostly Conservatives, and I used to think that the visits the Liberal Ministers paid him from time to time were of a political complexion. At any rate, the Brights, John and Jacob, and Mr. Morley—Honest John of those days—came to see him at work fairly frequently. As often as not my grandfather would send me to take them round the pictures. He would have the gout, either real or pretended. He disliked being interrupted whilst he was working—and particularly so when it was by the distinguished of any kind.

I don't think the politicians much liked his pictures. They were new-fashioned and realistic for those days. John Bright I only saw once. He seemed to be too distracted to pay much attention to the pictures or to me and hurried away before we had got round the hall. He reminded me of the White Rabbit in *Alice in Wonderland* as he scuttled through the swinging doors exclaiming that he was very late. But in a silver and pink way he was very beautiful, with his long white hair and high-coloured cheeks. He radiated benevolence. Jacob Bright gave the air of being more cultured; at any rate, he and his wife paid more attention to the pictures.

Morley I very much disliked. I have never had a more disagreeable half hour than that which I spent taking him round the vast hall. He comes back to me as having been at once reserved and disagreeable. He treated the details that I gave him as to the history of Manchester with contempt and said that the drawing of several of the figures was grotesque and impossible. He said—about Diderot—something that struck me at the time as curious and unsympathetic—as to the untidiness of his dress or his personal habits. That was because my grandfather's figure of Crabtree observing the transit of Venus struck him as resembling the encyclopædist. For some reason he took it for granted that I had not read his life of Diderot. I had. But when I heard him talk about his subject, I wondered he had chosen the French philosopher to write about.

My grandfather afterwards sent me to see him. He possessed a number of contemporary pamphlets about the Lancashire cotton famine during the Civil War. My grandfather had the idea of painting a fresco showing the first cargo of cotton arriving at Liverpool after the war was over. Mr. Morley did not seem to be more sympathetic than about the author of *The Parasite*. The pamphlets and papers that he asked his secretary to select to lend me were nearly all economic treatises or anti-Southern propaganda. He did not seem to understand that what my grandfather wanted was information about picturesque or tragic episodes that happened in Manchester. I cannot remember whether Mr. Morley said that he was actually present at the arrival of the first cotton bales. He certainly talked about the demonstration made by the crowd—as if with disfavour. The people waiting

on the wharf caught the ship's ropes and dragged her into
dock whilst they spontaneously sang the *Old Hundred*. During
the entire years that the American Civil War had lasted no
cotton had come to Lancashire and, as at least half Lancashire was engaged in the cotton mills, the destitution had
been terrible.

But the *Old Hundred* begins: "Praise God from whom
all blessings flow," and Mr. Morley seemed to dislike the
introduction of the Deity into the matter. I think he said
it would have been better if the Almighty had turned the
hearts of the South. Then there would have been no war
and no famine. I disliked that. Stonewall Jackson and Lee
were my heroes of that day. I daresay they still are. Mr.
Morley, even, did not wish me to take the newspaper reports
of the arrival of the cotton. I think he did not wish this
testimony to Lancashire's religious crassness perpetuated in
Manchester Town Hall. He would have preferred a fresco
to the glory of Free Trade with portraits of Bright and
Cobden—and no doubt of Gladstone and himself. He was a
dry-skinned, lean man with cold eyes and a trick of swallowing suddenly. But he was no doubt passionate enough.
At any rate I remember his making several passionate speeches
in the House of Commons.

I never spoke to Mr. Gladstone, but I saw him once
extraordinarily close to. I was in a train going North—I should
think in 1887. The train stopped at Swindon. Immediately
alongside my carriage was another that contained Mr. Gladstone. He was sitting reading a memorandum with his feet
on the cushions of the opposite seat. His face was expressionless, or rather morose. He was quite alone. He was wearing
a black woolen cap with ear-flaps tied under his chin. It
struck me that anyone could easily have assassinated him if
they had wanted to. And plenty did then!

I only once heard Mr. Gladstone speak. Then he was
in an outrageous temper. He was talking about Egyptian
finance and someone—I think Lord Randolph Churchill—

ejaculated "Remember Gordon!" Mr. Gladstone was apparently still sensitive about the accusation that he had allowed Gordon to be murdered at Khartum. He let out a perfect flood of invective as to the unmannerliness of the interjection and menaced his interrupter with a wagging forefinger. His voice was of extreme beauty and of an amazing carrying power. In the Stranger's Gallery you could hear his merely whispered asides—almost his very breathing.

He was said to resemble an eagle. But in his anger he seemed to be very much more like the eagle owl with all its feathers ruffled up into a shape like the sun. I would have sworn that his eyes were yellow. I wonder if anyone knows what color his eyes were. Nobody knows that of Napoleon's.

I wonder indeed if anyone today remembers who all these people were—Gladstone, Morley, Bright and the rest. The other day I happened to mention Mr. Gladstone before an American poet of great culture.

He said:

"Gladstone? Who was he?" He added: "Oh, the fellow who took two chops at a cherry."

I was puzzled until I remembered that it was once tremendously noised abroad that Gladstone—like Henry James—used to Fletcherise. He took thirty-two bites at every morsel of food before swallowing it. He also—like the Father of one Republic and the exiled Emperor of another—used to chop down trees for exercise.... But "two chops at a cherry" is pretty poor alms for oblivion for one whose voice could once shake the world. To balance the account, however, I later met a gentleman farmer of Tennessee who talked for a whole afternoon of the times and policies of Sir Robert Peel and Lord Palmerston, as if we were still living in 1842.

Mr. Morley's distaste at the idea of the intrusion of the Deity into mundane affairs reminds me of a strikers' meeting on Tower Hill during the great dock strike. News came during the meeting that the Government had taken some step that materially aided the employers. Mr. Ben Tillet—who was almost out of his mind at the news—raised his fist at the heavens and called on the meeting to curse God. Mr. Cunninghame-Graham who was on the platform quieted things down by saying that it was wrong of Mr. Tillet to throw imprecations at the Almighty. God was a man of the very best intentions who died young. The committee of the aristocratic Devonshire Club had put up with many of Mr. Graham's political eccentricities because of his illustrious birth and connections, but that was too much for them. They asked him to resign from the club. Mr. Graham answered that a committee nearly all of whose names ended in -schen, -baum, and -stein no doubt knew more about Jehovah than he did. But he had been speaking about the Son. He heard no more from that body.

The attitude of the militant atheist—or even that of the coldly rational agnostic like Mr. Morley has always been rather a mystery to me. But Mr. Tillet's emotion was comprehensible enough. Those were days when it might well seem that only the direct intervention of the Deity could much alleviate the lot of the underdog and Mr. Tillet's emotion was much more that of the despairing believer than that of the rationalist.

The world in turning towards universal industrialism was undergoing immense growing pains. The distress which goes with developments, as with stagnations of trade is accompanied by wide-spread and atrocious suffering. The hideousness of the poverty in the early nineties the world over would now be incredible were it not that some of them are only too visible today. And it is not merely that hunger, cold and squalour beset the actually destitute. It was the terrible anxiety that for ever harassed the minds of those who were just above the starvation line. You were in work one day; you were out the next. Thus even whilst you were in work you had no rest at the thought of the morrow. Worklessness meant the gradual disintegration of your home, the wearing out of the shoes of your children, if your children had shoes; it meant thus slow starvation, your moral decay, your slowly sinking away from all the light. I remember Charles Booth saying fiercely in 1892: "Do you realise that there are now in London 250,000 people—and in Lancashire God knows how many—who in this December weather have no fire in the grate, no meal on the table, no stick of furniture on the floor, no door in the doorway, no handrails to the stairs and no candle to go to bed by?" Mr. Booth was a great shipowner but he was also a statistician. His statistics affected him at that time almost to madness.

If that could happen to a very rich man with great powers of alleviating suffering, what would take place in the minds of those who, just not starving themselves, lived as if buried beneath the foodless, the unclothed, the unwarmed, who dwelt in darkness? And it is to be remembered that if things were that bad in London they were infinitely worse in every other country in the world. It was a day of nightmares universal and showing no signs of coming to an end. Nothing could happen but what did—a world-wide flood of disorder ending in Anarchism. That was inevitable.

The state of affairs in some of the Continental cities was incredible. I remember Paris in 1892 as being absolutely paralysed. I was stopping with American relatives who belonged to the rich Anglo-American Catholic circle that solidly ornamented in those days the French capital. That colony and the rich and solid French families with whom they mingled and intermarried lived again as if in the days of the siege. They dared not go to theatres, to restaurants, to the fashionable shops in the rue de la Paix, to ride in the Bois where there were Anarchists behind every tree. The most terrible rumours ran round every morning: the Anarchists had undermined the churches of Paris; they had been caught pouring prussic acid into the city reservoirs; the New York *Herald* came out one day with a terrifying story of Anarchists having been hidden beneath the seats of the tiny black and yellow fiacres and coming out and robbing and murdering rich American ladies in the Champs Elysées.

The Anarchists did not of course hide beneath the seats of fiacres because those little vehicles had no spaces beneath their seats. The axles of the wheels were there. Nevertheless today the catalogue of their outrages reads like an improbable nightmare. They bombed the cafés where the rich took their *apéritifs* and the more costly restaurants; then they bombed poor restaurants where their comrades had been arrested; they bombed theatres, railway stations, the Chamber of Deputies, the President of the Republic himself. Merely to consider how they could have done it in the face of the most skilful and remorseless police force in the world is an amazing speculation.

"Paris," says a contemporary journalist, Fernand Evrard, writing in 1892, "offers the spectacle of a besieged city: the streets are deserted, the shops closed, the omnibusses without passengers, the museums and the theatres barricaded. The police are invisible but ubiquitous; the troops assembled in the suburbs are ready to march at the first command. The rich foreign families take flight, the hotels are empty, the takings of shops dwindle. After some weeks of relative quiet the populace takes hope again and the red sequence seems at an end. Then the terrible bomb in the police station of the rue des Bons Enfants, followed immediately by the discovery of the dynamite cartridge in the Prefecture of Police causes new panic and despair.... There is cholera in the outskirts of the city, the Panama scandal within the walls ... one hundred and four deputies are suspected of complicity. The year 1892 may well bear on its brow the words 'Death to Society,' and 'Corruption to Politics.' "

The passion that inspired these paralysers of a whole society was probably nothing else but pity. Ravachol, who committed the outrage in the rue de Clichy, was arrested because he could not restrain himself from saying to a waiter in a *bistrôt:* "How can you call that an outrage when there is so much suffering in the world?" The queerly paradoxical and reckless speech might well stand for the philosophical basis of the whole movement, more especially when you consider that neither Ravachol nor Vaillant nor yet the assassin of President Carnot had suffered much themselves from poverty. And indeed the relative prosperity of England and possibly the more considerable voice that the poorer classes had in the government of the country may have been as much accountable for the absence of Anarchist activities in London as the fact that, the police letting them alone, the Anarchists were determined not to close to themselves their only safe refuge.

Kropotkin's was the only name of the movement that is likely to remain in the annals of those times. A prince and officer of the Imperial body-guard he was in addition a very distinguished scientist. His investigations led him irresistibly towards the frame of mind that is called non-resistance and he was one of the most determined opponents of the theory of evolution as one upholding conquests. Eventually, like Tolstoi and so many of the Russian aristocracy, he abandoned his career and his vast properties and lived the life of a poor man among the poor.

From that to the bombing of the commissariat in the rue des Bons Enfants may well seem a far cry but the workings of the human mind are always mysterious and when they take place under conditions of great stress there is no saying whither they may not tend. Kropotkin's great sympathy for the very poor and the very oppressed made him seek their company and they his. That he never counselled violence or excused it when it had taken place is certain enough, but the essence of his philosophy being that laws by their very existence incite to crime, it was not a great progression for a hunger-weakened brain to imagine that the destruction of those who benefit by or enforce laws will bring about a reign of peace upon earth.

I will not undertake to say that I ever heard him deprecating violence to Ravachol or Vaillant, though I certainly was in the same room with Vaillant if not with Ravachol on more than one occasion at a Socialist club, but I do remember Kropotkin speaking with great emphasis against physical force and even against revolution brought about by violence, the occasion coming back to me very vividly.

It was during the great coal strike of 1893 and Charles Rowley had invited me to dine with some other labour leaders with the idea of converting me to advanced opinions, such as they were in those days. The meal took place in the Holborn Restaurant, a haunt of everything that was middle-class and Free Masonic. There were present Mr. Ben Tillet, Mr. Tom Mann, Charles Rowley, the Manchester Socialist, and Prince Kropotkin, and since the restaurant was so very middle-class the presence of those notorious promoters of disorder created a sufficient agitation so that the management tucked us away into a quiet alcove where the waiters hovered about us with scared faces.

As long as the discussion remained on general lines of the relief of suffering or even of strikes these leaders of advanced thought got on very well together, and that stage lasted for the greater part of the meal. But the moment it came to the discussion of remedies Kropotkin's quietism acted like a bomb at the table, the Labour representatives being all for strong measures against authority. Kropotkin was all for non-resistance, meditation and propaganda so that eventually we broke up in disorder after a deadlock in which Mr. Mann, who was dark and of Celtic animation with an immense harsh voice, had gone on for a long time striking the palms of his left hand with the clenched fist of his right and exclaiming over and over again, "We must destroy! We must pull down! We must be rid of tyrants!"

Mr. Tillet, little, blond and virulent, echoing in a soft but even more destructive voice:

"Yes, we must tear down! We must make a clear space!" And Charles Rowley with his red beard and Lancashire

brogue, trying uselessly to quiet the noises. But always in the
pauses came the quiet, foreign accent of the Prince, who, with
the eyes of a German scientist behind his gleaming spectacles
fixed intently on his interlocutors, exclaimed gently and unceasingly:

"No, there must be no destruction. We must build. We
must build the hearts of men. We must establish a kingdom
of God."

That seemed to drive the others mad.

When the party broke up, I stood for a long time with
the Prince under the portico of the restaurant whilst the rain
poured down. He asked me what I was doing and I told him
that I was just publishing a fairy tale. He said that that was
an admirable sort of thing to do. Then he said that he hoped
the fairy tale was not about Princes and Princesses—or at
least that I would write one that would be about simple and
ordinary people. I have been trying to do so ever since. Indeed
I tried to do so at once with the singular result that although
my first invention had a great—indeed a prodigious—sale I
could not even find a publisher for the second. My subsequent
difficulties have been technical. I always want to write about
ordinary people. But it seems to be almost impossible to decide
who are ordinary people—and then to meet them. All men's
lives and characteristics are so singular.

I do not think I saw much of Kropotkin after that in
political gatherings though I must have seen him once at the
office of *The Torch* in Goodge Street. But I did not much frequent that establishment. Until my aunt's death, the Rossettis'
house being her property, my juvenile relatives carried on their
activities at home. Why my aunt permitted them to run in
her basement a printing press that produced militant Anarchist
propaganda I never quite knew. She no doubt would have
approved of any activities of her children, so long as they
were active in a spirited and precocious way. But I imagine
she would have preferred their energies to continue to be
devoted to the productions of the Greek plays which caused

me so much suffering. In any case the world was presented with the extraordinary spectacle of the abode of Her Majesty's Secretary to the Inland Revenue, so beset with English detectives, French police spies and Russian *agents provocateurs* that to go along the sidewalk of that respectable terrace was to feel that one ran the gauntlet of innumerable gimlets. That came to an end.

My uncle William was a man of the strongest—if slightly eccentric—ethical rectitude and, as soon as my aunt was dead and the house become his property, he descended into its basement and ordered the press and all its belongings to be removed from his house. He said that although his views of the duties of parenthood did not allow of his coercing his children, his sense of the fitness of things would not permit him to sanction the printing of subversive literature in the basement of a prominent servant of the Crown. *The Torch* then had to go.

It removed itself to Goodge Street, Tottenham Court Road —a locality as grim as its name. There it became a sort of club where the hangers-on of the extreme Left idled away an immense amount of time whilst their infant hosts and hostesses were extremely active over their forms. I did not myself like it much and only went there I think twice—to see about the printing of my first poem. This was not very Anarchist in coloration. It ran:

> *"Oh, where shall I find rest?"*
> *Wailed the wind from the West,*
> *"I've sought in vain on dale and down,*
> *In tangled woodland, tarn and town*
>   *But found no rest."*

> *"Rest thou ne'er shalt find,"*
> *Answered Love to the wind.*
> *"For thou and I and the great, grey sea*
> *May never rest till Eternity*
>   *Its end shall find."*

It seems to be a fairly orthodox piece of verse to find publication in a Red journal.

The other piece of imaginative literature to which *The Torch* committed itself was Mr. George Bernard Shaw's pamphlet entitled *Why I Am an Anarchist*. That had an amusing sequel.

When Mr. Shaw first came to London he was a true-red Anarchist. A little later he changed his coat and became a Socialist, at first of the William Morris and then of the Marxian school. In the early days of the nineties the quarrels between Socialist and Anarchist were far more bitter than those between either and constituted Society. These quarrels as often as not ended in free fights. I have said that I remember seeing several meetings in Hyde Park break up in disorder, the Socialists being always the aggressors and usually the victors. One meeting at Kelmscott House was brought to an end by someone—I presume an Anarchist—putting red pepper on the stove. Poor William Morris, with his enormous mop of white hair, luxuriant white beard and nautical pea-jacket, used to preside at these meetings of his group. I never heard him speak. But he walked up and down in the aisle between the rows of chairs, his hands in his jacket-pockets, with the air of a rather melancholy sea-captain on the quarter-deck. He disliked the violence that was creeping into his beloved meetings. He had founded them solely with the idea of promoting human kindness and peopling the earth with large-bosomed women dressed in Walter Crane gowns and bearing great sheaves of full-eared corn. On this occasion his air was most extraordinary as he fled uttering passionate sneezes that jerked his white hairs backwards and forwards like the waves of the sea.

Mr. Shaw imprudently addressed a meeting of Socialists in Hyde Park. It was perhaps his one mistake in tactics. As soon as he announced the title of his address which was *The Foolishness of Anarchism* childish voices arose on the silence. They repeated and repeated: "Buy *Why I Am an Anarchist* by the lecturer. *Why I Am an Anarchist* by the lecturer. One penny." The high skies towered above the trees of the Park; in the branches birds sang. Those fresh young voices mounted to heaven. Mr. Shaw's did not. Every time he opened his mouth that anthem: *"Why I Am an Anarchist* by the lecturer. One penny," began again. Every now and then they added: "And worth it!" I suppose it would be worth ten thousand pence today. And then some!

Those young people shortly afterwards arrived at the conclusion that they were being victimised, and *The Torch* was discontinued.

It had one other curious literary offshoot. That was *The Secret Agent* by Joseph Conrad. In one of my visits to *The Torch* office I heard the inner story of the Greenwich Observatory outrage. It was subsequently confirmed and supplemented to me by Inspector French of Scotland Yard after first my mother's and then my own house had been burgled by a professional cracksman employed by the Russian Embassy. I happened to tell the story to Conrad shortly after my burglary and, since he detested all Russians, and the Russian Secret Police in particular, he made his novel out of it. In his attribution to me of the plot which will be found in the Preface to the book he says he is sure that the highly superior person who told him the tale could never have come into contact with Anarchists. I have recounted above how I did.

A short time after that dinner at the Holborn Restaurant, I forsook London and took to agriculture.

CHAPTER III

THE OUTSIDE

It must have been in 1894 that I first left London to take up agriculture. I have done that three or four times in as many countries. Before then I must have formed nomadic habits, for I hardly remember a year of which I did not spend a great portion outside England until today when, rather to my surprise, I find myself a legally domiciled citizen of Gotham and I am again contemplating taking up farming—this time in Tennessee if not in Provence. At any rate I have never felt myself quite happy or quite a man when I did not possess and work at least a small piece of land. Then I would leave it to a bailiff and go to the other side of the globe.

Before I was twenty I had spent three winters in Paris and two summers in Germany. In Paris I studied agriculture, or rather kitchen gardening—at the Sorbonne under the great Professor Gressent. In Bonn I studied history under my uncle Hermann who was Professor of Canon Law at that University. Professor Gressent was the first exponent of the hoe. He used to begin all his lessons by saying, *"Messieurs, trois fois biner vaut deux fois engraisser....* Three hoeings are as good as two coats of dung." I remember sitting for hours of a morning outside the *Café des Deux Magots* in the Place St. Germain des Près. I was making, for an examination, a plan of an ideal kitchen garden *à la Gressent*. I can still see it. It had a dung-well in the centre. From that all its beds radiated.

But no bed was so broad that its middle could not be reached by a hoe wielded from the paths on either sides. So you did not tread on the beds when hoeing. It is a good plan for a kitchen garden. Try it if you are laying one out. I passed my examination.

Yes, I can still see my plan. I can see also the veins in the marble of the table at which I wrote. But indeed I saw them a month or so ago. The actual table is still in use.

My Uncle Hermann was the type of the absent-minded professor. My aunt, a very elegant and beautiful woman who had been a prima donna and had sung, my uncle used to say, before all the crowned heads of Europe, used to sew tapes instead of buttons on his coats. When lecturing he fingered his buttons in succession until each fell off. I was once walking with my uncle in the public gardens in front of the Kaiserhof Hotel. A lady passed us and smiled. My uncle said: "That is a very attractive woman. I should like to make her acquaintance." It was his wife.

Amongst my uncle's pupils in Canon Law at Bonn was the German Emperor, William II. Whenever, after his ascent to the throne, the Emperor passed through Bonn he made it a strict practice to call on any one who had ever given him a cup of tea when he was a student—even to the oldest of old maids. He usually avoided passing through Bonn. I was once in my uncle's house when the Emperor paid him a three-minute call. When, years after, at my solitary interview with William II, I ventured to remind him that I had once been in the same room with him in Bonn, he said that he of course remembered my uncle very well—but he did not remember me. I was reminded—conversely—of a professor in the University of California in Berkeley. He wrote an immense article about myself. In the course of it he said: "I have read over a thousand anecdotes by Mr. Ford but as he made no reference in any of them to me I can only believe that I made no impression on him."

It must have been in 1891—or possibly in 1892—that I

met Bismarck walking all alone in the Poppelsdorfer Allé. He was moving very slowly, leaning laboriously upon a cane—in the uniform of his old regiment—the Bonn Cuirassiers. His immense Great Dane, Tiras, the gift of the German nation, followed him, his great head lowered, so that his dewlaps nearly reached his master's heels. The Prince acknowledged my salute with a weary and as if distasteful raising of his heavy lids. It was as if he disliked me intensely. But I daresay it was only that, then, in the period of his fall and loneliness, he disliked the whole world. I remember thinking at the time: "It is queer he should wear a uniform when now he must be tired of all parades and ceremonies." But I understand it now. I should like to be wearing a uniform again myself. I suppose I never shall.

Later—nearly where my uncle had tried to make the acquaintance of his wife—I was witness of what I took to be a carriage accident. A tiny, incredibly smart dog-cart with a cockaded English groom and wonderfully shining harness was darting along the road outside the promenade rails. It stopped so suddenly that the groom appeared to be projected at the horse's head whilst his master, in the costume of a Borusser corps-student seemed to be thrown out of the other side of the cart. That was merely smart—*Schneidig!*

The Crown Prince had perceived, almost behind my back, the English lady for whom he was said to entertain a virtuous passion. He had pulled in his pony mercilessly and was flying to her feet. The groom had merely, smartly, taken the pony's head.

That afternoon I heard my Aunt Antonia comment that her life was indeed a hard one. My uncle was then Rector of the University. It was her duty to chaperon any Princes or Serenities who happened to be up at Bonn. She said:

"The Crown Prince is an admirable young man. But I do think he ought not to loll about on a sofa, at the Freifrau von——'s with Miss——. It is very wearing!"

Later in the same year strange rumours went about London. Little Willie was said to have thrown over the Imperial load and to have followed Miss —— to London. He was going to have done with the trappings of Royalty, to marry Miss —— and to settle down in a cottage in Surrey, poultry farming. He was persuaded to visit the German Embassy. When he came to, he was on an Imperial battleship, recovering from a heavy drugging, on his way to Kiel. I don't know if the story was true. I daresay it was.

It might have changed the history of the world if the German Crown Prince had had an English wife!

My early days in Germany were, however, passed in the society of Social Democrats rather than with Princes. That was still the old Germany of crow-stepped gables, black and white, half-timbered houses, swineherds, adventurous tailors, industrious apprentices, storks' wine-flagons and *Gemütlichkeit*. Nevertheless the new was already creeping in. I fought a duel in Bonn with a student who trod on the tail of my dog. It was not a *Mensur*—one of those affairs at which the *corps studenten* hack each others' faces to pieces and incur the scars of glory. No, it was a duel with rapiers such as soothes outraged honour. For, if in student Bonn of those days another student trod with intention on the tail of your dog, your honour was tarnished until blood had cleansed it. But to my astonishment—for I had regarded the contest as a necessary action—my young friends of the Intelligentsia regarded the proceeding with the greatest disfavour. In those days already the State universities—and particularly their customs—were regarded with great disfavour by the children of the professional classes. So I got no glory.

A little later I fought another with a young man in Paris over a celebrated professional beauty. I do not mean for a moment to assert that either of us had enjoyed the lady's favours. She was meat for our masters and is still a leader in the society of another capital. But I had actually spoken to the lady and my young friend thought he was better with the sword. So we went to the Bois de Meudon.

In each event the result was the same. I wounded my adversary in the forearm. I was so long in the reach that few men of my own class or near it ever got by me. But I was always so wanting in enterprise or ferocity that I never made much show in competitions, though I once won a pair of gilt-headed foils at London University. They were promptly pawned by a necessitous relative; so I got little good out of them.

I all but got into a duel later with a Polish enemy of Conrad's. That would have been a much more serious affair. But, as I have elsewhere related, Conrad's unfortunate opponent committed suicide in the train coming to the meeting. I think I was rather glad that that meeting did not come off. The poor man was too miserable to have been fought. But last spring I tried to fight one with a French man of letters who had said injurious things about Henry James—and that that did not come off I still regret. I wrote the most injurious things I could think of to that French gentleman—to the effect generally that dog does not eat dog if he is a gentlemanly dog and that one constructive imaginative writer should not write things against another. But the French gentleman told the friend of mine who went to see him that: firstly, the letter had not reached him; secondly, that he was too old to fight and that, thirdly, he should imagine that I was too. So I suppose he really had the laugh on me. For, alas, when I come to think of it, almost all the people I could now want to meet in mortal combat must be nearly past standing up!

I ought, I suppose, to be ashamed of myself. There are innumerable reasons against the duel. Yet there are certain things which the duel alone can satisfactorily remedy, though it is perhaps only a foreigner who can see that. For instance, against libel. If a man libels me I would rather have his life than his money.... Or if anyone libels a dead friend of yours what better can *you* do than pink the fellow in the forearm—as a gesture to indicate that you spare his life or that you have offered your life to the shade of your dead friend?

I can't expect Anglo-Saxons to agree with me.

At any rate, the Germany of my extreme youth was a land where one duelled, and it was patriarchal and archaic, and hoisted wheels to the tops of its crow-step gables, so that the storks might nest there. Framersdach near Lohrhaupten, where I stayed with my tutor, was a Bavarian community village. Our inn was a *Gemeinde-Wirtschaft*—a community hostelry. These institutions dated from the early Middle Ages. It was both inn and workhouse. If a tramp came along and asked for a night's lodging we had to turn out of our rooms or pay him two marks. He invariably accepted the two marks.

All sorts of horns blew in that village between the high black and white housefronts. Every quarter of an hour through the night the watchman made a series of grunts on a great wooden horn and cried out: "Three quarters of two and it rains.... Two and the moon is behind thick clouds.... Three and cock-crow approaches." He carried a lanthorn attached to a halberd like the man in the moon.

But, if he had a mind to nod at dawn when he woke he would rattle off all the quarters of the hours and the changes in the weather, gabbling them through like a cuckoo-clock running down, and ending: "God be with your awakening, gentlemen," and would hurry off to bed. He claimed to remember the Robbers of Hauff's *Wirtshaus im Spessart*.

Immediately afterwards a cow's horn would sound and there would be a crepitation like heavy rain, growing louder and louder and then receding; then a formidable sound from a horn of leather and similar rising and dying of pattering sounds; then the notes of a pan-pipe and more rustlings, then a shrill whistle often repeated and cackles and hisses. That would be the swine-, goat- and sheep-herds and the goose girl, summoning their respective beasts. Each animal came out of its own barn and fell in, for all the world like soldiers catching up after a halt in a village. So they went away up into the woods on the margin of whose shade they would graze all day, except during high noon—Pan's hour. Then they lay in the shadow. The shepherd read Goethe's *Faust;* the goat-herd slept, when he was not playing his pan-pipes, the swine-herd played the fiddle when he was not blowing his leather horn to keep his pigs together; the goose girl knitted, when she was not dreaming of marrying a prince. The shepherd was armed with an enormously long pole at the top of which there was an iron trowel. With this instrument he could dig up a clod of earth or a stone. He could hurl these to great distances and with astonishing precision of aim. This had been originally a weapon against wolves. Now it served against dogs, or against foxes who prowled after the lambs. He read *Faust* to improve his knowledge of wizardry. All shepherds from the Bavarian Spessart to Brittany have singular knowledges that go down from father to son, and they number their sheep in Gaelic. English shepherds do this last too—and so do we when we begin a counting game with: "Eeny, meeny, miny, mo."

I have already told—I think in one of my novels which was not otherwise autobiographic—how, having a guard to mount over a hospital tent of German prisoners, in France in 1917, I went into the tent and there, washed, in a white bed was a young boy like an angel. I asked him where he came from and he said: "From Framersdach near Lohrhaupten in the Bavarian Spessart." I asked him what he did at home and he said he was the swineherd. I asked him if he had ever been in a bed with sheets before and he answered: *"Niemals, Herr Offizier."* I asked him if he felt himself well there and he said: *"Es ist doch Himmel, Herr Offizier."*

It seemed to me, standing looking down on him and remembering Framersdach as I had known it, that he had gone from one heaven to another, for that nest hidden in the great Spessart Forest came back to me as like enough to an earthly paradise. It no doubt was not.

The long raftered upper room that we occupied, my tutor

and I, in one of the high gables of the inn had been the home
of an eighteenth-century alchemist who had died of starvation.
It contained great chests. They were carved and painted and
filled to the brim with the poor fellow's papers. There were
innumerable mouse-nibbled manuscripts and treatises on perpetual motion, the squaring of the circle, elixirs for the restora-
tion of youth—and, of course, for transforming base into
precious metals. The people of the inn used these for lighting
fires when they ran short of newspaper. I tried to buy some
of them. The village council met and decided that, as goods
of the community, they could not be alienated. I carried off
half a dozen of them however, nobody objecting, and presented
them to the British Muesum. There was a treatise *De Quadra-
tura Circuli* and another *De Perpetuo Mobile,* an account of
some one's journey into Persia in search of the Fountain of
Perpetual Youth which was to be found at the Court of the
Shah. We dream different dreams now, but some of us still
starve in the attempt to materialise them.

Our high window gave down on to the village ghetto, the
court of three or four houses round a stock-yard entirely occupied by an immense dung heap. Towards sunset little Jewesses
would come out and sit on the high steps. The eldest span and
the smallest blew dandelion clocks. They were ravishingly
beautiful in the low sunlight. They wore pigtails in knots,
little blue aprons and little white trousers.

The village Jews were not popular in those parts. There
was a strong anti-Semitic movement in agrarian Germany
and the Jews of Framersdach were said to have mortgages on
all the agricultural gear and the furniture and the bridal
chests of the village. The immense mound of dung in the
courtyard was said to be the interest paid by the peasants.
The peasants of those parts were jovial but improvident.
Bavaria was a lusty kingdom.

I went to a neighbouring village to see the Sedan *Feier
fest*—the celebration of the victory of Sedan. Veterans marched
in ranks; Chinese lanthorns were hung across the streets; the

housefronts were gay with green boughs and carpets were hung from the windows to give colour and be gay. The pastor, the forester, the policeman and the postman delivered orations from hustings—I suppose I wanted a row or did not like Sedan to be celebrated without striking another note. I went into the inn and played the *Marseillaise* at the top of my strength on the harmonium. It was forbidden to play the *Marseillaise* in Germany of those days—not so much because it was French as because it was revolutionary. The pastor, the forester, the policeman, and the postman, the barrelsmith, the geometrical instrument maker, the vintner, the master glass-blower all crowded into the room and applauded. More and more crowded in and I had to play the *Marseillaise* over and over again—varying it with singing *Die beiden Grenadiere*. Prussia was very unpopular with the Bavarians then and Sedan was regarded as a Prussian victory. The applause was uproarious. Finally the Village Jew poked his nose in at the door. They pelted him out of the room and the inn and down the street with stone beer jugs. They declared that they had killed him, but I daresay they were only boasting to the greater glory of God.

We went on to Soden in the Taunus, a little Bath whose guests were like a family party. I wore out the brims of several hats in a very short time. The band used to wake everyone in the place at an exceedingly early hour—at six I should say. It played very slowly and loudly *"Ein fester Burg ist unser Gott"* and other Lutheran chorales. They suggested funeral marches. Everyone turned out, provided himself with a glass mug and promenaded slowly around the bandstand. There were perhaps two hundred and fifty *Kur* guests. Each one saluted every one else each time that he passed. As the promenade lasted half an hour, every man must have raised his hat and every lady must have genuflected at least a thousand times apiece before breakfast. It was bad for hat brims and for ladies' knee joints but apparently good for the liver. I was supposed in those days to have both an enlarged liver and a defective heart. At any rate the doctors had rejected me on that score for both the Indian Army and the civil service. That put an end to my hopes of a military career. The Home Army in those days was too expensive an affair for a young man without considerable means. His only chance was to exchange into the Indian Army, where pay was better and social life was brilliant. So I became a writer. I still regret it.

I suppose that was why I was sent to Soden with my tutor. He lived there. He was a Lutheran clergyman and, like most of his brethren of that day, an atheist—a strange person to look after the scion of a Catholic family. He had extraordinarily blue eyes, very highly coloured cheek bones, stiff flaxen hair, a twisted, tow-coloured moustache, and a voice like the bark of a Prussian officer on parade. I heard him preach his sermon of induction in the village of which he was to become the *Pfarrherr,* near Soden. His sermon was about the *Barmhertziger Samariter.* He was in a long black gown and hung out over the little pulpit, wagging his finger at the congregation as if he were barking reproaches at them. I thought that if I were the Good Samaritan I should hate to be talked about in that tone. The congregation was very docile.

The church was one of those Box and Cox affairs to be found here and there on the Continent. Roman Catholics and Lutherans worshipped there in turn—a little, whitewashed, barrel-roofed edifice. The men worshipped on the right, the women on the left. I was put among the women. I thought at first that that was meant to prevent contamination by the coarser sex. But I found that it was only that I might express to the mother and sister of the preacher my admiration for his phrases. In the middle of the sermon, a peasant-girl sitting in front of me turned round and looked at the ladies and myself. She was rather comely, dark and blue-eyed. Her eyes began to roll in agony, her mouth was all distorted. She fell on her face on the ground in front of her chair. It appalled me.

The preacher's mother said:

"It's only an epileptic fit.... There, that is a well-turned phrase!" The preacher thundered on, still leaning half out of his pulpit and wagging his finger in condemnation, apparently because we were not pitiful-hearted Samaritans. They let the girl lie there till the end of the service.

I can still see that girl's face—the agonised eyes and the distorted mouth, as if she were looking into the pit of hell. It still, when I think of it, horrifies me more than many more ostensibly horrible things that I have since seen.

The great world-event of that day was the first electrical exhibition—at Frankfort. The great local social event was the billeting of the Bonn Hussars at Soden. Frankfort was only a few miles from Bad Soden and the Hussars had come for some ceremony at which Serenities were to be present. The exhibition was already sufficient excitement. We used to go in every evening in bands of students and studentesses and spend innumerable twopences in riding in the first electric tram that ever ran and on giving our first telephone calls, one to the other. The latter occupation was not so satisfactory. You had the conviction that whilst you roared soft nothings into the mouthpiece at one end of the building another young man in the other box would be squeezing the hand of the charmer to whom your words were addressed. But it was all very gay; the arc-lights stuttered like mad. None of us had ever seen so much light before.

But all that was as nothing to the excitement attending on the announcement of the *Einquartierung* of the Hussars. All the young men of the place at once joined the Social Democratic party; all the young women except the most serious-minded studentesses at once became Imperialists. You have never seen such re-furbishing of frocks and bread-crumbing of twenty-button gloves. That was for the officers and the junketings and the dances. We, on the other hand, the ununiformed youths, leaned with murder in our hearts against the door jambs. We went only to look on and quote Schopenhauer.

For myself, I seriously contemplated fighting one or all of the magnificent creatures. They glittered with sabres and spurs; they were perfumed and polished. And we outsiders jeered at the ridges that their corsets made in the backs of their tunics. They ignored us and twisted their moustaches and croaked: "Kolossal!" at every second word. When really impressed by a lady they croaked a language that was more than half French: *"Belle dame je vous assure que c'est une Kolossal richtig-gehende montre, foi de gentilhomme."*— "Beautiful lady I assure you that it is a colossally correct watch, on my faith as a gentleman." This mania for French expressions caused serious concern to the higher military authorities. I was sitting a little later on the stoop of the *Hirsch Hotel* at Boppard on the Rhine. The garrison commander of Ehrenbreitstein drove up with a tremendous escort of cars. He pointed to the sign "Garage" that protruded from the hotel and said that if that objectionable Gallicism was not removed and a German word substituted he would put the inn out of bounds for the officers of his garrison. That would have ruined the innkeeper. The word substituted was: *"Kraftwageneinstellraum"*—"Power-wagon-standing-in-place."

At Soden all the suddenly-become *Social Demokratische* young men also became violently Teutonic in their language— occasionally using English words. English also passed for an Allemanic tongue. There was a roistering, plump young man called Otto Stilgebauer who had written a book called *"Die Unbefleckte Magdalena"*—"The Unsoiled Magdalene." He afterwards became famous—at any rate to the extent of being suppressed by Authority. When the ball-room floor was not occupied by dancers he stumped about it exclaiming:

> "Ven shall ve sree meet acken
> In dunder lightening or in ren?"

This was supposed to give great offence to the military. A young law student called Arthur Ringer, afterwards celebrated for his defence of Social Democrats, caused even more offence by singing *Rule Britannia* with great clearness and an excellent accent. As at that time Germany was beginning her bid for maritime supremacy this was accounted treason. The Hussar-colonel, a lean dry man with a little tooth-brush moustache, appealed to the *Kur* authorities to have Mr. Ringer deported. I daresay he ought to have been.

But next day, whilst he was riding into Frankfort at the head of his regiment, the Colonel's horse put its foot on the rail of the electric tram. The horse fell dead; so did the Colonel.

This was regarded—at least by the Military Power—as the judgment of Heaven. Man had substituted for the time honoured beast of burden of the cavalry a means of traction that was impiously modern. It was no doubt Social Democratic in origin—if not that, then French. So the Almighty hit the cavalry Colonel with a thunderbolt. It seemed rather confused reasoning. At any rate, the catastrophe gave the ball-room floor over to the Socialist youths. The officers had to lean against the door posts in mourning for their chief. Then they rode away.

There was at Soden then a Russian-Polish Nihilist studentess called Magdalena Schabrowsky. Though Polish, she had been born in St. Petersburg and, getting into trouble at the university there, because of her political opinions, had come to Heidelberg to finish her medical studies. She must have been the first Slav I ever came across—certainly the first Pole, if I except an authentic Polish Count in exile who, when I suppose I was about eleven, used to clean our boots at Stratford School. That unfortunate nobleman, victim of the abortive revolution of 1862, used to seem to me the most romantic being. He taught us to cook hedgehogs in the forest. He daubed them, rolled up, in circular balls of clay and threw them into bonfires. When they were done, the clay came away hard, like earthenware, the spines all came away with the clay and there was the most wonderfully succulent meal of hedgepig inside.

I don't know why a Polish count should know how to cook hedgehogs in a forest. We used to imagine that that was how he had supported himself whilst in hiding from the Cossacks who had burnt his family mansion. But, with his flashing eyes, black hair and the scarlet ribbon of, I think, the order of St. Stanislas, that he wore on certain feast days, even whilst cleaning our boots or catching hedgehogs—with all that he comes back to me as the most romantic figure of my childhood. He was my first Slav romance.

Magdalena Schabrowsky was my second. As became a Russian conspiratress she wore on her raven locks a sealskin toque and on her tall person a sealskin jacket. Her eyes were very dark—all of a piece, the irises and pupils all black and soft like velvet. They gazed at you from very close—and very intently as if she were very short-sighted—from her oval, olive complexioned face. She always carried a book.

She comes back to me as calm Purity. She was always calm. Only now and then would she express any irritation— by slightly shaking her head. That would be when, for the fiftieth time in the same morning or evening, one of the students would boisterously address her as *"Unbefleckte,"* after the Unsoiled Magdalene of our friend Stilgebauer's book. For forty-nine times she would bear that without emotion; at the fiftieth she would shake her head and say: *"Dumme Buben."* Then they could run to another forty-nine. I don't know whether she was or was not a Jewess. One has the tendency to regard all Poles as Jews. But I suppose she could not have been because Magdalena is not a Jewish name. But she filled my soul with heroic resolves and all the bliss of calf love. I hasten to say that I was perhaps seventeen, and she probably twenty-seven. Indeed I believe that, somewhere in the background or in Hamburg, there was a *Brautgram*—a fiancé—whom, in my darker moments, I planned to kill.

I can't make up my mind whether I was a very good or a very bad little boy. Certainly, until this moment, I have always considered myself as having been an infantile prodigy

of virtue. Certainly also I was always head of my school classes
and the favourite of my masters. Although incorrigibly lazy,
thanks to an amazing memory—which, alas, deserted me in
1917!—I could do absolutely no work for a whole school term
and then, glancing at a text book or two, could pass examinations that amazed myself. But there come back to me, now
that I think of it, moments when I deliberately resolved to be
wicked—out of sheer boredom. Then I would incite a whole
class to mutiny, rob the head master's hen roost at midnight,
ring all the bells in the school-house at four in the morning.
And, looking back at this record that I am writing, I perceive
the story of a number of unhallowed moments.... There *must*,
I suppose, be such a thing as original sin, for I committed
those enormities quite without motive or volition.

Magdalena Schabrowsky certainly was my good angel,
as far as those distant days were concerned. She radiated
quietism with her Slav glances. She asked me once to recom-
mend her an English book and I said: why not the Authorized
Version? I got her a copy of the Old Testament. She returned
it to me next morning with horror and the only indignation I
ever saw her show. She said it was, with its holocausts, tor-
tures, and treacheries, the most terrible record she had ever
read. If men or God were like those that ruled in Judea, men
were devils and the world Hell. They must, she said, have
been even worse than the Russian Government, though that
was unthinkable.

So, when I had proposed to kill all these Hussars, she just
laid her hand on my Byronic sleeve and I became like a sitting
dove.

Those were, you know, the days when it was glorious to be
an English boy. You had God always behind you. You owned
half the globe; you were foremost in every manly pursuit;
you were clean, sober, honest; you hated injustice; by a
glance of your eye, you could reveal that any bully of a Hussar
was actually the merest coward; you righted wrongs, succoured

the oppressed. With your back to the wall you could stand against the swords of the officers of a whole foreign army!

So I have no doubt that Magdalena Schabrowsky, with her hand on my sleeve and her inscrutable eyes, kept me from an infernal scrape. I sometimes still feel it there. In those juvenile days she seemed to me to be like Copperfield's Agnes —Sister Agnes with her finger to her lips, pointing upwards. One was once ingenuous. I suppose everybody is!

Her end was sad. Going back to St. Petersburg to prepare for her wedding she got involved in one of Sergius Stepniak's conspiracies, was sent to Siberia and died soon afterwards in Irkutsk. Her charm and peace come back to me now when, of an evening, I read *The Diary of a Sportsman*.

I daresay—but I don't feel certain—that her memory was responsible for the attraction I have always felt towards Slavs—and for the cause of Poland. I suppose I have a certain proportion of Slav blood. Conrad, whose genealogical interests were deeper than my own, once rooted out that one branch of my family was from the XV-XVIII centuries—Ruthenians settled in the neighbourhood of Warsaw. I prefer to think that one of my great-grandfathers came from Poland in the ranks of Poniatovski's legion. Certainly I should prefer to consider that what Slav blood I had was Polish rather than Russian in origin. Ruthenians were Russians who settled in Poland in the Middle Ages and were a good deal persecuted and forced to relinquish Orthodoxy in favour of Catholicism. I suppose it does not matter but Poles seem more romantic than Russians.

Until Conrad came along, however, I saw a great deal more of Russians than of Poles. That was partly because Magdalena Schabrowsky's fate attracted me to Stepniak when I met him. He just remembered her as one of thousands of heroic young people whom his titanic conspiracies sent to die in exile.

But in great part, the prominence taken by the Intellegentsia and Nihilists in English intellectual—and certainly in my own—life was due to Mrs. Constance Garnett. That lady's family had long been engaged in Russian trade and she herself gave to the world one of its noblest literary monuments—her translation of the works of Turgenev. For me Turgenev is the greatest of all writers and Mrs. Garnett's rendering of his Russian into English is the most flawless and limpid of carryings across from one country to another of a literary masterpiece.

Her circle of friends and admirers was enormous and international—the foreign element being mostly Russian and thus a constant transfusion of Russian ideas into English life went on around the *Cearne*. In the meantime Mr. Edward Garnett was achieving one of his meteoric publishing successes. That was the *Pseudonym Library*—a collection of little yellow-covered books which spread all over England and the continent of Europe with a most astonishing rapidity. Its contents were largely Slav in tone—with stories of Russia or translations from the Russian.

What exact part the activities that went on round the *Cearne* played in Russian history I don't propose to estimate. Certainly it must have been considerable. English Left opinion heartily espoused the cause of Nihilism, supported it with funds, found houses and even wives for its more destitute exiles. My brother-in-law, Dr. Soskice, had been imprisoned without trial or charge in St. Petersburg. He was sent to Siberia, escaped and found himself in Paris with badly damaged nerves. He was recommended to work in the open air. He came to Limpsfield to work in the garden of the *Cearne* and indeed worked in the garden of my cottage which was next door. Eventually he married my sister. My sister helped Mrs. Garnett with her later translations of Dostoievsky, Mrs. Garnett's eyes troubling her. Soskice played a considerable part in the political events in Russia up to the ending of the Kerensky Republic.

A curious detail of life at Limpsfield comes back to me. The Garnetts had an odd-looking yellow dog. The dog met a fox in the deep woods of the Chart. The fox bit out one of the dog's eyes. Mr. Garnett dispatched the dog with an axe on the porch of the *Cearne*. This immensely impressed Bunny—afterwards David—Garnett, then aged perhaps four. His childish stutterings largely concerned themselves with the wickedness of foxes. Later he wrote *Lady into Fox*.

My own most glamorous connections with the Russian branch of the Slav family dated from earlier. They centred round Sergius Stepniak and Felix Volkhovsky, who were Nihilists, and as I have said, round Kropotkin.

Stepniak was huge, flat-featured, with small, fiery black eyes and an enormous dark beard. He was always serious. He once came to sit for my grandfather but could not sit still long enough. He carried always an enormous despatch case of great weight. I imagined it to contain the secret service money of the Russian Revolution.

Volkhovsky edited *Free Russia*. It was a rather lugubrious sheet. But he himself was small, lean, grey and always humorous. He told almost as many stories as poor Borschitzky and in much the same accent. Here is one of them:

"Zair vas once Gypsy and a Ukrainian. Ze Gypsies are very clever people and the Ukrainians very stchupid. Zay vas going along a road and zay saw a porg tchop lying on it. 'Zat is my porg tchop,' said ze Gypsy. 'No, zat is my porg tchop,' said ze Ukrainian. 'You poor Ukrainian,' said ze Gypsy, 'you are too stchupid to have ze porg tchop. Zay are for fine Gypsy fellows.'

"So zay agreed to go to sleep and zer one zat should have ze pudifullest dream should have ze porg tchop. In a little while: 'Wake up, wake up, you stchupid Ukrainian,' said ze Gypsy. 'I have had ze pudifullest dream. O it vas a lofly dream: I dream I come into a mos' lofly prairie; zer vas lofly green, green grass and flowers bright, bright like enamel. And zer came running to me like ze wind a mos' wonderful charger. And his saddle vas of silver and his reins of gold and fire flashed from his eyes and smoke from his nostrils. And he say: "Get up on my back, you fine Gypsy man, and I will carry you to ze Lord God," and I get up on his back and 'e run swift, like ze wind till he come to a mos' lofly golden ladder. An' ze angels of God was flying up and down it and they help me climb up it like it was no labour at all.

" 'And when I get up into Heaven zere I see ze Lord God sit at dinner. And He say: "Come an' 'ave dinner wiz me, you fine Gipsy man. It will be honour to 'ave you at my table." ... Vos zat not a mos' lofly dream, you stchupid Ukrainian?'

" 'Zat is very sdrange,' said ze Ukrainian. 'I also have a dream—but it vas a mos' wretched dream. I dream I come into a prairie but it was not a lofly prairie. It vas a wretched desert of dust an' dirt an' ol' rags. An' zer came toward me vairy, vairy slowly a miserable ol' 'oss. And 'is lungs wheezed an' ze tears dripped from 'is eyes an' 'e 'ad a rope of straw for 'is reins an' 'e 'adn't got no saddle at all. An' I git on 'is back an' 'e go vairy, vairy slowly till 'e come to a miserable old broken ladder and zer vas no angels going up nor coming down. An' I clumb panting up ze ladder till I come to ze back door of Evan. An' I see a fine Gypsy fellow sitting at ze table of ze Lord God.... "Zat was me," said ze Gypsy. "Yes, zat vos you," said ze Ukrainian. An' ze Gypsy he say to me: "You poor stchupid Ukrainian, I am 'avin' a fine dinner wiz ze Lord God, you can go down an' eat ze porg tchop." An' so I did! ..."You fool," said the Gypsy, "it vos only a dream." "Ow could I tell zat," said ze Ukrainian. 'E vos too stchupid.' "

Mr. Volkhovsky was a Ukrainian.

An examination of the amount of harm that the Russian Imperial Secret Police must have done to Russian international relations would be a very profitable and instructive proceeding. Every nation had, and still of course has, its secret police, *agents provocateurs* and bands of active semi-criminals, but these activities are as a rule limited to the territories and crimes of the nation itself and international preventive measures are carried on by officials of the respective police services. The secret police of Russia spread themselves in armies of spies and *agents provocateurs* over pretty nearly the surface of the habitable globe. They were most

active in England which had then a name for being the land
of freedom. I can remember about 1897 seeing shiploads of
Russian and Polish Jews escaped from pogroms in their native
lands and, as they came off the gangways of their ships in
London Docks, falling on their knees and kissing the sacred
soil of freedom—a thing that may be put to the credit of England who gets very little in matters international.

I knew, vaguely hanging about the skirts of the Russian
exiles group in London, a vague, quite not political Russian
then calling himself Grumeisen. He was the cause of Russia's
early failure to effect an alliance with France—a dim, stoutish
person with a grievance. There had been in the early eighties
some sort of attempt to de-rail an Imperial train in Russia.
Grumeisen was at that time a fur merchant in Paris. For
some obscure reason—Grumeisen said it was because he had
refused to pay money to a blackmailer who was also a Russian
agent provocateur—the Russian secret police insisted that he
was a perpetrator of the outrage. To please the Imperial Government the French police detained Grumeisen. M. De Frey-
sinet and Prince Orloff were then engaged in the lively and
picturesque conversation that would certainly have led to a
Franco-Russian alliance. But there was not a shadow of proof
that poor Grumeisen had had anything to do with the attempted outrage. The photographs supplied by the secret
police in no way resembled him; he was able to prove that he
had been in Paris at the time of the outrage. The French
police were forced to release him. The Russian secret service
was so strong in the entourage of the Tzar that the negotiations for the alliance were summarily broken off. The bitterness of the matter from poor Mr. Grumeisen's point of view
was that the French police released him only on condition
that he went to England. He did not want to go to England;
he was doing pretty well in the French fur trade and all his
friends were Parisians.

But the fact that England was the international refuge
for all exiles was not agreeable to the Russian police who filled

the country with an incredible number of spies. There must have been at least one for every political exile and the annoyance that they caused in the country was extreme. I remember between 1893 and 1894 going home for longish periods almost every night from London University to a western suburb with Stepniak, Volkhovsky or Prince Kropotkin who were then the most prominent members of the Russian extreme Left and who were lecturing at the university on political economy, Russian literature and, I think, biology respectively. And behind us always lurked or dodged the Russian spies allotted to each of those distinguished lecturers. Stepniak or Volkhovsky dismissed them at Hammersmith station, as often as not with the price of a pint, for the poor devils were miserably paid, and also because, the spies and their purpose being perfectly well known in the district where the Russians lived, they were apt to receive very rough handling from the residents who resented their presences as an insult to the country. One or two quite considerable riots were thus caused in the neighbourhoods of Hammersmith proper and Ealing.

Those matters caused at one time a very considerable friction between the British and the Russian courts. The redoubtable Azev, who was the Russian chief spy-master and *agent provocateur,* conceived the fantastic idea that an outrage in England might induce the British Government and British public opinion to decree the expulsion of all political exiles from their shores, the exiles themselves being remarkably law-abiding. He accordingly persuaded a half-witted youth to throw a bomb into Greenwich Observatory. The boy, however, stumbling over a tree-stump in the Observatory Park was blown to pieces and the whole matter came to light. For diplomatic reasons, the newspapers made very little of it. But the Home Secretary, Sir William Vernon Harcourt, made such caustic remarks over it to the Russian First Secretary of Embassy that Russian activities on the Afghan border became very marked for a considerable period.

I happen accidentally to know a good deal of these episodes. My own house was once—and my mother's twice—burgled by emissaries of the Russian Embassy in search of documents. In my case, I being the owner of *The English Review,* the above-mentioned scoundrel Azev sent me by one of his emissaries a volume of the diary of the late Tzar; he imagining that I might like to publish it—which I didn't. I didn't want to have it in my house for more than a minute and took it round to my bank for internment whilst I informed the police. In the interval between then and my return, a little after midnight my house had been carefully gone through and all my papers, which were very many, had been thrown all over the floor. In my mother's case, the same thing happened twice, during the time that Father Gapon, the heroic leader of the peasants to the Tzar's palace on Bloody Sunday, was being housed by her, my mother being very charitable but by no means interested in politics. Eventually Gapon was sandbagged outside the house and the burglar—a Russian—given a long term of imprisonment. The Embassy naturally denied all knowledge of or responsibility for him. I came in that way a good deal in contact with the Scotland Yard Inspector who had charge of that sort of case and he told me a great deal about not only the activities of the Russian spies but gave me an—I daresay highly coloured—account of what the Home Secretary had said to the Secretary of the Embassy. I may add as a note that the reputed Tzar's journal turned out to be nothing more than a list of trials and executions of Nihilists, with comments of an extreme naïveté in that sovereign's hand. Words like "Horrible," "Unimaginable," or "How can he speak thus of his Little Father?" being scrawled beside reports of Nihilists' professions of faith.

PART THREE

THE HEART OF THE COUNTRY

CHAPTER I

CABBAGES AND QUEENS

I AM going to give you some peasant biographies.

In the ten years, from 1894 to 1903, I was hardly at all in London. I had buried myself in the country and for three or four years hardly saw anyone but field-workers. These years were passed firstly at Bonnington, a lonely village in the Romney Marsh and then at the Pent—a lonelier farm-house at the foot of the North Downs. It was in 1897 that Mr. Edward Garnett persuaded me to come to Limpsfield but as I have said, I returned to the Pent. There Conrad came along.

I suppose that for seven or eight years we hardly passed a day and certainly not a month without meeting and discussing our joint and several works. For a number of years longer we remained on terms of the closest intimacy and community of interest. That was only interrupted by my frequent visits to the continent of Europe or to the United States. In Belgium we spent some time together, when we were working on *Romance*. On the publication of that book we went to London where I occupied a house on the top of Campden Hill. Conrad had lodgings round the corner.

I give so much of autobiography though these are reminiscences. In that form the narrator should be a mirror, not any sort of actor, but the reader may like so much of chronology. The people that I saw daily until the advent of Conrad and for long after that were all working farmers or farm labourers. There were Meary Walker and Meary Spratt and Ragged Arse Wilson and Farmer Finn of Bonnington Court Lodge and Parson Cameron and Muss Rayner of the Corner and Muss Diamond, who still wore a smock frock and a white beaver top hat, and Shaking Ben who had been ruined by the bad gels of Rye. And there were a whole countryside more.

Of course from time to time I was visited by persons from the outer world—relations, connections, members of the Garnett family, and most often by the Portuguese Consul-General, Señor Don Jaime Batalaha Reis, who seemed to en-joy my society and whose lovely daughter, Celeste, sat un-consciously for Seraphina, the heroine of *Romance*. Batalaha Reis was a bearded person with the most extravagant gestures I have ever met and I am afraid he sat for Tomas Castro in the same book. He became, after the Portuguese Revolution, Minister of the Navy, I think. Certainly if caution is desirable in marine affairs, he must have filled his job well. I remember at the very outset of our acquaintance he wanted to buy a torpedo boat. Apparently for the purchase of a torpedo boat a solicitor is necessary and the agonies that poor Mr. Reis went through in engaging one was such as in a lesser man would have accompanied at least a change of religion. He was of opinion that all lawyers are of the most desperate scoundrel-ism, concealing themselves in the garments of admirable fathers of families and behaving with righteousness for years in order in the end to bring off some atrocious coup. Finally I got him to engage one of the Garnetts who had long repre-sented my own family. Mr. Garnett must have done his job well, for I think he is still buying torpedo boats for Portugal. But after that terrible mental strain, Mr. Reis had to spend a prolonged holiday in Portugal. I met him at Dover when he came back and, to my astonishment, as soon as he had got into the carriage reserved for diplomats, he took from a Glad-stone bag and buckled round his waist an enormous revolver. He said that London, on account of blackmailers, is the most dangerous city in the world. I daresay it is, but I should hardly have thought that anyone as full of precautions as Mr. Reis could have come across them. Similarly he never went anywhere, even in the City of London or to the top of Primrose Hill, without an ordnance map which he searched for the dash-dot-dash sign which means standing water. He had suffered from malaria. So that his coming down so near the Romney Marsh was an act of friendship that truly resembled heroism. But in spite of his fears, all bearded and piratical in appearance as he was, he was very humorous and fantastically good-tempered. He got on far better with my peasant friends than anyone else and once, when he put on his preposterous Portuguese diplomatic uniform to please Mrs. Walker, he created a sensation in Bonnington that that village can never have gotten over.

Upon the whole, apart perhaps from Reis himself, those brown, battered men and women of an obscure Kentish countryside come back to me as the best English people I ever knew. I do not think that, except for the parson and the grocer, anyone of them could read or write, but I do not believe that one of them ever betrayed either me or even each other. If, as I undoubtedly do, I love England with a deep love, though I grow daily more alien to the Englishman it is because of them. Here are some of them.

About twenty-five years ago I wanted some mushroom catsup. Bonnington was in a scattered, little-populated village of the south of England. The village stood on what had formerly been common land, running all down the side of a range of hills. But this common land had been long since squatted on, so that it was a maze of little hawthorn hedges surrounding little closes. Each close had a few old apple or cherry trees, a patch of potato ground, a cabbage patch, a few rows of scarlet runners, a few plants of monthly roses, a few plants of marjoram, fennel, borage or thyme. And in each little patch there stood a small dwelling. Mostly these were the original squatters' huts built of mud, white-washed outside and crowned with old thatched roofs on which there grew grasses, house-leeks or even irises. There were a great many of these little houses beneath the September sunshine, and it was all a maze of the small green hedges.

I had been up to the shop in search of my catsup, but though they sold everything from boots and straw hats to darning needles, bacon, haricot beans, oatmeal and British wines they had no catsup. I was wandering desultorily home-wards among the small hedges down hill, looking at the distant sea, seven miles away over the marsh. Just beyond a little hedge I saw a woman digging potatoes in the dry hot ground. She looked up as I passed and said:

"Hullo, Measter!"

I answered: "Hullo, Missus!" and I was passing on when it occurred to me to ask her whether she knew anyone who sold catsup. She answered:

"Naw! Aw doan't knaw no one."

I walked on a little farther and then sat down on a stile for half an hour or so, enjoying the pleasant weather and taking a read in the country paper which I had bought in the shop. Then I saw the large, stalwart old woman coming along the stony path, carrying two great trugs of the potatoes that she had dug up. I had to get down from the stile to let her pass. And then seeing that she was going my way, that she was evidently oldish and was probably tired, I took the potato trugs from her and carried them. She strode along in front of me between the hedges. She wore an immense pair of men's hob-nailed boots that dragged along the stones of the causeway with metallic sounds, an immense shawl of wool that had been beaten by the weather until it was of a dull liver colour, an immense skirt that had once been of lilac cotton print, but was now a rusty brown, and an immense straw hat that had been given her by some one as being worn out and that had cost two pence when it was new. Her face was as large, as round and much the same colour as a copper warming-pan. Her mouth was immense and quite toothless except for one large fang and, as she smiled cheerfully all the time, her great gums were always to be seen. Her shoulders were immense and moved with the roll and heave of those of a great bullock. This was the wisest and upon the whole the most estimable human being that I ever knew at all well. Her hands were enormous and stained a deep blackish green over their original copper colour by the hops that it was her profession to tie.

As we walked along she told me that she was exactly the same age as our Queen who was then just seventy. She told me also that she wasn't of those parts but was a Paddock Wood woman by birth, which meant that she came from the true hop country. She told me also that her husband had died fifteen years before of the sting of a viper, that his poor old leg went all like green jelly up to his thigh before he died and that he had been the best basket maker in all Kent. She also told me that we can't all have everything and that the only thing to do is to "keep all on gooing."

I delivered up her trugs to her at her garden gate and she said to me with a cheerful nod:

"Well, I'll do the same for you, mate, when you come to be my age." She shambled over the rough stone of her garden path and into her dark door beneath the low thatch, that was two yards thick. Her cottage was more dilapidated than any that I have ever seen in my life. It stood in a very long narrow triangle of ground, so that the hedge that I walked along must have been at least eighty yards in length, while at its broadest part of the potato patch could not have measured twenty spade breadths. But before I was come to the end of the hedge, her voice was calling out after me:

"Measter! Dun yo really want ketchup?"

I replied that I really did.

She said:

"Old Meary Spratt up by Hungry Hall wheer ye see me diggin'—she makes ketchup."

I asked her why she had not told me before and she answered:

"Well, ye see the Quality do be asking foolish questions, I thought ye didn't really want to know."

I learnt afterwards it wasn't only the dislike of being asked foolish questions. In Meary Walker's long, wise life she had experienced one thing—that no man with a collar and a tie is to be trusted. She had had it vaguely in her mind that, when I asked the question, I might be some sort of excise officer trying to find out where illicit distilling was carried on. She didn't know that the making of catsup was not illegal. She had heard that many of her poor neighbours had been fined heavily for selling bottles of home-made sloe-gin or mead. She had refused to answer, out of a sense of automatic caution, for fear she should get poor old Meary Spratt into trouble.

But next morning she turned up at my cottage carrying two bottles of Meary Spratt's catsup in an old basket covered with a cloth. And after that, seeing her rather often at the shop on Saturday nights when all the world came to buy its Sunday provisions, and, because she came in to heat the bake-oven with faggots once a week, and to do the washing—in that isolated neighbourhood, among the deep woods of the weald, I got to know her as well as I ever knew anybody. This is her biography:

She was the daughter of a day labourer among the hop fields of Paddock Wood. When she had been born, the youngest of five, her own mother had died. Her father had brought a step-mother into the house. I never discovered that the step-mother was notably cruel to Meary. But those were the Hungry Forties. The children never had enough to eat. Once, Meary cut off one of her big toes. She had jumped down into a ditch after a piece of turnip peel. She had, of course, had no shoes or stockings and there had been a broken bottle in the ditch.

So her childhood had been a matter of thirst, hunger and frequent chatisements with the end of a leather strap that her father wore round his waist. When she was fourteen she was sent to service in a great house where all the maids slept together under the roof. Here they told each other legends at night—odd legends that exactly resembled the fairy tales of Grimm—legends of princes and princesses, of castles, or of travelling companions on the road. A great many of these stories seemed to hinge upon the price of salt which at one time was extravagantly dear in the popular memory, so that one princess offered to have her heart cut out in order to purchase a pound of salt that should restore her father to health.

From this house Meary Walker ran away with a gypsy—or at least he was what in that part of the world was called a "pikey," a user of the turnpike road. So, for many years they led a wandering existence, until at last they settled down in this village. Until the date of that settlement, Meary had not troubled to marry her Walker. Then a parson insisted on it, but it did not trouble her much either way.

Walker had always been a man of weak health. He had what is called the artistic temperament—a small, dark, delicate man whose one enthusiasm was his art of making baskets. In that he certainly excelled. But he was lazy and all the work of their support fell on Meary. She tied hops—and this is rather skilled work—she picked them in the autumn; she helped the neighbours with baking and brewing. She cleaned up the church once a week. She planted the potatoes and cropped them. She was the first cottager in East Kent to keep poultry for profit. In her biography, which I have related at greater length in another book, you could find traces of great benevolence and of considerable heroism. Thus, one hard winter, she supported not only herself and her husband, but her old friend Meary Spratt, at that time a widow with six children. Meary Spratt was in bed with pneumonia and its after effects, from December to March. Meary Walker nursed her, washed and tended the children and made the livings for all of them.

Then there came the time when she broke her leg and had to be taken against her will to the hospital, which was seven miles away. She did not want to be in the hospital; she was anxious to be with Walker who was then dying of gangrene of the leg. She was anxious, too, about a sitting hen; one of her neighbours had promised her half a crown for a clutch of chickens. She used to lie in hospital, patting her broken knee under the bed clothes and exclaiming:

"Get well, get well, oh, do get well quickly!" And even twenty years afterwards when she rehearsed these scenes and these words there would remain in the repetition a whole world of passionate wistfulness. But indeed, she translated her passion into words. One night, driven beyond endurance by the want of news of Walker and of her sitting hen she escaped from the hospital window and crawled on her hands and knees the whole seven miles from the hospital to her home. She found when she arrived in the dawn that Walker was in his coffin. The chickens, however, were a healthy brood. Her admiration for Walker, the weak and lazy artist in basket-making, never decreased. She treasured his best baskets to the end of her life as you and I might treasure Rembrandts. Once, ten years after, she sat for a whole day on his grave. The old sexton, growing confused with years, had made a mistake and was going to inter another man's wife on top of Walker. Meary stopped that.

For the last twenty-six years or so of her life she lived in the mud hut which I had first seen her enter. She went on as before, tying hops, heating ovens, picking up stones, keeping a hen or two. She looked after, fed and nursed—for the love of God—a particularly disagreeable old man called Purdey who had been a London cab driver. He sat all day in a grandfather's chair, grumbling and swearing at Meary whenever she came in. He was eighty-two. He had no claim whatever upon her and he never paid her a penny of money.

So she kept on going all through life. She was always cheerful; she had always on her tongue some fragment of peasant wisdom. Once, coming back from market, she sat down outside a public house and a soldier treated her to a pot of beer. Presently there rode up the Duke of Cambridge in his Field

Marshal's uniform and beside him there was the Shah of Persia. They were watching a sham fight in the neighbourhood. Meary raised her pot of beer towards these royal personages and wished them health. They nodded in return.

"Well," Meary called out to the Duke, "you're only your mother's son like the rest of us." Once, Batalaha Reis amiably told her that, in his language, bread was "pom" she expressed surprise but then she added:

"Oh, well, poor dear, when you're hungry you've got to eat it, like the rest of us, whatever you call it."

She was sorry for him because he had to call bread by such an outlandish name. She could not think how he remembered the word. Yet she knew that *Brot* was the German for bread and *Apfel* for apples, because, during the Napoleonic Wars the Hanoverian Legion had garrisoned that part of the country and there remained till the accession of Queen Victoria. One of what she called the jarman legions had murdered a friend of her mother's who had been his sweetheart, and when he was hung for it at Cantebury he asked for *Brot* and *Apfel* on the scaffold. She saw him hung, a pleasant fair boy, and when she looked down at her hands she said they were white as lard.

So she worked on until she was seventy-eight. One day she discovered a swelling under her left breast. It gave her no pain but she wanted to know what it was. So she put a hot brick to it. She knew that if it was cancer that was a bad thing to do, but she wanted to get it settled. The swelling became worse. So she walked to the hospital, the same hospital that she had crawled away from. They operated on her next morning—and she was dead by noon. Her last words were:

"Who's going to look after old Purdey?"

She was buried in the workhouse cemetery. The number of her grave is 1642. Mr. Purdey was taken to the Union that night. And there, the last time I heard of him, he still was, a disagreeable old man.

Meary Spratt was much more like the average woman of fiction. She was decidedly emotional; she was certainly not truthful; she begged, and when she begged she would scream and howl and yell in the highest of keys, pulling her gnarled, rheumatic fingers into repulsive shapes and screaming like a locomotive to show how much they pained her, or sobbing with the most dramatic emphasis when she related how Meary Walker had saved her six little children from starvation. On the other hand, she would relate with a proper female virtue the fact—I fancy it may have been true—that, at some portion of her career Meary Walker had a daughter by somebody who was not Walker and that the daughter was in service in Folkestone. She would also say that Meary Walker was an arrant miser who had saved up a large fortune in bank notes which were quilted into her stays. She said she had heard the stays crackle.

Meary Spratt had never had a child by anyone but a husband. But then she had had four husbands as well as nineteen children, all of whom had lived. She was quite a small woman with an appallingly shrill voice and her tongue never stopped. In the early morning among the dews you would hear her voice. She would be picking what she called mushrooms for her catsup. You would hear her all the while like this screaming quite loudly while you listened from your bedroom window, she being in the field beyond the hedge and it being four o'clock of a very dewy morning.

"He! He! He!" she would scream, "here is a nice little one, a little pinky one! Now I'm going to pick you! Up you come, my little darling! Ah, doesn't it hurt!" And then she would give a shrill yell to show the pain that the mushroom felt when it was being picked. And then she would continue: "Oh, oh, oh, Lord! Oh my poor shoulders! Oh! my poor legs! They do fairly terrify me with rhumatiz! Oh, oh, Lord!"

And you would hear her voice seeming to get shriller as it got fainter and she went over the marshy grass, into the mist, until she came on another little pink one. She was seventy-six and it was cold out on the marshes in that October weather.

Yes, she was decidedly feminine. She had only been married three years to Mr. Spratford. Mr. Spratford was eighty-two when they married. Between them they had thirty-one children. And they lived in a little brick cottage not much larger than a dog kennel. When you asked Mr. Spratford why he married—Mr. Spratford was a most venerable-looking peasant, like a Biblical patriarch, with very white hair curling round a fine bald head and with noble faded blue eyes; and when he spoke he always gesticulated nobly with one hand and uttered the most edifying moral sentiments. He was extremely dishonest and had three times been to prison for robbing poor old women. Indeed, when I first made his acquaintance, he did a week's work for me, charged me double prices and begged me not to tell anyone that I had paid him at all because he was on his club—and this is about the meanest crime that any peasant can commit. It was an offence so mean that even Meary Spratford—who, you will observe, was a woman and who would have had no scruple at all about pilfering from any member of the quality—even Meary Spratford was outraged and made him pay back his club money for that week. She could not bear to think of the members of the club being defrauded, because they were quite poor people. It is true that she came to me afterwards and, groaning and sobbing, she tried to get the money out of me to make up for her noble act—but when you asked Mr. Spratford why he married he answered:

"Well, you see, sir, in a manner of speaking us do be very poor people and us bean't able to afford more than one blanket apiece, and one small fire for each of us, coals do be so dear." (He got all his coals for nothing from the poor old parson and so did Mrs. Spratt.) "So if we do marry we do have two blankets atop of us at night and we have one big fire and sit on either side of it."

So said Mr. Spratford. But when it came to his wife she would scream out:

"Why did us marry? Why I, I like to have a man about the house and a woman looks better like among her neebours if she do have a husband." So that no doubt Mrs. Spratt was feminine enough, just as Mr. Spratford was undoubtedly masculine. He died raving on the mud floor of his hut. His wife had not the strength to lift him into bed and the four men who had held him down during the night had had to go to work in the morning. He tore his bald head to ribbons with his nails and Mrs. Spratt for years afterwards could make anybody sick with her dramatic rehearsals of how he died. When she was really worked up over this narration she would even scratch her own forehead until it bled. So perhaps she was really a more womanly woman than Mrs. Walker. She kept on going just the same. But she made much more noise about it. That, I believe, is what is demanded of man's weaker vessels.

But even in the village Meary Spratt was regarded as unusually loquacious, whereas Meary Walker attracted, as I have said, no attention at all. It was as if Meary Walker was just a woman, whereas Meary Spratt was at least a super-woman, or as if she were a woman endowed with the lungs of a locomotive whistle. Indeed, I am certain that anyone there would have told you that Meary Walker was just an average woman.

The most faithful soul I have ever known was Ragged Arse Wilson. His nickname was given him because of the frailty of his nether garments. His Christian name I never knew. He was singularly handsome, dark, with a little beard like Shakespeare's and that poet's eyes. He was slow, soft spoken, very gentle. In years I never knew him to run or lose his temper. And, for sure, he kept all on going.

I never knew that man not working. Even after supper in his great stuffed chair, between fire and lamp, with his pipe going he would be netting onion bags, making rabbit snares,

fashioning axe helves. Twenty years after—in 1917—I got a
singular shock. I had been taken to the Opera Comique by a
staff officer, the French Foreign Ministry shewing me the attention because of some work I had done for them. Major
B—— was then doing staff work for the French Territorials
and was very enthusiastic about them. He shewed me a photograph of an old Territorial in the parados of a trench. The
old man had been cutting the entrance to a dug-out in the
chalk of the parados. He had fallen asleep, sitting spread-
eagled—his hands and arms raised above his head the right
holding a great cold-chisel, the left a hammer, the legs stretched
out before him. At the time in the crowded foyer, I felt the
singular emotion that we all know—of having seen that scene
before. Now it occurs to me that that must have been a sudden
remembrance of good Ragged Arse.

I had taken him over to the Pent.

All my life I have had a singular complexity of possessions or have been singularly occupied in getting them ship-
shape. I seem to have leased, bought, inhabited, mended, extended, patched up, cleaned out more houses, households of
furniture, carts, harness, waggon-sheds, plots of ground than
there are years to my life or than would have sufficed for the
lifetimes of ten other men. One of these properties was the
Pent—the old farmhouse to which I went after living at Bonnington. This old place I pulled about for years, restoring it
on the most approved lines to its original antique condition
of great rafters and huge ingles with rackets and crocks. In
all these activities poor Wilson was my abettor. There was
nothing he could not do, patiently and to perfection. He was
a wonderful gardener; he could make a stake and binder hedge
better than any other man; he could get out of the underwood more of the fourteen kinds of woodcraft produce than
any other man in the weald of Kent, or Sussex too.... Hop-
poles, uset-poles, stakes, binders, teenet, faggots, wattle-gates,
field gates, clothes-props, clothes-pegs, gate-posts, kindling—
there was nothing he could not work up out of his or your

underwood and brush. He was an admirable thatcher, a careful waggoner, a wonderfully good shepherd. He could lay bricks, cut out rafters, plaster, hang paper, paint, make chairs, corner-cupboards, fish, poach, snare, brew, gather simples, care for poultry, stop foxes' earths. He could keep tallies and the most complicated accounts on notched sticks, cutting with a bill hook I II III IV V VI VII VIII IX X as fast as you could write them with a pen and adding up quite as fast. There was nothing he could not do but write, and late in life he taught himself to read—after he discovered that with the aid of a pair of my old spectacles he could tell a great A from a bull's foot.

I had taken him over to the Pent then. He did all the odd jobs, attendant upon settling into that old place that had been allowed to run to rack and ruin. His capacity for work was amazing. All daylight he worked in the orchard and gardens; when the lamps were lit he came into the house and did carpentering. He had his meals with me; where he slept I never knew—I suppose on some straw and sacks in the corner of a cow-house. One evening, after supper, he started to disinter an old ingle nook that had been bricked by previous farmers. I went to bed.

In the morning I came down and there was Wilson asleep on an old coffin stool in the opened-up ingle. His arms were above his head, one hand holding a great hammer, another a cold-chisel, his legs were extended before him. It was of that that I was reminded in the foyer of the Opera Comique in 1917.

I think he was happy. In fact I think all those people were as happy as they were wise and unlettered. They made good money; thirteen and sixpence—say three and a half dollars—a week with a cottage and garden for eighteen pence —say thirty-six cents! They would have a pig in the pen, a chicken or two, a poached rabbit, a hare when they were in luck, hopping money to pay the bills with at Michaelmas, a cant of underwood to work on for their own profit in winter when farm work was at a standstill. And American beef was fourpence—eight cents—a pound in Ashford market and fresh butter five pence at Grists on the Marsh. And you did not want for junketings; there were Fairday and Wood Sale-dinners and excursions got up by Parson for the whole parish. Every year a party went from Bonnington to Boulogne in France. You could see it from Aldington Knoll on a clear day. One and threepence return to Folkestone Harbour, five shillings return Folkestone Harbour to Boulogne and twelve hours among the Frenchies. You could take yourself, the mistress and a daughter there and back for a pound and have fivepence apiece left to buy shell boxes with views of the sea for the three other children.

No; it was not a bad life. I daresay it was as good a life as the world had to show—in the nineties in the English countryside when food was so cheap that even Shaking Ben got his bellyful twice a day from one cottage or another on his beat.

The village was full of sociability; you chattered over the hedgerows or from orchard to orchard. There was always plenty to talk about and plenty to do. You are not to think that Ragged Arse Wilson bemoaned his lot. He worked all daylight and all candle-light hours. But it was merely turning from one handicraft to another. Everything that he did interested him and everything that he saw—from the ice breaking up on the dykes to the green of Lenten wheat and the chaffinches nesting, the bees swarming, the apples ripening, the hopping, the October brewing, the wood sales, the work in the wood and so round to Christmas and the New Year frosts again. I daresay Wilson, fashioning his axe helve by the firelight was happier than any Wall Street operator in his box at the Metropolitan Opera or than I, with such cares as I have, sitting writing here. He was singularly carefree.

You would have believed that if you could have heard them up at T'Shop at Aldington Corner on a Saturday night. T'Shop was the village Club, the Emporium, the news centre, the employment agency, the bank. It ran away, back, back, from the mellow oil lamps in its two narrow windows, back into sheds, stables, cellars. From its rafters and the rafters of all the out-buildings hung a mysterious inverted forest of unassorted objects—boots, buckets, ploughshares, strings of onions, flasks of olive oil, red herrings, corduroy trousers, baggin-hooks, brill-hooks, tool-baskets, cradles, hams. There was no imaginable thing that you could not buy there—even to books. I once bought off the counter Dostoievsky's *Poor Folk*.

And when Saturday's dusk had settled down on the fallows and ridges and the dykes and the great marsh and the high downs, then tongues wagged in T'Shop. Everyone stood there, an immense market basket or a potato trug on the arm —stood and stood and stood and talked and talked or, into deaf ears, shouted. Farmer Borden had had a stroke: a judgment on him! Fifty years ago he had taken advantage of Dan Hogbin's gel an' tried to palm the chil' onto his waggoner's mate to make the illegitemacy 'lowance less. A judgment on him! Dan Rangsley, down to Coppin's he was the fellow. Keeper Finn and Policeman Hogbin they bursteses into his place when the smoke was coming out of the chimney. There set Mistress Rangsley rocking the baby to and fro an' the crock babble-babbling from the hook on the fire. Powerful keen eyes they has Keeper Finn and Peeler Hogbin. Sees a pheasant's feather on the floor by Mistress Rangsley's foot and a hare's foot on the gun-rack. They pounces on the pot and what does they find boiling? Tater-peelings! You see? Tater peelings for the peeler.... They had thought to find a pheasant or a hare of Earl Sonde's. Powerful ashamed they were. Show a tater to Policeman Hogbin and he'll clout you over the head or slope away round the corner according to the mood that is on him. How did Rangsley contrive that?— Picked up the feathers and the foot in game-dealer Vidler's shop up to Ashford market when he'd bin to sell his mistress's duck eggs. Heard the Quality had it in mind to git him out of his cottage. You KNOW WHO wants it for his doxy—her with the painted cheeks and don't you dare look at me manner. But they won't catch Dan Rangsley. So in the warmth and scent of sugar, spices, leather, onions, coffee and woolens the talk goes on and on, list after list of weekly supplies being filled by the grocer's men.

Outside, silhouetted against the lights that gleam away, away for miles over the low country round Smith Paddocks, stands Shaking Ben. He holds the stump of his pipe to his toothless jaws, shrugs his shoulders incessantly, his straw basket dangling from his wrist. Sometimes he gives an eldritch shriek, sometimes a low chuckle. As you come out to go away down into the marsh you say: "There Ben, you hain't no call to shriek. There's for you." And you give him a couple of onions, or a handful of apple rings, or a bit of pork, or a screw of 'baccy, according to your means or generosity.

There being no Squire for many miles round the community centred on the parson. An old man with a long light, white beard that blew away over his shoulders, you would see him striding over the fields in black shiny leggings, his black Inverness cape streaming out behind him. He had a way when he talked to you, holding the side of his spectacles and pushing forward his face which you might have called poking his nose into things. But nothing was further from Parson's habits. He let his flock alone—and was continuously consulted by them. His charities in the winter were very considerable. How he got along I could never understand; he had three large marshland parishes at a stipend of less than £250 a year—say $1,250. And he had several children and a parsonage that was falling to pieces. He was a most extraordinary preacher on occasion, though usually his sermons were above the heads of his congregation. But the country people would consult his children at T'Shop on a Saturday night and when the word went round that Parson was going to preach a stinger next day his tiny church would be packed, with people listening in at all the windows. I sat under him once or twice on these occasions. I have seldom been more uncomfortably moved. He had a low voice, hardly more than a whisper. He held the side of his spectacles and uttered intimacies of everyday life that made the farmers and their wives around him groan spasmodically. On special occasions he would be invited to Canterbury to preach "before the Archbishop and Sir Edward and they Lords," his parishioners said. But he never got promotion. On the death of his first wife, he had married his cook, the only recompense he could make her for devoted nursing during an illness lasting for years. But you must not marry your cook—not though you be St. Chrysostom of the golden words—if you want a house in a Cathedral Close among deans and minor canons.

A feature outside the country-communal life of that village was Grocer Rayner of T'Shop. Though he organised and ran that complicated place with a hand of iron, he was stone deaf. So he read. He read Henry James, Joseph Conrad, Stephen Crane. He had had no outside guidance to these authors. He read them with the passionate engrossment of a man in deep isolation. When I once went into his parlour I saw that he had complete sets of the first editions of those authors. He had bought them as they came out. They would have driven New York auction rooms mad a year or so ago. When Crane and Conrad came into his shop one day Rayner's emotion was so great that he was ill for some time—a dour, bearded, Scotch-looking grocer.

It is a great pleasure of the literary life to come thus right out of the blue on figures like that of the Aldington grocer. Writing books, as far as the great public is concerned, is rather like throwing them into a well. You write and publish—and nothing happens. That literary, or literarily inclined, people should here and there salute you is all in the day's journey. You think cynically that the salutation is interested in one way or another—because of hope of return, or boredom, or desire of social advancement. But one day to come across a village grocer, or a bank president, or a railway porter or a doctor, accidentally to find that they support what you stand for—your friends, your point of view, your Movement—that is a great encouragement. It has happened to me once or twice. Thus at Aldington, in a railway train, or aboard ship or in a Turkish bath. Once indeed, coming home on leave during the War, I was followed into the compartment of the civilian train by a dark man who was carrying some of my own books. I was a little annoyed; I thought he intended to scrape acquaintance. He didn't. Just before the train started a South African with the gilt antelope on his wide-awake, jumped in. The civilian began reading my collected poems. The South African began animatedly to tell me how he had traveled three thousand miles by canoe to join up. He had not heard of the War till six months after it started and then only knew of it because his black boys came rushing in to tell him that German troops were burning their huts. He had started at once.

Suddenly he turned on the studious civilian and exclaimed:

"You ought to join up too: a lusty young man like you. Why aren't you in khaki?"

The young man rolled agonised dark eyes and exclaimed:

"I'm a P—P—P—P—P—," grasping at his throat in the struggles of a hopeless stutterer.

"I don't care what you are," the South African shouted. "You may be a Pacifist, or a Papa, or a Potato-grower but your king and country need you."

The civilian repeated:

"I'm a P—P—P—P—," and the South African:

"Come now—you get out at the next station and join up. A young man like you! With civilisation at stake:—Look at that old fellow there—" meaning me! "with his service stripes. Doesn't it make you blush?"

They continued like that until a stop at which the South African got out. The other turned to me and, with all the signs of agony and an explosion of P's like the unsilenced exhaust of a motor bicycle, at last brought out:

"I'm a P—P—Peruvian!"

It appeared that, being a neutral, he had come to England to take a course in modern English Literature at London University. I presume my books had been prescribed to him but I did not ask him. I didn't even ask him how he liked them, but recommended him to read the South American books of W. H. Hudson and Cunninghame-Graham.

I wonder if that country group was happier for being unable to read. I fancy not. Imagination must be served or it feeds on itself; then superstitions come creeping in. And superstitions run like underground rootstocks throughout most countrysides—queer superstitions that the Quality neither hears of nor suspects. I had glimpses of them now and then. Once I was digging at Aldington in a bed near the corner of my cottage. Wilson and I were getting out a tree that was undermining the foundations. I dug up a small china doll and was about to throw it away. Wilson said with a queer dry manner:

"I wouldn't throw that away, Master. You'll be throwing away your luck. Us chaps buried that there when you bought this place."

I asked him if they always did that. He blushed shyly and at last said:

"Us allus does it if us likes the governor— Buries a maiden or a doll or a horse's skull if us can get it."

That of course was an unsuspected survival of the human sacrifice when men buried a slave or a captive beneath the corner-stone of a new house. "Maiden" is the Kentish for the mell doll of other counties—the last sheaf home of the harvest, tricked out with ribbons and given the place of honour at the thanksgiving dinner.

Once on the face of the cliff we dug up two very large skeletons in a burial niche. They faded away as the air got at them—all except the bright white teeth. Whilst they were crumbling Wilson looked at them pensively and said:

"Those be Denes—the gentry that jumps on your back like booboys and strangles you to death. In Aldington Knoll woods after dark."

The Denes were the unforgotten and still dreaded Danes. The skeletons were those of men who had on that spot fallen in a tenth-century battle between the sea-robbers and the Anglo-Saxons. In much the same way the inhabitants of the hinterland of the Riviera and the Camargue dread the *Revenants* of the Saracens. As the Danes ravaged the South shores of England, so the Saracens landed on those of the Mediterranean and burnt and slew and led away captives. And just as the South Wind which brought the Algerines is still endowed with mysterious evil qualities on the shore of the one sea, so the East Wind in Essex and Kent is accounted the root of all evil. It is best not to be born with those winds blowing. You *may* have the evil eye. And it is worse at night.

Indeed the night sheds terrors over some countrysides and many, many were the woodland paths and roads that Wilson and Meary Walker, and Meary Spratt and Mus Diamond and the others absolutely refused to take after sundown. Still more singular were the taboos that existed—the things that for indefinite and unstatable reasons you must not do—and the mascots! But these do not come into this book. Nevertheless, originating in the pre-historic days of the Great Trade Route from the Wall of China to the Scillies, they were still strong in the Kent of the nineties. And they crossed the water and obtained still in the United States when I first went there as a very young man.

One of the most curious instances of taboo in America I came across a little later in Philadelphia. I think I have already told the story in print somewhere but I cannot find it in any of my books and the whole episode impressed me a good deal. I was then—in a year that I won't specify—working on a small farm in the outskirts of Philadelphia. I did not want to work on that farm because though I was interested in American agriculture that was a type of farming with which I was very familiar—small mixed farming which might just as well have been carried out in England. The farmhouse and buildings went back to the early eighteenth century, the title deeds dated back to Penn's day and were of wampum executed by an Indian chief. The owner who was farming it was a direct descendant of the original settler and it had never been out of the hands of the family. It boasted a pasture lot, a field of corn, a pumpkin patch, a potato patch, and a small neglected orchard. The owner was of what they call in England the county family class. He was, that is to say, until misfortune overtook him, one of the most prosperous professional men in the city and kept his farm in hand for pleasure and the sake of sentiment.

The misfortune that overtook him had its grotesque side. He was swindled out of the greater part of his money by a confidence trickster. This happened in London. He had gone to England to buy a county property where he intended to settle down. He was an Anglomaniac who found even the Philadelphia of those days too bustling for him. I will call him Peter Dundee. That is not his name; he is still living.

He had returned to his native city. But his unlucky star had let him be induced by the London police to prosecute the swindler. This did him no good. His money was gone. But that case was widely reported in the English and American papers and poor Dundee on his return found himself laughed at as the foolishest man in Philadelphia. He found the place still more unbearable. Being very impoverished he settled on his farm which he intended to hold until on the spreading out of the city he could restore his fortunes by its sale as building land. But he could find no hired man. All the hired men of that day went west to the bonanza farms and, never making enough money to pay their carfares back, there they remained.

I met Dundee, whose family I had long known, in a bar on Chestnut Street. He was extremely downcast and to comfort him I offered to work for him until he could get help. We started at once cutting his corn. This we did with *machetes*— long-headed Cuban knives.

The sun has a peculiarity in Pennsylvania when you are cutting corn. It jumps straight up to the zenith and there remains until you have finished work. You have not even the meagre shadow of the corn stalks. We worked usually in a temperature of 117° Fahr. The papers put it at merely 106°. They were anxious for the credit of the local climate. But we knew.

Every quarter of an hour whilst we worked the sheep got out of the pasture into the pumpkin patch. We would run out and drive them back and then go into the hall of the farm and hack pieces of watermelon with our *machetes*. Then back to work, then after the sheep again and then back to the watermelon. And so round and round and round again.

This grew monotonous. One morning I got up before sunrise and started to mend the snake fences. I had been working ten minutes when the long shadow of the farmer in the rising sunbeams came to me over the dew-wet grass. He contemplated me mournfully and said:

"You can't mend fence or build wall before Thanksgiving."

I said:

"I damn well can."

He repeated mournfully:

"You *can't* mend fence or build wall before Thanksgiving."

I said:

"We shall be a twelvemonth cutting your corn."

But he would not let me go on. I said:

"Look here, Peter, you're such an unlucky man, you might as well chance the evil eye or whatever it is." But that taboo was too strong.

Whilst I was there the Seventh Day Adventists raised a tumult amongst the Pennsylvania Dutch. They declared that

an immense balloon would come down from Heaven. The oc-
cupants would let down ropes. Such men as could hold on to
them would be dragged up to Heaven. The rest would be lost.
When you drove through the Dutch villages you saw hefty
men practising for the ascent. They were swinging from ropes
in their shirt sleeves from elm boughs or the gutters and water-
pipes of their farms. The women were not invited.

Whilst I was working there I was asked by Miss Mary
Moss to a dinner at her house on Chestnut Hill. Miss Moss
in those days was the literary dictatrix of Philadelphia so I
suppose I was invited rather as a man of letters than a farm
labourer. I sat after dinner on the stoop between a daughter
of Lee and a daughter of General Sherman. I heard from the
former a story of Marshal Ney in New Orleans which afterwards formed the basis for an unfinished collaboration of Conrad and myself. What the story was I shall tell later when I
write of that collaboration. It was told by Lee's daughter.
And it seemed to me a romantic episode of my then young life
to sit there looking into the black night and listening to the
katydids—and in that company to stories about the old South.
It perhaps seemed romantic to others. For when I at last published the story, two years ago, I prefaced it with a note as
to where I had heard it. By a slip of the pen I made the lady
who sat on my right Sherman's niece. I received a little later
a letter from the right lady who said she was in truth the
daughter of the general and remembered the occasion—and
me!—very well. That was more than a quarter of a century
after its occurrence. So the daughter of a federal commander-
in-chief had more of the royal gift of memory than the ex-
Kaiser!

I don't know why I should have been remembered or
treated as a literary celebrity in Philadelphia of those days.
I was certainly being enormously boomed in England for
books which now seem to me to be trivially suave. None of
them had been published in the United States. But the Quaker
City certainly opened its arms to me. I was most amazingly

dined—coming out of the heat of the cornfields to go into the city and eat enormous quantities of planked lamb or chicken à la Maryland.

Philadelphia was then in the throes of a municipal reform. The streets were full of reformers, mild young men, much like the English Fabians. They marched about with drums and banners and were intensely moral. They succeeded in electing their own district attorney and in putting one of their opponents in prison. Both the reformers and the Clover Club gave me dinners and lectured me ferociously on their respective virtues. At the Clover Club festival I had my first experience of public speaking in America. I shan't forget it.

I had come in hurriedly to the city and taken an hotel bedroom. I did not know whether or not to dress for dinner and could find no one on the 'phone to ask. I adopted a subterfuge. I had a velvet dinner jacket. You wore them for informal dinners in England then. I put this on over the rest of what used to be called immaculate evening dress. I calculated that, if no one else was dressed, I would keep it closed and, with a black dinner tie, pass for nothing worse than an undertaker. If others were dressed I would open it and there would be the correct *plastron.*

Some were dressed and some were not. The table was in the form of a horseshoe. Political speeches—of an anti-reform eloquence—were made from the floor during the meal. We ate, truly, planked lamb, whole on the plank. It was admirable. The liquor was very good. A distinguished lawyer—the one who afterwards defended Mr. Thaw for killing Stanford White —made an impassioned appeal to us. He wanted his client, a politician, brought to speedy trial. The client was languishing on bail. The lawyer, in the height of his passion went down on his knees in the space between the tables. He implored us to have his client brought to trial. As it was the reformers who were persecuting his client his eloquence seemed useless. The Clover Club was the organisation of the then Philadelphia equivalent of Tammany.

I was seated on the right of the chairman. When the dinner was finished I tried to slink away behind his throne. But I was caught and brought forcibly back. The audience who had heard at least twenty speeches were insatiable. They were yelling: "English novelist. We want the English novelist." Then they began to shout a short chant in unison, repeatedly. I made out that they were shouting: "Little Lord Fauntleroy." That was because of the velvet jacket.

The reformers' dinner was more sober. The reformers were of course elated over their success at the polls. But their elation took the form of cold boiled salmon and coca-cola. I have seldom seen such virtue except at dinners of the Square Club, a similarly virtuous English coterie. I told them all about the Fabian Society. They didn't listen. They told me all about purity of elections. I don't think I listened much. The Mayor was there. He was an Englishman who had been pitchforked into the job as being the only man in the Quaker City who could be expected to act impartially. He slapped them on the back and they him and everybody everybody else.

What happened to the Mayor in the night I don't know. The salmon or the liquor disagreed with him. In the morning he issued a *pronunciamento* accusing those mild reformers of bribery. He said that in order to elect their uncorrupted district attorney they had bribed every inhabitant of the Thirteenth Ward. They admitted it. They said there was no other way to secure political purity.

Shortly afterwards my employer found a hired man and I rested from my labours. I was sitting on the stoop, stopping up a wasp's nest. The hired man was on the roof fixing the shingles. I heard him call:

"I'm coming down now."

I said:

"Wait while I fetch a ladder." When I came back he was lying on the ground. He said:

"I've bruck me leg."

I said: "What did you jump for?"

He answered: "Wall, I thought I'd see."

I told poor Peter Dundee that I could not go on working for him any longer. He was so persistently unlucky that I was afraid of his ill-luck rubbing off on me. I went back to England. Dundee, however, is now a rich man with property in the Shires. Perhaps if I had stuck to him I might also be that.

I shall add here a postscript, for I cannot see where else I shall get the matter in. I have suffered from many injustices and slights. There is one only that I cannot stomach. That is in the appropriation and mangling of the stories that I tell. At the dinner of the Clover Club to which I have referred I told the spinach story. By next morning it had been cabled not only all across the American continent but all round the world, reaching Australia two days after I had told it. It had come into my head at that dinner because, whilst talking very vigorously to some one next me, I nearly took some fish handed me by a waiter—with my fingers. My story was:

"An absent-minded man took a lady into dinner. Soles were handed round and he took one with his fingers. Seeing the lady look surprised he said:

" 'Oh, I thought it was spinach.' "

Now that story has been related to me in almost every large city of two continents. Worse! It has always been mangled so as to turn it into nonsense. And invariably it has been attributed to almost everybody else under the sun.

Again there is my tango story.

Just after the tango—it was really the *cielito*—had reached London it excited enormous controversy as to whether it was or was not shocking. I was at a dance given by Mrs. Ina Matthias—one of the three beautiful sisters of Sargent's *Misses Wertheimer*. Mrs. Wertheimer, who was then a very old lady, asked me to take her to see the tango danced. We stood in the doorway of the ball-room and she looked long and earnestly. She sighed and said: "Yes, I suppose it is *very* shocking.... But does it matter, if they really love one another?"

Now I considered that story to be the prey of *my* bow and spear. What was my astonishment to see it next day in a morning paper over the signature of the regretted humorist "Saki." When Mrs. Wertheimer made the remark it was already two in the morning; the paper had already gone to bed. Saki had not been to Mrs. Matthias' party. And, almost more extraordinarily, at lunch that day I met Saki for the first time. And he told me my own story.

Yes. I have suffered. In all sorts of ways. Conrad—as I shall later point out—took one of his stories from a story in a book of mine published in 1903. There was no reason why he shouldn't. My story was not fiction but a record of a grim fact that happened to the sole survivor of a shipwreck in the Romney Marsh which was then my home. I happened to mention the appropriation with no ill thought in my head, in the book I wrote on Conrad just after his death. At once all the world that concerned itself with Conrad seemed to go mad. A writer in the London *Times* abused me to the extent of half a column for having made the impious claim. Another in the New York *Times* took up the burden to the extent of nearly three-quarters of a page. He has returned to the charge twice yearly ever since in the same journal and at much the same length. I can't help it. Was it Damas or Daimas that was the unrepentant thief?

Let me pull another shower string.

In a book of mine published in 1926 there appears the story of a lady who kept the cloak-room in a Paris theatre. Now last year, five years after my story first appeared in serial form, a charming lady who, as Mr. James used to say, unites to considerable literary gifts an enviable, a world-wide popularity—Miss A...a L...s, in a work called G...n M...Y B...ttes, reprints my story all over again.

Oh dear! What will the London *Times* and New York *Times* and the *Temps,* and the *Secolo,* and the *Welt Am Mittag* and the *Literary Bulletin* do to me now?—*And* Miss A...a L...s?

CHAPTER II

PURE LETTERS

THE coming of Conrad into my life forced my nose hard down again on the grindstone of writing. At Bonnington and the Pent I had dug and hedged and thatched. When my *oncle de l'Amérique* had performed as American uncles should, I added golf to my occupations. I became in a small way very proficient in that game which was then little played in England. My cousin, George Wilkes of Hythe had just started a links at Hythe. The Pent was five miles from that Cinque Port. I played there a good deal with Dr. MacNamara, the Liberal Minister for Education, and with Charles Masterman with whom I was afterwards very intimate. He was Chancellor of the Duchy of Lancaster in Asquith's War Cabinet.

I made a great many notes for a life of Henry VIII which I never published and for my history of the Cinque Ports which I did publish in 1903. I wrote also some verse. I suppose I became tired of a life of leisure and golf and went to Limpsfield to be reformed by Mr. Edward Garnett and his friends. Limpsfield, however, disgusted me with the life of the Intelligentsia as lived in the London suburbs. So back I went to the Pent. I daresay I should have become finally a country gentleman historian. But a curious coincidence prevented that. I had got together all my material for the life of Henry VIII and had made a synopsis of the chapters and even a list of the illustrations. And I had chosen my publishers. The book

167

was to be heavily illustrated with reproductions of Holbein and the like. There was only one publisher in London then for finely illustrated books. That was the house of Virtue. I went up to London with my synopsis and specimen reproductions. I saw one of the partners of the firm and laid my plan before him. He said:

"You saw the gentleman who just went out. Do you know who that was?" I didn't, and he said:

"That was Mr. Pollard of the British Museum. Just before you entered we signed an agreement for a life of Henry VIII by him." Mr. Pollard's synopsis allowing for difference in idiosyncrasies was almost word for word the same as mine. His list of illustrations was identical.

The coincidence is not as surprising as it sounds, but the blow was none the less severe. It was not to be thought of that two books on exactly the same lines could appear almost simultaneously.... I had worked on my plan for a number of years. Now I had to drop it dead.

The coincidence was not so surprising because the great compilation called the *Catalogue of State Papers of Henry VIII Foreign and Domestic* had been appearing for a number of years. It had just reached Vol. XIII. I suppose Mr. Pollard and I had been working on the documents thus indexed for just the same number of years and with the publication of that volume had arrived simultaneously at the idea that we might begin writing our books. I felt stunned.

I should not have said that I cared much whether I wrote a life of Henry VIII or not, or even whether I ever wrote anything at all except now and then for a verse or two. The physical side of life had at that time gripped me. I wanted to hunt, to hit a ball and to make things grow. Writing seemed to me an unmanly sort of occupation. I still want to make things grow and indeed now again have my little plot of ground. But I no longer regard writing as an unmanly occupation, though I much dislike doing it.

The idea of putting tiny dark objects into the ground fascinates me. Over their germination and growth there is something mysterious and exciting. It is the only clean way of attaining the world's desire. You get something for nothing. Yes, it is the only clean way of adding to your store; the only way by which you can eat your bread without taking it out of another's mouth. I used to think that the arts and letters were also not only creative but non-competitive. An author—*auctor*—added to things and took nothing from anyone. But during the first battle of the Somme it was rumoured in my London clubs that I was killed or dead of drink or court-martialed and shot. Non-combatants said cheerful things like that of people in the line. A brother author on hearing this said:

"Killed! Good! I shall be able to afford a second lump of sugar in my tea!" The gentleman who reported this to me pointed out that it was not even an original sentiment. It had been uttered on a similar occasion by Theodore Hook or Douglas Jerold or someone of the sort. So there must be authors who regard their art as means to a competitive scramble.

In any case I was slightly stunned at hearing that Mr. Pollard was writing my life of Henry VIII. I drifted, as one did in those days, round to the British Museum to pour my woes into Dr. Garnett's ear. It was really like that. Dr. Garnett never looked at you. He presented his ear. He suggested that I should turn the fruits of my studies into novels. I didn't want to write novels—and particularly not historical novels. I knew he thought Mr. Pollard, who was one of his assistants, would be a more serious historian than I. He said: why not write a novel about pusses—pronouncing it to rhyme with busses? The amiable and cultivated Egyptians when their houses were on fire put a cordon round them to prevent their pusses dashing into the flames. There was a subject. I said I should hate to write a novel about pusses. He said: then, why not pirates? I ejaculated:

"Good God: Pirates! Why not palmistry?" Palmistry,

as I have said, was along with pusses one of that great scholar's infatuations.

We were standing in the embrasure of one of the windows in the Garnetts' great drawing-room. It was in the east wing of the Museum. The Garnetts had a tea party every day and an immense one every Thursday. The room was full of people. I knew I ought not to have monopolised the attention of their host. I was also aware that Dr. Garnett was lecturing me for my good. He had turned his spectacles towards the carpet and was speaking with his absent deference, fingering the revers of his frock coat.

Pirates, he was saying, were always very much in the public eye. Any details as to their lives and careers always attracted attention. *Treasure Island* was tremendously to the fore then. I knew he considered me an idle and presumptuous young fellow. He was intimate with all the elder members of my family. My grandfather and my Uncle William Rossetti always spoke of him as "young Garnett"—a stripling of promise. He was then perhaps fifty. My father and Mr. Gosse had done most of their courting in his hospitable drawing-room, neither of their parents-in-law much approving of them. So he was trying to give me good advice as to how to make a living with my pen. This annoyed me because I did not consider that I had to make a living.

He suggested that I should go into the Reading Room. There I should find the trial of Aaron Smith.

I saw Samuel Butler bearing down on us. I disliked Samuel Butler more than anyone I knew. He was intolerant and extraordinarily rude in conversation—particularly to old ladies and young persons. He had perhaps cause to be, for he was conscious of great gifts and of being altogether neglected. In those days he was almost unknown. *Erewhon* was nearly forgotten, *The Way of All Flesh* unpublished and not even fully written. Otherwise he was unfavourably known as having pirated the ideas of Darwin and as having behaved with extraordinary rudeness to that great and aged scientist. It struck

me that, as he was bearing down on us, he had the air of a
pirate. His complexion was fresh, his hair and torpedo beard
of silver grey; he kept his hands usually in his coat pocket.
His coat was a square blue reefer; his red necktie was con-
fined in a gold scarf ring. It is one of the regrets of my life
that I made nothing at all of two of the most remarkable
men I ever met casually and fairly frequently. Butler was too
arrogant, Synge too modest. I saw Synge rather often when
he was a journalist in Paris. He said very little and seemed
to be merely another, florid, tuberculous Irishman. Yet I
suppose that *The Way of All Flesh* and *The Playboy of the
Western World* are the two great milestones on the road of
purely English letters between *Gulliver's Travels* and Joyce's
Ulysses.

At any rate, as Butler drew towards that alcove I prepared to leave it.

As I was going Dr. Garnett, with his mild obstinacy,
again advised me to read the trial of Aaron Smith. He said it
concerned the last pirate who was ever tried at the Old Bailey.
The man had been acquitted but his case had caused a great
deal of controversy because party politics had come into it
and the case still had elements of mystery. For himself he was
inclined to think that Smith actually had been the victim
of governmental hard usage. Mr. Butler said that if there had
ever been a scoundrel who deserved hanging it was Smith.
It occurs to me now that that speech settled my fate. It seemed
to me odd that anyone so aged as Butler should take passionate
sides in a trial of a pirate sixty years ago. Butler then appeared
to me aged. I suppose I am older now than he was then, and
I don't feel old.

It occurred to me in the course of a sleepless night to
wonder how an aged fellow like Butler would regard his past,
supposing him to have been a pirate as a boy. I was sleepless
because the ceasing of my aspiration to write the life of Henry
VIII had left me at a loose end. I was accustomed to reflect
on that Protestant hero just before I went to sleep. I had

nothing else to reflect upon. So Butler and the pirate replaced the monarch. I wanted something controversial to tackle if not with my pen then at least in my half-waking thoughts. Smith was not so important as Henry VIII. But Henry VIII was not attacked by Butler. I wanted to defend anyone from Darwin to a pirate who was attacked by that fellow who himself looked and behaved, in conversation, like a pirate. So I began to wonder how Smith, when he was an old man, would have regarded his life. And I had to make him a nice old man because Butler was a nasty one.

I suppose I then fell asleep. Nothing further of that night comes back to me. But I will add a detail of literary life of that day. I had then a small apartment in John Street, Bloomsbury. It consisted of a living-room, a bedroom and a tiny kitchen at the top of an eighteenth-century house—one of those old houses that exactly resemble those in Greenwich Village or Chelsea on the west side of Fifth Avenue. I paid for it £30— $150—a year and as I shared it with the architect who built Edward Garnett's cottage at Limpsfield it cost me only £15— $75—a year to have that London *pied à terre*. Alas! I pay exactly double per month for the apartment of the same room and appearance that I occupy in Greenwich Village. But a pound was a pound then—a fat, shining, substantial coin.

Having then slept I awoke to a feeling of uneasy conscience. I thought I had been grossly rude and ungrateful to Dr. Garnett. The least I could do was to feign an interest in Pirate Smith. I went therefore to his intriguing private room in the Museum Library and asked him where I could find records of the Smith trials. When you visited him there you pressed on a button in one of the museum walls. A section swung out towards you and there was a passage leading to his room. He told me that I should find the record in *State Trials;* Volume So and So, Page So and So. But I could find a condensation in Dickens' *All the Year Round* for such and such a date. That was another coincidence. I do not suppose that I should ever have taken the trouble to look up the State Trial. But

I was going to write an article about my grandfather's wood-
cuts and several of these had been printed in *All the Year
Round*. I was actually in the Museum with the purpose of taking out all the volumes of that periodical. So, as it were against
the grain, I read the trial of Aaron Smith. In that way I came
to work with Conrad—and to write novels of my own! I may
add, as another coincidence, that last year I was recommended
to read and did read with enormous enjoyment Mr. Richard
Hughes' *High Wind in Jamaica*. It seemed to me the best thing
that had come out of Wales or the British Empire since the
War. I had not been reading very long before I discovered
that Mr. Hughes also had based his book on the trial of Aaron
Smith. But whereas I made him an agreeable person who ended
up as a country gentleman, Mr. Hughes made him a lousy
and lachrymose scoundrel who was duly hanged in chains on
Thames Bank at Gallions Reach. That shows probably the
difference between the pure Welch and the Polono-Cymric
imagination.

I shall probably not be mentioning Dr. Garnett again. I
should like to round off what I hope has been a tribute of gratitude and affection to that great scholar. He was, as I have said,
famous the world over for his Catalogue and is I hope still
so famous. But alas for the imaginative writer that was lost!
His industry was prodigious. He worked in the Museum day
in day out from nine o'clock till four. At that hour he attended
his wife's tea parties. Then he wrote till dinner time. He
usually went to some official, or City Company dinner. On his
return he worked again till far in the night. But every morning
towards six he went to Covent Garden market to buy the
family fruit and vegetables. He worked on the Catalogue; he
reviewed endless dull books; he collaborated on Histories of
Literature; he contributed serious articles to the heavy monthlies. The actual body of his writing must be tremendous. But,
again alas! he wrote only one *Twilight of the Gods*. That volume comes back to me as the most delightful of collections of
learned-whimsical stories. His verse also was dainty and

skilled. So, to gain an illustrious scholar, the world lost an Anatole France who should have been without mournful rancour and jejune cynicism. Destiny led him to sink his imaginative gift in the career of the *bon père de famille* who appears in French leases. For, when you sign a French lease, you have to undertake that you will conduct no business in your premises and will there cause no scandal. But you will occupy them like a good father of a family. I think Dr. Garnett felt some bitterness about it towards the end of his life. Imaginative work then came to have for him an aspect of far greater weight and certainly of vastly greater permanence.

He was a man of iron physique and was never ill till almost the day of his death. Once, as I have said, going to buy his morning fruit he was set upon by three roughs who tried to go through his pockets. He put his back against the market railings and beat them all off with his umbrella without calling for the police. He wrote a work called *Alms for Oblivion*—about the forgotten great!

I think he was the great literary-scholastic figure of London of those just-after-gaslit days. He certainly was, if to be great is to be one to whom one's whole world resorts for assistance in technical troubles. His position was almost unassailable but I think he had one enemy. This was a Mr. John Cordy Jeaffreson, a man of general letters, of boisterous and combative tendencies. I don't know how far the feud went but it must have been bitterish. Dr. Garnett had written a monograph on Byron which essayed to prove that Byron was a relatively respectable person. Mr. Cordy Jeaffreson replied with a violent monograph to prove that Byron wasn't. It was called *The Real Lord Byron* and made many personal attacks on the keeper of Printed Books. Dr. Garnett preserved a dignified silence. But looking through Mrs. Garnett's album soon after, I came across a picture of an owl screeching from above a bust of the poet. It was labeled "The Real Cordy Jeaffreson." So I suppose there had been subterranean irritation.

The other literary Popes of London were in the realms of

what was then called "Pure Literature," Mr. Norman Mac-coll of the *Athenaeum*. In "Mixed Literature" it was Mr. W. L. Courtney, the agreeable and rather *rigolo* figure who edited the *Fortnightly Review* and was the Literary Editor of the *Daily Telegraph*. The Imaginative-Literary Pope was my guardian, Mr. Theodore Watts-Dunton who was the Literary Editor of the *Athenaeum* and lived with Swinburne at a Putney villa called "The Pines." There were also Literary Religious Popes of varying denominations. Dean Farrar who wrote with the aid of Dr. Garnett a *Life of Christ* stood for Establishment. Mr. Frederick Harrison dominated Positivism, Dr. Robertson Nicoll, Nonconformity. Newman, I suppose, still dominated Literary Catholicism.

All these people for me were sixtyish, bad-tempered, formidable, and all, with the exception of Dr. Garnett, of the sort I did not like. They were united by contempt for novel writing which was perhaps why I insensibly disliked them. And the curious symptom of the time was that nearly all of them with the exception of Mr. Maccoll wrote novels before they died. Mr. Harrison's contribution to fiction was a portentous classical-historical composition whose name I have forgotten, Mr. Courtney's also I have forgotten. Dean Farrar caused misery to a whole generation of schoolboys by writing a lugubrious piece of fiction called *Eric, or Little by Little*. Mr. Watts-Dunton very late in life produced *Aylwin* a *roman à clef* introducing most of the characters of D. G. Rossetti's circle. It had a prodigious success. It was as if, with dying hands, they clasped at immortality.

But they were tremendously excitable. The appearance of the *Athenaeum* every Thursday set them scurrying to the bookstalls as today we run for news of the latest phase of a considerable murder. At every gas-lit literary tea excited whispers went round as to how in its columns one bearded and disagreeable pundit had flagellated another. And as every London literary man had—and very likely has—no one but himself for a friend amongst his confrères the *Athenaeum* was a popular journal. Its flailings might cause consternation in one poor lion's home but it brought joy to the dens of a hundred jackals.

I did my best to destroy it and, in my more sanguine moments, have imagined that with my friends I helped it towards its disappearance. But I don't know that I don't regret it, or that its successors have added gaiety to the literary landscape. I suppose—after having studied the matter all my life—that what is most necessary for literature—or for any art or for any human pursuit!—is a standard. That is something to kick off from or to kick. If it is good you work according to its dictates. If it is bad you gain inspiration from fighting it.

A body like the French Academy is probably more detrimental than not to the production of any of the arts or even the sciences. But its existence does this much good: it shows the State as honouring thought. The position of a writer, an artist, or a pure scientist is one of some dignity in France. I hear the Anglo-Saxon reader gasping with astonishment. Yet just above where I sit now writing lives a French naval officer of the rank of Vice Admiral. The day before yesterday somebody told him I was a poet. Yesterday he got out his Panhard and drove a hundred miles or so to a forest in Savoy and, with great labour of his hands and a tyre-wrench, dug up a root of asphodel. This he brought back to me that I might plant it in my garden. He said that poets ought to have asphodels in their gardens. I cannot quite figure any American Admiral thinking that my friend Ezra Pound ought to be supplied by the Navy with fabulous classical plants or any British one doing as much for that distinguished British Poet, Mr. T. S. Eliot.... But then French academicians wear swords.

England and America have no Academies or none that you would notice. But in England of the nineties the body of contributors to the *Athenaeum*, over whom ruled Mr. Maccoll, supplied something very similar. They wore no swords but they dipped their pens in gall when they wrote of outsiders and newcomers and in honey mixed with hyssop when they discussed the works of their confrères of the Heavies, the *Quarterly* or the *Edinburgh Review.*

As compared with the *Athenaeum* and the two quarterlies, the *Nineteenth Century* and the *Fortnightly Review* were light reading. The first was then conducted, I think, by Knowles. The second by W. L. Courtney. Knowles' hand was heavy. Courtney's rather light. Knowles was Olympian. I didn't know him and never knew anyone who did. Courtney I knew fairly well. He was accessible, a *bon vivant,* mixed freely with gayer literati and the Smart Set, wore evening clothes well and gave admirable lunches. I don't know that his *Fortnightly* did much harm to literature. It sometimes printed my poems and paid very well for them. But the harm done by Mr. Courtney's literary pages in the *Daily Telegraph* must have been incalculable. It heralded mediocrity to the sound of shawns and oboes; it never praised any writer of merit and originality until he had grown old and imbecile. Its influence amongst the middle classes was tremendous. The manager of Mudies' Circulating Library in the City told me that every Friday at lunch time he was inundated by the warmer inhabitants of the Square Mile. These chief city-men of the Empire would remove their silk hats. Inside the leather linings their careful spouses would have placed the list of books they desired to read during the ensuing week. Almost invariably these lists consisted of a clipping from the *Daily Telegraph,* made up of the names of books recommended on Mr. Courtney's Literary Page.

It is good will that is needed if the Humaner Letters are to come into their own. No amount of praise from academicians will make a bad book have a permanent life whilst ill-natured comment on a good one will delay its entry into its kingdom. Thus people die without having read it and the writer is discouraged. These are two of the worst things that can happen to humanity. You may die reconciled to your fate without having seen Carcassonne but what would it be like to leave the world without having read...oh, *The Playboy of the Western World?* And what is the place in the hereafter reserved for the gentleman who checked the activities of Keats? For myself, I would rather see the worst popular writer roll in gold than a fraudulent pill maker or a Wall Street bear. He at least is only doing what Shakespeare tried to do.

The only human activity that has always been of extreme importance to the world is imaginative literature. It is of supreme importance because it is the only means by which humanity can express at once emotions and ideas. To avoid controversy I am perfectly ready to concede that the other arts are of equal importance. But nothing that is not an art is of any lasting importance at all, the meanest novel being humanly more valuable than the most pompous of factual works, the most formidable of material achievements or the most carefully thought out of legal codes. Samuel Butler wrote an immense number of wasted words in the attempt to avenge himself for some fancied slight at the hands of Darwin. But, in spite of these follies *The Way of All Flesh* is of vastly more use to us today than is *The Origin of Species*. Darwin as scientist is as superseded as the poor alchemist in the Spessart Inn: so is Butler in the same department of human futility. But *The Way of All Flesh* cannot be superseded because it is a record of humanity. Science changes its aspect as every new investigator gains sufficient publicity to discredit his predecessors. The stuff of humanity is unchangeable. I do not expect the lay reader to agree with me in this pronouncement but it would be better for him if he did. The world would be a clearer place to him.

From that point of view the activities of the old *Athenaeum* under Maccoll were unmitigatedly harmful—and singularly adroit. Mr. Maccoll was, to all appearances, a nearly imbecile, blond, bald, whiskered individual. He wore black gloves on every occasion, indoors or out, and if you addressed him his eyes wandered round the cornice of the ceiling as if the mere fact of being spoken to had driven him into a panic.

As far as I know he never wrote anything except perhaps the biography of some obscure theologian or diplomatist but his bulky figure with its black kid gloves and its hand, in addition, always in the pockets of his reefer jacket as if he had doubly to hide some grotesque and shameful disease—his panic-stricken and bulky figure comes back to me as containing one of the most potent and disastrous forces of his day.

He had got his job I think from having been the travelling tutor of Sir Charles Dilke, the politician and owner of the journal. But having made his singular and bemused apparition at a public or private function he would return to his office and with unerring and diabolical skill would send out books to the reviewers for whom they were exactly unsuited. The policy of his journal was to regard all novels as tawdry trifles to be dismissed in a few notes. It considered that no poetry had been written or could have been written by persons born after 1820, except when Mr. Watts-Dunton got hold of a volume by D. G. Rossetti, whose solicitor he was, or by Swinburne, to whom he acted as keeper. The body of the paper was given up to tremendous and sesquipedalian reviews of works with titles like: *The Walcheren Expedition and the Manœuvres in the Low Countries* in three volumes, post quarto. If its reviewer could discover three misprints, the name of a Dutch village spelt wrong, two real inaccuracies and a nine which the writer had inverted in a date so that it looked like a six—then the joy of the journal was unmeasured. It pronounced in Olympian tones that this immense undertaking was completely worthless to the student of the subject, and nothing could better display its infallibility. It once reviewed a novel of mine with the words:

"From the fact that on page 276 Mr. Hueffer misspells the word *herasia* the reader will be able to judge of the value of his piece of fiction." And most novels received as summary treatment at its hands.

No, certainly if an attitude of friendship is productive of good literature the *Athenaeum* did little to help things. I remember hearing an immensely popular novelist recount how he paid a visit of reconciliation to Watts-Dunton at "The Pines," Putney. I do not think there were many pine trees there. The immensely popular novelist had once served D. G. Rossetti as factotum and body-servant. As soon as the breath was out of Rossetti's body Mr. Watts-Dunton, as solicitor and executor, had turned the novelist out of the house. The novelist had avenged himself by forestalling all the *Athenaeum* reviewers by a volume of personal recollections of the painter poet. All the reviewers of the *Athenaeum* had wanted to write volumes about Rossetti and all had wanted to be the first. They all eventually wrote their volumes, but the novelist's effusion took the cream off the market and established him in the public mind as being Rossetti's best friend. I daresay he really had been. Towards the end of his life Rossetti was a pretty forlorn figure.

Well, there was a devil of a bobbery over that volume. Every *Athenaeum* reviewer and all poor Rossetti's parasites and bottle-washers fell on it. When Mr. Maccoll thought he had given space enough to the attacks they overflowed into the most ill-assorted journals. I remember reading an attack on it years later in the correspondence column of the *Farmers and Stockbreeders' Gazette,* all of ten years later.

Mr. Watts-Dunton bided his time. The attacks on the novelist had the effect of conferring on him an extraordinary popularity. Every volume he wrote was received as if with salutes of a hundred guns by the circulating libraries. He was at once the greatest romanticist, the greatest moralist and the public figure who physically most resembled Shakespeare.

At last Mr. Watts-Dunton produced *Aylwin.* It must have had the largest sale of any novel published up to that date and for twenty years later. Its fame resounded round the world and back again and then back again. Then Mr. Watts-Dunton found himself secure.

He wrote to the novelist and invited him to visit "The Pines" in a pilgrimage of reconciliation. It was not a success.

Said the novelist, speaking very slowly as he always did, but with tones of bitterness and contempt that can seldom have been surpassed:

"I ... went ... to *Putney!*" Putney is an estimable suburb of London, the social equivalent of the Bronx, New York, in its more comfortable regions. I was born about two miles from there. But from the tones of the novelist's voice you would have taken it to be an open sewer and contemptible at that. "I ... took ... a ... *yellow* bus! .. and a *red* ... bus! .. and I changed ... into ... a *green* ... bus! ! !" All this to indicate how remote and unfashionable was Mr. Watts-Dunton's residence, the novelist inhabiting a feudal castle, nothing less! .. "I asked ... a po .. *lice*man! ... And a *fish* ... monger! ... And at a *cheese* ... shop! ... And at last in a dreary ... dilapidated ... forbidding ... Victorian villa ... in a dark ... gloomy ... obscure ... back room ... poring over a ... crabbed ... manuscript ... I saw an ... ugly ... yellow ... little ... evil ... crabbed ... hateful ... toad ... of a ... hunchback. ... And it looked up at me and said:

" 'Blank ... you left us ... you left ... Gabriel and me ... thirty ... years ... ago. ... And since then I see from the ... public ... prints ... that you have written a book!'

" 'So,' said the novelist, 'I left that ... little ... ugly ... yellow ... ,' " and he went through all his epithets and the vicissitudes of his return journey in inverse order.

That was how they managed things, Victoria being queen.

Amongst such people the conception of the novel as a work of art was unthinkable. Nor can I claim any greater enlightenment for myself. It was difficult in the England of those days to strike out on that path alone. I owe a great deal to Conrad. But most of all I owe to him that strong faith: that in our day and hour the writing of novels is the only pursuit worth while for a proper man. That was his strong faith and certainly it communicated itself to me.

Nothing was further from English belief in the dying years of the reign. The novel then was "fiction." It had sometimes a purpose, sometimes a key. But those very facts made it by so much the less a work of art. A gentleman who wishes to enforce a moral by means of fiction colours his facts and underlines his inferences. An art is unbiased rendering.

In the days of which I am writing, Meredith was writing probably *Lord Ormont and His Aminta* at Box Hill; Thomas Hardy thinking of *Tess of the D'urbervilles* at Dorchester; Mr. Kipling was contributing *Badalia Herodsfoot* to the *Detroit Free Press* and, amongst the quite young, Mr. H. G. Wells was turning from his marvelous semi-scientific short stories to the consideration of social injustices and writing the *Wheels of Chance* for a journal called *Today*. Conrad had as yet published nothing, but *Almayer's Folly* was about to appear. Mr. Arnold Bennett was still a hack-writer of appalling and obscure energy. Mr. Galsworthy, having met Conrad during a voyage to the Cape, was meditating the modest and amiable short stories and the charming novels which he eventually published under the titles respectively of *A Man of Devon* and the *Villa Rubein*—both by John Sinjohn. James was accepted as a moral prodigy by moralists among the Intelligentsia. Crane was about to appear. Henry Harland was just publishing an agreeable *pastiche* called *The Cardinal's Snuffbox.*

To say that none of these writers save Conrad and the three last named Americans had any artistic self-consciousness at all would be to exaggerate. Certainly Mr. Arnold Bennett united to an amazing business facility a really deep knowledge of French technical methods. I remember going to lunch at his Paris apartment in 1909, I should say. He was then relatively unknown. But the leg of mutton—with the clove of garlic properly tucked into the knuckle!—which Mrs. Bennett cooked for my benefit in that pretty little place near the Odéon is not more clear in my memory than poor Bennett's conversation. At first view, he was queerly cockney in appearance with the cowlick at the back of his hair, his ready-made bow riding up over his collar, and his front teeth protruding. But, when he spoke, he immediately—and again and again—gave me the impression that he was the wisest man not only that there ever was but that there possibly could be. And his pronouncements about writing—at any rate in conversation—seemed to me of an astounding justness. He disliked, it is true, the French from whom he had learned everything. But that seemed to be inevitable in the English Intelligentsia of his generation. Nevertheless his *The Old Wives' Tale* is one of the best artistic presentations of life in Paris that I have ever read.

I write thus at this point because I was only yesterday shocked to read in an English paper that I very rarely see, that his will had been proved. He must therefore be dead. I think that posterity will not willingly let his work die.

I think he was the only Englishman who ever talked to me about how books should be written, though I have talked to several with singular unsuccess in awakening interest in the subject. At that date the triumphant English slogan as to writing found vent in Mr. Kipling's verse:

> *There are five and fifty ways*
> *Of inditing tribal lays*
> *And every single one of them is right.*

That is true enough as far as it goes—but the corollary should be considered. The corollary is more important than the proposition. It is that for every subject there is one only best treatment.

There was, of course, even in the late nineties, a group of writers, mostly women, who by the shrillness of their voices or the exaggeration of their methods conferred on the "Nuvvle" —for you could not call it the novel—a certain fictitious prominence. There was Mrs. Mannington Caffyn who wrote, as Iota, a book called, I think, *The Yellow Aster* and Mme. Sarah Grand whose name I remember but whose titles refuse to come back to me. I think she wrote *The Heavenly Twins*. There was also a lady who wrote as George Egerton a book called *Keynotes*. She had real talent but a tendency towards bitterness enhanced by real or fancied slights made her give up writing.

Mrs. Olive Schreiner's *The Story of an African Farm* was also immensely read by the more serious. I could not say if it had any merit. There was also—more monumentally, Henry James' friend, Mrs. Humphry Ward, an Arnold who made you very aware of the fact.

This sudden appearance of women was an omen. The novel was a field in which till then they had made only solitary appearances. Sarah Fielding, Miss Edgeworth, Jane Austen, Charlotte Brontë, Mrs Gaskell and George Eliot occupied in the public estimation of that day about the positions of Mesdames Vigée Lebrun, Angelica Kaufmann and Rosa Bonheur in painting. They were patronised and hardly regarded askance.

But the appearance of this cloud of active and energetic sisters with their instinct for publicity, their pertinacious pronouncement of equal rights, their doctrines of liberty for the sex that till then had been calmly ignored—that was a very different pair of shoes. Rhoda Broughton, Mrs. Lynn Lynton, Mrs. Mona Caird, advocated, in novels, unheard of things. Miss Broughton even proclaimed that women—even young girls— should have latchkeys. You have no idea of the sensation *that* caused. To top it all Miss Fawcett was proclaimed Senior Wrangler—and her mother, Mrs. Fawcett, the wife of the blind Postmaster General, began the process of sitting in drawing-rooms and giving mildly as her opinion that the franchise ought to be conferred on women. Her more energetic ally, Miss Garrett Anderson, even proclaimed the same doctrine loudly in semi-public meetings. The cat was out of the bag and the epithet, the Shrieking Sisterhood, became sanctified in English middle-class vernacular.

The result was the formidable movement which twenty years afterwards brought English public life to a deadlock. That I shall talk of when I come to it. I played in that a certain part—all that my energies and passions for the cause of the stupidly oppressed would let me. For the moment I am only concerned to point out that the despised Novel—and the

"Nuvvle" at that!—played a very great part in giving public prominence to the movement.

That, then, was the general aspect of things literary at about the time when Conrad asked to be allowed to collaborate in the novel I was then writing. It was the novel about Aaron Smith. I must have told him the plot when he came to see me at Limpsfield. I had forgotten the fact and his letter to me making the proposition seemed to come to me out of a clear sky. I can remember to this day its aspect and how I read it in bed at the Pent with the robin that always accompanied the morning tray up the stairs, sitting on a comb on the dressing table.

CHAPTER III

WORKING WITH CONRAD

THE nature of my relationship with Conrad has been a good deal misunderstood by the general public and the press of this country and the one across the water. Just before my last departure from Paris for New York, I received a letter from a London editor asking me for my "account" of my "quarrel with Conrad" and giving me to understand that someone else was giving what he alleged to be Conrad's account of his quarrel with me. There never was a quarrel. Conrad never in his life addressed an irritated word to me about any personal matter, nor did I ever address one to Conrad.

I published three books in collaboration with Conrad, one of them of great length and calling for five years of work, joint and apart. For such work—work of such close texture—intimacy is necessary. That must be manifest to the most lay of intelligences. Intimacy calls also for a certain interchange of respect and affection. You cannot pass days and nights alone together worrying over words with an individual whom in your normal moments you regard as imbecile, a double-crosser, or, as for any other reasons, nauseous.

I was, then, for more than ten years, very intimate with Joseph Conrad; our friendship was never disturbed by any quarrel, and the last words of our last letters from one to the other were full of affection. Within a few weeks of his death, Conrad once more expressed the desire, against my own wishes, publicly to identify himself with me as collaborator. This he did. The proof of all this I am about to afford; the more impatient reader may see it by turning to the last sentence in the last paragraph but four of this chapter.

The personal record of Conrad that I wrote immediately after his death was impressionistic rather than factual. That was appropriate because Conrad was the greatest of impressionist writers and held that truly recorded impressions communicate impressions truer than the truest records of facts. The reasons for this are too technical here to go into, but that was what Conrad held and that was what he desired—to keep his memory sweet.

I was useful to Conrad as writer and as man in a great many subordinate ways during his early days of struggle and deep poverty. It was not merely that, from 1897 to 1909, I did, at such times as he was not himself equal to them, absolutely all of his literary dustings and sweepings, correcting his proofs, writing from his dictation, suggesting words when he was at a loss, or bringing to his memory incidents that he had forgotten. It was still more, perhaps, that I was large, blond, phlegmatic on the surface and had a good deal of knowledge of the practical sides of English life that Conrad naturally ignored.

That was a question of temperaments. Conrad passionately needed some moral support of the type that such an individual could afford him. Other people might have had the same temperament or temperaments very similar, but they had not the time to give nor the same taste in words. That last was the strongest bond. In all the millions of words that we must have written or pored over together we never once disagreed over the words a sentence contained once it was given its final form. You will say that that sort of statement is easy to write and difficult to prove.

Well, in my preface to *The Nature of a Crime*, which was our last published collaboration and the last finished work that Conrad signed, I made the statement that towards the end of our labours on those books, we had got so used to reading our own works aloud to each other that we finally wrote for the purpose of reading aloud the one to the other. That statement Conrad corroborated by passing it for the press—as it were with his dying breath. And that we should thus have written must have meant a similar taste in words, for it would be insupportable to have to listen, evening after evening, to prose that you did not like and almost as intolerable to read your own work to a person who did not like your turns of phrase.

I do not think that Conrad ever worked with a pen over manuscripts of a book of mine. He read them with minuteness, suggested emendations, and groaned over banalities—but he was always too harried by his own work to have a minute to give to writing into another's. My own books of that period are entirely negligible. They were not, however, neglected, for during a considerable part of the period of our collaboration I was not only much the more prosperous individual but greatly the more popular author; indeed at one period I must have been one of the most boomed writers in England.

Literary collaborations seem to present to the public aspects of mystery which they do not deserve. They are rare. It is unusual for two persons of inter-supportable temperaments to come together and bear each other's society, day in day out, for the long space of time that it takes to write a book. Few books can be written in a very short time; collaboration slows down writing, if only for material reasons. *Romance* by Conrad and myself was more than five years in the writing. Whether the book itself was worth the labour, it is for the public rather than myself to say. But that the labour in itself was worth while for us I have no doubt at all. I, at least, learned the greater part of what I know of the technical side of writing during the process, and Conrad certainly wrote with greater ease after the book had been in progress some while.

The desirability of that particular collaboration has been a good deal questioned. Indeed, it has been freely stated in the press that association with myself was the ruin of Conrad. That may have been the case; the penultimate sentence of my last paragraph may be claimed as an admission of Conrad's deterioration under my influence. For it is quite possible to advance the theory against Conrad or any other man that because he writes more easily he writes worse. Mr. Havelock Ellis did, indeed, advance that view as to Conrad in a letter he wrote to me for publication in *The Transatlantic Review*—that Conrad's early books written with great difficulty were masterpieces and that later his work steadily deteriorated.

I do not share that view myself, for, for me, *Under Western Eyes* is a long way the greatest—as it is the latest—of all Conrad's great novels. It is almost the only great one in which I had no finger at all. In looking at the list of books by Conrad opposite the title page of *The Arrow of Gold*, I see the names of only four others published after the beginning of my acquaintance with Conrad, with which I had absolutely no, however subordinate, connection. They are *Victory*, *The Shadow Line*, and *The Arrow of Gold*. As to *Within the Tides*, I am not quite certain. For all Conrad's other books I either corrected the proofs at one or other stage, or discussed the plots or incidents, or wrote passages from Conrad's dictation—or actually wrote in passages. What I actually wrote into Conrad's books was by no means great in bulk and was usually done when he was too ill to write himself and had to catch up with serial publication. Mr. Keating has shown me twenty-five pages of my manuscript of *Nostromo* which he lately obtained from M. Jean Aubry, Conrad's official biographer, who states that they were given him by Conrad. Thus Conrad could not have been ashamed of the fact that I wrote passages into his work and, I may presume that he would not now resent my mention of the fact. But, indeed, the importance of the passages I did write was so negligible, and they themselves were so frequently emended out of sight that they could not make as much difference to the completion and glory of his prose as three drops of water poured into a butt of Malmsey.

These pages of *Nostromo* were written at a time when Conrad was very ill and the next installment of the book, which was being serialised in *T. P.'s Weekly*, had to be supplied. Similarly a number of short passages in *The End of the Tether* were written by me after the manuscript had been burned and whilst it was running as a serial in *Blackwood's*. A little of *The Secret Agent* was written by me, sentences here and there, mostly about the topography of western London—which Conrad did not know at all—and details about policemen and Anarchists. That the plot of this story was suggested by me Conrad acknowledges in his preface.

Apart from the three collaborations, the plots of all of which were mine, I suggested the subject for *Amy Foster*, the outline of which I wrote in my *Cinque Ports* of 1902; and I suggested several of the episodes in a story called, I think, *Gaspar Ruiz*, which Conrad was desperately writing as an avowed potboiler. *The Mirror of the Sea* and *A Personal Record* were mostly written by my hand from Conrad's dictation. Whilst he was dictating them, I would recall incidents to him—I mean incidents of his past life which he had told me but which did not come freely back to his mind because at the time he was mentally ill, in desperate need of money, and, above all, skeptical as to the merits of the reminiscential form which I had suggested to him. The fact is I could make Conrad write at periods when his despair and fatigue were such that in no other way would it have been possible to him. He would be lying on the sofa or pacing the room, railing at life and literature as practised in England, and I would get a writing pad and pencil and, whilst he was still raving, would interject: "Now, then, what was it you were saying about coming up the Channel and nearly running over a fishing boat that suddenly appeared under your bows?" and gradually there would come *Landfalls and Departures*. Or I would say: "What was the story you told of the spy coming with a sledgeful of British gold to your uncle's house in Poland in order to foment insurrection against Russia?" And equally gradually there would come the beginnings of *A Personal Record*. There are no episodes of my past life more vivid to me—you must remember that I had a great enthusiasm for my collaborator—than those dictations that mostly took place on a little terrace of my cottage at Aldington, high up in the air, with the great skies over the Romney Marsh below. And in those days I had a very remarkable memory, so that if Conrad became too tired to go on I could complete a paragraph or episode in his own words —though they might have been words of a week, a month, or several years before.

It has been alleged that I started *The English Review* in order to print a poem by Thomas Hardy that had been refused by every magazine in England. It would be more just to say that that was the suggestion of my partner Arthur Marwood. My own most urgent motive was to provide some money for Conrad by printing *A Personal Record* and other things which I extracted from him. In one of his prefaces you can read how I did extract these books by what he calls "gentle pressure"; in the facsimile of a letter to me which was reproduced in the English edition of my *Joseph Conrad, A Personal Reminiscence,* you can read how I sat up nearly all night with him gently pressing him to write a review of Anatole France's *Isle des Pingouins* for the first number. That letter was written as a contribution to *The Transatlantic Review.* The first draft of that letter is still in my possession. Conrad added to it for purposes of publication and it is here printed from the original letter:

Oswalds,
Bishopsbourne,
Kent,
Oct. 13th, 1923

MY DEAR FORD,

Forgive me for answering your interesting holograph letter on the machine. I don't like to delay any longer telling you how pleased I am to know you have got hold of such interesting work, in conditions which will permit you to concentrate your mind on it in peace and comfort. My warmest wishes for its success. I won't tell you that I will be "honoured" or "flattered" by having my name included amongst your contributors, but I will tell you that I consider it a very friendly thing on your part to wish to do so.

I don't think your memory renders me justice as to my attitude to the early E.R. (*English Review*). The early E.R. is the only one I ever cared for. The mere fact that it was the occasion of you putting on me that gentle but persistent pressure which extracted, from the depths of my then despondency, the stuff of *A Personal Record,* would be enough to make its memory dear. My only grievance against the early E.R. is that it didn't last long enough. If I say that I am curious to see what you will make of this venture, it isn't because I have the slightest doubts of your consistency. You have a perfect right to say that you are rather "unchangeable." Unlike the Serpent (which is Wise) you will die in your original skin. So I have no doubt that *The Transatlantic Review* will be truly Fordian—at all costs! But it will be interesting to see what men you will find and what you will get out of them in these changed times.

I won't say anything about myself, for it wouldn't be amusing and not even interesting. We are still sticking in this house till next year. A novel of sorts will appear at the end of this year. Another, half written, has been stewing in its own juice for months and months. I suppose I may take it that Bd. Arago is a permanent address where you can be found from now on.

Yours,
J. CONRAD.

How the "gentle" pressure came through to Conrad I don't know; he would have been justified enough in hating me, for I know how one hates the people who, when one is ill, stand at one's bedside with food and say: "Just another spoonful!" And I certainly felt that that was what I was doing. I would say, "Now ... about the *Tremolino*" and look away over the Marsh at the great shadows of clouds that crossed. . . . Conrad rushing feverishly up and down the terrace! . . . There appears to be evidence that, at one point of that process, hate me temporarily he did, for M. Aubry in his official biography, prints what purports to be a violent letter written to me by Conrad, saying practically that he will not go on being connected with *The English Review* after about six installments of *A Personal Record* were printed. But that letter was never received by me —M. Aubry did not ask me for or print any of the letters that Conrad wrote me—so it was only a sketch of a letter that Conrad would no doubt have liked to have sent. That was a part of the inner politics of the day. Marwood and I being unable to continue the financing of *The English Review,* it was sold to a company whose members were mostly Liberal in complexion and whose managing director was a Russian, I remaining the editor. Marwood being a strong Tory and Conrad a Pole with a violent hatred for all Russians, they decided between them that Conrad's contributions should cease. Marwood had by that time taken my place as general cook and bottle-washer in Conrad's literary establishment. He also was large, blond, outwardly placid, and deliberate—and admirably and touchingly he performed his functions to the day of his death. I myself would have gone on editing the *Review* had its proprietors been military dictators and its manager a Turk. I was interested in helping on young talent and have never paid any attention at all to politics.

I collaborated, then, with Conrad officially in three books: *Romance, The Inheritors,* and *The Nature of a Crime.* The preface to this last, as I have said, was the last completed literary work from the pen of Joseph Conrad—our friendship and common work continuing thus till the day of his death. We contemplated, indeed, and talked for years about another collaboration, which was to have been about the execution—or rather the escape—of Marshal Ney after Waterloo. The book was to have begun with frigate warfare in the Mediterranean, the chief character being with Napoleon on Elba in 1814-15 and going to Paris for the Hundred Days and so coming in contact with Ney. In June 1916 when I was going out to the Front, during a valedictory interview with Conrad, we cleared up a number of outstanding matters, he consenting to become my literary executor and asking me to write a memoir of him if I survived, arranging that the collaborations were to appear in both our collected works and so on. Incidentally, we settled about the Ney collaboration. As I was going to a place where collaborations are not literary, Conrad was to take over the book altogether. This was only fair, for Conrad had done a great deal more reading for the book than I had. His power of consuming memoirs always appeared to me fantastic—and although I had read a good deal, he must have read five times as much. So eventually Conrad wrote *Suspense* which, alas, remains a fragment. It was whilst I was in the service or afterwards incapacitated for literary work, that Conrad wrote the four books with which I had no connection at all.

Our methods of collaboration were in no way mysterious and must have been those of most other collaborators. That is to say, one of us would write a passage, or a draft of a book, the other going through it and making changes or re-writing. In the case of *Romance,* I wrote the whole book first—I wrote it indeed before I had met Conrad. *The Inheritors* is almost wholly mine, so far as the writing is concerned, except in the last twenty pages of the book. As for *The Nature of a Crime,* when it was republished, twenty years or so after it was written, neither Conrad nor I could remember anything about it and both at first denied that it existed. I had, however, much earlier, written about half a long short-story having the same subject. The story was one my grandfather used to tell about one of his wealthy Greek art patrons who, imagining himself to be ruined, wrote a letter to his mistress to the effect that he was going to commit suicide rather than be detected in a fraudulent bankruptcy and then found that bankruptcy could be avoided.

As I have elsewhere stated, the idea of the Ney book came to me in Philadelphia in 1906, when a Southern lady told me that in the New Orleans of her youth she had seen—or her mother had told her of—an old, mild gentleman who said he was Marshal Ney and possessed a remarkable presentation sword. It was the sword that most impressed me because, when Ney was arrested in 1815, it was a sword presented to him by Napoleon that drew attention to him. On returning to England, I told the story to Conrad who was at once enormously seized with it as a subject—and when a subject got hold of him, his determination to treat it was as overwhelming as any tornado. If you like, that may have been the reason of our collaborations: that I had a knack of getting hold of subjects that appealed to him.

To the lay reader it sounds like tremendous presumption to claim to have suggested subjects to Joseph Conrad; and the chief onus of the attacks that were made on me in 1925 lay in the fact that I had, in my reminiscences, stated that I had done so. The experienced writer will know how foolish is that view. For you must get subjects from somewhere, except in tales depending purely on invention, and those have seldom any literary merit. Most, for instance, of Henry James' subjects were heard of from one lady or another at the dinner table. Many of Conrad's came from the memoirs that he so continuously read; I myself, as I have said, got the subject of the Ney collaboration from a lady in Philadelphia. For that matter, as too I have said, I had the story of *The Nature of a Crime* from my grandfather, and that of *Romance* was suggested to me by Dr. Richard Garnett, who recommended me to look up the trial of Aaron Smith published in *All the Year Round* if I wanted a real romance about pirates; the details of the story of *The Secret Agent* I heard from one of my cousins, who had something to do with the actual events; the story of *Amy Foster* was told me by Meary Walker on Romney Marsh in 1894.

No, there is no particular glory attaching to the suggestion of a subject, although I should be grateful enough to anyone who would suggest a subject to me now. But a temperament is necessary, and I suppose it was because my temperament caused me to select certain types of subjects for conversation or treatment that Conrad took forcible hold of so many of them.

I have written so much about the origins of *Romance* in my book on Conrad that I will only repeat here that it was some time after hearing me tell the story of the book—which I then called "Seraphina"—that Conrad wrote to me and asked to be allowed to collaborate with me in writing it. He said that he had consulted his friends and that they had strongly recommended the experiment because he wrote so slowly and with such difficulty.

I may as well dispose, once and for all, of the legend that I had any part in teaching Conrad English, though, on the face of it, it may well look plausible enough since he was a foreigner who never till the end of his life spoke English other than as a foreigner. But when it came to writing, it was at once quite a different matter. As I said elsewhere a little time ago, the moment he got a pen in his hand and had no eye to publication, Conrad could write English with a speed, a volubility, and a banal correctness that used to amaze me. So you have his immense volume of letters. On the other hand, when, as it were, he was going before the public, a species of stagefright would almost completely paralyse him so that his constructions were frequently very un-English.

In his letters, that is to say, he just let himself go without precision of phrase as without *arrière pensée,* pouring out supplications, abuse of third parties, eternal and unvarying complaints, so that in the end the impression is left of a weak, rather whining personality. But no impression could be more false. Conrad was a man, a He-man if you like, who fought against enormous odds with undying—with almost unfaltering —courage. And his courage was all the more impressive in that by birth, race, and temperament he was an unshakable pessimist. Life for him was predestined to end tragically, or, if not, in banality; literature was foredoomed to failure. These were his *choses données,* his only certain truths. In face of that creed, his struggles were unceasing.

And it was astonishing what small things could call down to his underlying buoyancy. I remember once we had been struggling with *Romance* for hours and hours, and he had been in complete despair, and everything that I had suggested had called forth his bitterest gibes, and he was sick, and over ears in debt, and penniless. And we had come to a blank full-stop —one of those intervals when the soul *must* pause to breathe, and love itself have rest. And Mrs. Conrad came in and said that the mare had trotted from Postling Vents to Sandling in five minutes—say, twelve miles an hour! At once, there in the room was Conrad-Jack-ashore! The world was splendid; hope nodded from every rosebud that looked over the window-sill of the low room. We were going to get a car and go to Canterbury; the mare should have a brand new breeching strap. And in an incredibly short space of time—say, three hours—at least half a page of *Romance* got itself written.

That was how it went, day in day out, for years—the despair, the lamentations continuing for hours, and then the sudden desperate attack on the work—the attack that would become the fabulous engrossment. We would write for whole days, for half nights, for half the day, or all the night. We would jot down passages on scraps of paper or on the margins of books, handing them one to the other or exchanging them. We would roar with laughter over passages that would have struck no other soul as humorous; Conrad would howl with rage and I would almost sigh over others that no other soul perhaps would have found as bad as we considered them. We would recoil one from the other and go each to our own cottage —our cottages at that period never being further the one from the other than an old mare could take us in an afternoon. In those cottages we would prepare other drafts and so drive backwards and forwards with packages of manuscript under the dog-cart seats. We drove in the heat of summer, through the deluges of autumn, with the winter snows blinding our eyes—always, always with manuscripts. Heavens, don't my fingers still tingle with the feeling of undoing the stiff buckles, long past midnight, of a horse streaming with rain—and the rubbing down in the stable and the backing the cart into the coach-house. And with always at the back of the mind, the consideration of some unfinished passage, the puzzledom to avoid some too-used phrase that yet seemed hypnotically inevitable.

So it went on for years—seven, ten, eleven—I don't remember how many. At any rate, it was after *Romance* itself was finished that Conrad wrote that "Ford had become a habit," rather wondering at it because, he said, no one liked me.

My early job was to get Conrad's work over. I do not believe that any other person could have tackled it then, though later on Marwood was quite as indispensable—quite as much of a habit. Given that you acknowledge that Conrad's professional career was fortunate from the date of our association, the conjunction must have been materially fortunate for him whether or no his work deteriorated. That it was fortunate for me I am sure, for if I know anything of how to write, almost the whole of that knowledge was acquired then. It was acquired at the cost of an infinite mental patience, for the process of digging out words in the same room with Conrad was exhausting. On the other hand, the pleasure derived from his society was inexhaustible; his love, his passion for his art did not, I believe, exceed mine, but his power of expressing that passion was delicious, winning, sweet, incredible. When —but how rarely!—a passage went right or the final phrase of a long-tinkered episode suggested itself, his happiness was overwhelming, his whole being lit up, his face became serenely radiant, his shoulders squared, his monocle gleamed like rock crystal. It was extraordinary.

And his delight was just as great if the *trouvaille* had been mine as if it had been his own. Indeed, the high-water mark of our discoveries was reached with a phrase of mine—"Excellency, a few goats!"—which so impressed him that twenty years later he was still chuckling over it. It was that generosity

. that atoned for, say, his abusive letters written about myself to his friends. After all, you cannot—nobody could—live with another man practically as a room-mate for years without occasional periods of exasperation, and if you have the habit of volubly expressing yourself, in unstudied letters, your exasperations will work through into print.

In one such letter Conrad alludes to our struggles over *The Inheritors* and ends with a burst of mordant humour at my expense. The reader may seek out the letter for himself because I do not choose to quote abuse of myself by Conrad. But in it he describes how I sat at the desk writing and reading out what I wrote whilst behind my back he stormed and raved and declared that every word I produced was the imagination of a *crétin*. That was all right between ourselves because he was accustomed to indict every word that he himself wrote even more incisively. It was the passion—the agony—of the idealist who, seeking with every fibre of his brain to express perfection, seems to see the fine gold turn to clay beneath his fingers. However, in this particular letter, he must have thought that he had gone a little too far, for he asked Mr. Garnett to whom it was addressed to burn it. Mr. Garnett preferred to publish it. The reader will find it in the collection of Conrad's letters to him that Mr. Garnett lately edited. It substantiates —if that is really necessary—the statement I have made that *The Inheritors* is practically all my writing. Or if the still skeptical reader continues to doubt, let him glance at the facsimile of the inscription by Conrad on the fly-leaf of that volume. Conrad wrote it for Mr. George Keating who has been kind enough to afford me a sight of it.

But in spite of these rubs of the game—and what a game for rubs it was!—our friendship remained unbroken and only interrupted by the exigencies of time, space, and public events. It is in the end better if the public will believe that version— for nearly ideal literary friendships are rare, and the literary world is ennobled by them. It was that that Conrad meant when, looking up from the play of *King John* at which he had been glancing for a little while, he quoted to me, who was writing and had to turn my head over my shoulder to listen:

> *Oh, two such silver currents when they join*
> *Do glorify the banks that bound them in—*

and he added: *"C'est pas mal, ça; pour qualifier nous deux!"*

And by that he meant not that we were producers of great books but writers without envy, jealousy, or any of the petty feeling that writers not unusually cherish, the one towards the other. That gave him lifelong satisfaction, and one of his last literary acts was to testify to that—to the public as to myself in his preface to *The Nature of a Crime*. For a reason that I won't go into, I was not myself very anxious that my name should be attached to that volume, even if it meant that the volume did not appear. I accordingly wrote to Conrad and suggested that that course should be pursued. He, however, wrote to me on May 17, 1924—three months before his death— "I have looked at the proofs (of *The Nature of a Crime*) and made a few corrections which escaped you. I have also considered your proposal of my writing a preface and I forward you here the outcome of it with the hope that you will act in the spirit of the last paragraph." In the last paragraph he had inserted a plea—that *coram populo*—I would contradict his more or less humorous account of the methods of our joint labours. He continues: "It seemed to me that neither of us (alone) could write a preface with propriety. Yet from the point of view of the book's future ... I think each of us may contribute a few words of introduction over our separate signatures. The enclosed is my contribution. I hope it will meet with your approval (I mean as to its being suitable from the point of view of the public)....

"If you are too full of work or do not want the bother or from any other reason, you may delete the last paragraph and move my initials up accordingly.

"But I hope you will not. For your contribution of an introduction will not only be valuable *per se* but may influence the fortunes of the book in a considerable way. After all, this is the last piece of our joint work that is likely to appear and it seems to me becoming that we both should be heard on such an occasion."

For the sake of sentiment and to please myself I will here add the last sentence of the letter that, four days later, I had from him: "As to the novel" (a book of mine that I had sent him) "I think that, between us two, if I tell you that I consider it *tout à fait chic* you will understand perfectly how much that *phrase d'atelier* means to the initiated."

Five days later, I again sailed for New York from Cherbourg. When, late at night, the *France* touched at its English port, I was seized with an overwhelming conviction that I should never see Conrad again. I got up and desperately scrawled to him a last letter assuring him of my for ever unchanging affection and admiration for his almost miraculous gifts.

CHAPTER IV

RYE ROAD

THIRTY years ago the novel was still the newest, as it remains the Cinderella, of art forms. (That of the "Movies" had not yet appeared.) The practice of novel writing had existed for a bare two hundred and fifty years; the novelist was still regarded as a rogue and vagabond, and the novel as a "waste of time"—or worse. And the idea of the novel as a work of art, capable of possessing a form, even as sonnets or sonatas possess forms—that idea had only existed since 1850, and in the France of Flaubert alone, at that. Writers had certainly aimed at "progressions of effect" in short efforts since the days of Margaret of Navarre; and obviously what the typical English novelist had always aimed at—if he had aimed at any form at all—and what the typical English critic looked for—if ever he condescended to look at a novel—was a series of short stories with linked characters and possibly a culmination. Indeed, that conception of the novel has been forced upon the English novelist by the commercial exigencies of hundreds of years. The romances of Shakespeare, novels written for ranted recitation, and admirable in the technique of that form, were moulded by the necessity for concurrent action in varying places; the curtain had to be used. So you had the "strong situation," in order that the psychological stages of Othello should be firm in the hearer's mind whilst Desdemona was alone before the audience. The novels of Fielding, of Dick-

ens and of Thackeray were written for publication in Parts;
at the end of every part must come the "strong situation," to
keep the plot in the reader's head until the first of next month.
So with the eminent contemporaries of ours in the nineties of
the last century; if the writer was to make a living wage he
must aim at serialisation; for that once again you must have
a strong scene before you write "To be continued," or the
reader would not hanker for the next number of the magazine
you served. But you do not need to go to commercial fiction
to find the origin of the tendency; if the reader has ever lain
awake in a long school dormitory or a well-peopled children's
bedroom, listening to or telling long, long, tales that went on
from day to day or from week to week, he will have known,
or will have observed, the necessity of retaining the story in
the hearer's mind, and to introduce, just before each listener's
head sank on the pillow—the "strong situation." Indeed, Sche-
herazade knew that pressing need.

It was against the tyranny of this convention that Conrad
was revolting, when he sought so passionately for the "new
form." How often, in those distant days, lamenting the unlike-
lihood of our making even modest livings by our pens, have
we not sighingly acknowledged that serialisation was not for
us! For I think we both started out with at least this much
of a new form in our heads: we considered a novel to be a
rendering of an affair. We used to say, I will admit, that a
subject must be seized by the throat until the last drop of
dramatic possibility was squeezed out of it. I suppose we had
to concede that much to the cult of the strong situation. Nevertheless, a novel was the rendering of an affair: of one embroil-
ment, one set of embarrassments, one human coil, one
psychological progression. From this the novel got its unity.
No doubt it might have its cæsura—or even several; but these
must be brought about by temperamental pauses, markings of
time when the treatment called for them. But the whole novel
was to be an exhaustion of aspects, was to proceed to one cul-

mination, to reveal once and for all, in the last sentence—or the penultimate—in the last phrase, or the one before it, the psychological significance of the whole. (Of course, you might have what is called in music the coda.) But it is perfectly obvious that such a treatment of an affair could not cut itself up into strong situations at the end of every four or every seven thousand words. *That* market at least was closed to us.

I have suggested that we were more alone in our search for the new form than, very likely, we actually were. Mr. Bennett, at least at that date, was engaged in acquiring the immense knowledge of French tricks and devices that his work afterwards displayed. And there was always Mr. George Moore.

In the meantime, magisterially and at leisure, in Rye, Henry James was performing the miracles after whose secrets we were merely groping. I don't know why—but we rather ignored that fact. For, in the end, Conrad and I found salvation not in any machined form, but in the sheer attempt to reproduce life as it presents itself to the intelligent observer. I daresay, if we could only perceive it, life has a pattern. I don't mean that of birth, apogee, and death, but a woven symbolism of its own. "The Pattern in the Carpet," Henry James called it—and that he saw something of the sort was no doubt the secret of his magic. But, though I walked with and listened to the Master day after day, I remember only one occasion on which he made a remark that was a revelation of his own aims and methods. That I will reserve until it falls in place in the pattern of my own immediate carpet. For the rest, our intercourse resolved itself into my listening silently and wondering unceasingly at his observation of the littlest things of life.

"Are you acquainted," he would begin, as we strolled under the gateway down Winchelsea Hill towards Rye ... Ellen Terry would wave a gracious hand from her garden above the old Tower, the leash of Maximilian would require several readjustments, and the dog himself a great many *sotto voce* admonitions as to his expensive habit of chasing sheep into dykes. "Are you acquainted," the Master would begin again, "with the terrible words. ..."

A higgler, driving a cart burdened with crates of live poultry, would pass us. The Master would drive the point of his cane into the roadway. "Now *that* man!" he would exclaim. And he would break off to say what hideous, what appalling, what bewildering, what engrossing affairs were going on all round us in the little white cottages and farms that we could see, dotting Playden Hill and the Marsh to the verge of the great horizon. "Terrible things!" he would say. "Appalling! ... Now that man who just passed us. ..." And then he would dig his stick into the road again and hurry forward, like the White Queen escaping from disaster, dropping over his shoulder the words: "But that probably would not interest you. ..."

I don't know what he thought *would* interest me!

So he would finish his sentence before the door above the high steps of Lamb House:

"Are you acquainted with the terrible, the devastating words, if I may call them so, the fiat of Doom: 'I don't know if you know, sir'? As when the housemaid comes into your bedroom in the morning and says: 'I don't know if you know, sir, that the bath has fallen through the kitchen ceiling.'"

It was held in Rye that he practised black magic behind the high walls of Lamb House. ...

I think I will, after reflection, lay claim to a very considerable degree of intimacy with Henry James. It was a winter, and a wholly nonliterary intimacy. That is to say, during the summers we saw little of each other. He had his friends, and I mine. He was too often expecting "my friend Lady Maude," or some orthodox critic to tea, and I, modern poets whom he could not abide. Occasionally, even during the summer, he would send from Rye to Winchelsea, a distance of two miles, telegrams such as the following which I transcribe:—

"To Ford Madox Hueffer, Esq.,
"The Bungalow, Winchelsea, near Rye, Sussex.
"May I bring four American ladies, of whom one a priest, to tea today?

"Yours sincerely, Henry James."

And he would come.

But in the winters, when London visitors were scarce, he would come to tea every other day with almost exact regularity, and I would walk back with him to Rye. On the alternate days I would have tea with him and he would walk back to Winchelsea, in all weathers, across the windswept marshes. That was his daily, four miles, constitutional.

But it was, as I have said, an almost purely non-literary intimacy. I could, I think, put down on one page all that he ever said to me of books—and, although I used, out of respect, to send him an occasional book of my own on publication, and he an occasional book of his to me, he never said a word to me about my writings, and I do not remember ever having done more than thank him in letters for his volume of the moment. I remember his saying of *Romance* that it was an immense English plum cake which he kept at his bedside for a fortnight and of which he ate a nightly slice.

He would, if he never talked of books, frequently talk of the personalities of their writers—not infrequently in terms of shuddering at their social excess, much as he shuddered at contact with Crane. He expressed intense dislike for Flaubert who "opened his own door in his dressing-gown" and he related, not infrequently, unrepeatable stories of the menages of Maupassant—but he much preferred Maupassant to "poor dear old Flaubert." Of Turgenev's appearance, personality and habits, he would talk with great tenderness of expression; he called him nearly always "the beautiful Russian genius," and would tell stories of Turgenev's charming attentions to his peasant mistresses. He liked, in fact, persons who were suave when you met them—and I daresay that his preference of that sort coloured his literary tastes. He preferred Maupassant to Flaubert because Maupassant was *homme du monde*—or at any rate had *femmes du monde* for his mistresses; and he preferred Turgenev to either because Turgenev was a quiet aristocrat and an invalid of the German bathing towns to the finger tips. And he liked—he used to say so—people who treated him with proper respect.

Flaubert he hated with a lasting, deep rancour. Flaubert had once abused him unmercifully—over a point in the style of Prosper Mérimée, of all people in the world. You may read about it in the *Correspondence* of Flaubert, and James himself referred to the occasion several times. It seemed to make it all the worse that, just before the outbreak, Flaubert should have opened the front door of his flat to Turgenev and James, in his dressing-gown.

Myself, I suppose he must have liked, because I treated him with deep respect, had a low voice—appeared, in short, a *jeune homme modeste*. Occasionally he would burst out at me with furious irritation, as if I had been a stupid nephew. This would be particularly the case if I ventured to have any opinions about the United States, which, at that date, I had visited much more lately than he had. I remember one occasion very vividly—the place, beside one of the patches of thorn on the Rye road, and his aspect, the brown face with the dark eyes rolling in the whites, the compact, strong figure, the stick raised so as to be dug violently into the road. He had been talking two days before of the provincialism of Washington in the sixties. He said that when one descended the steps of the Capitol in those days *on trébuchait sur des vaches*—one stumbled over cows, as if on a village green. Two days later, I don't know why—I happened to return to the subject of the provincialism of Washington of the sixties. He stopped as if I had hit him and, with the coldly infuriated tone of a country squire whose patriotism had been outraged, exclaimed:

"Don't talk such *damnable* nonsense!" He really shouted these words with a male fury. And when, slightly outraged myself, I returned to the charge with his own *on trébuchait sur des vaches*, he exclaimed: "I should not have thought you would have wanted to display such ignorance," and hurried off along the road.

I do not suppose that this was as unreasonable a manifestation of patriotism as it appears. No doubt he imagined me incapable of distinguishing between material and cultural poverties and I am fairly sure that, at the bottom of his mind lay the idea that in Washington of the sixties there had been some singularly good cosmopolitan and diplomatic conversation and society, whatever the cows might have done outside the Capitol. Indeed I know that towards the end of his life, he came to think that the society of early, self-conscious New England, with its circumscribed horizon and want of exterior decoration or furnishings, was a spiritually finer thing than the mannered Europeanism that had so taken him to its bosom. As these years went on, more and more, with a sort of trepidation, he hovered round the idea of a return to the American scene. When I first knew him you could have imagined no oak more firmly planted in European soil. But, little by little, when he talked about America there would come into his tones a slight tremulousness that grew with the months. I remember once he went to see some friends—Mrs. and Miss Lafarge, I think—off to New York from Tilbury Dock. He came back singularly excited, bringing out a great many unusually uncompleted sentences. He had gone over the liner: "And once aboard the lugger ... And if ... Say a toothbrush ... And circular notes ... And something for the night ..." All this with a sort of diffident shamefacedness.

I fancy that his mannerisms, his involution, whether in speech or in writing, were due to a settled conviction that, neither in his public nor in his acquaintance, would he ever find any one who would not need talking down to. The desire of the artist, of the creative writer, is that his words and his "scenes" shall suggest—of course with precision—far more than they actually express or project. But, having found that his

limpidities, from *Daisy Miller* to *The Real Thing,* not only
suggested less than he desired, but carried suggestions entirely
unmeant, he gave up the attempt at impressionism of that
type—as if his audiences had tired him out. So he talked down
to us, explaining and explaining, the ramifications of his mind.
He was aiming at explicitness, never at obscurities—as if he
were talking to children.

At any rate, then, he had none of that provincialism of
the literary mind which must for ever be dragging in allusions
to some book or local custom. If he found it necessary to al-
lude to one or the other, he explained them and their prove-
nance. In that you saw that he had learned in the same school
as Conrad and Stephen Crane. And indeed he had.

It has always seemed to me inscrutable that he should
have been so frequently damned for his depicting only one
phase of life; as if it were his fault that he was not also Conrad, to write of the sea, or Crane, to project the life of the
New York slums. The Old Man knew consummately one form
of life; to that he restricted himself. I have heard him talk
with extreme exactness and insight of the life of the poor—
at any rate of the agricultural poor, for I do not remember
ever to have heard him discuss industrialism. But he knew
that he did not know enough to treat of farm-labourers in his
writing. So that, mostly, when he discoursed of these matters
he put his observations in the form of question: "Didn't I agree
to this?" "Hadn't I found that?"

But indeed, although I have lived amongst agricultural
labourers a good deal at one time or another, I would cheerfully acknowledge that his knowledge—at any rate of their
psychologies—had a great deal more insight than my own. He
had such an extraordinary gift for observing minutiæ—and a
gift still more extraordinary for making people talk. I have
heard the secretary of a golf club, a dour, silent man who never
addressed five words to myself though I was one of his members, talk for twenty minutes to the Master about a new bunker
that he was thinking of making at the fourteenth hole. And

James had never touched a niblick in his life. It was the same with market-women, tram-conductors, ship-builders' labourers, auctioneers. I have stood by and heard them talk to him for hours. Indeed, I am fairly certain that he once had a murder confessed to him. But he needed to stand on extraordinarily firm ground before he would think that he knew a world. And what he knew he rendered, along with its amenities, its gentle-folkishness, its pettinesses, its hypocrisies, its make-believes. He gives you an immense—and an increasingly tragic—picture of a leisured society that is fairly unavailing, materialist, emasculated—and doomed. No one was more aware of all that than he.

Stevie used to rail at English literature, as being one immense petty, parlour game. Our books he used to say were written by men who never wanted to go out of drawing-rooms for people who wanted to live at perpetual tea parties. Even our adventure stories, colonial fictions and tales of the boundless prairie were conducted in that spirit. The criticism was just enough. It was possible that James never wanted to live outside tea parties—but the tea parties that he wanted were debating circles of a splendid aloofness, of an immense human sympathy, and of a beauty that you do not find in Putney—or in Passy!

It was his tragedy that no such five-o'clock ever sounded for him on the timepiece of this world. And that is no doubt the real tragedy of all of us—of all societies—that we never find in our Spanish Castle our ideal friends living in an assured and permanent Republic. Crane's utopia, but not his literary method, was different. He gave you the pattern in—and the reverse of—the carpet in physical life, in wars, in slums, in western saloons, in a world where the "gun" was the final argument. The life that Conrad gives you is somewhere halfway between the two; it is dominated—but less dominated—by the revolver than that of Stephen Crane, and dominated, but less dominated, by the moral scruple than that of James. But the approach to life is the same with all these three; they show you that disillusionment is to be found alike at the tea-table, in the slum and on the tented field. That is of great service to our Republic.

It occurs to me that I have given a picture of Henry James in which small personal unkindliness may appear to sound too dominant a note. That is the misfortune of wishing to point a particular moral. I will not say that lovableness was the predominating feature of the Old Man; he was too intent on his own particular aims to be lavishly sentimental over surrounding humanity. And his was not a character painted in the flat, in water-colour, like the caricatures of Rowlandson. For some protective reason or other, just as Shelley used to call himself the atheist, he loved to appear in the character of a sort of Mr. Pickwick, with the rather superficial benevolences and the mannerisms of which he was perfectly aware. But below that protective mask was undoubtedly a plane of nervous cruelty. I have heard him be—to simple and quite unpretentious people—more diabolically blighting than it was quite decent for a man to be, for he was always an artist in expression. And it needed a certain fortitude when, the studied benevolence and the chuckling, savouring, enjoyment of words, disappearing suddenly from his personality, his dark eyes rolled in their whites and he spoke very brutal and direct English. He chose in fact to appear as Henrietta Maria, but he could be atrocious to those who behaved as if they took him at that valuation.

And there was yet a third depth—a depth of religious, of mystical, benevolence, such as you find just now and again in the stories that he "wanted" to write—in *The Great Good Places*. . . . His practical benevolences were innumerable, astonishing—and indefatigable. To do a kindness when a sick cat or dog of the human race *had* "got through" to his mind as needing assistance, he would exhibit all the extraordinary ingenuities that are displayed in his most involved sentences.

I have said that my relation with James was in no sense literary—and I never knew what it *was*. I am perfectly sure that I never in my life addressed to the Master one word of praise or of flattery and, as far as I know, he called me *le jeune homme modeste* and left it at that. He did indeed confess to having drawn my externals in Morton Densher of *The Wings of the Dove*—the longish, leanish, looseish, rather vague Englishman who, never seeming to have anything to do with his days, occupied in journalism his night hours.

I daresay he took me to be a journalist of a gentle disposition, too languid to interrupt him. Once, after I had sent him one of my volumes of poems, he just mentioned the name of the book, raised both his hands over his head, let them slowly down again, made an extraordinary, quick grimace, and shook with an immense internal joke. . . . Shortly afterwards he began to poke fun at Swinburne.

In revenge, constantly and with every appearance of according weight to my opinions, though he seldom waited for an answer, he would consult me about practical matters—investments now and then, agreements once or twice—and, finally, unceasingly as to his fantastic domestic arrangements. He had at one stage portentous but increasingly unsatisfactory servants of whom, in his kindness of heart, he would not get rid until their conduct became the talk of the Antient Town of Rye.

So, one day he came over to Winchelsea to ask me if I thought a Lady Help would be a desirable feature in an eminent bachelor's establishment. . . . Going, as we seemed eternally in those days to be doing, down Winchelsea Hill under the Strand Gate, he said:

"H . . . you seem worried!" I said that I was worried. I don't know how he knew. But he knew everything.

Ellen Terry waved her gracious hand from the old garden above the tower; the collar of Maximilian the dachshund called for adjustment. He began another interminable, refining, sentence—about housemaids and their locutions. It lasted us to the bridge at the western foot of Rye.

In Rye High Street he exclaimed—he was extraordinarily flustered:

"I perceive a compatriot. Let us go into this shop!" And he bolted into a fruiterer's. He came out holding an orange and, eventually, throwing it into the air in an ecstasy of nervousness and stuttering like a schoolboy:

"If it's money, H..." he brought out. *"Mon sac n'est pas grand.... Mais puisez dans mon sac!"*

I explained that it was not about money that I was worried, but about the "form" of a book I was writing. His mute agony was a painful thing to see. He became much more appalled, but much less nervous. At last he made the great sacrifice:

"Well, then," he said, "I'm supposed to be.... Um, um.... There's Mary.... Mrs. Ward.... does me the honour.... I'm supposed to know.... In short, why not let me look at the manuscript!"

I had the decency not to take up his time with it.... *Les beaux jours quand on était bien modeste!* And how much I regret that I did not.

The last time I saw him was, accidentally, in August of 1915—on the fourteenth of that month, in St. James Park. He said:

"Tu vas te battre pour le sol sacré de Mme. de Staël!"

I suppose it was characteristic that he should say "de Mme. de Staël"—and not of Stendhal, or even of George Sand: He added—and how sincerely and with what passion —putting one hand on his chest and just bowing, that he loved and had loved France as he had never loved a woman!

I have said that I remember only one occasion on which Henry James spoke of his own work. That was like this: He had published *The Sacred Fount,* and was walking along beside the little shipyard at the foot of Rye Hill. Suddenly he said:

"You understand... I *wanted* to write *The Great Good Place* and *The Altar of the Dead....* There are things one

wants to write all one's life, but one's artist's conscience prevents one ... And then ... perhaps one allows oneself... "

I don't know what he meant ... Or I do! For there *are*
things one wants to write all one's life—only one's artist's conscience prevents one. That is the first—or the final, bitter—
lesson that the artist has to learn: that he is not a man to
be swayed by the hopes, fears, consummations or despairs of
a man. He is a sensitised instrument, recording to the measure
of the light vouchsafed him what is—what *may* be—the truth.
I fancy that that is why the idea of applying any theory of
art to the process of writing is so disliked by the typical English man of letters. For I assure you it was hated—that idea;
it was hunted; it was cried down—as if, in advocating the
research for form in a novel or the just word in a phrase, you
were not only advocating an unnatural vice or practising an
hypocrisy, but as if you were likely to cause certain pecuniary
loss to any one who followed, or even so much as listened to,
that *hæræsia damnosa!* How often have I not read sentences
like these which come back to me from a review in *The
Daily Telegraph* of those days.

Thank Heavens, we have outgrown the stage when English novelists bother their heads about the phraseology and
the shape of their fiction. Mr.—— writes a straightforward,
rattling tale in straightforward language....

The novelist—I forget his name—had, in fact, "selected
an excellent subject and treated it in a very spirited manner." (That was Henry James' sardonic politeness; he addressed it to novelists who sent him books he did not care
for.) The work (I now remember the book) may have caused
the author some intellectual struggles. The reading called for
none. I want to talk, however, of the "phraseology."

This author, then (*Please:* he was a modest, unaffected
English gentleman—I never in my life grudged him anything
that his simple, honest novels brought him in—the desirable
country place, the charming wife, the sons at Harrow. Nothing
have I ever grudged him!)—this author, then, had been edu-

cated at Harrow and Oxford. In consequence his "style" for pedestrian passages of narrative was that of the daily organ with the better type of social circulation. For descriptive passages he used the phraseology of Shakespeare, as it is found in the pages of Charles Lamb. He was fond of innocent quotations; when describing starlight he would talk of patines of bright gold. For his emotional passages, strong situations, or tragic moments—these, of course, were very rare in his work :— he and his characters had recourse to the "phraseology" and the cadences of the Authorised Version or the Book of Common Prayer. So that if the hero went anywhere he hailed a hansom or repaired to his tailor; but, if a ship took fire at sea, the conflagration illumined the heavens, and the heroine said, "Intreat me not to leave thee or to leave from following after thee...." A kindly and simple soul was here revealed.

Between that, then, and the "interjected finger" of Stevenson that "delayed the action of the timepiece" (and, for the matter of that, the stretched forefinger of Old Time that, I suppose, must go on sparkling for ever), we—Conrad and I— set out to search for a formula for *le mot juste*. Let me now particularise with great care, for, if I do not get this clear, all is indeed lost. This was how the world presented itself to our eyes: On the one hand, we had the respectable journal, critic and author whose desire was to make a not difficult living. On the other side of the fence were those literary alchemists who aim at attaining immortality by means of jewels five words long. The respectable journal could not wish to be forced to use any more actual verbiage than the *cliché phrase,* the phrase that has been mumbled so over and over by tired jaws that you can write it half asleep and "peruse" it without disturbance during the "degustation" of your "post-prandial port." Speakers according to this dialect were always cordially received; they did not anticipate a large exodus of Jews to Palestine; they opposed one thing or another "on the grounds that the proposals were novel and of a far-reaching character." And their hansoms always had to be hailed. The critics and supporters of these Respectabilia did not object to the fabricators of the jewels five words long; because when such a jewel had been a jewel for long enough, it could be imported into diurnal columns and be hallowed as a *cliché*. But they *did* object— and very wildly—to *le mot juste*. It was something foreign; it was indescribably troublesome. You had, they said, the "sound English" in which the daily, weekly, monthly, and quarterly periodicals are still written. You had also Fine Writing—to be used occasionally. That meant fourteen words, or forty, or half a page, of tired prose and then a shot at a five-word jewel. That was easy. But—so it seemed to them—*le mot juste* meant "every word a sparkler." That was a conception that appalled our friends. It subverted the ca'canny ideal; it was contrary to the rules of the Best of Trade Unions; it was a product of snuffy, foreign, affected or sexually perverted minds. Alas! for that miserable literary botcher who *péchait par pur snobisme*.

The trouble, however, with Conrad and myself was this: we could not get our own prose keyed down enough. We wanted to write, I suppose, as only Mr. W. H. Hudson writes —as simply as the grass grows. We desired to achieve a style —the *habit* of a style—so simple that you would notice it no more than you notice the unostentatious covering of the South Downs. The turf has to be there, or the earth would not be green.

Our most constant preoccupation, then, was to avoid words that stuck out of sentences either by their brilliant unusualness or their "amazing aptness." Either sort of word arrests the attention of a reader, and thus "hangs up" both the meaning and the cadence of a phrase. We wanted the reader to forget the writer—to forget that he was reading. We wished him to be hypnotised into thinking that he was living what he read—or, at least, into the conviction that he was listening to a simple and in no way brilliant narrator who was telling —not writing—a true story. Mind you, that was not easy; it was perhaps easier for me than for Conrad; or perhaps it would be more just to say that I desired it more than Conrad did. For, by sheer reaction of inheritance, I had even then an absolute hatred for the "toli-loll" Great Figure, the Quarterly Reviewer, the Bibliographer, and the ceaselessly mouthing Great Poet, who had overshadowed my childhood. Such disadvantages Conrad had not known, so that he had less of my hatred for "fine writing"; but his difficulties were greater. He was conquering—conquering, truly—a foreign language. And that language was particularly unsuited to our joint purpose, in that its more polite forms, through centuries of literary usage, have become absolutely unsuited to direct statement. You cannot make a direct statement in literary English. And Conrad came to it by way of Miss Braddon and the English Bible....

In the end, of course, he achieved both a form and a habit of language; he invented the figure of Marlowe. To Henry James, whose eye for other people's work was, strangely, too literary, Marlowe was always a fabulous Master Mariner. James refused to believe in him any more than he would believe in any other mechanical device. It was useless to argue with him; he used to groan over the matter, and, if I persisted at all, would end by saying that Conrad—or Marlowe, that Old Man of the Sea, that incredible but enduring vampire—was ruining my prospects.

He was wrong. Marlowe is a natural, simple and not at all unusual peasant type. He is wise as to human vicissitudes, as the simple or the merely poor are so frequently wise; but he is not over-read in the booklore that is so inevitably destructive of wisdom of that type. If I went up the hill from where I used to sit, I found an old shepherd. He was just as wise as Marlowe. And gradually, from this old man I learned the history of a fabulous farmer, Mr. Cummings. I knew already that in 1892 Mr. Cummings married his third wife. Till 1870 he still bred the old, horned, Wiltshire sheep that have now disappeared. About 1880 he ate five-pound notes between thin bread and butter—to annoy the Income Tax

authorities. In 1879 he married the first Mrs. Cummings;
she was still living when he married number two and number
three. Apparently all three ladies lived together in the great
old farm till 1900. He was a little, terrible, swearing man,
with a pimply face and no teeth. He was the first man to
use a steam-plough in those parts, and his eldest son went to
America because he didn't hold with it. That would be about
1894. In 1869 Annie Meggott drowned herself in the Arun;
Mr. Cummings never got over that. It was why he was like
what he was. For, in 1902, on his deathbed, he sent for the
old shepherd and said: "That Annie Meggott she was terrible
pernickety. But upstanding and with red cheeks." He had lost
the use of one eye by then.

You perceive that this is how Marlowe gets hold of and
tells the stories of exceptional men. And it is in that way that
life really presents itself to us; not as a rattling narrative
beginning at a hero's birth and progressing to his not very
carefully machined yet predestined glory—but dallying backwards and forwards, now in 1890, now in 1869; in 1902 and
then again in 1869—as forgotten episodes came up in the
minds of simple narrators. And, if you put your affair into
the mouth of such a narrator your phraseology will be the real
thing in *mots justes* for just so long as they remain within his
probable vocabulary. There will be no jewels five words long,
nor, for that matter, will the narrator ever say that Mr. Cummings hailed a hansom.

PART FOUR

THE BL—Y WORLD

CHAPTER I

COMPANIES AND KINGS

T HERE is a story which I am never tired—and which I hope I shall never tire, impenitently—of repeating. It belongs of right to Mr. Christopher Morley in one of whose books I read it. A Cockney in Canada was asked by a recruiting sergeant where he came from. He replied: "London." Said the sergeant: "London what? London, Ontario? London, N. Y.? London, Mass.?" "London the bl—y world!" the recruit replied with ineffable disgust. That is how it feels to the born Londoner.

I don't believe I am immensely delighted at having been born in England. But I know that I should feel as disgusted as the recruit if, after accusing me of being English, you should suggest that I was born anywhere but within sound of Bow Bells. To be born there is almost like being born in the United States. At the beginning of the century it would have taken you two hundred and forty-seven years walking at four miles an hour to cover all the streets of London on foot. What it would take now, goodness knows . . . A thousand very likely, I daresay it would take no longer to traverse all the mainroads of the United States. In any case it is good business to be born in London. You acquire very soon the knowledge that you are merely an atom amongst vastnesses and shouldn't take yourself very seriously. That is the first lesson the artist has to learn.

Romance was published in 1903, and shortly afterwards

Conrad and I determined to "shew ourselves"—that was Conrad's phrase—in London. I never understood Conrad's desire to shew himself with me. It certainly existed. When we had finally decided on collaborating on *Romance*, he insisted on driving the seven miles that separated the Pent from Spade House in order to break the news to Mr. H. G. Wells. I suppose he regarded Mr. Wells as the doyen of the younger school of writers. Certainly Mr. Wells had written of *Almayer's Folly* with extraordinary generosity. Anyhow, to my discomfort we drove in state in a hired fly, down, down, down to the seashore. When I come to think of it, it was not to Spade House that we drove but to a hired villa. The Wellses were living in it whilst Spade House was building. The landscape from the terrace of that villa—the shingle, the swains and maidens in bathing garb, the break-water, the as if tamed Channel—was exactly that of *The Sea Lady*. That romance for which Conrad had the most ardent and unrestrained admiration must have been the last novel of Mr. Wells' to be free of sociological speculation. Very shortly afterwards he told me that it was his intention to galvanise the Fabian Society into new life. I begged him not to. I had an admiration at least as ardent and unrestrained as that of Conrad's for Mr. Wells' work of that period. And I have always considered—and alas, observed— that the work of imaginative writers markedly deteriorates as soon as they occupy themselves with politics.

Mr. Wells got back at me by turning up at my cottage at Aldington and advising me not to collaborate with Conrad. He said that I should probably ruin Conrad's "delicate Oriental style." And, referring to the virulent controversy that was then raging between Henley and Mrs. Stevenson, he said that I should probably regret the step all my life. I can still see and hear him as he mounted his bicycle by the rear step.

I should like to add a pleasant detail with regard to that literary scrap. In the number of the *Pall Mall Magazine* which printed Henley's most outrageous attack on the Shorter Catechist, there appeared a collection of obviously fictitious epitaphs. And, as clearly as I remember Mr. Wells' departure, I remember the print of the magazine and the passion-flowers that trailed over the stoop of General Prescott's frame-cottage at Winchelsea where I read them and my delight at these anonymous fragments. One of them began:

> Here lies a most beautiful lady,
> Light of heart and step was she.
> I think she was the most beautiful lady
> That ever was in the West Countree....

And after all these years I still remember those verses and feel the same delight of discovery in them. They must have been the first that Walter de la Mare published.

Conrad's last request to me to stand side by side with him before the public I have already printed in this book.... I don't suppose he desired to exhibit me tied to his chariot wheels, though I should not have minded. But it occurs to me at this moment that his desire may have been solely for my good. The reader will remember that in a letter I have already quoted Conrad says: "Ford has become a daily habit with me," and adds that he is astonished because nobody liked me. No doubt he wished, in exhibiting me to his friends, to shew that I was not as black as I was painted. I remember his saying to me about that time: "Ford, your ruin will be that you cannot suffer fools gladly." I daresay it has been.

The house that I took in London presented an appearance of such immensity than when Henry James called his eyes rolled nearly out of his head and he exclaimed: "When you do go in for largenesses you *do* go in for largenesses!" He was accustomed to finding me in General Prescott's Winchelsea cottage. That did not contain at the time any one room in which you could swing a cat—whether the cat were the naval instrument of punishment or one of Dr. Garnett's pusses that you held by the tail. I had at that time lent the Pent with most of my furniture—which had descended to me from my grandfather and Christina Rossetti—to Conrad. He used to imagine pleasure at writing at a desk on which she had composed *Goblin Market*. But as a matter of fact that masterpiece—which contains the first rhymed Free Verse that was ever written in English—was actually composed on the corner of her washing-stand. She used to be banished to her bedroom, the other apartments of her father's house being needed for Mr. Ruskin and the pre-Raphaelites. They had to have space in which to shout the arguments for primitive and virtuous arts.

In revenge I had a Chippendale desk at Winchelsea and at that Conrad firmly refused to write. It had been given to my father as a wedding present by Thomas Carlyle. Conrad used to pretend that if he wrote at a desk on which *The French Revolution* had been composed it would ruin his style. So I had to hire across the road a two-room cottage in which he could write. He need not really have worried. I found in a letter of Mrs. Carlyle's a passage in which she complains of the trouble it gave her to go out and buy that desk as a wedding present for my father, so Carlyle could never have written on it. It came from a second-hand dealer's in the King's Road, Chelsea. It cost six pounds—thirty dollars.

It was in the cottage across the road that Conrad re-wrote the latter half of *The End of the Tether*. I have elsewhere related how that happened. A glass kerosene lamp had burst. It had belonged to my grandfather and was no doubt in a mind to revenge itself on the arts after a too-prolonged period of service. So at least Conrad used to say. It was in any case intended for colza oil which is a vegetable and non-inflammable liquid. So it burst and the flames destroyed Conrad's manuscript. He came over bag and baggage, horse and groom at once to Winchelsea, driving his old mare, Nancy of the long ears, in his old chaise. He brought such leaves of the manuscript as were decipherable.

We worked at the story day and night, Conrad writing in the cottage. In the house I wrote passages which he sometimes accepted and sometimes didn't. Mrs. Conrad typed—or perhaps I did. His groom—his name was Walter—a fresh-coloured chawbacon of a lad, relieved my groom who was a pasty-faced scoundrel called Ernest—in sitting up all night booted and spurred. The mare remained always saddled. The rest of my household made soup for the exhausted writers.

The occasion was thus tremendous because *The End of the Tether* was running in *Blackwood's*, then famous magazine, and the sun had better stop than that *Maga* should appear with an installment of its serial missing. So that cavalry was kept mobilised at night. At whatever hour the story was finished it must be galloped with to Ashford Junction to catch a mail train to Edinburgh. *Blackwood's* was published there.

The move to London was for me the beginning of a series of disasters. That was perhaps because the year was 1903. Those digits added up to thirteen. No one should have done anything in that year. Or it was perhaps because the house I then took was accursed. It was a monstrous sepulchre—and not even whitened. It was grey with the greyness of withered bones. It was triangular in ground plan; the face formed the nose of a blunted sedan, the body tapered to a wedge in which there was a staircase like the corkscrew staircases of the Middle Ages. The façade was thus monstrous, the tail ignoble. It was seven stories in height and in those days elevators in private houses were unknown. It was what housemaids call: "A murderer."

The happenings in that house come back to me as gruesome and bizarre. I daresay they were mere episodes in the chain of disasters, suicides, bankruptcies and despairs that visited its successive tenants and owners. My first party was distinguished by Conrad's attack on the unfortunate Mr. Charles Lewis Hind. This violent encounter took place in a circle of half-gay, half-morose celebrities. Mr. James had brought Mrs. Humphry Ward; Mrs. Clifford, who could be as awful as Mrs. Ward, had brought some mild and decorous young American—I should think it was Mr. Owen Wister. Mr. Watts-Dunton had brought a message from Swinburne, blessing me because he had known me as a baby. This Mr. Watts-

Dunton repeated *à tort et à travers* at the oddest and most inconvenient moments. He was deaf and accustomed to speaking to Swinburne who was deafer. I found myself again and again distracted by his rather snuffling, elevated voice exclaiming:

"Swinburne said in excusing himself for not attending this party of our gifted young host..."

He was a little dark man with an immense waterfall of grey moustache. Finally he settled himself—I think on the always patient Mr. Galsworthy—and repeated over and over again the message with which he was charged. Then I was aware that Conrad had hold of Lewis Hind's tie and was dragging him towards the door that gave onto the corkscrew staircase. If he had thrown Hind down it, the poor man would have been killed. I managed to separate them but I haven't forgotten and don't suppose I ever shall forget the look of polite incredulity of the more august guests. Mrs. Humphry Ward looked like a disgusted sheep. Mrs. Clifford, who loved the society of reviewers, was openly distressed at the disappearance of Mr. Hind. Mr. Hind was the editor of the *Academy*. The *Academy* was a rather livelier *Athenaeum*. A great lady of the Court of His Majesty put her lorgnettes up to her proud nose and weary eyes and exclaimed to me afterwards:

"Haw! Very interesting. But awkward for you. I suppose all literary parties are like that."

She added:

"I wonder you give 'em. I shouldn't. I once gave one but it did not work. Yet one tries to encourage...ah...these things!"

The Court in those days had to be interested in literature because Edward VII wanted to be told about books. I know this because I had at that date a secretary who was very highly connected. Her name was Smith and she was the daughter of a very famous soldier. She was one day sitting with the beautiful Lady Londonderry who was her cousin. Lady Londonderry was dying of a painful disease, but lay on a sofa. The

King came in. Miss Smith was the shyest human being I have
ever known. She desired to sink into the ground and made
for the door. Lady Londonderry told her to stay and pour tea
for them and presented her as

"Miss Smith, the daughter of the famous soldier." The
King said:

"Smith...ah, we all know *that* name." Royal politenesses
must exact a certain lack of the sense of humour.

I was once presented to the President of a Great Republic. He said he was delighted to see me and would never forget
a certain passage in one of my books. He recited the passage.
But the book was lying on the table behind him; with, in it,
a slip inscribed in the handwriting of the friend who had introduced me: "Try here!" They manage these things better
in France. At any rate, during the War I was sent for from
the line by M. Delcassé, then Minister for Foreign Affairs.
He showed a remarkable knowledge of a book of propaganda
I had written for his Government. He even suggested altera-
tions in certain passages. And the book was not to be seen
even in his bookshelves....

Well, the King asked Lady Londonderry if he might touch
the bell and ask the footman for some very dry toast, as he
was banting. Miss Smith poured tea. As she was finally escaping, the King said:

"Miss Smith, Lady Londonderry tells me you are interested in literature. I like books. I like boys' books.... Captain Marryat now. I have read all Captain Marryat. But I
find it very difficult to get books like that." He said that he
had asked all the Court but no one could tell him of books
like that. He added:

"If in the course of your researches at the British Museum, Miss Smith, you should come across any such books, I
should be very much obliged if you would jot their names
down on a postcard and send it to me, at Buckingham Palace."

Miss Smith said it seemed to her curious that he should think she did not know his address.

Alas: she found no books like Marryat's. All the horses and all the men of all the dozen sovereigns between the days of Shakespeare and our Roi Bonhomme had not sufficed to produce a second—nor all the wishes of Edward VII. It put him in the good books of Conrad at least, for Conrad considered Marryat to be the greatest English novelist since Shakespeare and always declared that it was reading *Peter Simple* and *Midshipman Easy* that made him wish to go to sea.

Edward VII put himself into my good books too. A little before he died I was at tea at the house of Mr. G. W. Prothers, the editor of the *Quarterly Review*. Mrs. George Keppel rushed in and exclaimed:

"For goodness sake tell me some stories for the King. I've got to tell him some in half an hour! Quick: lots of stories."

Mrs. Prothero turned me on to her and I told her the story of the "Seein' Eye" and the Lutheran Pastor on his honeymoon. She told me that the King had laughed very heartily at one of them. I can't repeat it here. But I was glad to know how a King goes towards death.

The husband of the great lady who came to my tea party was the official most closely in attendance on the King. The King, who slept very badly, had a private telephone from his bedside to that poor man's and constantly rang him up in the small hours to ask questions as to points of protocolar etiquette.

My poor friend—he eventually committed suicide—told me that three things passionately engrossed the King. In the first place, there was his foreign policy. Of this the chief note was of course the Entente Cordiale. Then came men's dress. The King would go on board a battleship with his mentor:

"Now Mr. ——," he would say, "I am naval, so I shall touch my hat on going on the quarterdeck. You are in civilian costume so you will take your hat off. And I should be obliged

if you would have the top of your waistcoat unbuttoned." . . .
In consequence every man in London would have the top of his
waistcoat unbuttoned for the rest of the season.

I suppose not everybody knows to what a king or a cabin
boy touches his hat when he steps on the quarterdeck. It is
done on the quarterdeck of vessels of war of nearly all nations.
It is a salute to the crucifix that used to hang on the mainmast
of the *Harry Grace de Dieu,* the galleon of Henry VIII which
was the first royal battleship. Before that fleets were hired by
monarchs from various maritime cities like the Cinque Ports
or the Hanseatic Ligne.

The third preoccupation of Edward VII was Acts of Gra-
ciousness. You would not think when a King or Queen gives
a cake to a little boy in the street or a kiss to a little girl on
a platform that the act is carefully discussed beforehand. Apparently it is. The case that of all others got on the King's
mind was that of the bridal tour of Mrs. Longworth. Over
that, my poor friend told me the King woke him up not once
every night but six times at least—and for a fortnight.

The case was a very nice one. The King wanted to do
everything that he could—and then some, as the saying is. But
it was difficult. Mrs. Longworth not being royal could not be
given a banquet in the State apartments. Presidents of Republics rank as semi-royal and Mrs. Longworth alone could
have passed as such. But Mr. Longworth could by no means
be regarded even as semi-royal, so a banquet could not be
given for the lady even in the semi-State apartments. You
could not give a banquet to a bride and not invite the groom.
The King would ring up my friend and chafe against the
Protocol that bound him in every imaginable manner. He
would say: "Mr. ——, if we gave a special drawing-room for
Mrs. Longworth, could the Queen take a step forward in
greeting her?" And the Earl Marshal's Deputy would reply:
"Quite impossible, Sir!" The King hit on the brilliant solu-
tion. He was permitted to get someone—the Duchess of Devon-

shire, I think, to give a dinner at which Mrs. Longworth was to be present. Then he himself could take the lady in to dinner. A bride takes precedence of all other ladies present.

After the King's death—so my friend said—the palace was one night thrown into a panic by the complete disappearance of Queen Alexandra. She had apparently slipped out by a back door, accompanied only by a maid and had mailed to the *Times* office her letter to the Nation on the accession of the present King. I don't think the Cabinet liked that very much. But after that no trace of her! She was at last found in Westminster Hall, where the King was lying in state. She was kneeling on the right hand side of the bier. Mrs. Keppel was kneeling on the other.

It is curious—and sad!—to think that but for his altercation in my drawing-room Conrad might possibly have become Edward VII's favourite writer. I was quite seriously given to understand later that he was then under the observation of the wife of the King's mentor. But apparently the works of a writer so inconsiderate as to make a fuss in a drawing-room might be considered to be bad for a King who was thinking out an Entente Cordiale. It would have made all the difference in the world to the poor fellow. He might have had fifteen years or so of comparative ease. For the literary examples of royalty in England are followed with extraordinary keenness by the King's lieges and they have a contagious effect on the United States. As it was, a little before his death, Conrad wrote to me that he had not made any money by his pen for nearly two years. He lived on royalties from his earlier books.

His estate was sworn at £50,000—a quarter of a million dollars or so. This may seem a large sum for a mere writer. But Conrad towards his death would have been pretty freely acknowledged to be the greatest member of his profession in Anglo-Saxondom—the greatest in the world with the doubtful exception of Anatole France who was then already becoming unpopular in France. Think then of the sums which are possessed at death by the greatest in the world of any other profession. Think of the greatest sausage-skin maker in the world, or rag and bone dealer, or automobile manufacturer or bucket-shop keeper. You will say that all these are purveyors of necessities. Well then, think of the greatest, or the greatest but one, beauty specialist or perfumer. What would the heirs of M. Coty think if they received but £50,000 at his death?

When I made my £5 bet with Conrad, in 1901 or so, that *Chance* when it came to be finished would sell 14,000 copies I was considering the fact that there are 14,000 railway stations in the United Kingdom. I said to myself that Conrad might well find one reader per town, village, or hamlet in the country of his adoption. But when, on the Somme in 1916, I received a money order telegram sending me, with the £5, the message: *"Chance* did 14,000 today," it seemed to me a very small figure. The population of the British Empire at that date was some 250,000,000. For the purposes of the hostilities in which we were engaged it could find seven million men and two or three million women—say one in twenty-five. For its intellectual Front line, that two hundred and fifty million could find only 14,000—one in 17,857. It is not much consideration to say that a large percentage of that 250,000,000 do not read English. If the greatest Empire the world has ever seen cannot induce its subject races to assimilate its highest form of culture its existence seems to be unjustified. And unjustifiable.

The question of whether one should or should not write for money seems easy to answer at first sight. But the moment you approach it practically it becomes nearly insoluble. For myself I should be very glad if I could earn with my pen as a regular salary as much as a New York street sweeper does. But I am aware that the attempt would be impracticable on my part. I will not say that I have never written with an eye to a great public and great publicity. I have. The attempts have always been my most dismal failures. When I have written the best that I knew how, I have now and then had very considerable successes. Shortly after the time of which I am writing, I became for a time certainly the most "boomed" writer in England. I had for one book fifteen and for another seventeen reviews on the day of publication. The review on day of publication was in those days the sign of popularity with the Press.

Yet in neither of those books had I ever thought of the public at all. Everything I wrote whilst I was looking after Conrad I wrote quite listlessly as far as the public fate of the work was concerned. What I wrote was almost always something in the way of experiment and I did not even send the greater part of it to any publisher. Indeed, as I have already said, most of what I wrote was produced with the idea of reading it aloud to Conrad. Beyond that I gave it little thought. I had no need to earn a living by my pen and Conrad's need was so insistent and clamant that I neither thought nor cared about my own.

Then accidentally I made the acquaintance of Mr. R. B. Byles—in a train going to Rye. We got into a talk about publishing in general. He was just starting, with Mr. Henry Bathurst and, I think, Mr. Archibald Marshall, the firm of Alston Rivers. I imagine that he was hoping to publish the work of Henry James. He never told me so because he was not one to talk about his failures, but Mr. James told me a day or two later that a publisher had been to see him. I do not see for what other reason Byles could have wanted to go to Rye, for he hated the game of golf and, even more than Stephen Crane, despised corner lots and battlefields.

In the event he asked to see what I was writing and I told Pinker to send him some of my MSS. Byles became one of my most intimate friends. His activities as a publisher were extraordinary and alas—meteoric. He was a small, grim, bronzed Sheffield man of the wildest prejudices. His real name was Boileaux, his original ancestor who emigrated to England having been a Huguenot. But—by Grimm's Law, I sup-

pose—the name had become Boilers, then Bilers, and finally
Byles. His parents had, however, conferred on him the fore-
names of Réné Boileau to his intense indignation and disgust.
He aspired to be the absolute, commonsense Englishman. He
refused to know any foreign language except Japanese of
which he had a few words. He ate daily the same English food
wherever he found himself—mutton chops, grilled without
condiments, potatoes boiled without sauce, a slice of apple
pie, some Stilton with pulled bread. He was a martyr to indigestion. He died too young.

But for him it is almost certain that I should have given
up writing. But his enthusiasm for my work was extraordinary
and infectious. He almost made me believe in myself. He certainly made the newspapers believe in me—and indeed in
many of the other books that he published. His office was a
queer one. His partner, the Hon. Hervey Bathurst, was the
casual peer's son who takes up publishing as being a pursuit
for a gentleman. He was lean, brown, with slightly curling
hair. He was one of those Englishmen who perpetually smokes
an enormous pipe and seems eternally just about to remove
it and let out portentous utterances. I never saw Bathurst
remove his pipe from his mouth.

Mr. Archibald Marshall, the novelist, the other partner,
was as English and almost as be-piped as Bathurst. He was,
however, larger, plumper, a little more curly haired and more
elaborately dressed. He was just as taciturn but gave the impression that his silences arose from bewilderment rather than
from profound, pipe-inspired cogitations.

I do not say that Mr. Marshall was actually bewildered,
merely that he had that air. But he might well have been.
For, before those tranquil, relative immensities, little Byles
buzzed about like an English wasp in front of the winged bulls
of Nineveh. There was nothing that he did not manage and no
member of the office staff that he did not anathematise for
incompetence. He must have been almost the first English

man of business to use a card-index and the introduction of that admirable, brain-saving device caused immense confusion in an office that only asked to be conservative. Byles only thought that he was.

CHAPTER II

"LET US TAKE A WALK DOWN FLEET STREET!"

THE devices of Byles for obtaining publicity were unusual and numerous and he followed them up with amazing energy. On the publication of the first of my books that he handled he went down with a copy of it to the *Daily Mail* office. He succeeded in buttonholing Lord Northcliffe actually in the composing room of that paper and then and there read him some extracts from my book. I am quite certain that no one ever before or since achieved such a feat. He managed to convey some of his enthusiasm to the Napoleon of Fleet Street and Lord Northcliffe promised to review the book himself on the day of publication and to give himself a column or more of the precious middle page of his journal for the purpose of expressing his enthusiasm. I think he did so, but I do not know. For early in life I began the practice of never reading reviews of my own work. I found with even my first book that all reviews affected me disagreeably. If they praised me I used to think that I could do it better myself; if they blamed me it upset me. Favourable reviews in consequence I never see but now and then especially unfavourable ones are sent me by third parties. I suppose they are meant to annoy me. They do.

When that happens I spend perhaps a fortnight composing and polishing up an answer to the strictures. I can be immensely biting in such letters. But I never send them. I am

pretty sure that I never wrote but once a letter to a newspaper
or any other periodical or person in defence of my work. When
the New York *Times* reviewer accused me of terminological
inexactitudes in my book on Conrad I waited some years for
the tumult to die down. Then I forwarded documentary proof
of my accuracy to that paper and to several others in New
York. The *Times* did not print my letter. The others did. The
reviewer afterwards wrote two attacks on me in the same
number of his paper. I should have thought that was bad
editing.

Armed then with Lord Northcliffe's promise, Byles went
round to Mr. Gardiner of the *Daily News,* the leading Liberal
organ, of the time. Mr. Gardiner was Lord Northcliffe's chief
rival in London journalism of the day. As soon as he heard
that the Harmsworth Press had discovered a new genius he determined not to be beaten and promised a column and a half.
With that promise my friend went to the *Morning Post,* the
chief Tory paper, not only of that, but of all time. If the
Morning Post had any enemies they were the *Daily Mail,* and
the Liberal organ. The *Morning Post* was the property of the
Bathurst family and the most scrupulously honest paper in
the world. Nothing would have persuaded it to go out of its
way to praise a book in which Mr. Hervey Bathurst was
interested. It despised news and all its foreign correspondence,
from however far, was always sent by post. But in its lordly
and condescending way it patronised letters and was indeed
a most valuable literary organ. I remember Mr. Ashmead
Bartlett going almost out of his mind. He was the *Post's*
correspondent in Constantinople at the time of the Young
Turk rising. The Sultan gave him a unique and amazingly
frank interview. The *Post* refused to pay cable rates for it.
But it promised Byles two columns for my book.

So Byles went from paper to paper till he had promises
of reviews from all the fifteen principal sheets in the Kingdom. All this was kept secret from me, so that on the day of
that publication I felt like a cat in a corruscation of fireworks.

I could not open a paper, morning or evening, without seeing my name in "leaded caps." And, hardened as I ought to be, I had never got over a feeling of shyness at seeing my name in print. Byles did even better for my next book.

I was singularly in harmony with him as a publisher. He accepted the books that I recommended him to publish and published them as I thought they ought to be published and advertised. I wish he could have gone on publishing me for good. But he met his Waterloo in the battle of the book clubs, and I with him. He went to Japan to run a mineral water business dealing in Tan San water. He did this with considerable success but returned just before the War, having quarrelled with the Japanese Government and the proprietors of the spring. The water had a considerable sale on the Coast, where there is little or no indigenous mineral water. Its advertising placards became familiar objects on the roadsides of the United States, and Byles might have been a rich man, for he had considerable interest in the spring. But the War made shipments from Japan to the Coast too costly, when they were possible, and no more was heard of Tan San.

Byles then tried publishing again, but for a hard business man was rather simply double-crossed. A couple of young men who were starting a publishing business pretended that they had a great deal of capital, whereas they had none at all. They engaged Byles as manager and the affair was a disaster for him—and indeed for me. I was anxious to help him as much as possible. I had a very good contract with very good publishers at the time but I broke it in order to give the book to Byles' firm—for nothing: that is to say without any advance. Byles sailed in with immense enthusiasm to provide publicity for me. The results were almost more painful than with the earlier venture. My book was called "Mr...." after the central character and Byles hit on the diabolical idea of hiring a carriage and pair with cockaded footmen and a passenger got up to resemble my principal character. This monstrosity drove all over the more aristocratic region of London leaving cards on which was engraved:

Mr....
Palatial Hall
Hampstead N.W.

I don't know how that would have worked as an advertising scheme. I knew nothing about it. On the day he had done it Byles told me rather nervously that he had adopted an advertising device that I might not like. He added that I must bear up under it. I had to.

That afternoon I went, as I frequently did, to tea at the G. W. Protheros'; I like Mr. and Mrs. Prothero a good deal. The editor of the *Quarterly* was not exactly my speed, as the saying is—a gentle, bearded, restrained, as if blighted, little man. But his conversation was, in a muted key, very entertaining and his comments on public affairs were singularly just and instructed. Mrs. Prothero also had great charm of a bird-like type. Dr. Garnett being then dead, the Protheros' household was the one I liked best to visit in London at tea-time.

That day I was received with very marked coldness. After a time Mr. Prothero took me into his study and, stroking his pointed little beard, said bluffly that my passion for publicity carried me too far. He produced one of Byles' cards which had been left at his door. I did not explain the mistake and I never went to the Protheros' again. I took the view that they ought to have known me better. Or perhaps they did not ask me. I suppose it doesn't matter. In the event, the book was seized by the sheriff's office because Byles' firm could not pay its printers' bills, so that it was never actually published.

Byles subsequently became the manager of the Socialist *New Statesman*. He filled the job with energy and distaste— for he was both loyal to his employers and a tremendous Tory. So during the War his was a tortured personality. His last letter to me was rather tart. I was in training at Cardiff and was appointed military prosecutor for the express purpose of prosecuting Mr. Bertrand Russell. Mr. Russell had been making what the authorities considered to be pro-German speeches in that city. I naturally did not like the job but having been pitchforked into it, I set about it conscientiously but with some listlessness. I wrote in due course to Byles, as manager of the *New Statesman,* and asked him to supply me with numbers of that paper containing articles on the War by the philosopher. Byles replied that if I wanted aid in that dirty business I had better apply to the police. Fortunately my difficulties solved themselves. I got my "last leave" notice three days before the trial of Mr. Russell, which was then postponed, and before he was tried I was already at the Front. Byles I never heard from again. He died shortly afterwards. In spite of eccentricities he was as good a publisher as I could want. He had great knowledge of the business side of book producing and great courage in backing his fancies. His honesty was absolute and his sympathy with the idiosyncrasies of his authors can hardly have been surpassed. He got me into a singular number of scrapes— but that is inevitable with a publisher of strong character.

He succeeded indeed in very nearly embroiling me with Conrad. Conrad wanted to sponsor a cookery book at a time when I was advising Byles as to the books he published. Conrad wanted £400 very badly at that moment and he insisted that I should make Byles publish the book and pay £400 for it. Byles did not want to publish a cookery book and very curtly refused to pay anything like £400 for it.

Authors have singular vanities as to recipes for cooking. I have my own. I have long wanted to write a cookery book. And I can cook. Once in a New York—say—restaurant, I cooked a meal so admirable that, at its end, not a scrap of the food I had treated remained in the casseroles. . . . But, still more important I can aver that having cooked for my family lately during a period of ninety days I only once repeated the same dish three times—and then by request of the consumers. There are very few cooks that can make that boast.

Nevertheless I have been quite unable to find a publisher for my cookery book.

Yet authors of a certain notoriety invariably believe that, if they will lend their names to, or write prefaces for, volumes of recipes for dishes, their names will give publicity to the compilations. They won't. Neither publishers nor public will believe that a novelist can know anything about cooking. We are supposed to live in garrets on a little thin oatmeal. But indeed I do not believe that I would allow any novelist save myself into my own kitchen.... I once arranged for a third party the sale to Mr. Pierpont Morgan of a cookery book compiled by George Meredith and his father-in-law, Peacock. They had collected recipes from the Greek Anthology, the Koran, the Torah, and every likely and unlikely source. It never found a publisher.

Conrad's culinary god-child did, I think, though I never saw it. Unfortunately, in rejecting the book, Byles put the two letters that he wrote into the wrong envelopes. Conrad was stopping with me at Winchelsea at the time these letters came but I was in town for the day. So Conrad, confidently expecting a cheque for £400 read instead a letter in which Byles asked whether I had gone mad or imagined that he had become a benevolent institution. Could I, he asked, imagine him, the smartest publicity man outside Coney Island giving £400 to one of my highbrow friends whose books had a sale of 2,000 copies—giving him £400 for a collection of papers only fit for—I forget what they were fit for. But I remember my homecoming. Conrad had already written to Byles. His letters could be violent. This one was more than violent. Now he wanted to return to town at once and horsewhip Byles. When Byles got Conrad's letter, he wrote to me that the only thing I could do was to horsewhip Conrad.

The matter settled itself, as far as Conrad was concerned, by my offering to guarantee the costs of publishing the book if some reputable publisher could be found to produce it. But no reputable publisher could.

The moral seems to be that one should not have friends who misdirect letters—or other friends who read letters not intended for them. What ought one to do in such cases? Very shortly after that Conrad-Byles affray, I was going through my morning letters half asleep in bed when I became aware that I was reading something that was certainly not meant for me. It contained information of singular delicacy and was—when I came to look at the envelope—addressed by a lady I knew well to a man who had just been stopping with me. I don't know what I ought to have done but I know what I did. I went half an hour later by train up to London. I got some envelopes to match the one I had opened. Then, at one of my clubs I imitated the address of that letter on those envelopes. I managed at last a fair likeness. Then I posted the letter to my own house in that envelope. It had thus the London postmark. Then I returned to Winchelsea, and, as soon as the letter arrived, I forwarded it to the addressee.

I might perhaps have spared myself the trouble. A little later that gentleman turned up at my house just half an hour before a big and rather formal dinner that I was giving to celebrities of sorts. He had been invited and had accepted. Now he said with signs of agitation that he couldn't come. He was very apologetic but assured me that in the end I should much prefer his empty place to his presence. It turned out that he had just been served with a notice of divorce proceedings by the husband of the lady who had written that letter. We had our delicacies in the early days of the century.

My mind keeps harking back to that sarcophagus of a grey house and its painful memories. I will mark time by dwelling on them so as to fill in the three or four next years. During these years I paid little attention to literary or other mundane matters. There was one pleasure—I used to go round to breakfast with Mr. Galsworthy. He lived *en garçon* in a little converted stable on the other side of the square open space formed by the waterworks on Campden Hill. My house was in the south side, his stable—it was very elegantly appointed—was on the north. We used to play lawn tennis on the great lid that covered the reservoir.

In those days Mr. Galsworthy was already writing, but I think as "John Sinjohn" in order to spare the feelings of his family. I do not think I ever disagreed with anyone more thoroughly than I did with Mr. Galsworthy as to the methods and functions of novel writing—but we disagreed very amiably —at least on my side. I wrote him immense and violent letters on the subject. For all I know they may have annoyed him, but he always smiled at breakfast.

Conrad, I imagine, was fonder of "Poor Jack" than of anyone else. Having much the same viewpoint about writing as mine, he must have differed as much as I from the author of *The Man of Property*. But his pleasure when Mr. Galsworthy announced by letter that he was coming down to the Pent was too ingenuous not to be genuine. He would jump up from the breakfast table with the letter in his hand and shout up the stairs to whoever was on the upper floor:

"Hullo ... Jack's coming down. . . . Poor Jack's coming down ... Hurray!"

Poor Jack was the name of one of Marryat's novels. Mr. Galsworthy was not lacking in resources or otherwise marked out by misfortune.

Conrad's account of his first meeting with Mr. Galsworthy always pleased me; it was like one of those fairy-tales of which there are too few in life. Mr. Galsworthy, I anticipate, will contradict it. I can only vouch for the way Conrad told the story.

Conrad then was first mate of a sailing ship called the *Torrens*. The *Torrens* was one of the famous, teak-built, clipper-rigged vessels that carried sea-loving or invalid passengers by way of the Cape to Australia with almost the punctuality of a steam liner. Ninety days out to Sidney Headland, ninety days back to the Thames Estuary—that was her schedule and she kept to it. Conrad already had ideas of leaving the sea and making a living by his pen. It was before the days of typewriters. He had begun a novel, writing trial passages on the fly-leaves and margins of *Madame Bovary* and *l'Education Sentimentale*. I used to possess his copy of the latter book. Whilst I was in France during the War someone relieved me of it along with most of my portable property. There was a passage, that was afterwards incorporated into *Almayer*, pencilled on the front and back of the half-title page.

On the *Torrens*, bound for the Cape, was a young, blond, modest and smiling barrister. He was bound on legal business for the Cape Copper Mines in which he had a family interest. The two young men—Conrad was still in his thirties—confided each to the other that they had literary ambitions. In the starlit silence of the dog-watches, Conrad descended to his cabin and fetched up the beginning of his manuscript. That young barrister who seemed to Conrad to possess all the gifts of Fortunatus must have been the first human being to read any of Conrad's manuscript—on a ship, in the starlight, running down off the coast of Africa. That romance would be almost enough for any one man's portion: That fortunate being was the author of—*The Silver Box*.

I say *The Silver Box* because it was the one of Mr. Galsworthy's writings for which Conrad had the most unbounded admiration. I went with him to one of its later performances and his enthusiasm was so vocal as to cause me considerable shyness. The people in the stalls round us now and then hissed for silence. And indeed *The Silver Box* is an admirable work. I would give no little to see it again but I suppose I never shall. The grim determination with which Mr. Galsworthy makes point after point always reminds me of a big trout lying in a stickle of a stream on his native Dartmoor. Fly after fly comes down on the water and not one, ever, does the grim speckled being miss. In that play at least you have an object lesson in what Conrad used to call catching a subject by the throat and squeezing the last breath out of it. And the original cast was admirable. I wish I could remember the name of the young lady who played the young lady. I will make the confession that she sat to me—she on the stage and I in the house—for the subsidiary heroine of a series of my novels. (It has come suddenly into my head at the moment of correcting the proofs of this page that the young lady was Miss Dorothy Minto.) The publisher insisted on calling that production of mine a "Saga" when the word surely should have been considered the sole appurtenance of the immensely known Forsyte family. I shall make, later, a few remarks upon publishers.... At any rate let me put it on record, as atonement for what it is worth, that except for *The Playboy of the Western World* no play ever gave me so much pleasure as *The Silver Box*. I mean no play at all.

Another play of its author's also pleased me very much indeed. That was *Joy*. It was not very successful—not one tenth as successful as it should have been, for it was full of charm and geniality. It contained one catchword of one character that has remained amongst my most valuable possessions. The story comes back to me as one of agitated matrimonial complications in which a number of characters confide their woes, to exact sympathy from, to a buxom and venerably placid family nurse who has seen them all in their cradles. As each finishes, breathless and a little uncertain of the justifiability of his or her position, the old lady affords them the balm of the same remark: "Yours, my dear, is a special case."

I have for my sins and in the course of a longish life received, always unwillingly, a great number of agitated confidences. I do not know how many times I have not called to my aid that magic phrase. Confidences are things that one ought to be called on to receive for they lead almost invariably to misunderstandings. An individual who will confide in one person will almost certainly confide later in two or three more. If he is agitated he will still more certainly do so. Then, though A may be as reticent as the grave, B, C, or D will almost surely commit some breach of the secret. A will be the one that will get it in the neck. I do not think I have ever violated a confidence. I know at least that I have fre-

quently made myself unpopular with members of my family—
by reticences at exciting moments. But I was once let down in
a most unfortunate way—and just after I had seen *Joy*.

There was in those days an eminent politician of very
wide knowledge and ability. He was then on the verge of a
disagreeable affair. He honoured me by a belief, that was perhaps exaggerated, in my knowledge of life and influence in
regions where he wanted influence exercised. One day he
asked me to go with him to the Zoo. In the Reptile house,
which also contained cages of bright tropical finches, he gave
me a most brilliant lecture on the protective colouring of
birds. It remains now vivid in my mind and has been of the
greatest use in helping me to form appreciations of more
modern art. On the face of it, the birds we were looking at
appeared, in their surroundings, astonishingly visible. But at
home they lived in tree-tops above jungles and had to fear
hawks above all. A finch with a scarlet stomach, sapphire blue
wings, and emerald green head and back is a striking object
in a dim London building. Seen from above in the tropical
rays of an immense sun the effect of the light and shadows in
the prismatic coloration of the tree-tops is completely to break
up the form of the bird.

My friend exhausted this topic and we looked at some
snakes. He then led me into the inner circle of Regent's Park—
a solitary promenade given up to lovers and a few horsemen.
Round and round this he took me for nearly two hours whilst
he told me the story of his life with all its vicissitudes, passions and triumphs. I particularly did not want to hear it. But
he said he had hanging over him a thundercloud that might
burst at any moment. If his friends did not stand by him he
must be swept from his public position and be irretrievably
ruined. He adjured me to tell his story as he told it—at my
fireside, in my clubs and in all public places where men talk.
I said I did not want to. He plunged at once into the story
of his affairs. It was complicated and tenebrous. I grew more

and more apprehensive but on he went—and on. At last he said: "Don't you think I'm justified?"

I answered gravely: "Yours of course is a special case." The answer gave complete satisfaction.

Alas, the matter did not end there! My poor friend's case was exciting a great deal of comment; he himself was much in the public eye. I could not go anywhere without hearing his affair discussed and himself usually unfavourably commented on. I seriously—and naïvely:—recounted his life in almost exactly his own words on every one of these occasions. I had my work cut out! He had—I daresay sagaciously—by no means spared himself in his narration. It is probably good policy not to make yourself out too much of an angel when mud is flying.

The result was embarrassing for me. The affair ended in nothing: its reverberations died away; my friend retained his public offices and at last reconciled himself to his most embittered opponents. This left them the embittered enemies of myself because, if the politician was able to forget their offences against him, I was not disposed to. And in defending him, I had caused them the deepest offence. I do not have to say that they are now members of the present British Government. Everyone I ever managed to offend in those days climbed afterwards into the seats of the mighty. I once dreadfully hurt a future Prime Minister during a game of golf by successfully using a wooden putter when he said an artist would have used a niblick. I was annoyed and told him that for him to talk to me about art was like a blacksmith telling a lace-maker how to make lace. He was one of several Ministers of War during the late hostilities. I have always thought that if I had compromised and used an approaching iron I might today have been a major-general. The most violent row I ever had in my life—I at least was more angry than I have ever otherwise been—was with the present representative of His Majesty in France. If I should ever get into trouble with

the French authorities, I don't know what would become
of me.

The incident of the politician's confidences did not, however, end merely with the enmity of his opponents. Some time
after, at a moment of political excitement, he made a speech
which was reported in the Press and in it accused me of going
about seeking his ruin by relating unthinkable things about
him. I was more than perturbed. I wrote him a mild letter,
more, as the saying is, in sorrow than in indignation. I reminded him that the horrible things I had related about him
I had from his own mouth and he had requested me to communicate them to anyone who was interested in him. I have
no doubt that by the time they got back to him the stories
were considerably altered. There is in the army a drill called
"message carrying." You line up a platoon and give the first
private a message, say, to the effect that the cylinders of
poisoned gas have not arrived. You tell him to repeat it to
his neighbour and his neighbour to number three. By the time
it reaches the end of the line it will take the form of, "the
general's wife has poisoned herself in a six cylinder car!" I
daresay that politician's autobiography by the time it re-
reached him had been as startlingly altered. He never answered my letter.

If you had asked me ten minutes ago I should have said
I was the mildest of men, but it occurs to me, after what I have
just written and considering what I'm about to write, that there
must be something wrong with that theory. My life through
I seem to have been mixed up in terrific rows with people
who appeared singularly touchy. That is probably my own
fault. I suppose I've always rather liked teasing public characters and public characters must dislike being teased more
than I imagined they did.

I am writing this section as if for the benefit of the literary aspirant and the young generally. I never myself took
anyone's advice and I do not imagine that many people will
take mine. But as an example how not to manage a career

my story may be almost as useful as Hogarth's cartoons of the Idle Apprentice.

I left that story some pages back at the point when, largely owing to Lord Northcliffe, I had become the most boomed author in England. Alas! A few years later Mr. Hamilton Fyffe wrote and asked me to go and see him at the *Daily Mail* office. He was Lord Northcliffe's mentor and quite a good friend to me. He asked me what I had done to offend Lord Northcliffe. Lord Northcliffe had had my name put on the black list of all his papers. That meant that not one of his papers was permitted to mention me for good or evil. He suggested that I should go then and there and apologise for what I'd done. His Lordship was in the next room. I didn't.

I have not to this moment the remotest idea of what I could have done to him. I had known him for a very long time —for long indeed before he was even prosperous. He was then Alfred Harmsworth and living with his wife in a couple of rooms in one of the Inns of the Court—the Middle Temple, I think. Mrs. Harmsworth was making in an album the collection of snippets that afterwards became the first number of *Answers*. She would read in a newspaper: "The largest haul of sprats ever made took place yesterday at Grimsby. It consisted of 90,000 tons, which is equivalent to eleven thousand million sprats." She would cut this out, stick it in her album and write above it: "Where was the largest haul of sprats ever made? And of how many did it consist?" She would then get Harmsworth to look up the distances of the planets from the earth and estimating a sprat at three inches he would dictate to her: "Placed head to tail they would reach from Fleet Street to the planet Arcturus." Mr. Harmsworth was at that time a barrister, but I fancy that making these calculations occupied the greater part of his time. He owed my grandfather a little money. It would have been singular if he hadn't, for my grandfather had a way of being owed money by the most dissimilar people. But he paid this back within a few days or almost within a few hours of the publication of the first number of *Answers*. He had borrowed the money to help in paying for the printer's bill. So I may say that my ancestors, who must have been in very queer places in their day, were in at the birth of the Harmsworth Press—which is the queerest reflection of all. I myself carried the cheque from my grandfather to that Inn of the Court apartment. I reminded Lord Northcliffe of this in the days of his splendour. I don't think he liked it very much. In those days half London said Lord Northcliffe was a Jew. The other half said he couldn't be a Jew because he was revengeful and Jews are never revengeful. Actually he was an Irishman. He knew my grandfather through William Allingham, the Irish poet who wrote "Up the Airy Mountains." I did not see Lord Northcliffe again for a good many years. Then he was buying papers right and left. He sent for me and peremptorily ordered me to buy the *Academy* but not to tell anyone I was buying it with his money. I really liked him very much upon the instant. He was an extraordinary and romantic figure in my eyes. He stood in the gorgeous drawing-room that was his editorial office, in front of his desk beneath a portrait of Lady Hamilton by Romney. But I think it ought to have been a portrait rather of the Empress Josephine, for he considered himself the Napoleon of journalism.

For the first time in my life I let myself be swayed by prudence. It was no doubt a mistake. He was the most talked about man in London of those days and what was most said of him was that he took up young men of talent, gave them small fortunes, worked them to death and then threw them aside. I was particularly swayed by G. W. Steevens' memory. He died in Pretoria in the service of the *Daily Mail* and his last words were: "This is a backstairs way out of it." I did not want those to be my last words.

Besides, I did not know that the *Academy* was for sale and I should not have known how to set about buying it, if it had been, nor how to edit it, if I should control it. I therefore did nothing about the matter and I suppose he forgot about it. I saw him rather often socially after that but he never mentioned the *Academy* to me again. A little incident occurred during that interview. The great man rang his bell and told the messenger to tell Mr. Someone to write the paper's editorial about the visit of the German Journalists' Deputation to London. The messenger replied that Mr. Someone was ill. Lord Northcliffe—I suppose he was actually still Sir Alfred Harmsworth—said, "Then tell someone else to write it. Tell him to look up the previous articles in the paper. Tell him to be civil but not to be too civil. You understand, civil but not too civil."

Some time later the editor of the *Daily Mail* rang me up about two in the afternoon and asked me to write a sonnet to the memory of Dr. Johnson. This was to be in the *Daily Mail* office by five o'clock that afternoon. The editor had just heard at lunch that the next day was the—I think bi-centenary—of the birth of Dr. Johnson and the office thought it ought, in some way or other, to commemorate that event. I had just won a sonnet competition in which most of the literati of London who could write verse at all engaged themselves. I had written my sonnet in two minutes and thirty-nine seconds, beating Mr. Hilaire Belloc by two seconds. Mr. Belloc sneezed twice whilst writing his sestette or else no doubt he would have beaten me. This achievement having been reported in the Press, Mr. Marlowe, who was then either the editor or one of the two editors of the *Daily Mail*, did not see why I could not write a sonnet and have it at the *Mail* office in three hours. I said I couldn't do it. It was one thing to write a sonnet to given rhymes about anything under the sun and quite another to write one about Johnson. All I could remember about Johnson at the moment was that he had kept pieces of orange peel and patted corner posts when he walked down Fleet Street. Mr. Marlowe offered me a large sum to write this sonnet. I said I couldn't possibly. He doubled his offer and I said it made no difference. He trebled his offer and added Lord North-cliffe's compliments, and the fact that his Lordship would be

much obliged. I will add for the gratification of the curious
the following statistics. If I could have written sonnets for
eight hours a day for three hundred days in the year at two
and a half minutes per sonnet and at the rate of pay offered
by Mr. Marlowe I should have been making two million, four
hundred and nineteen thousand—two hundred guineas a year—
or say twelve million dollars. I should not be making much
more if I owned Detroit's most famous industry. Alas, even by
that offer I was not tempted and, Mr. Marlowe continuing to
worry me I said good-humouredly: "You can tell Lord Northcliffe that if he offered me all the treasures of India I would not
write a word in any one of his papers." I was not intending to be
insulting but merely jocular. And indeed I said as much to Lord
Northcliffe himself because I was perfectly sure I could never
with my writing keep up to the pace of the Northcliffe Press. So
I do not think that that is what gave Lord Northcliffe the final
offence. Indeed, some time later when he asked me to assist Mr.
Archibald Marshall in editing that paper's literary supplement,
I consented to this. It meant that I could pretty well set the pace
of that periodical myself.

It was an unfortunate venture. The supplement had been
founded by Mr. Edmund Gosse who was then London's chief
literary pontiff. And very pontifical he was. Lord Northcliffe
had engaged him to edit the paper for exactly a year. When
the year ended he gave Mr. Gosse no notice that his job was
terminated but simply installed Mr. Marshall in the editorial
chair with myself behind him. Thus, one Thursday, Mr. Gosse
walked into the office and found Mr. Marshall sitting at his
desk opening the letters and dictating the answers to the
secretary. It was one of the most disagreeable episodes in which
I have ever been concerned. I used to write an article on some
writer or other every week for this journal. The supplement
had no connection with the *Daily Mail*. We had a very lovely
office of our own in an eighteenth century house. It had a
beautiful view of the Thames and no one connected with the
Mail ever entered it until one of the Harmsworth brothers—

I forget which—came into it one day and said that that journal was to be discontinued. It was at the time when the Sunlight Soap Company was victorious in the libel suit against the *Mail* and the *Mail's* advertisement revenue had diminished enormously. Lord Northcliffe was at the time ill in Spain. I protested vigorously against the suppression. When I had undertaken to help Mr. Marshall, Lord Northcliffe had promised to continue the supplement as a separate venture for at least two years. I did not like to be connected with failures. On the strength of this promise Mr. Marshall and I had got together a group of admirable but needy writers. We promised them each two years' employment. Now they were suddenly cast into Fleet Street.

The *Daily Mail* office ignored my protests. I wrote to Lord Northcliffe and reminded him of his promise. He answered that he could not remember it. But as a compromise the Literary Supplement was turned into a weekly page in the *Daily Mail* itself. The staff was thus retained in their employment which was what I wanted and I transferred my weekly article on books to an eccentric paper which was edited and owned and run with extraordinary profusion by a cotton millionaire called Thomassen. It is possible that this transference was what irritated Lord Northcliffe. But he never made any comment to me on the subject.

It is possible also that his irritation was caused by the part that along with Byles I took in the *Times Book Club* row. This was an obscure contest carried on between the Publishers' Association of which Byles was then the most active member and Messrs. Hooper and Jackson, a couple of American business men whom Lord Northcliffe had brought over from New York with the intention of turning them loose in the *Times* office in order that they might suggest economies in the running of that august journal. I do not know what irritated Byles in that arrangement or exactly what affair of his it was but I know that just before then I found myself engaged, more or less as a figurehead, with Byles behind me in bidding for the purchase of the *Times* as against Lord Northcliffe. I did not at first know where Byles proposed to get the money but he assured me that he could do so and I took his word for it. I forget exactly what sum we offered for it but it was certainly a matter of several million dollars. A little later I heard from Byles that his backers were a syndicate of London bankers. I then withdrew from the enterprise. I could not see myself editing any paper, much less a paper with the influence of the *Times*, in the interest of anybody connected with finance. The responsibility would have been enormous and my hands would have been tied. As between the two I would rather have edited the paper for Northcliffe. I always liked him personally and should at least have been able to gauge his motives, whereas I cannot imagine myself liking any banker, let alone a syndicate of them. And their motives would almost always have been obscure to me. In the end, Lord Northcliffe offered more for the paper and it became his property. Byles then turned his attention to Messrs. Hooper and Jackson in another capacity. Once in command of that paper those gentlemen set out to conquer the publishing world. They got out the ninth edition of the Encyclopedia Britannica and they fairly amazed London with a blaze of American publicity such as Europe till then had never seen. Then they started the *Times Book Club*, which was a much more serious affair. They began by saying that books ought to be cheaper. They then purchased the remainders and all the unsaleable books that all the London publishers had in their cellars. They bought books which had been published at a guinea for a few pence and resold them for a shilling or so. They showed an extraordinary activity in covering England with these derelicts of the book market. They sent salesmen in all kinds of tumble-down vehicles over all the country roads and got rid of their wares to the smallest grocers, stationers and chemists who had never before thought of selling a book. It was glorious while it lasted. It was then that I, as I have said, bought a copy of Dostoievsky's *Poor Folk* for six cents from Rayner's grocery store at Aldington. Yes, it was glorious while it lasted. Messrs. Hooper and Jackson loudly proclaimed that they were going to turn the English into a nation of readers. But they didn't. Nothing could. Messrs. Hooper and Jackson imagined that they would open new markets for books and with those markets once opened would go on selling them. They might have if they could have gone on supplying six shilling books for six cents. But they couldn't. The supply of publishers' remainders ran out and you could not in those days manufacture a new book for six cents. It was as much as you could do to put them on the market at six shillings.

I have always held that the unreasonable cheapening of the price of books is disastrous at once to authors and to the public. The author starves, reduces the quality of his work and eventually disappears. This in the end is bad for the public, since it reduces them to the state of savages. It is of course an admirable thing that the classics should be provided in the cheapest possible form. But if the public is to remain at all civilised it must pay for the turning of the attention of new and active brains towards contemporary problems. And the curious factor in the problem is that at any rate in England and America the public will not take with seriousness what it obtains at a very cheap rate.

And in England, but not quite to the same extent in America, the people who buy books are people who must buy them. The Englishman who buys books is taken for some one un-English, emasculated or detrimental to the public, so that anyone who indulges in this anti-national habit must of necessity have some very strong reason for so doing. To reduce then the price of a commodity that is a necessity to a restricted market is the action of a man without business sense.

Messrs. Hooper and Jackson's action was of a different nature. They were business men all right. They had no intention in the long run of producing books. Their aim was with the aid of the publicity that the *Times* could give them to start an enormous and glorified circulating library. Thus if they could force the price of books down their profit would be all the greater and they could go into the business with the aureoles of public benefactors.

Byles held very strongly the view that circulating libraries are the ruin of publishing. I held almost as strongly the view that they are bad for good literature. Byles thought—rightly or wrongly—that the fact that the public can get a new book from the library and read it at the cost of about three cents, prevented the average man from buying books at all and permitted even the rare men who had to read books to buy much fewer. I think that is probably true. The answer of the libraries was that in the case of books at all popular they actually purchased more copies than the publisher could by any means hope to disperse among the general public. That is true too. I have known instances of books of which the libraries had bought 15,000 copies before their publication. But these were practically never books that had any claim to the name of literature. At best they would be *romans à clef* or clever books dealing with passing topics. And they were of course few. The better book, on the other hand, suffered very badly. The type of books of which the libraries brought great numbers was one which had immediate appeal as a topic of dinner-table conversation. Its readers must have it at once or they would lose such social preëminence as chatter about the latest popular novel could give them.

The readers of better books, on the contrary, are in no such hurry. They will eventually have Conrad and will read him carefully and slowly but they have as a rule a program of reading and may not be at all ready to read a particular book at the time of its publication nor do they immensely object if a copy is not immediately available, when they apply to the library for it. At the time of which I am speaking or a little before it, Conrad's books were selling between three and four thousand copies each. Of these the great libraries, Mudie and Smith, took as a rule two hundred copies apiece before publication and purchased perhaps fifty copies more between them.

The small circulating libraries throughout the kingdom would take perhaps a thousand more. But as these were gradually put out of existence by Smith's railway bookstores or absorbed as branches of Mudie's, that market gradually closed itself. The general public would slowly absorb the rest of the books which would go on selling for three or four years. That meant to say that Conrad might get spread over a period of four years a hundred and fifty to two hundred pounds—say seven hundred and fifty dollars—or perhaps two hundred and fifty dollars a year. I once asked one of the managers of Mudie's how it was possible that they could take, say, five thousand copies of a work by Miss Marie Corelli and only two hundred of, say, *Typhoon*. He said: "Well, you see if we stocked any more of Mr. Conrad's books it would take up more of our warehousing space and warehousing space is one of our heaviest charges. With two hundred copies we can perfectly well supply any demand there is for Conrad." I asked him whether that did not seem rather lamentable from the point of view of the corruption of the public taste. He said rather animatedly: "No." He could undertake to say that Conrad got distributed by himself and the other libraries to everyone who could possibly be expected to read him. He added that the disproportion of copies sold was startling. But actually the difference between the number of readers of Miss Corelli and Conrad was nothing like so great and he referred to a table and told me that the average number of times each copy of Miss Corelli was taken out was not much more than five which might count for twenty readers, giving her a hundred thousand readers in that establishment. On the other hand *Lord Jim* had been sent out an enormous number of times, each copy in their possession being always sent out again as soon as it came back until it had to be re-bound or finally became too dirty for re-circulation. Then it would have to be replaced. In that way each copy of *Lord Jim,* if it was taken out two hundred and fifty times ... but I forget the exact figures. I know that this gentleman said that he thought a book of Conrad's might be counted on as having twelve thousand readers amongst his own subscribers alone. He pointed out another significant fact that when it came to disposing of second-hand copies that had got too worn for circulation Miss Corelli's books would hardly find purchasers at six pence whereas Conrad could not be kept in stock at a couple of shillings.

This was pretty poor hearing for anyone interested in keeping Conrad alive. Byles then had grown alarmed at the increase in the number of circulating libraries and at their insistence on cutting prices. He tried to induce the Publishers' Association to engineer a combine that should refuse to supply the libraries on terms at least as good or even better than they supplied the booksellers. I did all that I could to back him up with my pen.

The Publishers' Association was very weak-kneed. Its principal plea for not taking any action was that it could not do so without the consent of its authors. I wrote a number of articles in, I should think the *Tribune,* to induce my confrères to act upon the publishers. One or two actually took my advice. I think Mr. Shaw refused to let his books be supplied to the libraries except at the price at which they were actually sold by booksellers to the public. Byles himself took the drastic step of refusing to supply the books of his firm to the libraries at all. He had of course to obtain the consent of his authors and not nearly all of them consented. The others, however, were boycotted by those libraries. So they did not profit. I, of course, consented, and the sales of my books stopped dead. Byles had counted on the booksellers backing up the publishers and authors who had thus espoused our cause, but the booksellers were not minded so to do. Besides, there are practically no booksellers in England. In the City of Avignon with a population of 51,685 there are six first-class booksellers' shops. In the County of London with its then 10,000,000 inhabitants there were not twelve, nor was there one between Bumpus' which was the most westerly first-class book shop in London and the Land's End. Thus Byles had miscalculated the strength of the only support he could expect. That was his Waterloo.

It was also mine. For nearly twenty years after that no book of mine ever attracted any attention in the popular press or sold more than the most meagre number of copies. Byles said this was due to boycotting by the libraries. I don't know whether it was or not.

I am writing this chapter, as I have said, as a dreadful lesson in how not to manage a literary career. I don't exactly know what the moral is. I think it a duty for every author who is at all prosperous to take an interest in the politics of book producing—for the sake of his less fortunate confrères and for the sake of literature itself. But if he does so he will probably be ruined. I think it is the duty of the novelist to pay some attention to—not to take part in—the public affairs of his day because in the end it is to the novelist that the public must go for its knowledge of life. And if the novelist is to have and to convey that knowledge he must of necessity mix in public life. In that way too he is very likely to come up against one Lord Northcliffe or another and to have his ruin accelerated and increased. I do not think that I have any regrets except the regret that I had at the time of having upset Lord Northcliffe. As I have said I liked him as a man for his ingenuousness, his buoyancy, his boyishness and for the fact, naturally, that he did his best to be of service to me. I don't think I ever resented his afterwards trying to be of disservice to me. That sort of thing is all in the day's journey. And if I had it all to do over again, I do not see how I could now act differently.

But if I had to advise a literary aspirant as to his career and if he said that it was his career that interested him and that he was coldly uninterested in any other aspect of the literary life I should speak as follows:

"Your ideal of a career should be that it should leave you as is the case with all littérateurs of eminence in England on top of a hill at some distance from London and particularly at a distance as considerable as possible from all other littérateurs.

There you should lead the life as nearly as possible resembling that of a country gentleman as your comfortable means should allow to you. You should surround yourself with a retinue of body surgeons, consulting physicians, eminent attorneys-at-law, handy men to do what dirty work you have and a small cloud of devoted females to do the same. You will thus create around yourself an air of mystery, respectability, and even of awfulness. All your life until reaching that stage should have been devoted to that progress. You should have eschewed, as you would shrink from soiled underwear, all personal publicity. I am aware that this last course is not recommended in England and still less in America. Personal publicity is usually considered to be the first thing at which a writer should aim. But when you consider that at least half and very likely eighty per cent of the personal gossip about an author is likely to be detrimental you will, I think, see that though you gain on the swings you will lose a great deal more on the roundabouts. That at least is my conviction. And if you will consider the authors who together with some literary value have achieved great sales in both England and America you will see that the majority of them have been of extremely retiring dispositions. In my time they have been George Meredith of Box Hill, Thomas Hardy of Dorchester, Conrad of Postling, Arnold Bennett of Somewhere in Essex, Mr. Kipling of Burwash, pronounced Burridge, my dear lady, Henry James of Rye, Mr. Galsworthy of Somewhere in Devonshire, and one or two others. All these gentlemen have been … gentlemen. They have as far as possible avoided the public eye; they have deprecated personal publicity; they have mixed very little in public affairs and of them very little was known during their careers towards eminence except for their photographs. And a good photograph gives the public quite as much information as is necessary concerning an author's personality, *Who's Who* filling in all the other desirable blanks. You will perceive by glancing through my list of names that they include nearly all the great permanent sellers of both Great Britain and the United States. There are of course writers in America who have achieved great sales by means of permitting their publishers to indulge in orgies of publicity concerning their personalities, tastes, vicissitudes, earlier appearances in the bankruptcy, the divorce and the police courts, and the like. But these instances are so relatively recent that it is too early to say whether they will have any permanence. And my views on the subject are immensely strengthened for me when I consider the past. It is authors of whose personality very little is known whose books are widely read. Of Shakespeare we know nothing, of Homer less, of the writers of the Bible nothing at all. On the other hand, Dr. Johnson, who was when he chose to be a magnificent author, is completely swamped by Boswell's *Life* and for one person who reads the poems of Shelley probably a hundred read one or other concoction of chatter about Harriet. The fact is that people read consciously or unconsciously as much out of curiosity about the life and person of an author as for any other reason. If they can get that curiosity satisfied outside the authors' books they surely won't read the books."

I shall write a little more on the subject of other aspects of the literary career in a later chapter.

CHAPTER III

SOME CURES

F ROM 1903 to 1906 illness removed me from most activities.
The illness was purely imaginary; that made it none the better.
It was enhanced by wickedly unskilful doctoring. In those
days I wandered from nerve-cure to nerve-cure, all over England, Germany, Austria, Switzerland and Belgium—but mostly
in Germany. I suffered from what was diagnosed as agoraphobia and intense depression. I had nothing specific to be
depressed about. But the memory of those years is of one
uninterrupted mental agony and nothing marked them off one
from the other. They were lost years.

One single picture comes back to me. I had been trying
a nerve cure on the Lake of Constance. I had taken ninety cold
baths and thirty tepid soda-water douches in thirty days. I was
so weak that, even if the so-called agoraphobia had not inter-
fered with my walking I should hardly have been able to get
about. I had determined to pull myself together and had gone
to Bâle to write a life of Holbein.

I wrote the greater part of it in the house of a Swiss professor. He had lost his only daughter and could not bear the
silence of his immensely tall, gloomy, ancient and crow-stepped
house. He had filled it with clocks—every imaginable type of
Swiss clock. There was thus a continual ticking, striking, chim-
ing and cuckooing whilst the poor man continually wept. The
noise of the clocks was not disagreeable but the gloom of the

house was profound. I worked in a room high in the gable.
The upper stories of the houses in that street jutted forward
so as to come very close together. Immediately opposite me
lived a chimney sweep. He was jet black all over, wore a top
hat and carried behind his back a ladder and sacks of soot. His
apartment, which I could see into, contained a baby and a
blonde pink and white young wife. Apartment, baby and wife
were all spotless. On the edge of the window sill was a little
green and white fence, on one side of the window hung a
canary in a cage, on the other a goldfinch. The chimney sweep
never came home till dusk. By then the lights would be lit
behind a white blind. Then I would see the silhouette of the
sweep, framed by the window, in the black house-front that,
itself a silhouette, stood out with crockets and crow-steps
against the dark sky and the immense stars.

He would stride joyously into the room. His shadow would
catch the shadow of the baby from the invisible cradle and,
top hat, ladder, sacks all bobbing, he would throw the baby up
to the ceiling, again and again and again. I used to hang out
over my window sill and wonder with agony why God had made
it impossible to transfuse one's soul into another being. If
only I could have made my soul enter that chimney sweep's
body whilst his was absent in sleep! His could no doubt have
found a home.

I gave up Holbein and Bâle and went down the Rhine to a
Kaltwasser-Heilanstalt that seemed to me the most horrible
of all the monstrous institutions that had tortured me. They
fed you there on pork and ice-cream. On the Lake of Constance
they had given me dried peas and grapes—one grape every
quarter of an hour for sixteen hours out of the day. The
director of the *Kaltwasser-Heilanstalt* was an immense, thin
man with a long grey waterfall of beard through which he
passed his fingers, as if cautiously, before he ever made a
remark. He usually wore black spectacles. In the effort to
prove that my troubles had an obscure sexual origin, he would
suddenly produce from his desk and flash before my eyes

indecent photographs of a singular banality. He expected me to throw fits or to faint. I didn't.

In Austria, in an institution that became even more famous than the Rhineland *K.W.H.A.* they had attempted to demonstrate the same thing, with much the same primitive means and with similar unsuccess. One day my soul straightener had a ray of hope.

I had a friend in England who had had a child. He wanted me to be its godfather; I could not because he was Anglican. But I wanted to send the child a christening cup. As I had been going to the institution I had been into several jewellers' shops but could not see the kind of cup I wanted. At last, near the Kärntnerthor I had seen a very pretty, delicate cup in gold. I thought that silver was *de rigueur* for christenings. I was not certain that I could afford the gold one. I wondered if I could not have that golden cup reproduced in silver.

I was thinking about the golden cup in the anteroom of the nerve specialist's office, where I had to wait a long time and felt extremely melancholy. He put his head suddenly around the door and asked menacingly:

"Uber was speculieren Sie?" I said innocently and without premeditation:

"Eine goldene Tasse, Herr Wirklicher Geheimrath."

His face lit up with the pleasure of a cross-examining counsel who has caught out a hostile witness.

"Kurz und gut," he said, "you are suffering from..." some sexual disorder or other. As a matter of fact I was suffering from a slight fluttering of the heart which, after periods of intense overwork and fatigue, caused—and indeed does still cause—me to feel slightly faint for a second or two. This will naturally sometimes happen in the street. The result therefore a little resembles agoraphobia which is, in effect, a disease of the will-power and may be attributable to sexual disorders—but which equally well may not.

Those were the early days of that mania that has since beset the entire habitable globe. I went in those three years to nineteen specialists, all of them famous in their nations and some world famous. Not one of them examined by heart; everyone diagnosed my trouble as agoraphobia; sixteen or seventeen of them attributed it to sexual abnormalities and treated them as such. I am, however, bound to say for the Austrian practitioner that when I explained to him exactly why I was thinking about a golden cup he abandoned his theory. In those days—and I daresay still—a golden cup was regarded by those enthusiasts as a symbol of something improper. I use the last two words on purpose. I suppose the choice of the emblem is a hit at the Holy Grail.

The result of the efforts of these specialists was to reduce me in weight to nine stone two—one hundred and twenty-eight pounds. I am exactly six foot in height. When I went to New York next year the *Herald* had a caricature of me described as "The Animated Match."

The Rhineland *Kaltwasser-Heilanstalt* was the last institution of the sort that I endured. It was a vast, gloomy building, the former palace of a Kurfürst of sorts. I was fed on pork and ice-cream and salad made with lemon juice and white of egg. Oil and vinegar are said to be exciting—sexually. Three times a day I had alternately a boiling shampoo and a *fliessende Fussbad*—a footbath of iced water forced against the feet in a stream running ninety miles an hour. The *Dr. Kaltwasser-Heilanstaltiger Medizinrath* had by then come to the conclusion that my trouble was due to defective circulation. The blood had to be forced to my head by boiling it and then back to my feet by the reaction from their being frozen. It was a good idea but I lost weight. Then complete sleeplessness came to add itself to my pleasures.

My mother came out to me. She had been warned by the *Geheimrath* and members of my family who resided in the town overshadowed by the *Heilanstalt* that my case was desperate. For four nights running she read to me from Boswell's *Johnson*—through the entire night. She read on even when I dozed off.

There were two adorably old-maidish maiden ladies from Stamford, Connecticut, in the *Heilanstalt*. During the day, whilst my mother slept, they took me over, telling me of the glories of America before the Revolution. They were Tories. Their father had been horribly tortured because of his loyalty. Their drawing-room at home was decorated with portraits of General Braddock and Lord Cornwallis. American drawing-rooms they said were usually decorated with portraits of Washington and Franklin. I knew of course that they were not. Their pre-Revolutionary frame-house stood under enormous elms on the spot now occupied by the "Ambassadoor"—it is pronounced like that presumably to rhyme with Commodore—apartment building. I re-located it the other day. It is a pity they had to cut down the elms. There is much too little timber in New England.

Miss Hurlbird and her sister, in the immense, shadowed drawing-room of the *Heilanstalt* promised me that if I would visit them at Stamford and eat their peaches and frozen cream for breakfast I should be restored to complete health. I eventually did so and the promise came true. It was not, you understand, ice-cream, but fresh cream frozen thick and eaten with fresh peaches, peeled and cut in half.

At the time I said that I did not suppose I should ever see fresh peaches again. It was getting on to be the week before Christmas—1904, I should think. I had lost all count of time and cannot now re-capture those years. Then the doctor heard that my mother was reading all night to me. He forbade her to read to me later than ten. I had to face the thought that I should not any more go strolling down Fleet Street with the doctor rolling and muttering and fingering the post-tops. Perhaps still more I regretted that I might never again meet the fellow who said that he tried hard to be a philosopher but cheerfulness would come creeping in. I always imagined he must have been an ancestor of my own. I said: "That finishes it." To have to face nightly ten hours of sleepless agony was more than I could endure. I told the doctor that I was going back to London for Christmas. He said: "You will probably die if you do," and added that if I did not die, he would not again receive me amongst his patients. Even that consideration did not deter me.

When I got to London, Conrad begged me to see his family doctor—Tebb. I hope Tebb is still practising and may thus receive an advertisement that the Royal Medical Association would prevent his giving himself. He was the only doctor I ever heard of who always cured his patients at one sitting—or told them they were incurable. He nearly starved. I last heard of him during the War. He was managing a government hospital for consumptives.

He was the most mournful looking man I have ever imagined. He was thinner than seemed possible—thinner than myself! He wore extremely powerful glasses that dilated his eyes to extravagant dimensions. He could cure all his patients, but he had at home a child he could not cure. It was a most tragic story.

He came into the room where I lay. My uncle, William Rossetti, who was away from London, had lent me his house for the winter. I was lying on the sofa on which Shelley had passed the last night of his life. The room was a museum of Shelleyan and pre-Raphaelite relics. Tebb with his stethoscope in his top hat was like a ghost.

He sat beside me for more than two hours. He hardly spoke at all. Now and then he asked a question. It was as if his voice came from a tomb. My mind was full of finishing my life of Holbein that had been interrupted at Bâle. The *Wirklicher Sanitäts Rath* had told me that if I worked at it I should die. My mother had brought me out a copy of one of my books. It had seemed to me stupendous that I could ever have written a book. This one had been published just after the beginning of my illness and I had never seen it. It seemed to me that if I could write another book I should at least have justified my existence.

After Tebb had been silent for an hour and a half, I said:

"Doctor, I know I am going to die. Mayn't I finish a book I have begun?"

"What book?" he asked cavernously. I said it was a life of Holbein.

Half an hour afterwards he said:

"Yes, you may as well finish your life of Holbein if you have time. You will be dead in a month." He said it with a hollow and mournful vindictiveness that still rings in my ears. He told me to go to Winchelsea to do that work. If I was alive at the end of a month I could come and see him again. He went away, leaving no prescription.

As soon as he was gone I jumped up, dressed myself and all alone took a hansom to Piccadilly Circus. You are to remember that my chief trouble was that I imagined that I could not walk. Well, I walked backwards and forwards across the Circus for an hour and a half. I kept on saying: "Damn that brute, I will not be dead in a month." And walking across the Circus through the traffic was no joke. Motors are comparatively controllable but the traffic then was mostly horse-drawn and horses in motion are much more difficult to check than automobiles.

That afternoon—or almost immediately afterwards—I went down to Winchelsea. I was accompanied by Mr. Walter Jerrold, the grandson of Douglas of that name. Mr. Jerrold was a good and patient friend to me. He became annoyed with me because, afterwards, I did not offer him the sub-editorship of the *English Review*. I should have done so, but I thought he was too important and valuable a literary man to be offered a sub-editorship. I never saw him after that. There are many ways of losing friends.

In the company of Mr. Jerrold I all but finished the Holbein book down in the winter silence of Winchelsea. I still suffered a good deal from depression but as I could take a good deal of exercise I slept well. I ate hardly anything. One day in desperation I ate a hearty meal of ham and eggs. To my astonishment the depression temporarily disappeared. I did not then take the hint. But I plugged away stalwartly at Holbein. I was determined to justify my existence.... I may say that an artist who was reading the book only a week ago tells me that I shall not certainly be justified by that alone. That is probably true.

At the end of the month, I saw Tebb again. I said triumphantly:

"You see, I am not dead."

He answered as mournfully and hollowly as if he were in despair at the falsification of his prophecy:

"If I hadn't told you you would be dead, you would have been dead." He was no doubt right.

I am recounting this medical history for the benefit of poor souls who may be passing through similar experiences. So I hasten to say that from that day to this—except for the inevitable happenings of the late War—I have never spent a day in bed. Doctors have occasionally ordered me to and I have tried to obey but I never managed to get beyond four in the afternoon.

I have all my life been incapable of inaction. I could count on my fingers—on the fingers of one hand—the number of hours' rest, sitting in a chair, that I have taken this year. I must work. And I think no department of human labour below me. I would as soon wash dishes for the household as cook and as soon cook as read a book unless it be extraordinary —or a really ingenious detective story.

By analogy I suppose, I have the profound conviction that there is nothing I could not do if I tried—supposing it to be humanly possible. And, at that, if you really got it home to my conviction that I could not do something impossible, I should certainly have a try at it and be very mortified at failure. Of course, I am not good at higher mathematics.

I do not think I would even change the period of overwork in that London mausoleum of 1903. It cut two or three years out of my life, but I do not know what I should have done with them and it probably hardened my character. I had neither aims nor strong motives before that. I have had some since.

So, if I had to advise, I should say: "Work yourself all out, to the limit of your passion for activities. Then take what you get for it." Doctors will not advise you to do that; but doctors look for the large profits that come to them with quickish—but not too quick—returns. I broke down pretty badly after a period of fantastic overwork, but since then I have emerged pretty scatheless from periods of overwork. When I had the *English Review*, when I was interested simultaneously in the Suffragette Movement and in the Irish Theatre, when I worked in the army and at the same time wrote propaganda for both the French and British Governments, when I had the *Transatlantic Review* and simultaneously wrote a series of long novels about the War—all those were periods of really extreme strenuousness. They had, however, less attendant mental strain.

In 1903, as I have said, I used to breakfast very frequently with Mr. Galsworthy. I breakfasted indeed as frequently as he would let me. That was more for the mental relaxation than for the faultless and shining meals that come to me always as having taken place in sunlight falling through the rolled back door of his stable. But indeed to come in contact with the young man about London Town, with his moderate and easy views, his moderate, easy and perfectly appointed mode of life, his amiable insouciance and his kindly interest in all the arts—that was for me something remote and like a fairy tale. It has remained unique. I never knew at all well any other member of the English leisured class.

I broke my friendship with him—I daresay to his relief—over a public matter. It was a matter about which I have always been a little mad—the question of the humane slaughtering of cattle. Or rather it was the question of how to bring about in England legislation enforcing the humane slaughter of cattle over which we differed.

Just before the War I spent a good deal of time in

Belgium near the German frontier. There was then at Spa a queer, heavy, retired English lancer captain called Campbell. He was not otherwise distinguished by any great appearance of intelligence. But he deserves to be remembered and honoured along with St. Francis of the Birds—when the cattle at midnight on Christmas Eve talk from stall to stall and in the byres, surely they remember his name. He was the apostle of the four-footed dumb beasts.

It was impossible to understand how he did it. I toured with him a good deal of Belgium, notably in the Ardennes which is famous for its hams. He had practically no French, no Flemish, no signs. He was inarticulate even in his own tongue. But he carried a thermometer and a sort of blunderbuss. Exhibiting these with a series of grunts to the pig-slaughterers of the Ardennes, the ox-butchers of Flanders and the sheep-killers of the Walloon districts, he succeeded in getting all their suffrages for a bill in the Belgian Parliament. It made the slaughtering of cattle by as humane a process as is humanly possible obligatory in Belgium. He did this almost completely single-handed.

In, I think, 1913 I introduced him to C. F. G. Masterman, the Chancellor of the Duchy of Lancashire, who had been touring South Germany with me. He was looking for details of the German State Insurance Scheme in order to amend the measure of State Insurance that the Liberal Government were passing through the House of Commons. We had been up the Rhine, in Bavaria, in Metz, in Trêves and had finally arrived at Spa.

Masterman was at least as much impressed by Captain Campbell as I was. His extraordinary passion burning through a heavy and slow body was something hardly to be believed in. Masterman too made a tour of inspection of the model *abattoirs* that Campbell had induced the Ardennes ham-curers to erect. Eventually that Minister not only facilitated Campbell's return to England—Campbell had exhausted most of his resources in his campaign—but promised to give government support to a measure for humane slaughtering if Campbell could obtain in turn the support of British humanitarian societies.

Campbell came to England. I wrote a letter to the *Times* putting Campbell's arguments for him. The *Times* did not print it but the government organs did. Masterman lent Campbell someone—I suppose a drafter—to help him in preparing the bill. I then wrote to Mr. Galsworthy asking him to obtain the support of the various humane societies of which he was a distinguished member. Mr. Galsworthy replied that Captain Campbell would receive no support. His bill might even be opposed in Parliament by Societies like the Royal Society for the Prevention of Cruelty to Animals. Masterman then withdrew his promise of government support. The bill was dropped.

To understand this it is necessary to know a little of the English parliamentary system. A government bill stands or falls as a government stands or falls. Private measures depend for their passage on the introducers' being able to get behind them certain interests that may or may not be affected by the proposed legislation. I have only twice been interested in private bills in the English Parliament. On each occasion my interest arose from the sufferings of cattle. One was Captain Campbell's bill, the other a measure introduced by the parliamentary representatives of the Pharmaceutical Society. This aimed at preventing the sale of arsenical sheep-dips by unqualified persons. A packet of arsenical sheep-dip could be sold by any grocer or sweet-shop keeper. It contained enough arsenic to kill at least five thousand people. It cost a few cents. I had had a dog and cows poisoned at the Pent. They had drunk out of a rainwater butt in which the tenant farmer had mixed sheep-dip. The sight and still more the sound of those cattle dying in agony was so horrible that I swore I would leave no stone unturned in the effort to prevent the sale of the poison not only by, but to, uninstructed persons. The bill of the Pharmaceutical Society confining the sale to chemists was thrown out by the opposition of three interests in the

House of Commons. The sheep-dip manufacturers opposed it because it might limit the sale of sheep-dip; the doctors' representatives opposed it because they wanted the support of the railway interests for a bill for limiting the number of medical practitioners; the railway interests opposed it because they always acted in concert with the chemical manufacturers and finally the almost all-powerful License Victuallers' interests opposed it because they wanted the support of the railway, medical and chemical interests in opposition to a measure of local option that the government was proposing to introduce. So that bill was thrown out and cattle went on being poisoned by careless farmers.

I do not know exactly what political pull the humanitarian societies of Great Britain may have in Parliament. It must be fairly strong. Otherwise Masterman would not have withdrawn his promise of government support for Captain Campbell's measure. Almost miraculously the representatives of the butchers, stockbreeders and grazers who stand next to the publicans in political pull—those bucolic representatives who might be expected to do the stupid and cruel thing in such a situation—signified that they did not intend to oppose the bill. That was because Campbell had made the singular discovery that the flesh of an animal slaughtered humanely is in better condition and in consequence more valuable than the flesh of one that has been tortured before its death. With his thermometer he had been able to prove to the pork-butchers of the Ardennes and the calf-slaughterers of Flanders that the temperature of an animal that is tortured before death rises to such an extent that the animal is in a fever. The flesh of such enfevered animals is less firm and less easy to preserve than that of animals dying with normal temperatures. It is also relatively less fit for human consumption. The method of slaughter of calves in Belgium was as follows before Captain Campbell's pilgrimage through the Low Countries: The slaughterer would hang from sixty to a hundred calves up by one of their hind legs to a bar. He would then walk in a leisurely way down the line, cutting the tortured animals throats and pausing to re-light his pipe between each second or third calf. The pipe was supposed to be a preventive of the homicidal mania from which most slaughterers suffer before their own ends. Captain Campbell proved—I have seen him do it—that the temperature of the calf at the end of the line was frequently as high as 113° Fahrenheit before the butcher even reached it, whilst the lowest temperature of any of the animals was never less than 106°. On the other hand the temperature of a calf or other animal conducted without incidental brutality to a scientific slaughter-house, prevented from coming in contact with the smell of the blood of its fellows and stunned suddenly before being bled to death —the temperature of such an animal is seldom more than a degree or so above normal. Its flesh also is firmer and, in the case of calves or swine, whiter. Campbell proved to the Flemings and Walloons that the flesh of humanely slaughtered animals fetched from a halfpenny to twopence halfpenny— one to five cents—more than that of animals tortured before death.

There was a further aspect of the matter that used to drive me half mad when I thought of it in relation to England. In that country the great majority of slaughter-houses had no supervision of any sort. In one village in which I was interested the village butcher's shop abutted on the village infant school. Beasts were slaughtered by the butcher in his yard beneath the eyes of the school children who sat on the wall above. My attention was called to this—and to the whole horrible matter—by hearing a number of little girls crying in the playground when I passed. They were crying because they were too little to climb up the wall.

And there was no getting that changed. The school marm was too old and feeble to stop the children doing it. The school council were all farmers who thought, like Homais, that it did children good to be acquainted early in life with *les émotions fortes*. One farmer told me that he had seen every beast his father had sold slaughtered from the time he was eight till he had a farm of his own. And, he said, it had done him no harm. I could not allege that it had. He was quite a good man, as men go. But that children who in after life will normally have at their mercy generation on generation of dumb beasts bred for human food—that such children should from an early age be taught to find enjoyment on the sight of animal suffering... that seems to me a terrible thought.

Mr. Galsworthy's friends took the view that to prove to farmers and butchers that it paid to be humane was not the right way to go to work in securing humaneness. They said that that end must be secured educatively. The moral sense of butchers must be worked on so that freely and without constraint they had mercy on their victims.

I do not know how far Mr. Galsworthy endorsed these views. I was put into such a state by the part of his letter that stated that the Societies would not back the bill that I did not read—or have forgotten—the rest of it. The bill had to be dropped. There was no chance of its passing without government support. I argued for a whole week-end with Masterman, begging him to change his mind. But it was at a time when the government was in difficulties with its land policy. Mr. Lloyd George had just made his unfortunate speech about the starving farmer ruined because the wicked landlord's pheasants had eaten his mangold wurzels—a plant which, as I have said, the pheasant eschews. That speech made Masterman himself lose his seat for a rural constituency. He was at the time Mr. George's right-hand man and the High Street of the town which he sought to represent was entirely draped with mangold wurzels. It was, I think, Ipswich.

So the government did not want to be burdened with another topic which in the end mainly affected the agricultural community.

I passed a time of really considerable mental agony. At last I wrote to Mr. Galsworthy and said that I could never

see him again. And I never have, though he wrote to me a
kindly letter when I was in the Red Cross Hospital Number
Two in Rouen in 1916.

I had another curious difference with Mr. Galsworthy
about animals. At a time when he had just published one of
his books against English Country Society I met the editor of
an organ that represented that class of English individual. He
said that he was just going to review Mr. Galsworthy's book
and was going to abuse it at the top of his lungs. I said that
was rather a shame and, in the end, got him to let me review
the book for him. I wrote quite a nice review, alluding to
the charm of the style and sentiments and the amount of
knowledge that Mr. Galsworthy had gained from the study
of Turgenev. Then, as a sop to the poor editor, I put in a
mild protest. Mr. Galsworthy had spiritedly described a bat-
tue at a covert-side. Hundreds of beasts had been shot. At
the end of the chapter he made a poor little wounded rabbit,
when all the shooters and beaters had gone, creep out into the
twilight open to die. I pointed out that wounded rabbits never
came into the open to die but died in their buries. Mr. Galsworthy wrote to say: How silly of him. Of course he knew
that rabbits died in their buries. Another correspondent of
the paper wrote furiously to say that wherever rabbits died
they never did in their buries. A dying rabbit was always
turned out by its comrades in a natural fear of death or of
the infection of a corpse's decay. I duly made the note: How
silly it was of me not to have thought of that. Other corre-
spondents again wrote in to say that that was quite a mistake.
In digging out wounded rabbits or ferrets they had frequently
come on the skeletons or decaying corpses of other rabbits.
Altogether the editor came in for a great deal of free copy
and was pleased.

I suppose the truth about the deaths of rabbits varies.
I never myself dug out a dead rabbit though I have opened
a good many buries. And actually the dying rabbit, like most
other dying beasts, seeks to die in the shade of a bush and

in woodlands. But I suppose that if a rabbit is wounded and is a big, heavy animal that its comrades cannot eject, supposing it to have the strength to reach its hole, it will die there and the others will not be able to turn it out. In captivity a doe will usually eject its sick young from breeding boxes. Indeed most gregarious quadrupeds or birds will get rid of a sick comrade if they can. I remember at the Pent, Conrad's mare, Nancy—or it may have been an animal of my own— slipped into a brook and lay, belly upwards, kicking frantically. All the other horses in the field at once attacked it shewing every sign of indignation and terror, and as it was firmly wedged between the narrow brook banks we had the utmost difficulty in driving them off and getting it out. As soon as it was again on its feet the others ran up and smelt it and gave the usual signs of affection.

In any case I wish I could have again breakfasts like those Mr. Galsworthy used to give me—and not for the kippers, kidneys, sausages, soles and silver-ware alone! For it was rare in London then to find that *décor* and at the same time a love for Turgenev.... It is perhaps rarer nowadays to find either! ... I differed violently with my host as to the purposes, and, if not quite so violently as to the methods of the art that he was later to dominate in several continents. But one's differences in those days were merely the expression of enthusiasms. They come back to me as passing in the sunlight.

The shadow used to fall on me as soon as I left the Mews. Going back to my own house was like returning to a prison of illnesses and mental strains almost too heavy to be borne. And the pavement along the blank wall that supported the reservoir of the waterworks would be littered with hairpins. You can have no idea how that circumstance added to my depression.

Some time before I had come upon Zola seated on a public bench in Hyde Park. He had been gazing gloomily at the ground and poking the sand with the end of his cane. It had been at the time of his exile during the Dreyfus case

and no gloom could have ever been greater than his. He said
wearily: "What was one to think of a country where nurse-
maids dressed their hair so carelessly that he had found as
many as eighteen hairpins on one morning in front of one
park bench? A city so improvident must be doomed."

The memory of Zola so depressed me that merely to be
reminded of him by those hairpins was saddening. He had,
at any rate during that stay in London, so many phobias.
I remember riding with him in a hansom cab, conducting him
somewhere at the request of someone who had undertaken to
look after him but was prevented. I think it must have been
Mr. R. H. Sherard, whom I knew slightly at the time. I did
not much want to ride with Zola. I suppose I was the only
Englishman who differed from him as to the Dreyfus case, yet
he was so deeply miserable that it would have been unthinkable to argue with him. Nevertheless I felt the matter very
deeply. He said very little, taking it for granted that I knew
no French. But eventually I found that he was counting the
numbers on the registration plates of the cabs that were in
front of us. If the added digits came to nine—or possibly to
seven—he was momentarily elated; if they came to some in-
auspicious number—to thirteen I suppose—he would be pro-
longedly depressed. I supposed him to be thinking of the
Affaire and was not rendered any more gay.

He was very carefully looked after by various littérateurs
whilst he was in London, so he can hardly have had call to
depreciate the spirit of hospitality he found there. Its manner
I believe was less to his taste. He had a singular misadven-
ture in a house a few yards from the one I then inhabited on
Campden Hill. He was in some club and the editor of a famous
political journal of the Right said to him: "Ha, Zola, all
this visiting of Clubs gives you very little idea of England.
What you want is a taste of English home life." So he invited
the unfortunate Frenchman to take pot-luck with him one
evening and share a boiled leg of mutton and caper sauce.
To reach Campden Hill is a confusing affair for foreigners in

London. Zola set out about a quarter past seven and towards eight found himself in Camden Town, a poor quarter, nine miles or so from the lordly Hill—as if one should seek in Clichy or the Battery a house actually situate in Passy or Park Avenue. He reached Campden Hill about ten thirty. The house to which he was invited was in darkness and he spent more time in the shrubbery in the front garden. When he reached the front door he found it open and myopically entered the dark hall. He was normally very shortsighted and at the time was suffering from something like conjunctivitis, so that he had to wear black spectacles. Suddenly he was confronted by a lady in a yellow flannel bed-wrap, with her hair in curl-papers. She was on the landing above him and held over her head a flat candlestick. She called: "William! When are you coming to bed?"

Zola, who had lost himself in the dark hall, tried in confusion to escape from that apparition. He fell over a prostrate body. It was that of the editor. The editor had been consoling himself for the absence of his famous guest. He had gone down to the cellar to fetch another bottle and, reascending, had fallen over the top step of the kitchen stairs—in front of the garden door which was open. Zola therefore pitched down the garden steps. He had had more than enough of English family life.

I had had myself before my tenancy of the murderous house was up. But I had it from another angle. I have said that there is no department of human labour that I should be afraid or ashamed of tackling. That house made me prove it, on the domestic side of life's activities. It was one of those years when influenza—it was then called the Russian influenza—struck London as if with an immense hailstorm. That house, as if because it stood on a hill-top looking over a great part of the city, it struck as if with iron bullets. Member after member of my family went down, then the children's governess, then one by one of the servants except the cook, then the temporary servants and charwomen. No one was left on his feet except the hospital nurse I got in—she was an added flail!—the cook and myself. The cook, the nurse and I, ran the family meals. There was fortunately a sort of dumb-waiter hoisted by ropes that ran up several stories of the house. It made a rumbling like intoxicated thunder but would carry several trays of food at a time. Conrad came in to lunch every day because he was trying to work very hard in his lodgings round the corner. He could not eat English food cooked as he there found it. On the other hand he revelled in Johanna's cooking.

Johanna was an extraordinary personage from the hinterland of Hamburg. She exactly resembled Thackeray's caricatures of German peasants in *The Kickleburys on the Rhine*. If you had taken five balls of putty, rolled round in your hands as you used to do at school, and had stuck them together to represent trunk, arms and legs, and if you had taken a penny bun, stuck in two currants to represent eyes and painted the cheeks vermilion and varnished them, and if you had gummed a handful of unarranged straws on the back of the bun—then you would have had Johanna. I knew several German *platts* but she spoke in a series of loud, cheerful and animated grunts of which I never understood a syllable. She grinned perpetually except on the rare occasions—say once every six months—when she would run amok with a carving knife and barricade herself in the kitchen for twenty-four hours. There appeared to be no reason for these outbreaks. I suppose, like many Germans, she was of Celtic descent. Next morning she would open the kitchen door and appear with her usual grin.

So Johanna cooked, and, in the bowels of the earth, I washed up the plates and dishes when there was no charwoman. And we hauled that dumb-waiter up on its loud ropes like gnomes making thunder and hauled it down again with even greater labour until it reached the first floor. Then it would decide to crash down with a sound greater than that of the artillery during the first battle of the Somme. Then I would go up and lay the table in the dining-room and Johanna would cook for Conrad and me as we sat in state and discussed nice shades in sauce flavours. I do not think that Conrad ever noticed that anything was amiss—or at least unusual. He was much worried over *Nostromo*.

Then one day no voice from the kitchen answered mine in the speaking-tube. Johanna was lying face downwards on the kitchen table with her varnished scarlet cheeks in a great sieve of flour. She had been cooking against influenza for a fortnight. We used to have in those days a contraption with which, by spinning an arrow round a dial, you could call firemen, or cabs, or a doctor or ambulance. I spun it round and an ambulance turned up. The bearers said as they carried Johanna off that there were many houses like mine in London then. I could hardly believe it. London presented its usual grey and stolidly sane aspect.

I took up the cooking too then and Conrad noticed no difference as long as I imitated Johanna. But once I cooked a *civet de lièvre à la Parisienne*. That is not jugged hare as you have it in Anglo-Saxondom but has a sauce that is almost jet black with richness. Conrad inspected it as he always did, carefully and with his monocle screwed into his eye. He rubbed his hands and with enthusiasm unfolded his napkin. When, with head on one side and a look of pleased anticipation, he had tasted it, he started slightly. He said:

"My dear faller.... The admirable Johanna has of course surpassed herself.... But ... eh ... my gout! ... *Une telle succulence, mon cher....* Tebb says the greatest abstinence...." He added that ... if there remained a little of the admirable saddle of lamb of the night before ... a small slice, cold, with a leaf of salad....

I went down wearily into the kitchen, put the remains of lamb on the dumb-waiter, washed a lettuce and beat up some dressing.... I imitated Johanna from then on.

I was in addition doing double tides of writing. I had decided that I must do something of my own—I forget what it was—in order to defray the extra costs of that barrack.

And Conrad had to be constantly bolstered up, to dictate, to have passages written into *Nostromo*. It was at that time that I wrote the pages of *Nostromo* that Mr. Keating possesses. I also had the influenza.

CHAPTER IV

INTO DEPTHS

CONRAD, I think, was at that time my greatest cause for anxiety. As far as a man more than usually sane and practically wise can be temporarily unbalanced he was then unbalanced. He had of course great and many troubles. But the greatest were his detestation of the serial appearance of *Nostromo* in *T. P.'s Weekly* and his almost maniacal hatred of English as a medium for prose. He was ill himself; the illnesses of members of his family were causes for great anxiety; he was bitterly poor and forced to expenses altogether beyond his means. Those things he bore with great fortitude. The others caused him to be really unbalanced.

The passions into which he flew with inoffensive individuals over the publication left him gasping for breath and me trembling. I was never with him with third or more parties without going in dread that they would mention that unhappy series of agonised chapters. Merely to tell him that you admired the current instalment was enough. And the faintest suggestion that he was doing that work for money set him gesturing apoplectically. I remember a dinner at Mrs. W. K. Clifford's, and the memory still harrows me.

I stood to Mrs. Clifford a little in the relationship of a son. My father had been of great service to her after the death of Professor Clifford, and she was accustomed whenever she had any excuse at all to declare that he had saved her

life. So at her dinners, when I was invited I was told to take
the head of the table when the ladies went up to the drawing-
room. I wonder, do they still do that in London?

At that dinner the guests were Maurice Hewlett, Richard
Whiteing, one of H. M. Justices of the High Court, Conrad,
and myself. The Judge—I forget which it was; I think Lord
Darling—naturally had the right to lead the conversation.
As naturally he chose to talk about the easy way we writers
made money as opposed to members of the bar and judges.
On that subject Conrad could be politely instructive whilst
being deferential to a wearer of ermine. The Judge said that
he worked all day and most of the night, taking the shortest
of intervals for meals. When he left that table he would have
to go to his study at home and work till far into the small
hours preparing a judgment for delivery on the morrow. He
descanted on the anxiety that attended even on preparing
directions to the jury. By taking a wrong view a Judge might
ruin or endanger the life of an innocent party. The night
before a verdict in a murder trial he never slept. If he had to
deliver a death sentence, on the following night, after having
put on the black cap, he had to drug himself with veronal.

Conrad replied politely: The writer's work is never done;
if he is conscientious he thinks all day and all night of what
he shall say. Even during casual conversations and walks in
fields he is for ever turning phrases on his tongue. He will
pass whole nights awake thinking over a situation for treatment on the following day. And is his responsibility not far
greater than that of a Judge? By inconsiderate counsels or
wrong presentation of characters he may influence to their
ruin not one individual alone but a generation.

The Judge listened as politely as Conrad had done. I
daresay he was weighing that evidence. Hewlett, who was a
good fellow and a lean man of the world, with a dry, wry
face and a small twisted moustache, occasionally interjected
sounds of agreement. I saw a good deal of him in his beautiful
mediæval manor at Broad Chalke at a time when Hudson had

his hiding hole in the valley behind—the valley with the rook's nest. He was at the time a rival historical novelist, nevertheless I liked him very much and he supported my society with apparent resignation. I think he must have been very much more sincere in his historical novels than I and, in consequence, have done better work. With me the historical novel was always and almost of necessity a *tour de force*. I took historical characters, invested them with entirely modern psychologies and the appropriate trappings for which my once prodigious memory gave me great facility and so launched them on the world. That part of the world that consumed them seemed to find them very convincing. I was once told by a young man at the Record Office that he and some of his colleagues had read all my historical novels with minute attention and had failed to find any historical slips, wrong verbiage or sentiments that were anachronisms. All the notes I ever made for such a novel were contained on the backs of three or four visiting cards and then were only dates. For those things I have no head at all. So I was rather proud of my mnemonic feats.

But Hewlett was at great pains to study his periods minutely, to catch singular and characteristic phrases and to keep his characters well within their historic *cadres* in the matter of psychology. I think he loved the Middle Ages better than I. I was more interested in humanity. His *Little Novels of Italy* come back to me as passionate and remarkable. I hope they are still read. His *Queen's Quahir* came out in the same season as my most popular book. It had a similar name. We were thus subjected to all the minor vexations of being mixed up the one with the other. I felt no great annoyance. If he did he was vicariously avenged.

He had a son who greatly distinguished himself in an air-raid in the early days of the War. I think he dropped bombs on Cuxhaven or some other German port. As a reward he was given a job that spelt almost certain death. It was that of testing planes at the Severn Tunnel testing station. When I was sent up there for instruction in observing trenches, which was part of the education of an Intelligence Officer, it was he who took me up. He said as we stepped into the machine: "I have never been up in this old bus and a wing may drop off at any moment!" I passed the three quarters of an hour that ensued whilst he did stunts with that machine in an agony of dread. I have never since been able to enter or remain in an aeroplane without a return of that fear. I imagine that if he had not said that to me I should have been less cowardly. So, if his father needed revenge, he had it, for I had to go up several times after that.

On the occasion of that dinner at Mrs. Clifford's at least I had the greatest possible reason for gratitude to Hewlett. Conrad and the Judge were continuing to exchange polite generalisations. Suddenly Richard Whiteing burst in. He was a would-be bluff, white-haired septuagenarian...Scotsman, I think. For an immense number of years he had pursued a peaceable Grub Street career. He had written political articles of a Radical complexion for most of the Left weeklies and dailies. Then unexpectedly and at a very advanced age he had written a novel. *No. 5 John Street,* as far as I can remember it, was a romantic affair of poverties, loyalties, Bohemianisms in Bloomsbury and the like. It was a perfect honeycomb for dripping sentimentality. It met with extraordinary success and, for a season, Mr. Whiteing was a white-haired lion who roared prodigiously and with innocent gusta in literary drawing-rooms.

"Ho! Ho!" he burst in as Conrad was dilating on the sacred nature of the writer's calling, "That's all nonsense. We all write for money and nothing else. I write for money. You write for money. Hewlett does. You, Judge, write your rulings for money. What's the good of pretending anything else?"

Conrad had stopped as if a charge of buckshot had hit him.

I could not say now precisely how Conrad regarded this subject. I have heard him talk often enough of the misery of our profession—*le métier d'un chien,* the dog's life, with its solitude, its misgivings, its poverties. I know that at times he was intensely miserable at the thought that he, a Pole of aristocratic lineage, should have to use his pen for a living in a country where the arts are despised beyond all other human manifestations. And certainly for the ten years or so when I saw him daily he longed to go back to the sea though actually he hated the sea. He made several attempts to get a ship, but they always came to nothing.

Mr. Whiteing's outburst made him more than ever determined either to give up the calling of a writer or to leave the country for another. His dislike for the English mind and the English language which in those days was always near the surface became for a time, after that, almost intolerable. Fortunately, at Mrs. Clifford's the offensive brusqueness of Whiteing's attack was so gross as to leave Conrad for the moment breathless. He could not believe his ears. He screwed his eyeglass into his eye, poked his torpedo beard over the table and stared at that old man as if he had been a fabulous monster. His face became suffused with scarlet. He began:

"You mean to..."

But I had had time to whisper to Hewlett:

"Head him off, for heaven's sake," and myself addressed Whiteing with a volubility that must have been all the more singular because it was completely breathless. I don't know what I said. I had to save my hostess' beautiful glass, her admirable naperies and shaded candlesticks, and above all to stall off from that small dining-room that had known nothing but suavities, the profanation of a vulgar literary brawl. It was accomplished. Hewlett went on talking to Conrad, I to Whiteing. At last I heard my voice saying:

"Then is it your advice to me, a much younger writer, to write entirely for money? With no eye to anything else? No matter how vile or corrupting I may think the stuff I have to write in order to make money?"

The old man humped himself in his chair and said angrily:

"Of course I don't mean anything of the sort."

But the rest of the table was peaceful, the Judge, Hewlett and Conrad having got to talking about the old *cause célèbre* of the smashing of the Portland vase. The Judge collected Greek and Etruscan pottery...I felt I could suggest that we join the ladies. The situation was saved.

But the mental strain on myself had been very great. It continued for a long time, Conrad growing mentally and physically always sicker. He used to come in in the mornings and, having climbed the many stairs to my small, dreadful study, would sit for hours motionless and numb with a completely expressionless face. Every now and then he would say:

"I can't do it. It can't be done. *Je suis foûtu!*" Then he would launch out into a frightful diatribe against the English language. It was a language for dogs and horses. It was incapable of conveying human thoughts. He had given up the attempt. For good. The damn paper must go without its damn serial. Who would care? No one.

I would stand in the window, looking right over London: a grey expanse with sparkling points. From there—in the middle west—one could see Greenwich Observatory in the extreme east. It was looking over that view that I first told Conrad the story that he turned into *The Secret Agent*.

But in those moments I would have a perfectly vacant mind. It just stopped. There was really nothing to say. English is not a good language for prose. You cannot make a direct statement in literary English. At any rate in those days you could not and I doubt if you can now—in English English. In American English you almost can, but you shock elegant ears. Conrad's English, however, was literary. I had nothing with which to console him.

He would declare that he had written the last word of that serial. I would manœuvre him towards writing as the drake manœuvres the sitting duck back to the nest when she has abandoned her eggs. I would read over his last sentence to him. If it provoked no beginnings on his part I would dis-

place him at the desk and write a sentence or two. There
are five words that seem horrible to me.   They are "the silver
of the mine." That was the title of the part of *Nostromo* over
which we then wrestled.

He would groan:

"No, it's no use. I'm going to France. I tell you I am
going to set up as a French writer. French is a language; it is
not a collection of grunted sounds."

I would say:

"*Nostromo* would go admirably in French. Let us get it
blocked out. Then you could re-write it very easily in French."

The hospital nurse would come in:

"Now, Mr. Ford it is time you got back to bed again."
I would have been up an hour.

Conrad liked the society of that nurse. Inscrutably. She
was a flail. She had a face like a cockney camel. There poured
out of it incessantly words that I hardly understood. Conrad
however did. He had served before the mast with cockney
deckhands. He would ask her how the other patients were.
That would give her an excuse to get going.

"Last peetient I 'ad wus Lord Northcliffe. Hoperishun
on 'is leg! Lie in bed 'e would wiv the telephone on 'is chess.
Sweer into the telephone 'e would. Sweer ... somethin' awful
... Sweer w'en hi chinged im ... oh terrible! Sweer at the
pines an' then onto the telephone. At the *Dily Mile* ... Sech
lengwidge. Houtrageous. Then wen hi was going: 'Nurse,' 'e
sez to me, Nurse ... Whenever you 'ear men speak against me
you will say: 'He bore his illness like a Christian and a gentleman.' ... Peetient bifor that was an old maid ... bifor er
they 'ad swingin doors. Between the quality staircase and the
servants. ... Green b'ize ..."

She had been standing on the top landing of the house.
A servant let the green baize door swing against her. It had
precipitated her down several flights of stone stairs. She
lay at the bottom with her skull smashed and her brains
protruding. The servants put sheets of newspaper under her

head. They wanted to protect their mistress's stair carpets. When the surgeon came he could read the imprint of the paper on her brain—an account of the dispersal of the works of art from the collection of the Hon. Matthew L. Oldroyd.

That was her story—one of hundreds. Of thousands, perhaps. Her appearance used to drive me frantic. It meant that Conrad would not get to work for hours. Neither could I. I need a certain period of quiet before words will come.

I would slip away downstairs and dust the dining-room against lunch. When I returned, Conrad would be writing contentedly at my desk. The nurse with her lack-lustre eyes and untidy strands of hair hanging from beneath her cap was detrimental to all her patients. Conrad she seemed to stimulate. He would listen to her singular tarradiddles for hours with an expression of the utmost interest and deference. Perhaps *Nostromo* would never have got itself written but for her. Or perhaps Conrad's next book would have borne a Parisian imprint.

His dislike of England acted as a powerful depressant on me. I took the view that, for good or ill, we must write English and in England. If then the public and the critics were as dense as he declared in his passionate outbursts, what chance was there for us? I certainly shared his view, but it was as if I could not bear to hear my own view confirmed. We were once at a music-hall. I used to like music-halls myself. They took for me the place of the cafés one for ever misses when one is out of Paris or the French provinces. You can sometimes see there remarkable pieces of juggling which I very much enjoy. Occasionally there will be a good singer. When there is nothing to claim your attention on the stage you can talk to your neighbour, read a newspaper or even correct proofs. Conrad did not much share my tastes, but he went with me now and then. On this occasion the visit was not a success. The principal turn was by a lion comique of considerable notoriety. He was dressed as a miserable charwoman with a red nose, weeping eyes and straggling red locks.

He described how when young he had been seduced by a lodger, had several children by him; was deserted, went on the streets, took to gin and now did charing.

The house rocked and roared with laughter—an immense house: the old Empire, I think. It was almost impossible to hear the mincing comedian for the laughter. Between two verses, Conrad turned to me and said:

"Doesn't one in spite of everything feel a stranger in this beastly country?" That was just what I had been thinking. But, as I have said, it depressed me to have my thoughts so exactly confirmed.

I daresay London is changed. Perhaps there are nowadays no wretched tweenies and miserable old people to form the staple butt of her humour. Certainly the Empire of Leicester Square is not what it was. But in those days the black and bitterly cruel note of English humour might well make two novelists of foreign extractions and of perhaps too high sensibilities despair that their particular note could ever make itself penetrate through those gross roars. They made an immense building reel above its foundations. It was too much. The crash came soon afterwards.

I opened my front door with my latchkey one day and met my eldest daughter coming downstairs with her hair and clothing on fire. I put the flames out and, as they had been streaming behind her, she was not hurt. She said that, as she had done nothing to hurt the fire-fairies, she could not see why the fire-fairies should hurt her. So she had no mental disturbance.

The education of children is one of the few subjects on which I have no settled opinion whatever. I do not see how anybody can have.

Admirable theorists from Solomon downwards have from time to time convinced the public that various eccentricities in the upbringing of children will lead to the salvation of the republic. But, as these theories can only be arrived at in old age, the theorists never see the results of their tuitions. For

myself I incline to think a child's education should follow
in petto the history of the education of mankind. It should
be taught to believe implicitly in fairies until it outgrows that
belief naturally. Then it should be carefully instructed in one
or other of the forms of revealed religion, the instruction being
exact and absolutely orthodox to whatever the form may be.
For the child's good, the form should be that of the majority
of the inhabitants of the country in which the child is born.
Or it should be in a form avowed by a minority sufficiently
large to be able to take care of itself. A sense of persecution
is bad for a child's mental development as a rule.

After that, it simply remains a matter of whether a child
does or does not jump off from revealed religion. If it does,
the jump should be as clean as possible. That is why I should
advocate all children being brought up as implicit Roman
Catholics. If you disbelieve any article of the Roman form
of faith your whole faith falls. That is a good thing if you are
fated not to continue in a form of belief. Protestantism is a
continual and gradual refining away of beliefs. You refuse
to believe in the Immaculate Conception, but, for the time
being, believe in the Virgin Birth. Then you find yourself no
longer believing in the Virgin Birth but believing still in the
Divine Origin and the Holy Trinity. Then you no longer believe in the Divine Origin but in Divine inspiration. So you
whittle away and your thought has a continued timidity. I am
inclined to believe that the happiest—and even the best—
members of a society are those who retain their religious
beliefs intact. But I am certain that only harm can come
from want of clarity in thought or of courage to face the
issues. And I am equally certain that such religious instruction as a child has should be authorised by parents or the
State. Otherwise the child will for certain come in contact with
the most odious, ignorant and bigoted forms of revelation.
I had a friend who—in the days when it was the fashion to
bring up children in militant atheism—rigorously enacted that
his children should have no religious instruction whatever.

The servants, the elder members of his family, his friends were all forbidden so much as to mention the Deity. One day he stopped outside the open bedroom door of his nightnursery. He heard the eldest little girl say: "They say God is everywhere." All the children answered in chorus: "Yes, God is everywhere." The first child said: "Is God in the cupboard?" The second answered: "I don't know. But if you hold my hand I will see." The servants had been attending to those children. Servants will, forbid how resolutely you may. Then your children will be estranged from you to the extent of having secrets.

Unacknowledged superstitions are even more difficult to deal with. I have always been superstitious myself and so remain—impenitently. Each month at the turn of the moon I go to great trouble not to see the new moon through glass and I prefer to be in a house that does not face towards the west. Nothing will make me go under a ladder. I cannot bear to sit in a room with three candles or to bring snowdrops, may or marigolds indoors.

That is not foolish. An ill omen will depress you. However little it may depress you, it will do so. It is bad to be depressed. Nor can you stand absolutely unmoved against the tides of human opinion. The most rationalist of human beings does not pass his life without saying: "I am in luck today!" It is as irrational to believe in good luck as to believe in shrouds in a guttering candle. The doctrine of chances will tell you that there is no greater chance—and no less chance—of fortunate events following each other in a sequence than of unfortunate events alternating with others. Yet you *know* that fortunate and unfortunate ones do follow one another in sequences. The doctrine of chances is none the less not at fault. It is operating in an atmosphere of loaded dice.

When you feel you are passing a lucky day you will be resolute, keen, active, awake to proper courses to pursue. You ensure luck. When you are depressed by ill omens you are less resolute, you are despondent in the degree however small the weight you attach to the beliefs of your fellow-man. You give your dice a bias towards the lower numbers. I have found this again and again. The longest and most disastrous runs of ill-luck in my life have followed the one on the presentation of an immense opal to a member of my household; the other on a lady who was driving with me and others in a closed automobile exclaiming in an open space in Harlem: "Look at that immense crescent!" She was indicating the new moon which in consequence I saw through the front glass.

From that day for a long time—indeed until about a year ago—I experienced nothing but disaster: in finances, in health, in peace of mind, in ability to work. It was a run of ill luck similar to that, a quarter of a century ago, that attended on the acquisition of that large opal.

That was followed by every imaginable and unimaginable disaster. Improbable illnesses, unreasonable breakages of limbs, financial losses in affairs that seemed as stable as the Bank of England and a similar falling off in ability to work. At last it landed me in that improbably murderous house on Campden Hill.

I finally disposed of it with as many rites as I could think of.

To wash off the ill luck attendant on the possession of opals, it is necessary to give them away. A sale is not always efficacious. To give one away is to pass on the ill luck to a friend. That, in this case, I was not disposed to do. Neither was I prepared to sell it and pass on the ill luck to an innocent and unsuspecting jeweller. There remained the one alternative of throwing it into running water. Witchcraft, ill luck and the supernaturally disagreeable in general cannot operate through, and sometimes not even across, running water. Immediately after the accident to my daughter I determined in that way to dispose of that stone. But running water is not easy to find. The nearest of which I could think was the Thames. I put the stone in my pocket and set out for Hammersmith Bridge.

At once an indescribable lassitude fell on me. I was

almost unable to drag my legs along and quite incapable of getting to the Thames. I thought of dropping the opal down a gutter grating. Sewer and flood water is disagreeable, but at least it runs. But near every grating that I passed in returning, a large policeman was stationed. It was not to be thought of to drop a large opal in a ring down a sewer in presence of a policeman. He would be sure to think I was disposing of stolen property.

I got home and found that a large hole had been burned in the revers of my dress suit. I was going to a dinner and then to a concert given by a sister of Mr. Galsworthy, who was a leader in the musical society of that day. I had to borrow a dress coat from that unfortunate friend who can hardly have been able to wear it again. My circumference must have been twice his.

Next morning, in an interval of sweeping out the triangular drawing-room, I looked out of the gloomy window. It commanded views not only up and down Campden Hill Road but right down a long street called Bedford Gardens. Some nuns were going in and out of the garden gates of that street. They were Little Sisters of the Poor, begging.

I sat down at once and wrote to the Mother Superior of a convent of that order that was not far away. I told her the history of the opal and asked if she would have the courage to accept the stone for her poor. She accepted with enthusiasm and added the charming sentence: "Be sure the running water of your charity will ward off any ill luck from the purchaser I may find as well as from yourself."

Alas! I don't know how it may have been with the purchaser. But as to myself: I immediately wrapped the stone up and took it to the nearest post office. I handed it to the young woman in charge of registrations with an immense sigh of relief. Alas again! I had no sooner turned the corner of the post office than I found myself almost completely unable to walk. Campden Hill Road assumed an aspect as steep as the side of the Righi. I could hardly drag my feet along. There began the long illness of which I have already written.

Now I am not going to allege that the large crescent of the moon that I saw through the automobile actually caused the Wall Street crash that has been the cause of most of our troubles since then. And I am not anxious to make you believe that it was the opal that made Conrad arrive at the hatred of the English language that was at the root of most of my troubles on Campden Hill. But I am perfectly certain that the thought of both those portentous objects did from time to time interfere with the keenness of my thoughts and in consequence with my efficiency. I know this. Almost immediately after seeing that orange luminary two distinguished surgeons misdiagnosed a small swelling caused by the bite of an insect. They declared that it was a terrible and mortal complaint and insisted on operating at once. I retained even then the strength of mind to resist them but I know that the remembrance of the orange crescent over Harlem immensely depressed me at that moment. It rendered me incapable of working for a number of months during which it was very necessary that I should work. And almost every determination I arrived at during that period turned out in the event to be disastrous and always, whilst arriving at those determinations, I was certain in my subconscious mind that I was making a mistake. The stars in their courses were against me.

There is another aspect in the matter. A novelist had better share the superstitions of, than high-hat, humanity. He will thus more understand his matter. I remember once dreadfully shocking Mr. Edward Garnett. It was at the time when Limpsfield was disturbed by my wearing a cloth cap. I said it was my ambition to pass unobserved in a crowd. Mr. Garnett never forgot that. Years after he cited it against me as a proof of my bourgeois nature.

And indeed it is so. Yet the novelist must pass unobserved in a crowd if he himself is to observe. And the crowd is his clay; of his observations of it he will build his monuments to humanity. The social reformer may—and usually does—render himself conspicuous by singular garments that express his singular personality. It does not matter how humanity reacts towards him. He can make capital out of persecution.

But the first thing the novelist has to learn is self-efface-ment—that first and that always. Not for him flowing locks, sombreros, flaming ties, eccentric pants. If he gets himself up like a poet, humanity will act towards him as if he were a poet ... disagreeably. That would not matter were it not that he will see humanity under a false aspect. Then his books will be wrong.

His effort should be to be at one with his material. With-out that he will not understand its emotions and reactions. Superstitions, belief in luck, premonitions, play a great part in human motives. A novelist who does not to some extent enter into those feelings can hardly understand and will cer-tainly be unable to render to perfection most human affairs. Yes, you must sacrifice yourself. You must deny yourself the pleasure of saying to your weaker brothers and sisters: "Haw! No superstitions about me." Indeed you must deny yourself the pleasure of high-hatting anybody about anything. You must live merrily and trust to good letters. Besides, super-stitions will come creeping in.

I was one night at the house of Mr. Edward Clodd at Aldeburgh, in Sussex, on the sea-shore. There were present, besides Mr. Clodd, Thomas Hardy, Mr. Hilaire Belloc, Mrs. Belloc Lowndes, some more novelists, and Professor Gilbert Murray. Mr. Clodd had been one of those who, with Huxley, Bradlaugh, Foote the atheist, Ingersoll and others, had, in the eighties of the last century, destroyed revealed religion. The night was airless. On the black squares that the windows made, the lights of solitary fishing boats hung themselves out. As was natural the talk fell on religion.

Thomas Hardy avowed himself a believing communicant of the Established Church, Hilaire Belloc, his sister and other novelists were Papists. Professor Murray had some sort of patent faith of which all I can remember is that a black velvet coffin played some part in it. Some other form of spiritualism was also represented.

At last, valiant old Mr. Clodd threw his hands up above his white hair.

"Was it for this," he exclaimed tragically, "that we fought and overcame the priests in the eighties? You would think we had never lived. Here is a collection of the representative thinkers of Great Britain. Every one of them has his form of mumbo-jumbo. The old devils have all come creeping back and brought worse with them!"

After that Thomas Hardy told us the story of Wild Darrell.

I owe it to New York that the last vestiges of my depressions of twenty-five years ago left me for good. That occurred suddenly in the Players' Club on Gramercy Park in October, 1906.

After Dr. Tebb's summary treatment of my case I had no longer any doubts as to my ability to walk. But I remained appallingly hypochondriacal as to diet. The admirable and long-suffering Tebb took me into his house and saw to it that I ate everything that was set before me and that in considerable quantities. If I asked him for a dietary schedule, he used to grunt contemptuously: "If you think things will hurt you, they will hurt you. If you don't, they won't." He said the same as to liquor and tobacco. And, as long as I was under his eye, I behaved like any one else.

But let me merely go out to lunch with anyone and I would make a meal off three grains of rice and a handful of pepsin tablets washed down with water. And suffer agonies of indigestion. On the *Kaiserin Augusta Victoria* the menu sheet must daily have included at least three hundred dishes. Somewhere off the Banks there appeared on the eastward horizon a plume of smoke. It overtook us as a greyhound overtakes a fat spaniel in a forty acre field. It was the *Campania*. She passed us quite close and our passengers aligned themselves along the rail and shouted:

"Ohjé! We haf ze pedder grub!" I remember how devoutly I wished that I was on the British boat. They would there know how to make thin, dry toast. Often out of the three hundred items of our menu there would be not a single thing that I dared eat and I would get up from table starving. I had also no pepsin tablets and the German doctor had none in his dispensary.

Tebb invented one of the most ingenious lies about me that I have ever heard. He said that whilst I was stopping with him, at breakfast, I would mark my place in his priceless first editions and incredibly sumptuous large-paper copies with a slice of bacon. He had a remarkable collection of Odilon Redons. I have often wondered why he did not allege that I used to cut them out of their frames and use them for patching my riding breeches.

I rode a great deal in those days. Tebb had the theory that to become strong-willed one should control physically something stronger than oneself. He insisted therefore that I should ride disagreeable beasts with hard mouths. That afforded me an instance of how minutely one is watched in London. In those vastnesses one has the impression of being infinitely alone. When you get out of the Paris train at Charing Cross, it feels as if you sank down like a plummet into dim depths and were at once lost to sight. But one day I was riding in the Row a coffin-headed, enormous, clumsy beast with a horrible pace. I dropped my crop and had some difficulty in re-mounting after I had picked it up, the place being solitary in the early morning before breakfast and no one in sight to give it me. The animal backed away and I could not get onto him until I had his stern against the railings.

That evening I was dancing with a young woman whom I did not know and who, as far as I knew, knew nothing about me. It was in a Park Lane mansion that no book seemed ever to have entered. She said:

"You dropped your crop in the Row this morning."

I asked her how she knew. She only said she knew. I accused her of not even knowing my name and she said that was true too. Some time afterwards I got out of her that her old nurse who was still looking after her younger brother and sister had been crossing the Row that morning. She had seen me going up the stairs to the drawing-room before dinner and had told that young woman about my dropped crop whilst buttoning her frock.

No, I imagine that, in spite of the theories of detective writers, it is difficult to disappear in London. I was accosted in Soho, about that time, by a Frenchman who said he had known me as a student in Paris. I dimly remembered him and he told me a hard-luck story of being starving in London and anxious to return to France. I found I had no money in my pocket. I told him to come up to Tebb's that evening and I would telephone to Cook's to send up a ticket for the night boat to Paris. When I had left him, I found that I had forgotten to give him my address. I was annoyed because, as far as I could remember, he had been rather a good designer and I believed his story to be true. He had been induced to come to London by a fraudulent agency that had taken a large commission from him for finding him a highly paid job as drawing master—in a non-existent school in the Midlands.

I finally went to the police-station nearest to Tebb's house in Hampstead and explained the matter to the sergeant in charge. The London police are always anxious to get penniless people out of London. They will on occasion lend you your fare home if you find yourself accidentally without money in that city. So the sergeant at once started to telephone to Soho. All I could remember of the man was that he was thin and was wearing a bow-tie of green and white vertical stripes.

The police had him on Tebb's doorstep within two hours— in quite good time to catch the Paris train. He afterwards opened a life-class in Paris. It is still well-attended by English amateur painters, mostly of astonishingly advanced ages.

I have come across so many cases in which a little relief at odd moments has set destitute men on their feet that I have very little hesitation in advocating almost indiscriminate charity even where the donor's purpose is utilitarian rather than the self-satisfaction of giving relief. Remembering back, as I am doing at this moment, I seem to call to mind a whole legion of down-and-outers. Someone or other helped them and they afterwards did good work. They were mostly artists of one kind or another. I suppose the artist is more likely to know poverty and can know it with less despair or loss of self-respect than the layman.

I remember finding a man lying in the church square at Winchelsea. He had, beside him, an Amati violin of extraordinary beauty and consequently of great value. He was completely penniless and had fainted from hunger. I got the people of the inn to house him for a couple of days. He proved to be extraordinarily sanguine, uncowed and entertaining. He was a most beautiful violinist and an organist of great reputation.

He had come to London in July with the idea of giving a series of violin recitals. That, of course, was madness but he was a man of less knowledge of the world than was imaginable. He was not without resources in his own country. But that was somewhere in Middle-Eastern Europe and he had had no idea of how to touch it in London. The hotel at which he had stopped had seized all his luggage for non-payment of his bill after his money had run out. The few people to whom he had had letters of introduction had all been out of town. He had set out to walk home—to Central Europe.

I lent him the money to get as far as Paris, where he said he had plenty of friends, and I helped him to send a telegram to his home town, asking that supplies should be sent to him at Paris. A little later he repaid me; a little later I had the programme of a concert he was giving in Paris; then enthusiastic press-notices. Then, a good deal later, he let me know that he had been appointed a professor at the Conservatoire. He turned out several famous pupils before his death.

I had a similar contact with a similar affair. It ended, however, tragically and was the most inexplicable occurrence with which I ever had any connection.

I was walking along the Rye Road from Winchelsea one very hot day. A long way ahead of me, over the streaming waves of heat that distorted the view, there was hopping along a queer black object. As I came up with it, it assumed the aspect of the back of a very small man in disproportionately long-tailed evening dress. He said to me without preamble:

"*Leihen Sie mir fünf Mark.*" "Lend me five marks."

He appeared cheerful but distracted.

He was the son of a *Zucker-Bäcker*—a confectioner and candy maker who was also a Court actor to the Grand Duke of Sachsen-Weimar. The *Zucker-Bäcker* had brought up his son to his two professions. He made the young man wait in his restaurant by day and act as super in the Grand Ducal theatre at night. The son detested both occupations. He had saved a little money and started off for New York where there are golden side-walks and diamonds as big as pigeon's eggs in every garbage pail. As he was going onto the steamer at Liverpool, he had his pocket picked. He lost not only his ticket but all his money. The ticket did not so much matter. But in those days you had to be able to shew $50 or you could not land in America. The shipping people turned him back.

He pawned the contents of his valise and—he too—determined to walk home. Someone told him that the German Consul at Dover would pay his passage from there to Hamburg. From Liverpool to Dover is, I suppose, five hundred miles. He must have made it longer for he had certainly been to Southampton and Brighton. He said he had met with a good deal of kindness on the road. One gentleman had asked him into his house and given him wine. I gathered nevertheless that it had been a pretty terrible experience—for most of the time in the worst heat wave England had known for a long time. His only pride was in the retention of his evening dress. He called it his uniform. A German waiter, he said, would part with everything else before parting with that.

He wanted me to give him five marks so that he could take the train to Dover and he promised that, if I would give him my address, he would return the money to me.

I took him into Rye, gave him a good square meal, took his ticket for him and gave him enough for a night's lodging in Dover. I saw him off, curled up in the corner of a railway carriage and already asleep. He struck me as being a little mad in spite of his cheerfulness. I did not give him my address because there was at that time in London a German-Alsatian-Swiss waiters' club whose members gave me a good deal of trouble by begging from me and asserting that they knew members of my family in Paris, or Alsace, and I did not want my country address to reach them. So I never expected to hear of him again.

Years after, I was staying in a town about twenty miles from Frankfort. I had gone into the city for the opera and after it was over had to wait half an hour for my train to the other town. I ordered a cup of coffee and read a newspaper. The waiter came, as I supposed, for his money. Instead I heard the sound of coins on the marble table-top and a voice said:

"That makes four marks seventy-five that I owe you."

It was my waiter of the Rye Road. He had got safely back to Hamburg. He had resumed his profession and had risen high. He was now second head-waiter at Frankfort Station restaurant—a position of great honour in the Empire of table attendants. He was earning large sums of money, had a beautiful apartment, a lovely *hausfrau* and three blooming children. His emotions at seeing me were almost ecstatic. He called me his benefactor, asked the other waiters to come and view the man of whom he had so often spoken, implored me to visit his home. The one thing wanting to complete his happiness had been the repayment of his debt to me.

The dreadful sequel was this:

I went back to the town where I was staying. Next day at

lunchtime I read in the third or fourth edition of the *Frank-furter Zeitung* that that man had gone straight home after seeing me and had cut the throats of his wife, his children and himself.

There was no explanation. The police reported that he was an admirable father of a family, had no entanglements, a substantial sum on deposit in his bank, was industrious, sober, honest and in every way to be looked up to. The only imaginable reason might have been that he had suffered more intolerable mental agony on his long pilgrimage through England than any one had any idea of. The sudden sight of myself may have recalled to him emotions too terrible to bear even in the recollection. And having paid his debt, he may have considered himself at liberty to depart from a world of insufferable memories.

It was, as I have said, in 1906 that I met Mr. Gilbert Hare in the Players' Club in Gramercy Park. It was during that visit that I first considered New York seriously. It was characteristic that twenty-five years ago one did not consider the United States herself very seriously. She presented the aspect of a raft hung in space, inhabited by ninety million inhabitants who did not matter. New York before that had been a place through which one passed as rapidly as possible to reach the Old South. The Old South perhaps mattered in my green salad days. It had traditions, courtesies, old houses. Even Philadelphia mattered. She had red brick houses with, before them, white marble mounting blocks. It was aristocratic to suggest riding and the etiquette of card-leaving and calling or refusing to call was strictly observed in the surrounding country. Boston was rather funny and disagreeably serious. The Hill was in every way a replica of the intellectual suburb of Hampstead in London. You could not take its red brick sidewalks very seriously, but it did. Lowells spoke only to Cabots and Cabots only to the Almighty —but the names of neither Lowells nor Cabots conveyed anything at all.

But New York.... One heard its inhabitants call it little and old. One saw that it was quite little and undoubtedly old. If Gramercy Park or Washington Square had been in Charles-

ton or New Orleans, one would have taken them very seriously
indeed as monuments. But one went on.

By 1906, however, something of what Gotham was going
to become was beginning to manifest itself. She was still more
like London than any city outside London—and indeed she still
is. There was about her—and particularly about her old families, a staid old-fashionedness and a personal individualism
that you would not have found even in London. It was the note
almost of Dickens. It would not have astonished you to find in
Washington Square society in 1906 the Cheeryble Brothers. It
would have astonished you if you had ever found them in London. Broadway was already the Great White Way—but with
what a dim whiteness. In Newport, R. I., that year, New York
women with names advertised by new millions dined and went
to the opera with sucking pigs under their arms. Their palaces
along Ocean Drive were exact reproductions of the British
Museum in pink marble. These abutted on lawns without wall
or hedge, on stone for stone and tile for tile replicas of Haddon
Hall. They were New Yorkers, but of the new fashion. In the
bulk, New Yorkers remained the inhabitants of something little
and old. They set out in one horse broughams from brown stone
houses in East Fourteenth Street or took the three horse stage
up Fifth Avenue. The Flat Iron building, just run up, was at
once the cynosure and the scandal of Christendom. And very
beautiful it used to look, towering up, slim and ivory white
when you saw it from the Fifth Avenue stage or from on top
of a trolley descending Broadway.

But in spite of that sky-scraper, the light-signs on Broadway and the scandals that the younger members of the Four
Hundred families caused in remote New England, it was still
only in remote New England that they caused scandals. What
they did in Newport, they were hardly even beginning to do
in New York. The note of the dominant Gotham city father
was still staidness. The younger set might act the road-hog in
automobiles, but their severe sires in high hats with mourning
bands drove in landaus and pairs from their mansions on Staten

Island to the ferry. At the Battery they would be met by other carriages and be conveyed to Wall Street or its neighbourhood in an attitude of awfulness that much resembled that of my relative Mr. Justice Ford North of the Court of Chancery. He was the last of Her Majesty's judges to carry out the once universal habit of going on horseback to the Royal Courts of Justice. Mr. Justice North had to be translated from the more active courts of criminal jurisdiction because he sentenced Foote, the atheist, to penal servitude for life. Foote had stated in print that he did not believe in a Deity and Mr. Justice North had found an old statute that justified his inflicting that penalty for that crime.

I fancy the older inhabitants of Staten Island at the beginning of the century would have sentenced Foote to death. I visited quite lately the mansion of one of my deceased American uncles, a forty-niner who eventually settled on Staten Island. It was a mansion that resembled for all the world the residences of London Aldermen and those who have "passed the chair." There were the hothouses, the stables, the "sweep" or horseshoe-shaped carriage-drive. My aunt used to wave from the stoop or verandah to her husband as he stood on the ferry making the dangerous transit to Manhattan. My uncle was a top-hatted "character," all his friends were top-hatted characters, and New York itself was a city of characters just like the London of Mr. Pickwick. There were notorious barbers, bootblacks, restaurateurs like Mouquin, waiters full of quaint humour, actors, literati, divines, millionaires—and all were well known by sight to all New York. In 1906 you could see people on the sidewalks. You could recognise Mr. John Drew, or Richard Mansfield, or Blanche Bates, or W. D. Howells in his white ducks, from a distance of a quarter of a mile up Fifth Avenue. You saw all New York not only at the Players' Club but also at five o'clock in the tea-shop at the corner of Fifth Avenue and East Twenty-seventh Street. I have seen Mr. Poulteney Bigelow at that time New York's star international reporter and intimate of the German Emperor having tea outside the Waldorf-Astoria with Mrs. Lily Langtry and, I think, Mark Twain. They were on the sidewalk behind a privet hedge in green boxes for all the world as if it had been Paris.

And most of New York's fixings were little and, as it were, domestic. The hermetically sealed office note was still wanting in the great majority of offices when I first trod the streets of God's Own Country (Western Division) as opposed to God's Country (England). Naturally my first action was to go down town on a horse-trolley through the Dickensian landscape. I clung precariously to its hind-brake. You really did that in New York of those—ah, so distant, days! You desired to travel by one of those always packed vehicles. You stood far out in the roadway and extended a hand, displaying in its palm a dime. That was a lot of money in those days. If the driver deigned to slacken his pace for you to make a grab at any portion of the vehicle the dime became his.

I was going to a down-town bank to change some money. The bank was like a drawing-room. It was carpeted with great Oriental rugs and warmed by what appeared to be an immense wood-stove. I daresay it really burned anthracite. Beside it stood two gentlemen picking their teeth. They wore perfectly elegant costumes. From time to time they conversed. A quarter of an hour passed. I ventured to "hem!" slightly. One of them strolled, still using his toothpick, over to an isolated counter of unimaginably polished mahogany. He looked sceptically at my letter of credit, initialled it. He opened a drawer beneath the rear of the counter, slammed some notes down before me and then without a word returned to the stove. It was just before lunch.

I went into the churchyard beside Rector Street to count my notes. I was very young and diffident and notes of any denomination were unfamiliar to me. Gold and silver were almost the only European coinages of those days. According to my calculations—at fifty pence English to the dollar—I was about $5.75 to the bad. I returned timidly to the bank. The personnel of the establishment had completely changed. I said:

"Your Mr. Brown has given me five and three quarter dollars too little on my letter of credit."

Mr. Brown's substitute replied:

"Smart man, Mr. Brown," and that was all I got out of *that*. A U. S. N. bluejacket sat in my lap and smoked a stogie as far as Union Square. I reflected that New York was indeed little and old and went south that afternoon.

But by 1906 the domestic note was vanishing even from New York offices. The one that comes most vividly back to me was that of the S. S. McClure Company. That, as I have said, was panelled with polished tulip wood, which gave it a very pretty effect. Pretty is the exact word. It was certainly not august, neither was it opulent, nor yet drawing-room-like as was the case with Lord Northcliffe's private office in Carmelite House. It had already a number of shining, nickelled and black celluloid instruments. But still panelled room opened out into panelled room. There was not a sea of instrument-operating young women in shirt waists or any glass cases.

Sam McClure was then the dominating and romantic figure of the New York magazine-and-literary world. He was florid and stout and fond of relating to you how he had landed, a barefoot Belfast boy, in New York years before. His anecdotes for and against himself were innumerable. He would relate how, coming over on a German boat, he had looked one dinner-time at the music programme. There was no Wagner on it. He got up and approached the band.

"I am S. S. McClure," he said. "There is no Wagner on your programme. Play nothing but Wagner tonight. Wagner was the McClure of music."

He occupied the Imperial suite on the *Kaiserin Augusta Victoria* and had an enclosed space on the sun deck where he sat all day in his pyjamas. He would take you into his suite and ask:

"Notice anything?" Then he would point out that the corners of all the tables were rounded off. "That was ordered by the Kaiser." When the German Emperor had inspected the vessel he had noticed that all the tables had sharp edges. They would hurt you if you ran against them during a roll of the ship. Immediately the corners of all the tables on the ship were rounded off. McClure added the comment: "Sam McClure is the Kaiser of American magazines." Sometimes he would change it to: "The Kaiser is the Sam McClure of the Concert of Nations." That, in those days, seemed nearer the mark.

McClure's Magazine was at that day a power in America such as, I imagine, no other magazine or periodical ever since became. America was passing through a fit of misgivings and *McClure's* harped brilliantly on that note. It exposed everything and everybody with ability and insistence. Its denunciatory writings were called "muckrake articles." They were written or inspired by Miss Ida Tarbell who had an admirable pen for the purpose and a sombre passion in doing it.

I passed the greater part of my time in New York in McClure's office not because I wanted to work for the magazine but because I liked the editorial staff. It consisted of Miss Tarbell, Miss Willa Sibert Cather, and Mr. William Aspenwall Bradley, who was then a slim young poet and is now a substantial literary agent in Paris. Miss Isabel McClung, who is now Mrs. Jan Hamburg, was also on the staff, as, I think, assistant to Miss Cather.

McClure I had known in England. I had seen him maybe three times but you got to know him well in less than that. Pinker had tried to make him believe that he ought to publish Conrad in America and had got me to meet him and persuade him to that effect. I was glad enough to try. It did not prove very easy. McClure did not understand Conrad's books very well. But he prided himself on having discovered Robert L. Stevenson for America and was anxious to be in at such another discovery. Pinker, I and I daresay other people all swore to him that if he published Conrad he would. He grew nervous and several times described how he had made R.L.S., giving each time a slightly different turn to the narrative, so that I confuse one version with another. I know that at one date he bought a prodigious number of umbrellas, in San Francisco, and gave them to bootblacks with instructions to lend them to their clients gratis on the occasion of sudden thunderstorms. At the next downfall that city found itself confronted with hundreds of umbrellas each one bearing on its distended upper surface the inscription: "READ TREASURE ISLAND."

I fancy it was really some other product that McClure thus advertised, but when he was in the mood for greater glories, he usually said it was some book of Stevenson's. But the question of taking up Conrad caused him a great deal of perplexity. I remember dining with him one night at the Ritz in the company of, I think, Percival Gibbon and his beautiful wife and some other people. Percival Gibbon was one of McClure's most popular English story writers.

The occasion was not one on which one could very well discuss the selling qualities of Conrad's work. To get it over McClure asked me to return to the *Savoy* where he occupied an Imperial or Royal or Grand Ducal suite. Mrs. McClure was there, a simple, old-fashioned, admirable body. She appeared to be dazed as McClure, walking frantically up and down, threw wad after wad of banknotes into her lap, ordering her to buy all sorts of rather fabulous objects that I imagine she did not want. McClure kept on pushing his fingers through his forelocks and saying that he did not know whether he wanted Conrad or not. At last Mrs. McClure said:

"Well, father, if this gentleman says you ought to have him, maybe you ought, though to be sure I have not heard him say anything." I had not as yet been able to get a word in. I assured her that to publish Conrad would be to gain at least as much honour as to have published R.L.S. She said that that appeared to settle it. So the honour of being the first country fittingly to have appreciated that great writer was earned for the United States by that comfortable and charming lady.

The struggle was by no means over. Conrad had to be brought to accept McClure. This was by no means easy. He had his own opinions of American publishers. I don't know

how he had formed them, for he had not yet come in contact
with any. But he had the settled opinion that all American
publishers asked you to lunch and over that meal made you
enormous offers which they afterwards repudiated or forgot
about. He was not inclined to go up from the Pent to London
on any such fool errand. McClure, on the other hand, would
not sign any contract before he had had a sight of Conrad.
He wanted to see how he liked him personally and he liked
of course what glory was to be had out of meeting distinguished
authors.

The difficulty was solved by Conrad's inviting McClure
to lunch at the *Cecil*, which was almost next door to Pinker's
office. Conrad made a judicious choice of wines with the idea
of stimulating, but not too much stimulating, McClure. Then
he ordered Pinker not to go to lunch at all but to sit in his
office waiting for Conrad's phone. During the lunch McClure
made his offer. It was considerably better than anything Conrad had hitherto either received or expected and Conrad was
sure that McClure, who had actually drunk whisky and Perrier, was under the influence of liquor and would certainly
repudiate the contract as soon as he was sober. He therefore
said to McClure:

"Mr. McClure, is this your firm offer?" and McClure said
it was.

Conrad excused himself and went to the telephone to call
up Pinker. He dictated the terms to a subordinate, Pinker being
engaged, and ordered Pinker to come straight round to the
Cecil with a contract ready for signature. He himself would
hold McClure until Pinker arrived.

Pinker was there, contract and all, in the surprising time of
four minutes or four minutes and a half. As a matter of fact,
he had not chosen to go without his lunch but had gone to the
Savoy Grill which was next door to the *Cecil*. He had already
fully discussed the terms with McClure and so had a contract
all ready in his pocket.

I do not know how many books of Conrad's—or indeed of

mine—were published by the S. S. McClure Company. Mc-
Clure had his vicissitudes and lost his control of the Company
and the magazine. The firm became known as McClure Doubleday and Co. and, after other changes, as Doubleday Page. As
such it continued to publish Conrad. I had, however, a singular encounter with Mr. Page. I had published a historical novel
in which one of the characters said—in order to indicate extreme rarity: "You will find a chaste whore as soon as that."

Mr. Page told me that his firm certainly could not publish
such a phrase. I said:

"Oh, well, Mr. Page, make it 'a chaste dash'...'You will
find a chaste ——— as soon as that.'"

Mr. Page said:

"We certainly could not print the word 'chaste.' It is too
suggestive."

I said that in that case Mr. Page's firm should not publish
my book. That ended my publications in America for a good
number of years.

I had later a curious encounter with Dr. Page, then United
States Ambassador to Great Britain. It was at the time when I
was editing the *English Review*. Ezra Pound came into my
office in a great state of excitement. An American poet had
come to England as a stowaway and had been imprisoned on
the arrival of the ship at Plymouth. I was to go at once to the
American Embassy and make them get the poet out.

I obeyed. I thought the Embassy would be delighted to
help release a poet. I could not even see why I was needed.

Dr. Page received me politely but coldly. He evidently
remembered my face with dislike but was vague as to my
identity. That is not to be wondered at. Ezra had explained
who I was, and Americans never understand his particular
dialect. They don't understand either that in him they possess
the greatest poet of our time—and of several other times. Dr.
Page probably imagined therefore that I was an assistant
professor in English whom he had met at Chautauqua.

I explained my case. Dr. Page at once became colder—
but infinitely colder! He said:

"Young man. Do you know what my position is in this
country?"

I said I was under the impression that His Excellency was
United States Ambassador at the Court of St. James.

He said: Yes, but did I understand what that meant?

I said I understood that His Excellency was there to
protect the interests of oppressed citizens of the United States
in the country to which he was accredited.

He said: not at all. His position in Great Britain was exactly that of the King. He represented a sovereign State. It
was not his province to interfere in the criminal affairs of the
country any more than it was the King's.

I said that an American or any other foreign citizen was
only in Great Britain or any other country to which he was
not subject by favour of the Prince—*"par faveur du Prince"*
was the technical term. I did not see why Dr. Page, as royal by
his functions, could not intercede with the local royalty in
order to obtain additional favour for a national of his own
who had got into trouble.

Dr. Page exclaimed:

"Young man. If you were a British subject and you got
into trouble in a foreign country you would not expect your
King to interest himself in your case."

I said:

"Dr. Page, if I got into trouble in a foreign country and
my King did not interfere by his representative to my advantage my King would not remain for three weeks on his throne."

Dr. Page said he supposed I must be a British subject. But
he still refused to interfere in favour of his poet. I daresay he
was technically right. And no doubt as a publisher he had
reason to think that prison is quite a good place for poets.

The immediate sequel was amusing. I went round to the
Home Office and found C. F. G. Masterman, who was not yet,
I think, a Cabinet Minister but had already the ear of the All

Highest in England. Indeed, even then amongst the younger politicians he was considered to be well in the running for next Liberal Prime Minister. They had forgotten David.

I told him about the American poet's trouble and he scribbled something on a piece of paper. We got into one of the interminable arguments that I always had with him on every subject under the sun except politics. I knew him at that date very well but was not as intimate with him as I was later. But I had played a good deal of golf with him at Hythe and he professed a great admiration for my writing. He must have read some of my books, for he was always quoting from them catchwords that amused him.

We argued for a long time and then went out to dinner at the *Mont Blanc*—a famous semi-Bohemian restaurant of those days. Afterwards he asked me to go back to his office and, whilst he was talking to someone in the hall, told me to go up and ask his secretary if he had anything for me. His secretary gave me an official telegram addressed to the Home Secretary. I took it down to Masterman in the hall and he told me to read it and give it to Ezra. It was from the Governor of Plymouth gaol or the Chief Constable and announced that that poet had been released before dinner.

Masterman stood leering at me in that hall, his queer long nose very much to one side, his top hat extraordinarily ruffled and the invariable rag of satin hanging from the skirt of his governmental frock coat. He was the worst groomed politician I have ever even imagined.

"There, you old fruity Tory," he jeered, "don't say a Liberal Government does not appreciate the great authors of the country. We would not have done that for any other soul in the world but you."

I said that rather tore it. I had just told Dr. Page that they would do as much for the meanest Briton. He said:

"You take all the butter you can get, sonny. Your parsnips will be pretty dry if you don't." I told him of Meary Walker's saying:

"Pity without relief is like pudden without fat—very hard!"

He said:

"You've had all the relief you're going to get this sitting. Go away. I know you're going to ask me to make Ezra Pound Poet Laureate."

I met the poet himself some time later. It then appeared that he had never been to prison at all. He was met on the dock by a detective. The detective said:

"You are a man of education. How could you do such a silly thing?"

The poet said that he had been in Japan and Siam and Providence, Rhode Island, and a great many other places. But he had never been in England. As he had not had the money to pay his fare he had decided to come and see England without doing so. The detective said he would not see anything of England except the road to the gaol and its interior. That seemed to be a pity.

Suddenly he said:

"Have you the money to pay for a taxi drive round the town?"

The poet said he had. Then the detective said:

"It does seem a pity you should not see anything of England after going to so much trouble. If you like to pay the taxi I will pay for drinks. In that way you will see something of England."

So they drove all round the countryside and spent the day mostly in village ale-houses. When they arrived at the prison, the order for release had already come.

What pleased me most in New York was not so much its littleness or its oldness. It was the attention that those of its citizens who dealt with or in the printed word paid to the practical side of the literary job. As early as 1895 I had been aware that that was the fact. I bought at a Kentish farm sale about that time a great many numbers—sixty or seventy—of the *Atlantic Monthly* of the eighties. It was astonishing to buy those periodicals beneath the high skies off the grass of an English farm. Heaps of them had been thrown down between the coulters of ploughs and eider tubs on the trodden green turf. But it astonished me still more to find that correspondent after correspondent had written to the editor from Boston or Philadelphia to ask *how* to write short stories—not the moral attached to this or that specimen of that difficult form but quite simply how such stories should be written.

I had never heard that question asked in England. Yet here were questions being asked not about the codes of ethics of James or Howells or Maupassant or Turgenev but as to their literary methods. About that time American letters began to differentiate themselves from English work and to identify themselves much more closely with the main stream of international literature. And, as I have already pointed out, with James and Harland and various artists from Whistler to Sargent and various enormously popular writers like Mark Twain, Bret Harte, and even Miss Alcott, America was already in the nineties beginning to influence even England quite as much as England had formerly influenced that country. Till then people like the Concord group of authors had been merely English writers of great solemnity and some provincialism. The new movement, if it were largely under French influences, was an almost entirely native phenomenon. But indeed, even Poe was largely a French product. He was almost the only English critic who ever paid any attention to the technical side of writing. To the Concord group Poe was merely a bad man.

In 1906 there were still literary papacies even in the Eastern States of the North American Republic. But they were mild and hopeful institutions. There was about them little of the mournful and stupid upholding of vested interests that I have described as dominating the English literary world. No poet in New York was being killed by John Keats; no poetry could live in England because Keats had lived.

The imaginative-literary papacies of New York and Phila-

delphia were divided by the gentle figures of W. D. Howells
and the lady who ran the book department of Wanamaker's
store. W. D. Howells was a lovable figure whom one met on
summer evenings, clothed, as I have said, in white ducks, and
strolling, recognised and respected by everybody, down Fifth
Avenue or across Central Park. Wanamaker's lady chose books
to boom a little under the influence of Miss Mary Moss and a
little under that of Dr. Talcott Williams. But mostly she chose
them under her own inspiration. I remember the elation of Mr.
Harcourt, now of Harcourt, Brace & Co., when she decided to
"put over" *The Divine Fire* by Miss May Sinclair. She made
her customers buy it to the tune of I don't know what ... a
quarter of a million copies? Six hundred thousand? Seven?
Then New York was forced into buying, so as not to be behind
Philadelphia. Parties were given at which examinations were
held as to the speeches of the characters in Miss Sinclair's book.
At others you had to wear about you some attribute suggesting
its title. I went to one in a fireman's helmet. When I told that
afterwards to Miss Sinclair she was extremely angry with me.
I took her home in a hansom from the house of one of the
Garnetts in Highgate to her house in Kensington—a distance,
I imagine, of ten miles but seeming a hundred. She refused to
speak at all to me after I had told her. I daresay she was
justified but—to use the slang that we used to use in those
days—I got it in the neck both ways. It was bad enough to
have had to go to a party in a fireman's helmet. But Miss
Sinclair's silence was even less supportable. I suppose I ought
to have gone in horns and a tail.... Eventually *The Divine
Fire* reached even Boston.

Of Boston I refuse to say anything. I dislike the Hill as
much as the Hill dislikes me. It was in those days—and I
daresay it still is—an architectural imitation of the intellectual
suburb of London called Hampstead, N.W. It still had imitation English writers, imitation disagreeable old gentlemen who
wrote articles in imitation of those in the London *Athenaeum*
and imitation formidably disagreeable Duchesses who sat about

in rooms whose furniture scantily imitated that of their English predecessors. . . . It had of course William James. But do you believe that one just man could have saved *that* Gomorrah? I do not. And the accent! . . . When a real Boston man used to approach me uttering sounds like those of a brick-throated bull-frog it used to occur to me that if the Cabots really had the ear of the Almighty, He must bitterly have regretted that He ever invented the vocal organs of humanity.

I except of course from these insults Mr. Ferris Greenslett and Mr. James B. Connolly and indeed anyone else with whose personal acquaintance I was ever honoured in the Hub. Mr. Greenslett, who is now a pillar of the august and ancient House of Houghton Mifflin, was then a poet and gave me one of the queer sensations of my life. For the matter of that, he has given me three. But the first marks the progress of history. He was talking about the delights of an old house he had bought somewhere in Massachusetts. It had ingles and beams and lawns and old walls and everything that a poet should have—except asphodel! But a sad look came into his eyes. He said:

"The nigger in the woodpile is that it has only seven bath-rooms!"

It was not merely that that was the first time I was forced to consider aspects of what has since become a serious menace to world peace—I mean the American bath-room. It was that it seemed preposterous that it should be a poet who first presented the idea to me. Imagine a poet with seven bath-rooms! I suppose he was doomed even then to become a publisher.

At a later date I came back from Corsica to London, especially to be in time to give an entertainment to Mr. Greenslett, who was then in London. I tried to bring *bouilla-baisse* from Marseilles, but Pascal said it would not keep. I assembled London's wisest and fairest and they stood in a half ring as was done in New York receptions at that date, their faces all being towards the door. I thought it would make Mr. Greenslett feel at home. It didn't.

There were Mr. and Mrs. Arnold Bennett, and Mr. and

Mrs. Galsworthy, and Mr. and Mrs. Ezra Pound and Miss Rebecca West and other odalisques, and there was I painfully conscious of the impatience of my redoubtable Mrs. Melhuish and her assistants chafing in the kitchen and the caviar going tepid on the dining table and the Welch mutton being roasted to a cinder and the imbecility that had taken hold of me. For Mr. Greenslett was late. He was extravagantly late. He must have thought the party was in New York ... until he got to it. Then embarrassment overcame him. He marched into the half circle like a grenadier going to death and loudly and distinctly exclaimed:

"Why have all English women got red arms?"

The ladies present exclaimed that they hadn't and the men made appropriate murmurs.

"Well," said Mr. Greenslett, "the Miss G——'s have."

It was as good a recovery as Mr. Greenslett could have made if he had thought for a week of Sundays. He had just been having tea with the G—— family. And Mr. G—— was the most unpopular man in the world with the group whom Mr. Greenslett was addressing.

A little later it was I whom the sight of Mr. Greenslett covered with confusion. It was in 1917 and I was returning from Belgium with a report of a confidential nature but not of earthquaking importance. It was to be enshrined in a ministerial pronouncement in the House of Commons that evening and to form part of a reply to the German Government as to the treatment of German prisoners in the lines of communication. German Zeppelins searching for an ammunition dump many miles behind the Front had succeeded in killing a number of prisoners over whom I commanded the escort. They had also killed several of my men. No one had bothered much about them, but I had to be tried by a court of enquiry for being short in the roll-call of my wards. And I may say that at that time the prisoners were being a great deal better treated than my unfortunate men. So I was not in a very good temper. I had not yet had time to write my portion of the report, which was to be addressed to the Ministry of Information. I was irritated by the whole affair and I had private worries unconnected with the War. A special compartment had been reserved for me and I was writing away in a corner long before the train started. I was suddenly aware that there was a stranger in the carriage and, without looking at him, I said to the guard who was outside:

"Guard, remove this civilian. You know you have no right to allow civilians in a messenger's compartment." I had not indeed the right to allow civilians in it myself.

I heard a faint protesting noise. It was made by Mr. Greenslett.

My relations with Mr. Connolly, my other Boston friend of those days, procured me also several strong emotions. The most piquant of these goes back to Rome in I forget what year. At any rate for hours of a summer night Mr. Connolly and I walked up and down in front of the Foreign Ministry in Rome debating with such passion that, Mr. Connolly having been a footballer and pugilist, I fully expected to end the moonlight night in a battered condition. We were debating as to whether cricket or baseball were the better game. Mr. Connolly had never played cricket; I had never played baseball. In England baseball is called "rounders" and is only played by small children.

Mr. Connolly had many and overwhelming athletic qualifications and was an intimate friend of President Roosevelt. I imagine I owed to him that President's amiable words about my books. The President sent him round the world with the United States Navy, so that he might obtain inner light on the condition of that service. I visited with him some battleships off Newport, Rhode Island. It seemed to me that, by comparison with our own, the condition and discipline of the United States Navy must have made the service a comparative heaven. I am bound to say that I changed my mind on coming into contact with the U. S. land forces in France. If the discipline of our regulars had been in any way as strict as that of the

U. S. regular army we should have had a mutiny within a week. That is no doubt one of the advantages of the Feudal System.

Mr. Connolly was the hero of one of the most amusing scenes that I ever saw. It was in Rome in the low, dark and mysterious apartment of a Monsignor of Irish birth. The Monsignor was one of the most influential people behind the scenes at the Vatican and the apartments were full of priests and monks of any and every description. The talk fell on the personal magnetism of the Holy Father, then on personal magnetism in general. Mr. Connolly had a high opinion of that fluid. Said he:

"There's nothing like it. When I made my record long jump at the Olympic Games at Athens, I was standing between Prince George of England—him as is now the King—and Prince George of Greece. And the personal magnetism of those two gentlemen was so strong that I said: Here's for the honour of County Galway.... And I jumped twenty-nine feet."

The Monsignor said:

"How is it, Jimmy? Do you think you could jump that far now?"

"No," said Connolly, "the sight of all you fat priests in these tiny rooms is very depressing and saps my personal magnetism. I could *not* jump now."

"Well," said the Monsignor, "let's have a jumping competition."

"Not for me," said Jimmy.

But they all went down to the courtyard. The Dominicans tucked the slack of their robes into their girdles and jumped three feet, the Monsignors took off their coats and in their purple jumped three feet and a half; the Jesuits removed nothing and getting their toes a little over the line jumped three feet and nine inches. I jumped I don't remember what and turned my ankle.

Then said Mr. Connolly:

"The sight of all you fat old seggarts hopping and skipping about has revived my personal magnetism so powerfully, I think I could jump a little now."

He jumped twenty-eight yards two feet and nine inches. ...Or perhaps it was feet, not yards.

That Monsignor had a sister who, with his old mother, kept house for him. His sister was reputed a saint and certainly she was as beautiful and mysterious as a saint should be—with her pale gold hair and her silver face shining in the shadows of the dim rooms. She told another of those stories that have very much helped me in life. She said:

"An English bishop came to call on brother the other day. He was one of those proud persons. My brother has a great deal of influence here, as you all know, and is anxious that it should be used on all occasions when it can be useful. So I said to the bishop: 'The Monsignor is not in. But though not the rose I am very near the rose and if you will sit down I will try to entertain you to the best of my abilities until the Monsignor's return.' The bishop sat down as stiff as a ramrod.

"I was as entertaining as I knew how for two mortal hours. And you know I can be very entertaining when I please. At the end of that time the bishop rose as stiff as a ramrod. He had neither smiled nor made any sign of pleasure. My brother had not returned. So the bishop said:

" 'Ve..rry inter-resting!' and went on his way.

"He was one of those proud persons. My brother says I must not say that because the bishop is one of the shyest and most nervous men that he knows. But I am getting tired of having people excused for nervousness when they are so proud that they push you off the pavement every time that they meet you.

"Well, next day I was at the Church of Santa Maria Trastevere, waiting to go up to take the Blessed Sacrament. And the bishop was sitting on a stool in front of me. He removed his stool to make way for me and when he sat down again he forgot that he had removed his stool. So all I saw was his two soles sticking in the air. And you know it is very difficult to know what to say to a gentleman when all you can see of him is the two soles of his feet. So, as I passed, I looked down and said:

" 'Ve..rry inter-resting!' And then I went on and took the blessed sacrament."

So I tell the story of the Monsignor's sister who was a saint and of the bishop whenever I am told that someone who has been excruciatingly rude to me is really suffering from the extremes of nervousness. I was once seated next a bishop, but not one of the Roman persuasion. It was on a leathern sofa with a high back. The bishop had been reading a paper but had dropped it and was looking at nothing. My watch had stopped. I was waiting for a friend. I could not see a clock. So I asked the bishop the time. His lordship started, pointed at a placard inscribed SILENCE, and exclaimed in stentorian tones after a pause of indignation that I indicate with dots

"............ASK A WAITER!"

I told the story of Miss —— and the bishop to the next person I met. It was in the same exclusive London institution that Herbert Spencer made his famous remark to Edward Harrison, the brother of Frederick, the Positivist pope. Edward Harrison was rather a mild, shy little man but he was a pretty good billiard player. The philosopher on the other hand liked to play billiards for his health. They played a game and Edward Harrison won by a hundred points to forty-five: Then Mr. Spencer said:

"A moderate ability to play a game of skill is an excellent thing but such a proficiency as you have displayed argues a misspent youth."

That is, I believe, the accurate way to tell the story of which there are many versions. It was told me by Mr. Edward Harrison himself. He had a house at Winchelsea. He had been a West—or East—India merchant and was lavish in his hospitality. I dined there once, when there were present Harrison's brother Frederick, Henry James and someone else in whose eyes I know I was anxious to shine, though I forget who it was. The occasion was just after the accession of Edward VII. The Paris *Figaro* had come out with some not ill-natured but piquant anecdotes of the King's adventures in that city. It was therefore unobtainable in London. The Customs House officials had seized all copies of the journal coming to England. They gave as the reason for the seizure not the paragraphs about the King but the account of some quite ordinary divorce case which they said was too indecent to be allowed to appear in the country.

I happened to mention this to Mr. Frederick Harrison. He was one of the tremendous Victorians who always aroused rage in me—and in whom I always aroused rage. He had a great, square, white beard, flashing eyes and a really tremendous voice. He at once got onto his Victorian high horse. He exclaimed:

"What! You dare to say that? Infamous. Nothing of the sort can have happened. This is a free country. It would be contrary to all the laws. It is impossible. You are not telling the truth. I will ask my friend Lord Salisbury. I will get Arthur Balfour to ask a question in the House...."

I said I had only asserted what was a fact as a testimony to the tact with which British officials could sometimes act. It was undoubtedly true that the Customs House officials could seize and destroy anything that they alleged to be indecent. In that, England resembled China. In China, music was a part of and under the superintendence of the Customs, in England it was morals. Mr. Harrison grew more infuriated. He said:

"Nonsense. You are talking rank nonsense. You are not telling the truth (I shall get back to New York immediately) ... James, listen to what this young fool is saying.... Edward, you know all about the Customs.... Listen to this.... He says...."

I do not as a rule pursue arguments beyond the table at which they take place. On this occasion I determined to put Mr. Harrison definitely in the wrong. I was anxious to prove my reliability to James and other members of that company.

I wrote to my uncle, William Rossetti, to come to my rescue.
He replied that the Customs had seized that copy of the *Figaro*
under the orders of his own office acting as directed by the
Inland Revenue Act, 18 Vict. cap. 36, or some such number. I forwarded that letter to Mr. Harrison. He answered that,
of course, he was intimately acquainted with the provisions of
18 Vict. cap. 36, but our argument had had nothing to do with
it. He added, *"Patrem et avum habes, eos exorna!"* As who
should say: "Your father and grandfather were all right. Try
to live up to them!"

These amenities of the great are, I think, limited to the
English great. They are probably caused by indigestion, due
to bad cooking. Possibly they are due to the fact that the duel
was abolished in England before other countries. At any rate,
nowhere else, except when English people were present, have
I heard personal rudeness addressed to the face. Even the
German distinguished are usually, if formally, courteous, and
Americans are so careful of giving offence in private or family
life that I must confess never to have been able to keep up
with them. Even in 1906 I was struck—and pleased—by the
amenities of social manners in New York. At certain instances
of the characteristic I have never given over wondering. And it
went even deeper than I knew.

Some time ago I met in Paris a lady who was astonished
that I did not recognise her. She said:

"You ought to because you changed the whole course of
my life."

I expressed astonishment.

"Well," she said, "twenty years ago you came to call on
me with Miss Cather in Bronx Park. I was going to elope with
a married man but you stayed so long that I could not make
the train. So I have never married."

I imagine almost any lady of any other country would have
got rid of her guests earlier. She said that she could not have
thought of being as awkward as that. At the same time she
said that she could not expect a gentleman who had given

you a date on which to elope with you to give you another if you were so rude as to miss the first. I said that I should have thought that relationships having so approached intimacy as to permit of the arrangement of an elopement, the mere missing of a train should surely not be taken as the occasion of a life-long separation. She said that that was quite wrong. Intimate relationships, and especially family ones, call for the most ex-quisite of politenesses. You might risk being rude to a gentle-man whom you did not expect to meet again but he would be a very imprudent gentleman who took up permanently with you if you were remiss in manners on the occasion of your early acquaintance. That reminded me of a note in an early edition of Baedeker's guide to New York. "Tips," this organ declared, "are of an appallingly high scale in this city and must by no means be omitted if efficient attention is desired. If, however, the traveller does not intend again to visit the establishment the formality may be omitted."

Another New York lady wanted to give a tea for me. As we were both very dated up, it was difficult to find an after-noon on which we were both free. There was only a Thursday and I said, "Let's make it Thursday."

She said:

"No, I could never give a tea on a Thursday. Sadie always has her nervous headache on a Thursday."

I pointed out that her sister Sadie lived in Pittsburgh and that was New York. She repeated:

"No, I could never give a tea on a Thursday. Sadie would be dreadfully hurt if she ever heard that I had done it. None of our family ever gives an entertainment on a Thursday. Some of us do not even eat our full meals."

Family unity could hardly go further, yet the case is by no means an exaggerated one, for New York, and still less so for the rest of the vast territories of the North American Republic.

McClure's staff was certainly a happy family. On the occa-sion of that visit I had taken no letters of introduction. I do

not know that I ever took any anywhere. They are usually a
nuisance both to the giver and to the person for whom they
are destined. And I think they give you a false view of the
country you visit. A person receiving a letter of introduction
presented by the friend of a distant friend is apt to stretch his
hospitality. When such persons are many and influential the
result will be a quite distorted view of life. You are run from
banquet to banquet and allowed behind scenes of which a
normal person will only see the public side. So I think I have
seen America from an angle at which the visiting celebrity
never sees it, and therefore I like it better. America seen from
the platform of public banquets and the homes of hospitable
millionaires is a pretty overwhelming affair. You become fairly
aware that all this blaze of machined hospitality is not in the
end that something for nothing that is the lure of the world.
So your gratitude is an equally mechanical emotion. To be in
America as a public character used to be to be aware that you
were marketable goods being exploited as if you were a brand
of ham or molasses. But to be there in private was pleasant.
You received sufficient hospitality to let you know that you
were personally appreciated by cordial people whom you liked.
And the hospitality was not of such a nature as you could
never aspire to return. That is the first attribute of hospitality,
if it is to be satisfactory.

I lounged, then, in and out of McClure's office, getting in
the way of Miss Cather and Miss Tarbell, being taken about
by one or the other of them to tea parties or to lunch at
Mouquin's by Mr. Bradley. I bantered S. S. on the Napoleonic
nature of his policies and was taken by him to baseball matches,
the Tombs and the Night Court on Sixth Avenue. He wanted
me to write muck-rake articles for him. One article in particular that he wanted me to write was as to the comparative
statistics of crimes of violence in various countries. For this
he wanted me not only to get up an enormous body of statistics
but to interview thugs in the Tombs and, in the Night Court
prison, ladies who had stabbed with hatpins other ladies or

their gentlemen friends. I was, of course, to make it hot for the United States. In that respect America was, and is still, I believe, very far ahead of every other civilised country and of several uncivilised ones. According to McClure, crimes of violence were then most frequent in God's Own Country and least so in the Green Isle of his birth. In between came the following countries in their order of precedence: the German Empire, Italy, Spain, France and Great Britain. But Mr. McClure gave to his statistics a human twist. Thus the German Empire came next to the United States in crime because of assassinations of minor officials—postmen, most usually, because they carried objects of value; policemen because they were hated; and firemen because, extinguishing fires, they robbed the public of the chance of profitable insurances. These Mr. McClure included as ordinary crimes of violence, whilst recognising them as being largely political in character. On the other hand in his consideration of Ireland, he omitted assassinations and attempted assassinations of landlords, agents and constabulary because they *were* political.

His proposal was that I should travel in all these countries and, whilst interviewing murderers, collect statistics of all and every sort that could help in denouncing the United States from every angle, material and intellectual. For this he offered me what in those days seemed a princely fortune and he went on making it more and more princely as I successively refused and the hour grew later.

I had of him much the same sort of fear as I had of Lord Northcliffe. I instinctively distrusted mass production whether material or of printed matter; I did not believe I could make the pace of Twenty-third Street any more than of Carmelite House. And, in McClure's case, I could not see that denouncing the United States was any affair of mine. I was in a stage—that has not yet exhausted itself—of being delighted with New York. In and around McClure's office itself I came across what I most wanted. McClure and his young friends who made up his gang were as full of intellectual curiosity as an egg is filled with its contents. It was of intellectual curiosity and a distrust of vested interests that I was most in search. McClure wanted me most, I gathered, to help him attack the American administration. He did not care from what point of view. I could, if I liked, prove that American arts were no good and the American intellect non-existent because of the faultiness of American State education. I could make out elaborate tables to prove anything I liked, as long as it was to the discredit of American authority.

Nothing could have been farther from my inclinations. I was suffering at that time—and I have suffered ever since—from a violent reaction against vested interests in the arts and matters intellectual. In New York I could see no vestiges of the trail of that serpent. Except for the South I knew nothing of America outside New York. But the intellectual and artistic future of Anglo-Saxondom seemed to be in the hands of New York. I could not therefore have attacked what I discerned as the only sign of hope for the race that my skies shewed.

McClure then got it into his head that it would be a good idea to start a muck-rake magazine in England. England surely had political abuses that needed exposing. He suggested that I should start with his capital such a magazine in England. When he came to the country he would edit it as long as he was there. I could edit it for the rest of the time—in conjunction, perhaps, with Percival Gibbon, who knew his mind.

That suggestion, too, I turned down. I could see no need for a muck-rake magazine in England. English political institutions seemed to me—and still so seem—as nearly perfect in their workings as such things can be in this vale. It was only from the æsthetic and intellectual side of English life that I was growing daily more alien. In America the moment I had passed the imitation English cottages on Sandy Hook my heart always seemed to sink a little. I thought that from there to the Golden Gate there was not an old house, nor a mellow one. It was a terrible depressant. But the moment I struck Tilbury Dock and crossed over to Greenwich on my way back to Kent,

I knew that a much greater feeling of depression would descend on me. It was the thought of intellectual precedent narrowing down to precedent. From there to John o' Groat's House in the extreme north I should not find one soul who could think without calling on authority.

I had perhaps better illustrate what I mean by a couple of stories.

One Miss Cather told about herself and Miss McClung. Last year I re-related it to both ladies. Miss Cather made no comment, but she never does make any comment. That is perhaps why she is one of the greatest novelists of the present day. Miss McClung said it was very much exaggerated. It is at least very nice.

In Pittsburgh, then, in early days there was a *Shropshire Lad Club*. Beneath the palls of smoke that hang over that terrible valley and in among the slag-heaps that are its most marked features, there existed valiant spirits in large numbers who met for the daily study and reading aloud of Mr. A. E. Housman's volume. (I daresay some of them inhabited one or the other of the rather beautiful hill suburbs of that city. There must have been some such members, since the club was possessed of considerable resources.) But I like to think of them meeting under the presidency of Miss Cather on the sloping side of a conical slag deposit.

In due course, as they would, they decided to do something to make Mr. Housman aware of their admiration. They subscribed therefore for a solid gold laurel wreath and deputed Miss Cather and Miss McClung to carry it to the poet and explain suitably why it was sent.

The ladies got off the boat at Liverpool. They knew Liverpool to be near Chester and Cheshire to be the county next to Shropshire. They visited all the villages whose picturesque names give so much colour to the poems. They called at innumerable parsonages to ask for information as to the poet. The parsons, they said, all seemed to come to their doors carrying napkins and smelling strongly of lunch. Some of them even invited them to share their meals. But none of them had heard of Mr. Housman.

The two ladies then got as far as Shrewsbury—pronounced Shrowsb'ry. They went to the public library and asked their embarrassing question. The librarian had heard neither of book nor poet. After a considerable pause he said: "Ah, wait!" And consulted his catalogue.

He went away and came back with a copy of the book. It was covered with dust, inscribed: "Presented by the Author," and uncut. But the librarian could tell them no more about the author.

They went to the British Museum and consulted the quite courteous Principal Librarian. Sir E. Maunde Thompson said that he too had never heard of Mr. Housman but would be glad to read the volume of verse that they left with him.

A few days later they had from him a note running:

"Sir E. Maunde Thompson presents his compliments to Miss McCrather and Miss Lung. He has read the work submitted to him by those young ladies and begs to ask: Is there not Milton?

"If the young ladies nevertheless desire to prosecute their search he suggests that they should apply to the publisher of the fascicle. He is Mr. ——."

The young ladies would have done that before but the copies of *The Shropshire Lad* that they had possessed had all been of the American edition. No English bookseller had heard of the work and all refused to book an order for poetry unless the publisher's name could be supplied. They then found their way to Hampstead.

A teeny-tweeny maid opened the door of a boarding-house to the extent of a crack large enough to shew her nose. They were inspected by a landlady from an upper landing. At last they were admitted to a parlour. Its principal ornament was an immense, shiny and very cold-looking grand piano.

They waited a long time. At last there appeared the poet. He exclaimed:

"Oh! If I had not thought you were my American cousins I would never have seen you," and disappeared.

They laid the solid gold laurel wreath reverently on the grand piano and departed.

You perceive in the "Is there not Milton?" of Sir E. Maunde Thompson the grand style manner of using "Isn't there?"—the words that are used as ratsbane against the arts in England. Rat-catchers less Olympian employ the more plebeian form.

I have for many years had an immense admiration for a French writer called Réné Béhaine. Along with M. Léon Daudet I consider him to be the greatest of French—almost the greatest of living—novelists. That admiration finds few to share it. So, in New York, I say everywhere I go, that M. Béhaine is the greatest living novelist. Now and then I persuade a periodical to let me write an article about M. Béhaine. After such activities on my part the New York booksellers sell about one hundred and twenty copies of M. Béhaine's last published work. The purchasers are New York publisher's advisers, critics and members of the public interested in keeping in touch with developments of the French novel.

I once tried the same thing in England. I had just returned from New York and was feeling sanguine. I did not speak about M. Béhaine to London critics or publishers, for I knew none. Nor did I speak to more than one London editor. He, I had heard, was—almost anti-nationally—open to new ideas. I took my courage in my hands and approached him. I had some difficulty in getting to him because he supposed that I wanted to sell him an automobile and he already possessed a Lanchester twelve years old. I said I wanted to write something about M. Béhaine. He looked at my card with some curiosity. He said:

"You, er ... *write.* ... As well as. ... I thought. ... You Americans are said to be ... er ... so. ... Your automobile, you call them sales. ..."

I said I wanted to write something about M. Béhaine.

He was the greatest of living novelists. He expressed perturbation.

"An . . . er . . . novelist?" he asked. "A *novelist*. . . . I thought. . . ."

He lost words altogether.

"The greatest *living* novelist?" he asked. He placed the tips of his fingers together, leaned back in his chair and brought his palms one against the other.

"Isn't there . . . er . . . Mr. . . . ," he looked down again at my card and went on hopefully: "Mr. . . . er . . . Ford. . . . Surely not the greatest *living*. . . . Isn't there . . . E. Phillips Oppenheim?"

I mean of course no disrespect for a novelist with whose works I am hardly acquainted. The younger members of my family assure me, he—oh, unites to great literary ability a very enviable gift of popular appeal. I understand also that he, in conjunction with Mr. Charles Chaplin, is responsible for the fact that the Inland Revenue authorities make it almost impossible for English novelists to live abroad whilst the circumstances of the country make it quite impossible for them to live at home. But I imagine that Mr. Oppenheim himself would not be grateful to the English literary magnate who uses him as an excuse for not investigating the claims of a brother— even if a foreign—novelist.

It was the absence of that habit of mind in New York that first gave me the idea that I might leave England for good. No doubt it was also the feeling of well-being that first, after years, came to me in that city.

I have said that in October 1906 Mr. Gilbert Hare asked me to lunch at the Players' Club. I found him sitting already at table. A heat wave was raging and the club rooms were agreeably shady. Mr. Hare said:

"Have a devilled lobster!"

I shuddered and said that I never ate anything at lunch but boiled rice. He said:

"Have some beer!"

I screamed. I said that I should drop dead if I put my lips to the edge of a pewter pot. He said:

"That is because you do not drink enough."

He then unfolded his theory of life:

If you like things, eat them. The fact that you like them is nature's sign that you need them. If at first they disagree with you go on eating them till they do agree. Your digestion needs disciplining, just as if it were an unbroken and untrained horse. If you like grilled lobsters and they disagree with you, eat a grilled lobster every night for a fortnight just before getting into bed. The first time you will be uncomfortable but not so very because you will not be worried by the thought that you ought not to have done it. The second night it may be as bad. By the third or fourth night you will see a marked improvement. At the end of the fortnight you will eat lobsters without alarm or ill effects. As for things that you do not like there is no need to drill yourself into eating them.

But never, never eat when you do not want to. Even to please the most charming of hostesses never take a spoonful more of a dish than you need. That is fatal. Your appetite and your appetite only should be your guide. It is infallible. Never listen to a doctor who forbids you to eat this or that—and never listen to a layman. If someone tells you something will disagree with you, it will—to the measure of your respect for or fear of their opinions. Otherwise nothing need. Have a grilled lobster. Waiter, give this gentleman a quart of Scotch ale.

"By what right," I said hollowly, "do you counsel suicide to a compatriot in a strange land? Are you a doctor?"

He said: "I am."

I had thought he was an actor. He was that, too. His father, Sir John Hare, immensely popular in old men's parts, was then touring in the United States with his own company.

Mr. Hare was the only soul I have yet met whose early destiny paralleled my own. Just as in youth I had desired to be a soldier he had determined to be a doctor. The instinct to slay is inborn. But just as my grandfather had threatened to turn me into the streets if I did not become an artist of one sort or the other, Sir John insisted that his son should abandon medicine and embrace the art of acting. I never heard of any other parents insisting on their children becoming artists.

Mr. Hare is now, I believe, professor of biology or something of the sort at the University of Cambridge. There is then some hope for humanity. Oxford is the home of lost causes, but Cambridge may yet save western civilisation. I doubt if anything else will. The knell of Occidentalism and the industrial system was struck not on the fields of Flanders nor was the doom pronounced in Leningrad. Our civilisation died when first in a laboratory the word "vitamine" was pronounced. The dreadful word "enzyme" of my young manhood was bad enough because it tended to make western mankind self-conscious about its food. It had at least the merit of telling you not to eat refrigerated or canned foods. But the vitamine has at last broken the spirit that manifested itself on the peak of Darien or the field of Plassy. We shall never again see a Cortes or a Clive. Not even perhaps a Custer!

At any rate my debt of gratitude to Mr. Hare is immense. For twenty-five years after I began to follow his counsel, I never knew indigestion or any other illness. On the day of our meeting I weighed one hundred and twenty-eight pounds and was caricatured, as I have said, as "The Animated Match." At various dates since then I have tipped the scale at two hundred and fifteen pounds.

I will not say that never since my meeting with Dr. Hare have I known indigestion. Nearly twenty-five years later I was hospitably entertained at Dartmouth during Christmas week. One morning for breakfast I was given twelve Cape Cod oysters, three grilled sausages served on griddle cakes and concealed by maple syrup, and about a pound of pumpkin pie with a quarter of a pound of loaf cheese. The whole was kept down by a great deal of hot bread. Towards eleven I had a pain —of the sort that makes you believe that the doctor will pronounce on you the most dire sentence that that body of In-

quisitors has at its disposal. I hastened as well as I could to
the head of the University's medical faculty. He said:

"What have you been doing?" I said I had been breakfast-
ing. He said: "Describe the meal." Then he asked:

"Do you know what is the matter with you?" I really
trembled, as I said I did not. I seldom believe a doctor's diagnosis, but the meanest of the profession can make me afraid.
He said:

"That's indigestion." I said I had heard of that complaint.

I deserved it. The sternest of Mr. Hare's injunctions had
been never to eat a morsel more than you feel the need of.

It isn't then to be wondered at that I liked New York. I
found there new health and a new hold on life. I do not believe
that since that time I have ever feared anything *very* much—
except of course what *King's Regulations* calls "the exigencies
of active service."

One of the last things S. S. said to me—it was of course
later, after he had published a couple of my books—was:

"H——, the Americans will never read you because they
cannot tell whether you are in earnest or not and the English
will not because they know you are too damn in earnest. You
will have to find another country." I daresay what he said was
a true diagnosis. Nevertheless little old New York has remained
good enough for me.

I had a curious reminder of the Left of my earlier youth
on the *Kaiserin Augusta Victoria*. The boat had stopped at
Cherbourg—I had sailed from Hamburg. It was late and I had
gone to the purser's office for something. The purser was not
there but two men were trying to make themselves understood
by an assistant who did not speak French. They were Russians.
They wanted a passage to New York and were ready to pay
any price for it. I interpreted for them and the assistant said
you could not do things in that way. It was almost a scandal to
stroll onto the chief vessel of the German mercantile marine
and expect to sit down as if you were on a tram-car. The ship
had been booked up full to the davits for two months. The

Russians were extremely eager and agitated. They said they had a great deal of luggage on the tender as if to assure the assistant-purser that they would not leave without paying their bill. The assistant purser said that if they had had the Imperial crown jewels they could not have found a berth on that boat. One of the Russians was heavy and fair, the other thin, dark and magnetic. They began to upbraid each other violently in their own language.

The purser came in. He had two telegrams. One was from some American—I think it was Harriman, the railway king. He said he was prevented from using his reservation which was an extraordinarily gorgeous suite on the Sun Deck. Would the purser dispose of it for anything it would fetch? The other was from the German Embassy in St. Petersburg, ordering the purser to do anything that he could to find berths for a Count W—— and Mr. M——. They would be boarding the boat at Cherbourg.

Count W—— was the fair one, Mr. M—— the lively and elegant South Russian. They got berths in Mr. Harriman's suite for £16 a piece, and they had the whole place to themselves. They were the most amazing travelling companions I ever had.

Count W—— was a colonel of artillery in the suite of the Tzar; Mr. M—— a chamberlain of the Empress. They were thus of a very different type from Prince Kropotkin or Sergius Stepniak. But a more incredible picture of Russian Court habits and affairs than was revealed in the violent conversations of those two courtiers could not have been afforded by either revolutionist in his most heated moments.

Their conversations were always violent and nearly always in French. They carried them on at the tops of their voices, usually over a chess-board whilst they moved their men as violently as they spoke.

"The Tzar . . . ," W—— would shout. "Check and I win in three moves. . . . The Tzar is a *cretin.* . . ."

"Not at all," M—— would exclaim, "you do not win in

three moves and the Tzar is not a *cretin*. He is a congenital idiot."

"A *cretin* !" W—— would roar.

M—— would spring up and gesticulate over the board.

"You misuse terms," he would cry. "You do not know what a *cretin* is. The Tzar presents all the technical symptoms of inherited mental weakness."

"Check to the Queen," W—— would declare. He slammed his knight down on the board, as if he were trying with its base to kill a wasp. "You could not pass your medical examinations. You know less about technical terms than I do. I can at least apply a tourniquet. The Tzar is in every symptom and particular a *cretin*." He would lean over to me.

"Figure to yourself," he said. "I commanded the Emperor's own regiment of artillery at Vladivostok. We had the most magnificent guns and the most superfine breech-blocks. Only the breech-blocks would not fit the guns. We telegraphed to Petersburg for new breech-blocks. As his Imperial Majesty was Colonel of the regiment his leave had to be asked before the breech-blocks could be sent. He could not make up his mind because he disliked to be reminded of the War. By the time he did resolve to have them sent, the Japanese had cut the Trans-Siberian Railway. So my guns were never fired till the end of the siege. When I applied to the Tzar for permission to prosecute the scoundrels, the Tzar would not permit it. He said the war must be forgotten. I had an officer who deserted and went back to Petersburg. He got himself appointed to some high place in the civilian service. When he went to kiss hands on his appointment, the Tzar said to him: 'You did quite right to desert. You know how I hate war. I shall watch over your future career with special benevolence.' Yet we poor devils were endangering our lives. To be sure, not one of my officers had ever seen a gun fired. Every one of them knew Herbert Spencer by heart; not one of them ever went to bed sober.... But is that speech not the speech of a *cretin?*"

"You," M—— would declare, "were never sober on your feet

or in bed and you have never seen a gun fired either. The only
difference between you and your officers is that you have not
the intelligence to understand a sentence of Herbert Spencer.
I tell you the Tzar is a congenital idiot. A *cretin* technically is
a Swiss who has become deranged after suffering from a *goître*.
The Tzar is not Swiss and has never suffered from the *goître*.
He was born what he is—deficient in intellect." He would lean
over to me.

"Listen to this. Then you will say that the Tzar is not a
cretin. You have not heard of his book that was suppressed by
the censor? It was like this.... Every year the Tzar gives a
dinner and makes a speech to the cadets who are about to join
the Imperial body-guard. Every ten years those speeches have
to be printed in a volume. This year the Tzar's speeches were
printed as usual. The gorgeously got up volume was never
issued. Just before the copies were to be sent out, somebody
looked at it. The speeches ran: 'Cadets! You are about to enter
the service of your sovereign and your country. I drink this
glass of wine to you.' That was the first year. The second it
was: 'I drink this glass of wine to you, cadets. You are about
to enter the service of your sovereign and your country.' The
third: 'To you cadets, about to enter the service of your sovereign and your country, I drink this glass of wine.' So it went
on to the end of the volume. Is that not typical of mental
degeneracy?"

I passed practically the whole of my time on that voyage
with those two and became intimate as one does on ocean
voyages. W——, late one night, told me that they were actually
conveying, if not all the imperial crown jewels, then a great
number and a prodigious quantity of deeds and stocks. The Imperial family did not expect to remain long on the throne;
Bloody Sunday was not far off. They had suddenly decided to
send a great part of their negotiable property to New York for
safety. Count W—— and Mr. M—— had been awakened in
the night and told to start at once without even packing their
grips.

Loyalty takes queer forms. I am sure their imperial master had no more passionately loyal subjects than those two. I heard that they were both killed during the revolution, but, as I am not certain of the fact, I suppress their names, one of which was very famous.

I never saw them after we landed in New York. I heard that one of the Imperial spies in that city warned them that I was a disguised Nihilist.

PART FIVE

THE LAST OF LONDON

CHAPTER I

REVUES

A CURIOUS incident recalled itself to me whilst I was writing the portion with which my last chapter ends. I tell it here as much to symbolise the change of atmosphere which will now come over this book as to enforce a moral. The moral has none the less its value. It enjoins, if a little invertedly, the lesson to be learned of the fable of the mouse and the lion.

I had been then to the *Empire* to see Miss Génée dance. At that time seeing Miss Génée dance was one of the great pleasures of my life. There used to be, next door, to the old *Café Royale* a German beer house called *Gambrinus*. There I always went after the theatre, at least when—as I usually was —I was alone. It was vast, decorated with antlers, helmets, morgensterns, owls, the light of whose eyes went in and out, and the usual decorations that made for a simple Teutonic atmosphere. There was an end, giving on Glasshouse Street that was rather smart and an end towards Regent Street that was rather Bohemian. When I was in one mood I would go to one end, at other times to the other.

I was sitting towards the Regent Street end about one in the morning. Towards the other end of the place there was a group of perhaps six or seven waiters, the proprietor, Mr. Oddenino and a member of the public. They were moving chairs, displacing guests and looking carefully on the floor. I observed near my feet what looked like a large fragment of a beer mug—a dull piece of glass in the sawdust. Then I saw, after I had poked it with my stick, that it was faceted. I picked it up. It seemed duller in my hand than on the ground. It seemed too large to be valuable. I had two regular waiters under whom I sat in that place, the one at one end, the other at the other. The one on the Regent Street side was old, North German and extremely ugly, the one towards Glasshouse Street was young, Austrian and cherubic. I asked the old man what the group at the far end were looking for. He said:

"The gentleman has lost a diamond out of his tie-pin."

I got up and strollel over to that civilian. I say "civilian" because waiters always impress me as being military overlords of their domains. I held my open hand towards him. I said I supposed that what was in my palm was what he had lost. He jumped at it, as it were, and for a moment was too excited, shewing it to the waiters. His tie-pin was noticeable as being, on top of its stick, a large, empty circlet of gold. At last he said to me, quite inoffensively:

"I suppose I could not offer you anything for finding it?"

I said he could not. Then he asked me to sit down and have a drink with him. I said I would prefer not to. I do not think I ever took a drink with a stranger. Then he said:

"You *must* have a drink with me. Do you know what that stone is? It is the —— diamond."

It comes back to me as having been the Hope Diamond but I daresay it wasn't. It was at any rate one of the famous diamonds of the world of that day. I said that having held the —— diamond in my hand was sufficient reward for having strolled across the café to restore it to him. He said:

"Then come back to Claridge's with me and taste my champagne. I've got some..." He named some fabulous brand and vintage year.

When I still refused he said:

"But I'm Harriman." He added: "T. E. Harriman...."
I think those were the initials. At any rate they were those

of the then railway king of the United States. I said I was as
glad to have seen him as to have seen his diamond but that
champagne disagreed with me. As a matter of fact, I dislike
champagne almost more than any other fluid.

I strolled back to my place. But here is the point: I was
not half across the café when my little Austrian waiter ran
after me and said:

"How could you do it? How *could* you do it? How
could you?"

I expressed astonishment. He said, almost crying:

"Why did you give him the diamond? Of course, you
could not take a reward. But if you had given it to me to
give to him he must have given me three—four—five hundred
pounds, by law. Then I could have opened my café in Wien
and marry and be happy for ever."

I was never so ashamed of myself. I have not got over
being ashamed of it. Since then I have eaten I suppose the
majority of my meals at restaurants—and that lesson I have
never forgotten. Waiters, I mean, are human beings and the
wise man remembers it.

It is good to attach yourself to one waiter in a place in
which you are settled and to one in every place to which you
go frequently. Then—if you remember that he is not only a
military dictator but a human being—you will have a most
valuable friend and mentor. In the town near which I am
living I have been attended by a chief waiter for eight or ten
years. I go to him for advice as to every imaginable con-
tingency—as to where to buy hens, rubber piping, clocks, as
to the real characters of servants, lawyers, bank managers, as
to the most ornate church services, as to the dates of birth
of great men, as to which paper has the best account of such
and such a case, as to postage on parcels to the United States,
as to the foibles of the tax collector in my district. But from
time to time I give him little presents—or accept them from
him: a bunch of carnations from his or my garden, a duck's
egg or so, once one of my own books that had pictures in it.

I once gave a waiter—but a head, head waiter—advice. He was the incredibly all-knowing, bearded, inscrutable *maître d'hôtel* of the Carlton Grill Room. He positively came to me one day when I was lunching and asked me if I could give him advice how to find the house in which Casanova lived in London. Even the bibliophile Jacob had not known where it was except that it was in Soho. He wanted the information for some American clients who were making a pilgrimage to all the places dwelt in by Casanova—and if possible to the very house. I happened to have the information, so he was saved further trouble. He was suavely grateful.

Later he came back to my table and leaning one hand on the cloth said:

"Why do you ever lunch anywhere else but here? This is the best grill-room in the most famous hotel in the world. It should be good enough for you." I used the word "expensive."

He looked down sardonically at my *couvert*.

"Yes," he said, "but what do you want with a lunch like that? Half a dozen oysters, that alone is enough for a lunch for a young man like you. But you follow it by paté de Périgord and quails stewed with grapes. And you drink a half *Berncastler* and a half *Pontet Canet* 1906 ... What sort of lunch is that and can you grumble if it costs you the eyes out of your head?"

I said I was very busy and needed sustaining. He said:

"A lunch like that will not sustain you. After it you will be sleepy and your business will be a battle. Do you suppose I could do my work if I lunched like that? No, take my advice. Lunch here every day. We do not ask you to spend enormous sums but to have a good lunch. You will take a chump chop, or a steak, or some kidneys or any other thing of the grill. You will have some Stilton or Cheshire cheese, butter and the choice of twelve different sorts of bread and cheese biscuits. You will drink iced water or a half bottle of Perrier or, if you like, a half bottle of our *vin ordinaire rouge*

which I drink myself. It costs one and ninepence. If you
have mineral water you will save a shilling. So your lunch will
cost you two or three and ninepence. The chop and the cheese
cost two shillings. You will have the same seat and the same
waiter whom I will choose for you myself. You will tip him
fifteen shillings on the first of every month. You will be
troubled by no tiresome suggestions to take more costly food
and you will be under no sense of obligation. I have several
of the richest and most distinguished men in London amongst
my regular clients and they never spend or tip more."

It was kind and valuable advice to give a younger man.
I suppose I was thirty-three or -four then. But you have to be
older before you can dispense with a *maître d'hôtel's* or even
a waiter's advice. I should think you would have to be a
hundred.

You are to think of me then as rather a dandy. I was
going through that phase. It lasted perhaps eight years—until
Armageddon made one dress otherwise. Every morning about
eleven you would see me issue from the door of my apartment. I should be wearing a very long morning coat, a perfectly immaculate high hat, lavender trousers, a near-Gladstone
collar and a black satin stock. As often as not, at one period,
I should be followed by a Great Dane. The dog actually belonged to Stephen Reynolds, but he disliked exercising it in
London because he was nervous at crossings. But a policeman
will always stop the traffic for a Great Dane to cross. I carried a malacca cane with a gold knob.

I would walk up Holland Park Avenue as far as the
entrance to Kensington Gardens, diagonally across them to
Rotten Row where I would chat with the riders, leaning on
the rails. I would cross to St. James's Park and the Green
Park, cross them and reach one or other of my clubs about
half past twelve, read the papers and my letters until one.
Then I would lunch at the club or the Carlton and take a
hansom—later a taxi—back to my apartment which I would
reach about half past two. At five I would go to or give a

tea party. Before dinner I would take a bath and a barber would come in and shave me. I dined out every day, but very occasionally, for someone special I would cook a dinner myself in my own flat, putting a chef's coat over my evening things. I had two boasts—one that no one had ever seen me work, the other that I walked four miles every day on grass. That was in crossing the parks. In Central Park, New York, I had been apostrophised by a policeman who said:

"Get off the grass, same as you would in any other civilised country." I used my second boast usually on New Yorkers of whom I saw a good many.

My father used to say that he was the laziest man in the world, yet he had done more work than any man living. I could almost say as much of myself. I fancy that for ten years—say from 1904 to 1914—I never took a complete day's rest. I worked even on the trains in America at a time when that was less usual than it is today. My record in the British Museum Catalogue fills me with shame; it occupies page on page with the mere titles of my printed work. Even at that it is not a complete record; it omits several books published only in America. I do not imagine that any one not a daily journalist has written as much as I have and I imagine that few daily journalists have written more.

I am not proud of the record. If I had written less I should no doubt have written better. Of the fifty-two separate books there catalogued, probably forty are out of print. There is only one of those forty that I should care to re-publish and, of the remaining twelve, there are not more than six of which I should much regret the disappearance.

This great body of work was produced without any feeling of fatigue. At the time of which I am writing I used to work with great regularity from nine to eleven, when I went out to lunch, and from half past two to half past four, when I would go out to tea. After I was eighteen I never wrote at night and except for a week or so before the publication of the first number of the *English Review* I never did any work at all—even editing or proof correcting—after dinner. In the four hours of work I turned out exactly two thousand words. Of these I would condemn about half. This left about a thousand words for the day. A thousand words a day is 365,000 for the year—enough to make over four novels. Of course, I never published four novels in any one year. Only twice indeed have I published as many as two. The usual tale was one novel and one book of the type called in England "serious." There the novel cannot be heralded as "serious." It would give the public cause to think the writer was in earnest, which to the Englishman is insupportable. In the United States books that are not novels are classed as "non-fiction." The classification is perhaps not accurate but it is more complimentary to the novelist. That I suppose is why I have latterly published more books to the West than to the East of the Atlantic. Earnestness *will* come creeping into what I write.

But by far the greater bulk of what I wrote from, say, 1905 until the War went into ephemeral organs—mostly into the Saturday editions of weekly papers, into the editorial columns of monthlies that I owned or edited, or into weekly papers. At the time of the Suffragette agitations I wrote a great deal that Miss Pankhurst published, where and how she liked. Apart from that, most of my periodical writing was critical and mostly about the work of young writers, though I was always given a free hand and wrote a good deal about more revolutionary painting and sculpture. Latterly I wrote a weekly causerie about anything I liked to write about for the *Outlook* whose editor, Mr. Oliver, was very sympathetic to me. He let me write whatever I liked about any subject under the sun. As I was never a very good conversationalist, I enjoyed getting my say without interruptions.

I went on writing until well into the War. A suggestion of mine in one of those causeries—that the reports of German atrocities were probably a good deal exaggerated and that if we could fight the War in terms of the "gallant enemy," it would be better for all parties—caused the paper to lose some readers, but Mr. Oliver neither asked me to resign nor to change my note. That called for rare courage at that date. I continued writing government propaganda in his paper till I went to the Front.

I wrote a great deal of propaganda during the first year of the War. What I wrote was certainly the mildest in tone as it was probably the most instructive that was written for the Allies. I read the great bulk of it through the other day and saw nothing that I should now wish to alter. I had the rare honour of receiving sheafs of anonymous letters from both English and German patriots who all said they desired to murder me.

But at other times I wrote about English or foreign writers who did not appear to me to be receiving the attention they deserved or about curious points in the civilisation of the day. The only time I wrote about anything political was during the Marconi case. Of that I attended the hearings fairly regularly. I was shocked at the deterioration that appeared to have begun in English public life since the Boer War and the death of Queen Victoria. Before that time, a Minister of the Crown was expected to—and usually did— lay down office a poorer man than when he entered public life. That was true too of Germany. Both Bismarck and Gladstone died poorer than they had been on coming into their inherited wealth. A number of ministers of the first Asquith Administration did not, however, see why a minister should not use government information when making investments. They did not indeed see why they should not let their friends in on a good thing. I mean that they really did not see it. Nor did they see any necessity for concealment. Their relatives and intimates called inside financial information one to the other up the very staircases of their clubs.

There was nothing very wonderful in that. After the South African War a wave of financial gambling overcame the country. The great houses in Park Lane fell into the hands of the "Randlords"—South African speculators. They were received familiarly at Court, became intimates of the highest in the land, won classic races and became national heroes.

I suppose it was no affair of mine. But perhaps the certainty that the poor old Queen was turning in her grave got on my nerves. At any rate I wrote some impassioned articles, backing up Mr. F. W. Wilson, the financial editor of the *Outlook*. It was he who really brought about the exposure of the Marconi Affair.

The Postmaster General was at that date negotiating with the Marconi Company to make a network of Marconi Stations connecting the Dominions of the Empire. That much was known to the public and the shares of the Marconi Company rose sympathetically or fell, according as the negotiations progressed or stood still. But the relatives and intimates of the Postmaster General put it about with very little caution among *their* relatives and intimates that the Chancellor of the Exchequer—who ought to be a financial expert—was buying shares in a company subsidiary to the Marconi Company proper. The shares of everything connected with wireless telegraphy began extraordinarily to boom and Mr. Wilson began his attacks on the Chancellor of the Exchequer, the Postmaster General and a number of their relatives. The government at first pooh-poohed the matter. But the agitation spread to other papers and quarters. It became so intense that they had to appoint a Royal Commission to enquire into the whole matter of the sales of Marconi shares.

As I have said, I attended a number of the sittings of this body. I had before then attended, usually as a witness, a few Royal Commissions. They were non-political and seemed to be conducted with decorum and a fairly efficient if somnolent desire to obtain information. But the Marconi Commission must have been one of the most farcical bodies that ever met. There were seven Liberals and five Tories. They voted with the unanimity of the clockwork soldiers of the Russian ballet, each party against the other. The Tories voted that any evidence that could be helpful to the Ministers concerned should not be heard, the Liberals that it should. When evidence unfavourable to the Ministers was being heard all the Liberals went to sleep in a body; when anything that could be dug up seemed to be favourable to them, all the Tories seemed to have been drugged. In addition Lord Robert Cecil, who presumably suffered from a bad throat, constantly took out an atomiser and opened his mouth extraordinarily wide. The noise of the spray and his vocal garglings would extraordinarily disconcert any ministerial witness.

The evidence was extraordinarily prolix, the repetitions interminable. Gentleman after gentleman swore that he had heard ministerial relatives shouting financial information up the marble staircase of the National Liberal Club; gentleman after gentleman swore that he had not. Financial experts deposed that the shares of the companies subsidiary to the parent company would be advantaged by the contract given by the Postmaster General to that parent company; financial experts deposed that they would not be in the least advantaged. Every one in London or New York who had ever heard of any one else purchasing anything called after Marconi was examined by one side or the other.

At last came the turn of the editor of the *Financial News*, the journal and its editor having the greatest possible weight in the City. His evidence was not immensely important, mainly because he had been in South America during the greater part of the time when the case had been brewing. When he had finished, the President of the Commission put to him the formal question: Had he anywhere, at any time or in any circumstances heard the name of any other minister who was said to have bought shares in any company connected with Marconi. The editor said that he had not. The chairman who was bald, white-headed and stout repeated with extraordinary solemnity, whilst all the Tories snored:

"You have never—at any time, in *any* circumstances, in any place heard mention of any minister except those whose conduct is here under enquiry as having purchased any shares in any company in any remotest way connected with Marconi's?"

The editor said that he had of course heard another minister mentioned but it was idle gossip. He had means of knowing the names of all purchasers of such stock and knew the gossip was absolutely untrue. All the Liberal members became at once as if galvanised. They insisted on having the name of the accused minister.

The editor energetically refused to give it. The gossip was perfectly irresponsible. He had heard it in a bar in Buenos Aires from a person who, in the nature of events, could not have private information about the case. And he repeated that he knew the allegation was absolutely untrue.

The Liberals went on pressing him. A Conservative, Mr. Amory, made a pointed and impassioned remark about the waste of the Commission's time. The editor refused still. He said he could not as a gentleman be asked to give currency to gossip that he regarded as pestilential lying by the worst type of bar-loafer. His emotion was impressive. The Liberals continued to press him, the Tories to protest. At last the room was cleared for the Commission to put the matter to the vote. The seven Liberals voted for the evidence, the five Tories against its being heard.

The editor was pallid. He protested against being coerced into dishonouring himself. It was no good. He was threatened with the Speaker's writ committing him to the Clock Tower. The whole room hung on his lips in an intense silence. Lord Robert Cecil's spray sounded like artillery; his hanging open jaw gave him the appearance of being about to die. At last the witness said:

"The name was that of Winston Churchill ... But I protest...."

That Committee Room at once became like pandemonium. At last the Chairman could be heard to say:

"Mr. Churchill must be written to to attend before us," and we all adjourned to lunch. When we came back there was a long pause, some minutes being inaudibly read. Suddenly there was a roar like that of a charging wild boar. Mr. Churchill was pushing aside the people in the doorway as if he had been a forward in a game of football and near the goal. His top hat was pressed down over his ears, his face was as pallid as wax, whiter than the paper on which this is written. His features were so distorted that he was almost unrecognisable. He dashed himself at the chair that was in the horse-shoe-shaped space before the Commissioners. He shouted:

"If any man has dared to say that I would do such a damned swinish thing as to buy any share in any filthy company in any way connected with any governmental action.... If any man has dared...."

The chairman said:

"There, there Mr. Winston we all know your admirable record." The Tories shouted in unison: "An outrage...."

Mr. Churchill slammed his fist violently on the table before him and began again:

"If I could get my hands on his throat... To say that I could be capable of such infamy...."

Mr. Lloyd George's private secretary dashed up behind him and whispered in his ear. Mr. Churchill said:

"I don't care.... *Infamy*...." Other minister's secretaries had a try at him, the humour of the scene being added to by the fact that there was a tangle of acrimonious divorce cases going on among the ministers' secretaries. Mr. Asquith was having a great deal of trouble and putting himself to some expense in order to prevent charges and cross-charges making a very pretty scandal and to provide incomes denied to erring partners by recalcitrant and disagreeable parties. I had not considered till then that it was part of the Prime Minister's duties to provide for the lame ducks and divorced wives of his more immediate supporters. But apparently Mr. Asquith took the view that it was and behaved with great generosity and kindness. I know this because I was engaged to persuade one of the more unreasonable parties to one of the cases to behave with some moderation.

The final comic relief to the situation was provided by one of the Liberal members who, having begun life by pushing a costermonger's barrow had lately been ennobled. This knight, who was very handsome in a dark and bearded way, had a singularly sentimental manner and a strange accent. He leaned romantically over the table towards Mr. Churchill and made an elaborate oratorical effort. He begged Mr. Churchill to be sure that no one in that assembly could so much as most distantly suspect a Churchill of financial irregularity. How, he said, could any suspicion of dishonour attach to one descended from the heroic John Churchill, Duke of Marlborough and, one of the greatest generals the world had ever seen?

John Churchill, Duke of Marlborough, had to the common knowledge been one of the greatest eighteenth-century exponents of the art of what is today called grafting. So the handsome knight's speech proved too much for the gravity of the meeting and the sitting broke up in some disorder. Mr. Churchill with tremendous emphasis had assured the members that, since his taking the smallest office under the crown he had not bought a single share in any company whose destinies could be affected by government. Before taking such office he had disposed of every such share as happened to be in his possession.

Mr. George's speech of exculpation was one of the most marvellous feats of oratorical pathos that could be imagined. Certainly I have never heard on the stage or read in any book anything much more moving. He made no attempt to deny having purchased shares that he ought, strictly speaking, not to have bought, but he said he had bought them in the usual course of investment and on the advice of his usual financial adviser. He had had nothing to do with any attempts to influence the market. Was, he said, a career of sedulous devotion to the service of his country, to be broken because of a mistake that could be made by any one not born to opportunities of great experience in the manipulations of shares?

As he went on he moved the House to deep emotion. A great many of the members—Mr. Balfour was one—were moved to tears. I know that I came very near crying myself, and in that matter I was as bitter an opponent as Mr. George ever had. After the first five minutes of the speech there could be no doubt that the division would be a triumph for him. And it was. He carried practically the whole House with him.

The Marconi Commission had been a grotesque affair and, after the sitting which I have described, it was summarily brought to an end. But it did undoubtedly have the effect of restoring English public standards to their earlier strictness. I do not believe that any minister of the Crown has since bought any shares which could in any way be questioned. The horror of having such a body sit interminably on your case must be enough to deter you from the most minute of irregularities.

With such preoccupations and employments I passed my working hours. The second reverse of my medal—if a medal can have two reverses or a lump of amber contain two flies—presented itself when I took my morning walks abroad. When I left my doorstep I would perceive bearing down on me from opposite directions Mrs. Gwendolen Bishop and Mr. Ezra Pound. Mrs. Bishop was a lady of striking appearance—of great beauty, indeed. I think she danced snake dances and made pottery. Mr. Bernard Shaw broke up the City Socialist League because he drank champagne from one of her shoes on the premises of that body. But no one could have drunk anything from her shoes in those days for she habitually wore sandals on bare feet. In addition, she wore a very short blue skirt. It would be entirely covered by a leopard skin that descended from her shoulders; her head would be bare and she carried a string bag filled with onions. I had, as a matter of the merest courtesy, to take the string bag. Ezra, on the other hand, would approach with the step of a dancer, making passes with a cane at an imaginary opponent. He would wear trousers made of green billiard cloth, a pink coat, a blue shirt, a tie hand-painted by a Japanese friend, an immense sombrero, a flaming beard cut to a point, and a single, large blue earring.

Mrs. Bishop would fall in on my right, Ezra on my left, and the great Dane would adjust its nose so as just not to touch my heel. So arranged we would proceed up Holland Park Avenue towards Bond Street. I did not mind ... much. Sometimes I used to wonder why Mrs. Bishop should want to carry—or want me to carry—exposed onions to that fashionable thoroughfare. Indeed I used to wonder why she carried onions away from rather than towards her home which was in the other direction, though I never quite knew where it was. In any case we went on the way in concord, discussing *vers libre,* the metre of Arnaut Daniel or the villany of contributors to the front page of the *Times Literary Supplement.*

Ezra, the most erudite of poetic beings and the most poetic amongst the erudite, danced, fought and swashbuckled his way into my friendship through the medium of *The English Review.* He once challenged a *Times* reviewer to a duel because the reviewer had too high an opinion of Milton. I cannot imagine any better reason. The *Times* at least ought not to be kind to non-Conformists. And he gave a good deal of pain to many worthy and pompous people. But the only thing I have against him is that he never once offered to carry Mrs. Bishop's string back. And since that is the only thing I have against him during a friendship that has lasted nearly a quarter of a century it may well pass for very little. Ezra was brought to my office by Miss May Sinclair who said she wanted to introduce the greatest poet to the greatest editor in the world. She could invent these courtesies when she wanted to. She must by then have forgiven me for the fireman's helmet. But she afterwards wrote a book whose villain was a striking likeness of myself. So perhaps she really had not.

There are three people in whose deaths I have never been able to believe. They are Conrad and Arthur Marwood and

Mrs. H. G. Wells. It seems to me impossible that I shall never drive over to the Pent and ask Conrad some question, or never listen to Marwood encyclopædically and brilliantly laying down the English Tory law on something or other. And though I shall never again take tea with Mrs. Wells I can not believe it and I should not thank you if you proved the fact to me. I will pay to her my little tribute before going on to Marwood and the *English Review*.

She had an extraordinarily delicate talent and contributed to both *The English* and *The Transatlantic Reviews* while I edited them. I still occasionally meet someone who remembers those stories as standing out from those periodicals. I used to urge her to write more and I still possess a number of pages of her sketches for poems or stories. But she felt that her star rose to be obscured. The little she wrote was exquisite but it was very little indeed. Her achievements as a hostess were as extraordinary as they appeared to be effortless. There can have been very few men or women of talent or distinction in England for whom she had not at one time or another provided delicate and charming entertainment and the number of the unfortunate who had cause to bless her for her care was legion. Her domesticity was conducted with a fierceness of conscience that can never have been surpassed. How she achieved what in one field or the other she contrived to achieve was incomprehensible. Yet she seemed to be always at leisure and always full of humour. I remember that the first time I stopped at Spade House I was sent to take a walk with Mrs. Wells whilst Mr. Wells wrote. We got as far as Folkestone post office. Here she purchased a number of stamps, postcards and stamped envelopes that would have seemed to be excessive had she been purchasing a week's supply for the house of Rothschild. Her other purchases were on a similarly impressive scale. Years after—twenty perhaps— I reminded her of that walk in what was, I should imagine, the last of the few letters I ever wrote her. She replied, yes, she remembered. She had been told that I was a very haughty, ostentatious, and disagreeable sort of person. She had therefore

made a list of things that could be bought in bulk without
deteriorating and had taken me out for the sole purpose of dis-
gruntling me whilst she bought a whole year's supply of articles
necessary in the household. She wrote that she rejoiced to think
that she *had* impressed me. Ah, but indeed she had.

At Winchelsea a little later I had noticed for some time a
powerfully built, leisurely man who sauntered about the town
and the circumjacent marshes with a lady and, I think, a dog.
I do not remember the dog at all, so it must have been either
non-existent or a fox-terrier, a breed that I dislike for its rest-
lessness. How we became acquainted I do not remember, but I
do remember very vividly interminable conversations that we
had almost immediately after we did meet. There was nothing
under the sun that we did not discuss and no topic on which he
could not in some minute particular at least correct my asser-
tions. He would wait for a long time and then rather jestingly
drop his correction into the middle of a quite unrelated topic.
The first time he did this he filled me with a confusion that I
can still feel. By a feat of mixing up names of which I am at all
times capable I assigned Laura to Ariosto and spoke of Valence
instead of Vaucluse as Petrarch's place of exile. Marwood made
no immediate protest. A long time after we were talking of some
parliamentary candidate who had written an extraordinary
number of addresses to the electors of the Cleveland Division of
Durham. Marwood said:

"They were about as useful as the stuff *P*etrarch wrote to
Laura in Vaucl*use*," as it were underlining the names a very
little.

He possessed the clear, eighteenth-century English mind
which has disappeared from the earth, leaving the earth very
much the poorer. It was not merely that his mind was encyclo-
pædic, it was that his information was all arranged. I knew
Valence and Vaucluse as well as I know most places that I have
not inhabited and I knew and disliked the Petrarchan sonnet
as well as I know and dislike any literary form, but nothing
can prevent my mixing up names. I suppose I inherit the char-

acteristic from my grandfather who had it to a dangerous degree. I would come in and say to him:

"Grandpa, I met Lord Leighton in the Park and he sent his regards to you." He would exclaim with violence: "Leighton! How dare you be seen talking to him. And how dare he presume to send messages to me. He is the scoundrel who . . ." I would interrupt:

"But, Grandpa, he is the President of the Royal Academy. . . ." He would interrupt in turn: "Nonsense. I tell you he is the fellow who got seven years for. . . ." A few minutes after he would exclaim:

"Leighton? Oh, Leighton? Why didn't you say Leighton if you meant Leighton. I thought you said Fothergill-Bovey Haines. Of course there is no reason why you should not be civil to Leighton."

Marwood's mind connoted and arranged names, verb sounds and cyphers with such accuracy that it was impossible for him to make a slip. I got over my confusion about the Laura affair next day. The Ninth Edition of the Encyclopædia Britannica had just appeared and he had borrowed a copy of the first volume from the village library and covered it with a newspaper jacket so that no one should know that the objectionable volume was in the house. I found him going through the first page wtih a pencil and note-book. He had discovered thirty-seven errors in that page. In the paragraph about Arminianism alone he had found seven slips, misstatements and inaccuracies in terminology.

He had other and singular gifts; how many I never fathomed. He was a higher mathematician of considerable renown at his university. He was determined not to be Senior Wrangler because he disliked the idea of having a title that he considered ridiculous. The betting at Cambridge was five to one that he would be. He had to sit for that distinction. He deliberately set down five cyphers wrong, wrote them down on a piece of paper apart, and, as he came out tossed it contemptuously to his principal backer, saying:

"Sorry, old fellow. I'll shew you how to get what you've lost back at roulette." He was most interested in the theory of waves which I think occupied the greater part of his mind. But in an off moment he had invented a modification of the martingale that he said was infallible at Monte Carlo. He communicated it to me but warned me not to use it. It needed so much application for its proper working that you were certain to get impatient and plunge, losing all your small gains. I tried it when I was in the Red Cross Hospital at Mentone in 1917. We had leave to go into the Principality after lunch and, if we changed into mufti, might play at the tables, as long as we were back in hospital at seven. I played for a great many afternoons from about three till about half past six—and always with the result that Marwood predicted. By a quarter past six I had always won anything from five to thirty pounds. At a quarter past the hour I would be sick to death of the system and would plunge. The atmosphere was stuffy, the occupation too monotonous. One said the equivalent of today's "To hell with it!" and plumped all one's winnings on a number. If one won one plumped it all on another number. It went.

It was whilst I was thus passing my time that it occurred to me to wonder what Marwood would have thought about the War and the way it was conducted. In the attempt to realise that problem for myself I wrote several novels with a projection of him as a central character. Of course they were no sort of biography of Marwood. He died several years before the War, though, as I have said, that is a fact that I never realise.

It was the peculiar, scornful, acute quality of his mind that did that for me. I do not know that I ever consulted him over any of my personal difficulties as I invariably consulted Conrad—and indeed, rather often, Mrs. Wells. It was much more as if I "set" my mind by his. If I had personal problems I would go and talk to him about anything else. Then the clarity of the working of his mind had an effect on mine that made me see, if not what was best to do then, what would be most true to myself. In much the same way when I was at

Walton Heath during the first days of the War in attendance on Masterman I played a daily round of golf with George Duncan—for a fortnight or so. I was not taking lessons. Duncan paid no attention to me and gave me no hints. I merely paid him for his time. But I played really extraordinary golf for me —with disastrous results for Masterman or any other members of the Cabinet who played against Masterman and me in the afternoon.

I do not believe that Marwood had much sense of humour, but his dry statements of essential facts were so strange to the greater part of English humanity of his day that he could keep a roomful of men laughing as long as he was in it. He said one afternoon at Rye Golf Club to the Conservative member for that borough:

"You know,"—he was speaking as a Tory—"we ought to have had Lloyd George to do our dirty work. We have always had to have someone to do our dirty jobs. We had Disraeli and we had Chamberlain. We ought to have had Lloyd George." The Conservative member laughed as if he thought Marwood an amiable lunatic. His mind was incapable of making the jump of seeing Mr. George as anything but a Radical devil with hoofs and tail.

From the beginning of the period of which I am talking— from 1907 to 1914—I worried myself with the idea that I ought to have a periodical of my own. Lord Northcliffe had wanted me to run one under him. That had not impressed me so much. But, when the Transatlantic press-Napoleon urged me to adopt the same position under himself, I had had serious thoughts of doing something of the sort. S. S. McClure had sketched out a programme for a journal that should consist as to half of pure literature and criticism and as to half of muck-raking. If he had suggested giving me the opportunity of doing something of the sort in the United States I daresay that I should have stayed there for good. But I could not see that the employment of the muck-rake could do any good in political England and there were a number of monthlies in America all devoted to imaginative literature and technical criticism. I cared nothing about politics. If McClure had proposed to set me up in a periodical that was half political of either camp and half æsthetico-critical—in England—I daresay that I should have accepted his offer. But he said that English party politics meant nothing to him and that he did not, as a foreigner, think himself justified in taking part in them.

There entered then into me the itch of trying to meddle in English literary affairs. The old literary gang of the *Athenaeum-Spectator-Heavy Artillery* order was slowly decaying. Younger lions were not only roaring but making carnage of their predecessors. Mr. Wells was growing a formidable mane; Arnold Bennett if not widely known was at least known to and admired by me. Mr. Wells had given me his first novel—*A Man From the North*. Experimenting in forms kept Conrad still young. Henry James was still "young James" for my uncle William Rossetti and hardly known of by the general public; George Meredith and Thomas Hardy had come into their own only very little before; Mr. George Moore was being forgotten as he was always being forgotten; Mr. Yeats was known as having written the *Lake of Innisfree*. It seemed to me that if that nucleus of writers could be got together, with what of undiscovered talent the country might hold, a movement might be started. I had one or two things I wanted to say. They were about the technical side of novel writing. But mostly I desired to give the writers of whom I have spoken a rostrum as it were. It was with that idea that I had returned from America. England, I knew would always regard me—rather comically and a little suspiciously—as too damn in earnest. The others it might listen to and I might slip a word in now and then.

The nature of the periodical to be started gave me a good deal of thought. To imagine that a magazine devoted to imaginative literature and technical criticism alone would find more than a hundred readers in the United Kingdoms was a delusion that I in no way had. It must therefore of necessity be a hybrid, giving at least half its space to current affairs. Those

I did not consider myself fit to deal with. I knew either nothing about them or I knew so much that I could not form any opinions. The only public matter as to which I was determined to take a line was that of female suffrage.

I dallied with the idea for some time. Then I came across the politician who had insisted on telling me his life history. I do not remember if he approached me or I him. At any rate, we quickly came to an agreement. He was a virulent Tory of the new school, and he wanted an organ of his own. He was to provide half of the capital necessary which we agreed was to be £5000, I the other half. He was to edit half the magazine which was to be a monthly, I, the other half. Being a business man as well as a politician, he was to manage the business affairs of the concern, I to see to its make up, proof-reading and other details of publication. It was a good arrangement. I liked him very much. He was too brilliant to like me extremely but he tolerated me more than he tolerated most people. He had an exaggerated idea of my omniscience and political influence.

I had arranged with the house of Duckworth to publish the review and had commissioned a number of stories, poems and critical articles. He came to me one day and said he could not supervise the business affairs of the concern. That was rather a heavy blow because I knew enough about business to know that I should make a muddle of that side of it. I sighed, cabled to Byles who was then in Japan to come back and take on the business of the *Review,* and consented to continue the enterprise. A little later my friend came to me and said that he could not undertake to do half the editing. A General Election was in the offing; he had neglected his constituency; he would have to go perpetually into the North to kick off footballs, open flower shows, subscribe to fox-hounds and utter verbal coruscations. He suggested that I might find someone else of his school of thought to direct the political policy of the review; I sighed again and consented. For that Marwood was indicated. He was an old, rather than a New Tory and he was incurably indolent. But he consented to suggest from Winchelsea the sort

of article that should go into the review and in most cases to
indicate the writers who should be invited to contribute. My
political friend proposed in fairness that if so much of the
labour was to fall on me he should increase the amount of capital that he found, whilst I should retain my full half share of
the control of the periodical. I was glad of that because I had
lately had rather serious financial reverses.

The dummy of the first number approached completion; I
had announced the name of the periodical, *The English Review,*
in the press. It was Conrad who chose the title. He felt a certain
sardonic pleasure in the choosing so national a name for a
periodical that promised to be singularly international in tone,
that was started mainly in his not very English interest and
conducted by myself who was growing every day more and
more alien to the normal English trend of thought at any rate
in matters of literary technique. And it was matters of literary
technique that almost exclusively interested both him and me.
That was very un-English.

A couple of presumably needy journalists, both of very
great ability, conceived the idea of making me, who was pre-
sumed to be rolling in wealth, pay for the use of that title. They
registered it as soon as I had announced it in the press and then
asked me to pay a prodigious sum for its use. I offered them
half a sovereign apiece. They then published a single-sheet
broad-sheet under the title of *The English Review.* Its letter
press consisted of virulent attacks on Lord Northcliffe and me,
promising extraordinary revelations as to both of us in their
next number. I fancy they imagined that Lord Northcliffe was
financing the review. The main allegation against myself was
that I was a "multiple reviewer." The charge was true enough
but only as far as one book was concerned. That was Charles
Doughty's *Dawn in Britain*—an epic poem in twelve books
and four volumes. I had a great admiration for Doughty who
was the author also of *Arabia Deserta* and I read his poem
entirely through with a great deal of pleasure. No reviewer in
London had leisure for that task. The book looked as if it might

go unreviewed, so I asked a number of those gentlemen to let me review it for them. Others, hearing that I had volunteered to do it, also asked me to relieve them of the task. I do not remember how many reviews I wrote; it was a considerable number and some of them were quite long. I pleased myself by finding that I could do them all without once repeating a sentence or even an idea. At any rate I was quite unrepentant. I do not see why you should not write more than one review of a book for which you have a great admiration. I have written several times about *Ulysses*.

I continued to take no notice of the other *English Review*. My telephone became a constant worry because those two gentlemen rang me up at all hours of the night, asking me to buy the title for sums that gradually descended from a thousand pounds to five. Lord Northcliffe, on the other hand, applied for an injunction against my rivals in one of the courts—I forget which. The injunction was granted and the other *English Review* disappeared. The real joke was that I had lent one of those lively persons the money with which he paid for his broadsheet. At any rate, just before he printed it, I had met him looking very destitute in Fleet Street and had lent him exactly the sum with which he paid his printer's and papermaker's bill.

A little later I went to a Trench dinner. A Trench dinner was a Dutch treat presided over by Herbert Trench, the Irish poet. They were agreeable affairs and attended by most of the brilliant people in London. I was only asked to one. On this occasion I was set at a round table with Mr. Hilaire Belloc, Mr. Gilbert Chesterton, Mr. Maurice Baring and Mr. H. G. Wells. My politician was at another table with Mr. Trench, the Marchioness of Londonderry and other notables.

Amongst all these celebrities I felt nervous. Celebrities are always rude to me. That has been the case from my tenderest years. I can hardly think of one that has not, at one time or another, said rude things to me. I ought to except politicians. I can hardly remember a politician who has not said nice things to me about my books—as soon as he heard that I was a writer.

I suppose they learn that when canvassing for votes. Mr. Balfour once asked me to send him my books as they came out. I did for years. He always wrote politely thanking me for the volume "from the reading of which he anticipated much pleasure." The letters were always marked: "Not for publication."

I knew I should not get through that dinner without discomfort. It came. Mr. Belloc was late. I had written an article about him a day or two before. It had been published that morning. I had classed him among the brilliant *jeunes* of the day and had expressed the really great admiration I felt for his wit, sincerity and learning. He hurried in, saw me, stopped as if he had been shot, thrust his hand through his forelock, gave one more maledictory glance at me with his baleful, pebble-blue eyes and then sank wearily into his chair next to Mr. Maurice Baring. He looked anywhere but at me and began an impassioned monologue about the misfortunes of historians. They wore themselves out searching for matter in the British Museum Library and other stuffy places; they toiled till far into the night putting the results of their researches on paper. After infinite tribulation they published their books. Then along came the cold-eyed critic.

I forget what Mr. Belloc said that the cold-eyed critic did to the historian but I realised that it was my eyes that were frigid in his. In my eulogy of him I had amiably found fault with some gigantic exaggeration in a book, I think, about the Cromwell family. What exactly Thomas Cromwell had done to our co-religionists or how Oliver had sinned against the Church of Rome I forget. Heaven forbid that I should set myself down as good a Papist as Mr. Belloc, but I dislike to think of myself as a worse. I consider that there are only two human organisations that are nearly perfect for their disparate functions. They are the Church of Rome and His Britannic Majesty's Army. I would cheerfully offer my life for either if it would do them any good and supposing them not arrayed the one against the other. But I could not see that the cause of the Church was advantage1 by gigantically exaggerating the confiscations from which she has suffered any more than it would help the Old Contemptibles to represent them as having been without exception teachers in Sunday Schools. I had said this mildly in my article. As a matter of fact I wished that Mr. Belloc would write novels and leave propaganda to the less gifted.

The affair ended dramatically in nothing, for before ending his monologue Mr. Belloc suddenly burst out to someone whom I could not see at the chairman's table beside us:

"Our Lord! What do you know about Our Lord? Our Lord was a gentleman."

After that I escaped notice in the shadow of Mr. Chesterton. Mr. Chesterton and Mr. Belloc were one on each side of Mr. Baring. They occupied themselves for some time in trying in vain to balance glasses of Rhine wine on his skull. That gentleman comes back to me as having been then only a little less bald than an egg. The floor and his shirt front received the wine in about equal quantities. But he did not seem to mind. Something I said about the two Russians of the *Kaiserin Augusta Victoria* set him corroborating their stories and telling amazing stories of his own about the Russian Court. He had been, I think, Secretary to the Embassy in St. Petersburg.

Suddenly Mr. Belloc was at me again. He said that I would not dare to print in my review any article that he sent me just as it stood. I said I would. He repeated that I would not and I that I would. He was in those days almost as vigorous a muckraker as S. S. McClure and hardly anyone had the courage to print him in his more coruscating moments. I may say that I did print his article. It contained the most amazing accusations against bishops, keepers of the Crown jewels, West Indian Governors and other apparently unoffending and unimportant beings. So I made the printer black out the names and functions of everybody concerned. Those pages of the review startlingly resembled newspapers in Russia after they had received the attention of the censor. They startled Mr. St. Joe Strachey, the editor of the *Spectator* to some purpose. He confused my *English Review* with the broad-sheet promoted by the two journalists and supposed that either I or Mr. Belloc intended to threaten the owners of the blacked out names with exposure in another number if we were not bought off, and solemnly and weightily he protested against this growing tendency in British journals. He seemed to me to be a mild and doting old gentleman, so I wrote to him amiably and told him that he had accused me of being a blackmailer and would he kindly refute himself in the next number of his journal. He did so and wrote me a very agitated letter saying that he had meant nothing of the sort. He did not say what he *had* meant.

That Trench dinner, different as it was from the Trench dinners that we afterwards ate, came also to an end. I was going towards the Piccadilly tube. It was pouring and Mr. Belloc was begging me not to believe that he was in fact the light-hearted being that he appeared. Actually he was filled with the woes of all the world.

I was beginning to assure him that from then on I would regard his as a figure of the deepest tragedy. We were just turning into the tube station when my politician, ex-fellow-editor and business manager, came running up rather breathlessly and caught hold of the arm of mine that Mr. Belloc was not imprisoning. He said:

"Fordie, I'm very sorry. I can't find my half share of the capital for the review."

I said:

"That will be all right." He disappeared and I went on assuring Mr. Belloc of my appreciation of his pessimism.

It appeared subsequently that my friend was suffering from the same financial disaster that had hit hard not only myself but many other people. It was the case of a disappearance abroad—with an expensive young woman—of a man, the bearer of a very honoured name in whose faith too many had reposed their trust. He subsequently committed suicide.

There seemed to be nothing to do but to close down that periodical, pay off the contributors whom I had already commissioned and realise my dream of retiring to a little farm in

Provence. I had of course to tell Marwood, who was by that
time as enthusiastic about the review as he could be about anything.

He agreed with me. There was nothing to do but to shut
it down. He made a good many caustic remarks about Young
Tories in general and my friend in particular. I disagreed with
him. That politician was no more guilty than I. Marwood, however, was certain that he had never intended to find the money.

I returned from Winchelsea to Aldington where I had by
now bought a cottage. There remained, it seemed, nothing for
it but to emigrate to Provence and there seemed to be nowhere
else to emigrate to. As the world then appeared to me I could
support living in London, if I had the review. Without it, I
couldn't.

I was writing to a friend I had in Tarascon—a *notaire,* to
ask about small farms that might be for sale in his neighbourhood. It was a Sunday. Marwood was suddenly on the terrace.
He was pale with indignation and brandished a crumpled newspaper. He panted:

"You've got to carry on that review."

I had never seen him agitated before—and I never did
again. He must have got up at four that morning to catch the
train from Winchelsea to Aldington.

The newspaper announced that the *Cornhill Magazine* had
refused to print, on the score of immorality, a poem of Thomas
Hardy called *A Sunday Morning Tragedy.* All the other heavy
and semi-heavy monthlies, all the weeklies, all the daily papers
in England had similarly refused. Marwood said:

"You must print it. We can't have the country made a
laughing stock." He was of opinion that the rest of the world
must guffaw if it heard that Hardy could not find a printer in
England. Marwood was accustomed to say that nothing worth
the attention of a grown man had been written in England since
the eighteenth century. Clarendon's *History of the Great Re-
bellion* and the Jacobean poets were his reading. He made a
great concession to modernity when he read Maine's *Ancient*

Law and Doughty's *Arabia Deserta*. Yet there he was mad to spend several thousand pounds in order to publish one poem by a modern poet who as poet was hardly known at all. For of course he found the money that hadn't been found by my other friend.

That was *my* Sunday morning tragedy. But for that I should have been saved a great deal of labour, a number of enemies. I should have been, now, twenty years instead of only six months, a kitchen-gardener in Provence.

CHAPTER II

REVIEWS

I MUST run only cursorily through the years from 1911 to the last days of peace in 1914. Too many controversial matters began to appear. The end of yesterday was at hand and I am not one to write controversially—or not at this moment. The sea is too smooth and blue; the sunlight too bright and the islands across the bay too gay. And I have really nothing against anyone.

The English Review duly appeared. It was a source of a· good deal of amusement and some profit to certain people and of a good many worries to myself. They are not yet even ended. The other day in Chicago an editor-professor introduced me to an audience largely consisting of editors and editresses. He said I was the greatest editor the world had ever seen. It will take me a long time to live that down. The editresses in particular have said worse than hang of me ever since.

Our first two numbers were made up, perforce of works of the then distinguished. After that we tried to let the distinguished drop out gradually, so as to publish the unpublished. We published contributions of one sort and another by Thomas Hardy, George Meredith, D. G. Rossetti—posthumously, Swinburne, Anatole France, Gerhart Hauptmann, Henry James, Joseph Conrad, W. H. Hudson, W. B. Yeats and even President Taft. Of the then youngish—speaking in terms of career—we published Mr. Wells' *Tono Bungay* serially in four numbers

and a short serial of Mr. Arnold Bennett in two, as well as
Messrs. Galsworthy, Belloc, Chesterton and others of then similar standing. Then what I wanted came. I think the only work
of an unpublished author that we had secured before going to
press for the first time was *The Mountain* by Stephen Reynolds.
Reynolds was a most original figure. He lived with a fisherman
somewhere in the West and appeared in London usually in the
garb of the trade of Peter. He wrote a book called *The Poor
Man's House* which was a success and died much too young. I
had engaged him as sub-editor before the review started, but he
did not last long. He knew nothing about sub-editing, was of
too independent a nature and became afraid of London. He
would have been a very great writer, could Fate have seen her
way to spare him. His books are full of faults and arrogances.
But a young writer's future work will deteriorate if his first
books are not full of faults and arrogance. I have found that an
invariable rule. On the whole, I should say that his death was the
greatest loss that has befallen English literature for many years.

Then came Ezra, led in by Miss Sinclair. His Odyssey
would take twelve books in itself. In a very short time he had
taken charge of me, the review and finally of London. That will
appear later. When I first knew him his Philadelphian accent
was still comprehensible if disconcerting; his beard and flowing
locks were auburn and luxuriant; he was astonishingly meagre
and agile. He threw himself alarmingly into frail chairs, devoured enormous quantities of your pastry, fixed his pince-nez
firmly on his nose, drew out a manuscript from his pocket,
threw his head back, closed his eyes to the point of invisibility
and looking down his nose would chuckle like Mephistopheles
and read you a translation from Arnaut Daniel. The only part
of that verse that you would understand would be the refrain:

"Ah me, the darn, the darn it comes toe sune!"

We published his *Ballad of the Goodly Fere* which must
have been his first appearance in a periodical except for con-

tributions to the *Butte, Montana, Herald*. Ezra, though born in Butte in a caravan during the great blizzard of—but perhaps I ought not to reveal the year. At any rate, Ezra left Butte at the age of say two. The only one of his poems written and published there that I can remember had for refrain

"Cheer up, Dad!"

As a reaction against a sentiment so American, he shortly afterwards became instructor in Romance languages at the University of Pennsylvania. His history up to the date of his appearance in my office which was also my drawing-room comes back to me as follows: Born in the blizzard, his first meal consisted of kerosene. That was why he ate such enormous quantities of my tarts, the flavour of kerosene being very enduring. It accounted also for the glory of his hair. Where he studied the Romance languages I could not gather. But his proficiency in them was considerable when you allowed for the slightly negroid accent that he adopted when he spoke Provençal or recited the works of Bertran de Born.

His grandfather I understood was an unsuccessful candidate for the Presidency in the time of Blaine, his father assayer to the Mint in Philadelphia, a function requiring almost incredible delicacy of touch. His grandfather, as was the habit of millionaires in the America of that day, made and lost fortunes with astonishing rapidity and completeness. He had promised to send Ezra to Europe. Ezra was just making his reservations when his grandfather failed more finally and more completely than usual.

Ezra therefore came over on a cattle boat. Many poets have done that. But I doubt if any other ever made a living by shewing American tourists about Spain without previous knowledge of the country or language. It was, too, just after the Spanish-American War when the cattle boat dropped him in that country.

It was with that aura of romance about him that he appeared to me in my office-drawing-room. I guessed that he must be rather hard up, bought his poem at once and paid him more than it was usual to pay for a ballad. It was not a large sum but Ezra managed to live on it for a long time—six months, I think—in unknown London. Perhaps my pastry helped.

Shortly after the arrival of Ezra a young woman wrote to me from Nottingham. She said she knew a young man who wrote admirable poems and short stories. He was too shy to send them to me himself. Might she send them?

In that way we came to publish the first writings of D. H. Lawrence. They were some of his poems and a magnificent short story called *Odour of Chrysanthemums*. In Lawrence I knew at once that we had a writer of the highest genius and solidity. I do not think that he ever surpassed his first two books, *The White Peacock* and *Sons and Lovers*, but that must be largely a matter of taste. What is certain is the authenticity of his gifts. He suffered from the second of the two major perils that lie always in wait for the English novelist—the first being the desire to establish a claim to gentility. That did not trouble Lawrence. He was the son of a Nottingham coal miner and knew that there was nothing better that one could be.

In that respect he marked the passing of a very distinct phase. There had been before him novelists the sons of working men or of lower middle class origin. Their characters, at any rate in their earlier works, were always portrayed as of those classes and concerned, even to paroxysms of confusion, over social minutiæ. They wilted under the eyes of butlers and waiters, were horribly confused over the use of fish-knives and aspirates. About Lawrence there was no sign of that either in his characters or in his personal life. His characters are perfectly self-sufficient and unembarrassed by the sense of class. They move with freedom in a world that seems to belong to them alone; they are beings of complete ignorance of class fetters and of confidence that they and their likes are the only persons that matter in the world. It was the same with Lawrence himself.

He came to dine with me and some people I had asked to meet him. He brought with him the young lady who had sent his manuscripts. But there was no confusion about them. The young lady asked the housemaid whether she was expected to take off her hat; Lawrence asked the servant who waited at table what knives he was expected to use with fish or asparagus. That being settled, he went on to talk and was completely at his ease.

He was at that time a teacher in a school at Croydon. The confinement in a close atmosphere had caused him to have tuberculosis and he was about to be forced to give up that career. The fatigue of it he found in any case to be terrible. Had the school in which he taught been in the administrative County of London he would have received substantial compensation. But, though undistinguishable from any other London suburb, Croydon is just inside the County of Kent. The school board of that division made no provision for disabled teachers. Lawrence had been very distressed at the thought of having to return home and be a burden to his parents. Masterman, who had a great admiration for his work of that date, approached the Ministry of Education on Lawrence's behalf. I think he did eventually receive a small sum for medical treatment and the ministry put pressure on the East Kent School Board to make them improve their treatment of their teachers.

Lawrence I think went home. At any rate I visited him in Nottingham and was astonished at the atmosphere in which he lived though less astonished by then as to the great sense of culture in his work. Lawrence's father, of French extraction and great force of character, was a buttyman down the mine and one of his brothers also worked underground. His sister I think was, like Lawrence, a school teacher. Other young people from down the pit or from schools and offices drifted in and out of the Lawrences' house with the sort of freedom from restraint that I have only seen elsewhere in American small towns. I have never anywhere found so educated a society. Those young people *knew* the things that my generation in the great English schools hardly even chattered about. Lawrence, the father, came in from down the mine on a Saturday evening. He threw a great number of coins on the kitchen table and counted them out to his waiting mates. All the while the young people were talking about Nietzsche and Wagner and Leopardi and Flaubert and Karl Marx and Darwin and occasionally the father would interrupt his counting to contradict them. And they would discuss the French Impressionists and the primitive Italians and play Chopin or Debussy on the piano.

I went with them on the Sunday to a non-conformist place of worship. It was the only time I was ever in one except that I once heard the Rev. Stopford Brooke, who was a Unitarian, preach a sermon on Tennyson. The Nottingham chapel—it was I think Wesleyan—made me of course feel uncomfortable at first. But the sermon renewed my astonishment. It was almost entirely about—Nietzsche, Wagner, Leopardi, Karl Marx, Darwin, the French Impressionists and the primitive Italians. I asked one of Lawrence's friends if that was not an unusual sort of sermon. He looked at me with a sort of grim incredulity.

"What do you suppose?" he said. "Do you think we would sit under that fellow if he could not preach like that for fifty-two Sundays a year? He would lose his job."

I asked him if the elder generation liked it. He said that of course they liked it. They wanted their sons to be educated people. And they liked it for itself. They could do their religious thinking without help of preacher.

The fact is that that atmosphere was normal life to those young people. They could not imagine any other way of living. They lived like that "of course"—and that ended it. By the Monday of that week-end I was pretty certain that the days of middle-class government in England were numbered. The time was passing when Mrs. Sidney Webb would say that one person or another would not be able to be an official of the Fabian Society because he was not a gentleman.

I mentioned my astonishment to Mr. Wells as soon as I got back to Town. He said:

"Didn't you know? English public education is the best in the world. There was never anything as good at any time, anywhere. But you must not say so in public for fear of the rate-payers."

I suppose I may say so now that it has done its work.

I will permit myself thirty-odd lines of sermonising.

When I saw the environment in which Lawrence lived I learned at once the lesson of my life. Prosperity depends on culture. Here were people absolutely prosperous, not of great means nor yet of very small ones but having sufficient education to expend those means frugally and so as to obtain the greatest amount of rational pleasure out of life. That is the chief function of education. A society, a coterie, a nation, a civilisation so equipped is bound to outlast nations or classes within a nation whose idea of prosperity—nay, of culture itself—is that of material hegemony of the world. I read this paragraph yesterday in a Paris-American journal:

"The body of a woman was found floating in the Seine off Suresnes. As the fingers of the body were covered with costly rings and the neck and breast with very expensive necklaces and brooches it is evident that she was a woman of culture."

It isn't. A culture that is founded on the activities of the applied scientist, the financier, the commercial engineer is not only very little elevated above the state of savagedom, but it is foredoomed. Armageddon, as it was called, came upon us because of those activities. We fought so as to determine which set of savages should decorate the corpses of its women with the more costly rings and their necks and breasts with the most expensive necklaces and brooches.

The little society in which Lawrence moved was a microcosm of what the world must come to if it is to be permanent. Its existence foretold to me even then the disappearance of the ruling power of the middle-classes as they then were and even of the class that in England was called the ruling one. The disappearance of Eton as the educational home of the nation's legislators was there as plainly foreshadowed as was the fact that England's victories would never again be won on Eton's playing fields. The one was to go down before the type of edu-

cation that had produced Lawrence's small coterie and nour-
ished the genius of Lawrence himself. The other was just as
surely to disappear before wireless telegraphy, the aeroplane,
motor traction and the other wonders of science. You cannot
fight an atmosphere of poison gas with the rules of cricket any
more than you can expect to rule cultured people—or any people if you are unacquainted with the highest imaginative
thought of the world of your day. This Anglo-Saxondom has
never believed. That is why Anglo-Saxondom is crumbling as
Rome did to its doom. Even in the Middle Ages they knew
that. They used to say:

> *When lands are gone and money spent*
> *Then learning is most excellent.*

I will relate two incidents.

At a time when France was in very dire financial straits,
the franc tumbling to nothing in value and panic beginning to
appear in the land, I had to wait for an hour in the railway
station of a village only just outside the devastated districts.
There was around the station door a queer collection of vehicles
from the oddest of farm-carts to small motors and push bi-
cycles. There was also a small crowd of pedestrians. They were
waiting for the train from Paris. It came; they crowded to
the station bookstall and each came away with a paper. It was
the first number of a new literary review. I asked a man I knew
what this meant. He said:

"Well, I have had to put down my motor car. So I read
more." The other purchasers were peasants, graziers, small
tradesmen and the petite bourgeoisie in general. They had all
had to put down something, so they read more and wanted
instruction as to what to read. The first number of that journal
sold a prodigious number of copies throughout France.

I was stopping with the late Sir Alfred Mond—afterwards
Lord Melchett and probably the richest man in the world, if
riches be counted by possession rather than the control of
securities. It was at the time when the Liberal Government had

introduced the super-tax into the country's financial system. Panic was supposed to be besetting British industries.

I was talking to him before dinner about Marwood's sole contribution to *The English Review*. The government was then preparing its scheme of national insurance and Masterman had asked me to persuade Marwood to prepare an actuarial insurance plan for Masterman's private satisfaction. Marwood had protested violently. He was not the sort of fellow to do that sort of thing. He hated the government in any case. Why should he do anything towards the private satisfaction of Charles Masterman? In the end the fascination of the actuarial problem had proved too strong for him. He began making a few notes and gradually produced a complete scheme. I am too inexpert in mathematics to know if it had any influence on the government's legislation, but Masterman told me that it had some. Marwood's own proposal was that every employer of labour must be prepared to assure to every workman he employed, £400—$2,000—a year before being granted a license to start a company or build a factory. He assured me that that was perfectly practicable. Of course, as a Tory of the landowning class, he had a special distrust of all employers of labour and a special affection for the workingman as individual —if not for the working classes in the mass. He began to work out a complete survey of the trade of the United Kingdoms in order to prove his contention, but he died before it was finished. He used to assert that such a scheme was the only thing that would save western civilisation from inevitable Communism. I daresay he was right. On the other hand he saw no great reason why he should exert himself to save us from Communism. He was not really interested in the world after, say, 1668.

I met Mr. Bonar Law, afterwards Conservative Prime Minister, at a party at Lady St. Helier's at about that time and called his attention to the existence of Marwood. I suggested that his party might at least give Marwood secretarial assistance. He said depressedly that the Party had no funds for the purpose. It had more than a million sterling in its party chest

at the time. It was always called the Stupid Party—and proud
of it! It preferred giving the working classes beer about election times.

Well, Sir Alfred Mond had read Marwood's actuarial
scheme for State Insurance. It had appeared in two numbers of
The English Review. He discussed it with acumen, for he was
a man of extremely great intelligence. The only objection he
found to it was that he foresaw that it would not please the
Labour supporters of the government who by that time were
numerous and intelligent. They wanted the famous ninepence
for fourpence. Marwood's scheme worked out at something like
ninepence for something like 5.333 pence. I had asked Mr. John
Burns, the President of the Board of Trade and the first workingman to occupy a seat in the English Cabinet, what he
thought of the figures. He said that for his part they seemed
to him to be good enough but he agreed with Mond. The
extreme left of the Parliamentary Labour Party led by Messrs.
Keir Hardie, Ramsay Macdonald and Ponsonby would never
agree. They were the tail that wagged the Liberal dog.

When, then, Sir Alfred had finished his remarks on Marwood's scheme I congratulated him amiably on being one of
the too rare subscribers to the *Review*. He said that he was not
a subscriber but had read Marwood's article at his club. He
said that times were very bad owing to the super-tax and its
effect on business; his family insisted on having a new Rolls
Royce so he was cutting down his subscriptions to such periodicals as he did take in. He could not possbly contemplate paying half a crown a month for another. I took it that he was
half joking, half acting the part of the bluff Briton.

That was before dinner. After dinner, whilst the other
members of the house-party were playing billiards, I asked him
if the super-tax would really make any difference to him. He
said:

"Difference! What difference could it make? It will cost
me about £50,000 a year. I can make £100,000 by working five
minutes longer every day if I want to." I believe that was true.

Mond under a grotesque exterior had a supreme intelligence in the matter of commercial—and indeed of national—finance. And he had considerable æsthetic intelligence. His largesses to distressed practitioners of one art or the other were very great and they went to good people. He eventually bought *The English Review* and tried to run it on serious business lines. The affair was not very successful. It must have cost him a good deal more than the half-crown a month that he at first did not want to spend on it.

To me it had been obvious that the *Review* could not be run on any sort of sound commercial lines. Certainly I was not the person to attempt the feat. If Byles had been there to run it on the business side it might have done well enough. Or if Marwood had done it. But Marwood was physically prevented from doing anything of the sort. As a result of the cramming he had undergone at Clifton and Christ's College he had contracted tuberculosis of the bladder. The greater part of that organ had had to be removed with the result that he could not possibly live any sort of town life. He used therefore to come up and stay with me for a day or two every month whilst I was engaged in making up the month's number. But as to in any way taking part in business interviews outside my office that would have been impossible to him.

It was almost equally impossible to me. I have always given anyone any price they asked for anything and have always accepted any price that was ever offered me for my services. That does not work out very satisfactorily. I find that I am usually charged more than other people and the offers that are made to me for quite considerable labours are not unusually nothing at all. In addition, when making our joint agreement for the *Review*, Marwood and I had both undertaken not to take any profits, or any pay for contributions that we might make to the *Review* itself. If the undertaking made any profits, they were to be distributed to any of the contributors who cared to ask for them.

That was not unsatisfactory from the point of view of the

review itself. I used, pointing out that fact, to ask contributors to demand any rate of pay they liked, leaving it to their consciences to ask a fair average price for their work. That too worked out very well. One or two certainly asked for and got a great deal more than they had ever before imagined getting. On the other hand, many of the wealthier—and not a few of the quite indigent—writers wrote for me for nothing. I might however add as a corollary that a good many of these afterwards tried to get payment out of Lord Melchett, alleging that I had offered to pay them but had not done so. I suppose that that was in strictness true. It caused me to be a good deal discredited. I don't know what Lord Melchett did about it.

Once you sit in an editorial chair you conceive for contributors a singular dislike. They become "They." I used to receive on an average twenty manuscripts a day from the first day the periodical started to the day when I gave it up. Every one of the contributions I read myself. I had of course readers who went through the whole and proposed a number of them for acceptance. But although I would read those first I always later read and not infrequently annotated the others for the benefit of the writers. Then "They" would reply, and re-reply and re-reply until my patience and that of Miss Thomas, my admirable secretary, gave out altogether. When I proposed for the fifth time to answer a lady who remonstrated with me for refusing to publish a paper of verses on the solar system, whereas the Archbishop of Canterbury had praised a volume she had sent him, Miss Thomas absolutely refused to take down my letter. We hit at last on a scheme that considerably alleviated *that* trouble. If a person once written to wrote again, repeating his previous letter with variations, Miss Thomas without asking instructions would simply send him a carbon copy of my first letter. That must have caused a great deal of irritation. It was usually successful. Once it was not.

I had written to ask Mr. Arnold Bennett, who was then in Paris, to give me something, saying that I would pay him anything he liked to ask, but that I left it to his conscience to ask a fair average price. He wrote back that he never did business with editors direct. Presently arrived Pinker, the agent, with a short story, magnificent in execution but quite unsaleable to the commercial magazines owing to its length. Pinker asked me £40—$200—for it. I gave him thirty saying that Mr. Bennett had never received anything like that sum before for a short story. Pinker went off with the cheque quite contentedly.

The story duly appeared. On the day after its publication, I received a letter from Mr. Bennett:

"My dear H——. You owe me ten pounds. That story for which you paid Pinker thirty pounds was honestly worth forty."

I answered:

"My dear Bennett, I offered to pay you any sum you liked to ask for a contribution. You preferred to send me your agent. Agents are created by God to be beaten down. He sold the story to me for thirty pounds. I do not owe you anything."

Two days later I got a letter from Mr. Bennett. It read:

"My dear H——, You owe me ten pounds. That story for which you paid Pinker thirty pounds was honestly worth forty."

I told Miss Thomas to send him my first answer over again. I added: "H. G. tells me you are coming to London next Thursday. If you will dine with me that night and meet some friends I shall be delighted."

On the Thursday we were working in the office when there walked in a youngish man who said something I did not catch. Miss Thomas said:

"He says he is Bennett."

I said:

"Oh, yes, the hats are on the stairs."

In those days I used to have a great number of top-hats, so as to be assured of having always a newly ironed one to wear. They were supplied by the classic firm of Lincoln and Bennett who used periodically to send someone to take them away and iron them.

The stranger said:

"You owe me ten pounds. That story you bought of Pinker for thirty pounds was honestly worth forty.... If you will give me a cheque for ten pounds I will go home and dress and come back and dine with you. If you won't, I won't."

I was so overcome that I said to the inaudibly protesting Miss Thomas that she had better give Mr. Bennett his cheque. He took it and went off with grim satisfaction. He duly came to dinner. It was honestly worth ten pounds. I took peculiar pleasure in Bennett's company and conversation. I printed a good many things of his after that—notably his business play. I never paid him another penny and he never protested. He told me his scheme of life. He was going to have twenty thousand pounds in his bank before he had any relaxation of any kind, if he had to write day and night for it. After that he would splash. I used to see him on the Lower Corniche when I was at Mentone in the Red Cross Hospital. He would be walking slowly along with a magnificent carriage and pair following him. It would pick him up when he got tired or bored. He was splashing. I hope he liked it.

I went down with him one day by tram to dine with Thomas Seccombe who lived away to the devil, as the saying is. I think it must have been in Ealing. Seccombe was an industrious and wonderfully learned man whom we all loved. He did at the time enormous jobs in the way of writing encyclopædias which better known pomposities signed. He was afterwards instructor in military history to cadets at Camberley and died, I think, Professor of English Literature at McGill University in Canada. He was a good man.

We came back on top of a bus, Bennett and I. In passing a trolley car the bus ran into an electric light standard. A girl sitting on one of the forward seats began to scream. I went to her and she said that her side had hit the side-rail of the bus and hurt her terribly. A crowd had collected below including a couple of policemen. I told one of them to take the girl to the nearest doctor. The policemen said:

"You don't know the lower classes, sir. Sharp as weasels they are to get damages out of the great companies." I said:

"Take the girl to the doctor as I told you. I will pay his fee if she is not hurt."

There was a doctor's house just across the way. We streamed across it; the doctor examined the girl and found she had two of her short ribs fractured. The police then behaved like angels of kindness to her and conveyed her at their own expense to her home, since she refused to go to a hospital.

When I got back to the bus there was Arnold Bennett. He was standing on the top of it with his jaw hanging down. He said:

"You dare to talk to the police like that?"

I said: "Why not? Aren't the police there to do what you tell them to do?"

He said:

"In my walk of life as a boy and my father's as a grown workingman if we saw a policeman we got round the corner as quickly as we could. I still do. The idea of speaking to a policeman makes me shiver."

He was exaggerating of course, so as to impress me. His father could hardly be described as a workingman. He was I believe a lawyer's clerk and lawyer's clerks can usually manage the police very nicely, being certainly their social superiors in that singular maze of social strata, where the bricklayer will not eat at the same table with the bricklayer's labourer and the plasterer will not let his wife go out with the bricklayer's. But no doubt he had once had something of the feeling. For myself I have always regarded the policeman at the corner as a man who would fetch cabs for you if it rained, or post letters, or do any little job for the price of a pint. Once, just after the declaration of war, when Holland Park was picketed because anti-air guns were posted there, a policeman startled me as I was going home by jumping out of the shadows and exclaiming:

"Halt. Who goes there?" I said: "God damn and blast your

something eyes what do you mean by startling me?" He said: "Beg pardon, sir, I did not know that you were a gentleman."

The move of the hands in the clock was marked at that date by the attitude of D. H. Lawrence towards the guardians of order. For him they did not exist. He had never known any impulse to crime nor had anyone that he had ever known. The street in which he lived was so orderly that the police never patrolled it, and its inhabitants were not rich enough to need protection from burglars.

The last time I saw Bennett was towards the end of the War. I was sent for from my regiment to the Ministry of Information. They wanted me to write about peace terms. Masterman had asked me to prepare a plan for peace terms to submit to the Asquith Cabinet at the beginning of the War. I think they asked a number of other persons and collated their reports. My terms included the creation of a neutral federation of nations that should extend along the Rhine from Holland to Switzerland so as to serve as a buffer between France and Germany. It also provided for the creation of independent Republics round the Dardanelles, so as to protect Turkey from dismemberment. The creation of an independent Zionist Republic was also a part of my scheme.

I found Bennett in charge at the ministry. He asked me for suggestions for propaganda. I replied with a suggestion that the food supplies of the country could be immensely increased if agricultural labourers were provided with pigs and fowls to raise. He said that the farmers would never stand for it. They would be sure that the labourers would steal their grain to feed their own stock with. I said that now he had become a landed proprietor and put on flesh he had forgotten democracy. Then he asked me about my plan for a peace settlement. Was I prepared to write up Mr. George's proposals for a settlement? They were much less favourable to France. I said I had proposed to make a great strip of Alsace Lorraine an independent neutral Republic. He said that it would be in practice so under the thumb of France that it would serve merely as a jumping off ground to get across the Rhine into Germany. I began to lose my temper. He put me into communication by telephone with Sir William Tyrrell at the Foreign Office. My temper went altogether. I never spoke to anyone as I spoke to that invisible gentleman and I hope he never spoke to anyone else as he did to me about our allies. I was before then a Francophile, possibly of an unreasoning kind. I have been ever since a Francomaniac.

Bennett, who had been listening in on the conversation with attention and amusement, asked me nevertheless to write an article about the terms of peace. I said they would never print it. He said he would see that it was printed if it reached the Ministry. I went back to my regiment and between my duties wrote that article with despair and enthusiasm. I mailed it to the Ministry. It was lost in the post. There are things they manage very smoothly in England. Immediately afterwards the colonel-in-chief of the regiment reminded me that as a British officer I was forbidden to write anything.

His Excellency the Rt. Hon. the Lord Tyrrell is enormously popular as Ambassador to-day in Paris. I attended as a spectator the marriage of his daughter last year. It took place in Notre Dame de Paris. She was—and infinitely sympathetically—the first English woman to be married there since the days of Joan of Arc. May it be a firm omen!

I do not remember ever to have seen Bennett again.

The next contributor whose first writing we published in the *Review* I do not propose to mention by name. He came romantically—almost in answer to a prayer. But he subsequently waited on the editor of the *Times Literary Supplement* and threatened to horsewhip him if that gentleman allowed me to review any of his books in that organ. I cannot imagine myself writing for it and it is almost more impossible that it should ask me for contributions, so the threat was difficult to understand. I will call the Gentleman D. Z.

The efficacy of St. Anthony in guiding his votaries to lost objects has been doubted. I have màny and singular reasons for believing in it. Miss Thomas was the pearl of all secretaries. She could shorthand in seven languages and was so untemperamental that the only difference I felt between her presence and her absence was that I seemed unable to do anything right when she was not at the bureau that Carlyle had given to my father. She had just one defect. She never mislaid anything but the manuscript that at any given time I needed to go through. That went on for some time.

At last I sent her to Burns and Oates to buy a little image of St. Anthony. I ordered her to say a prayer in front of it every time she mislaid a manuscript. She never mislaid one after that. That was either because of the miraculous powers of the saint or because, being a strong Protestant, she was determined never to pray to him.

One day Marwood, she and I were lunching as we daily did in my dining-room which was above the office. I said to Marwood:

"The *Review* is rotten this month." He said:

"You might call it putrid."

So I asked Miss Thomas to be good enough to go down into the office and say a prayer to St. Anthony. He was to find a good contribution for that month's number.

From down stairs we heard her give a little squeak. It could not have been fear, for Miss Thomas was so expert at jui-jitsu that she could throw both Marwood and myself through the office window. But she came up again, saying rather agitatedly that there was an extraordinary looking man on the stairs.

He was extraordinary in appearance. It was just after Azev had tried to sell me the Tzar's diary and I was determined to have nothing to do with Russians. He seemed to be Russian. He was very dark in the shadows of the staircase. He wore an immense steeple-crowned hat. Long black locks fell from it. His coat was one of those Russian looking coats that have no revers. He had also an ample black cape of the type that villains in transpontine melodrama throw over their shoulders when they say "Ha-ha!" He said not a word.

I exclaimed:

"I don't want any Tzar's diaries. I don't want any Russian revelations. I don't want to see, hear or smell any Slavs." All the while I was pushing him down the stairs. He said nothing. His dark eyes rolled. He established himself immovably against the banisters and began fumbling in the pockets of his cape. He produced crumpled papers in rolls. He fumbled in the pockets of his strange coat. He produced crumpled papers in rolls. He produced them from all over his person—from inside his waistcoat, from against his skin beneath his brown jersey. He had no collar or I am sure he would have taken that off too and presented it too to me and it would have been covered with hieroglyphs. All the time he said no word. I have never known any one else whose silence was a positive rather than a negative quality. At last he went slowly down those stairs. I had the impression that he was not any more Russian. He must be Guy Fawkes.

He had thrust all those rolls into my arms. I went up again into the dining-room and dropped the rolls before Marwood. He looked at one of them for no more than a second and said:

"We are saved. St. Anthony has answered our prayer."

The article was called *Poles*. It was not about hop-poles or rods, poles, or perches. It was about the indigent Slavs or make-believe Slavs who victimise willing boarding-house keepers in the French capital and Provinces. I became then certain that Mr. D. Z. was himself a Pole. But he wasn't. He was actually born in the Western Continent and his costume was the usual uniform of the Paris student of those days. His writing was of extraordinary brilliance. He practised several arts.

I apparently conspired against him, so he threatened the editor of an Academic journal. That was rather like the action of the Almighty in killing the German colonel and his horse in Frankfort. I did not for many years—twenty at least—know how I had conspired. At last Ezra told me.

I had said to D. Z. one day:

"I wish you would give up your other arts and concentrate on writing. The other arts can look after themselves but in England writers are desperately needed." That proved that I was conspiring with Academicians to suppress his activities. There was nothing very singular in Mr. D. Z.'s suspecting me of willing his undoing. It was merely the form that his vengeance took that seemed to me singular. As far as I can remember, except for Ezra, not one of the writers whose first manuscripts I printed or whose second efforts I tried to give lifts to—not one of them did not in the end kick me in the face, as the saying is. Indeed if you believed my record as set down by my so-called protégés I must be the spider of my grandfather's image. It fell into an inkwell and then sprawled all across the whole ten commandments. That is Nature asserting itself. In the end the young cockerels must bring down the father of their barnyard. Without that the arts must stand still.

Mr. Norman Douglas walked into the office more normally with an introduction from Conrad. He came with an essay called *Sirens* which was, I think, the most beautiful thing we printed. It was his first work. Mr. Galsworthy introduced Mr. Mottram, now well known as the author of *Spanish Farm*.

The work of the *Review* grew harder, money grew scarcer. I secured a business manager in the person of my brother-in-law, Dr. Soskice, who put my accounts into some sort of order and found some fresh backers. As these were all of the moderate Left type, they did not like me much. I could always get on with the Extreme Right or the Extreme Left; moderates of any type I have always found insupportable.

It was not long before those gentlemen took over the *Review* leaving me as the nominal editor. Marwood resigned his share in the *Review* to me; Conrad refused to continue serialising his reminiscences in it. My controllers established a committee of censorship over my editing. They knew how to make censorship irritating. They had suffered from censors.

I saw that the end was not far off and took a flying visit to Provence. When I came back I found Mr. Galsworthy installed in my editorial chair. He had been nominated editor by the committee of censors. They had told him that I had gone for good. He resigned on my return. He had introduced one or two writers into my number which had gone to press before I left. I forget who they were but they gave the *Review* a distinctly more Left aspect. Its sales diminished very considerably. There was a small public for imaginative literature plus more or less imaginative handling of public matters but they were frightened away by moderate Left propaganda. The supporters of the moderate Left could not bear imaginative literature in their houses.

I raised money in various disagreeable ways—by impignorating my furniture and paintings, by borrowing from my father's richer relatives and others, by writing extremely bad novels at a very great speed. Count Metternich, the German Ambassador, suggested amiably that his government might like to hire the services of the *Review* and myself. He wanted to come and see me but hearing that I had lately had influenza he sent some Prince in a gorgeous carriage and pair. I think it was the hereditary Prince of Wied. I said that the German Government might if it liked buy the *Review* if it would pay off its creditors but it could not have my services. Prince Metternich then asked me to go and see him as soon as I could be quite certain that he would not catch influenza from me. He repeated his offer and paid me a number of compliments. He said that his Imperial master had sent me a personal message asking me to do my best to improve the relationships of the two countries. I said I had been doing it already but I could not carry it any further. I repeated that he could buy the *Review* but not my services.

The atmosphere of the Embassy alarmed me. The Am-

bassador had an odd, cautious way of speaking. I suppose it
was only the diplomatic manner. I got out of the Embassy
as quickly as I could and wrote an editorial to the effect
that any man who succeeded in cutting down the British navy
by as much as one howitzer would have about his head
before the decade was out, a cloud of human blood. Mr. Lloyd
George was then trying to whittle down the Navy Estimates.
I think that that was the first political article I ever wrote, but
I felt at the moment an overwhelming sense that an absolutely
omnipotent British Navy was the only guarantee of the peace
of the world as it was then constituted.

I saw shortly after that in a small German town—Hilde-
sheim, I think, a curious film. It was produced under the
auspices of the German Naval League. It represented wicked
conspirators, presumably British spies, trying to steal the
plans of the latest thing in German torpedo boats. The conspirators wore square beards, slouch hats, black spectacles
and all the paraphernalia that in England we gave to foreign
spies. It struck me as curious and it went on getting more and
more curious until at last a naval port, stated to be Kiel in
the close-ups, turned out to be a view of Spithead, with the
British Fleet, whilst sentries with hat-bands bearing the inscription "H.M.S. *Lion*" walked up and down in the foreground.
The German Naval League had hired a film promoted by their
British rivals. That was true economy.

My leader about the Navy shook out my Left-Centre supporters altogether. I struggled on but at last the struggle grew
impossible. For some reason in his inscrutable mind Marwood
rather counselled me to accept Count Metternich's offer and so
did Conrad. I suppose they thought that the *Review* would
have been more bearable under German auspices than under
those of a Left committee with a Russian president. I daresay I might have taken that view if it had not been for Count
Metternich's manner. As it was, I gave up and let the *Review*
go to Sir Alfred Mond who promptly installed a son of
Frederick Harrison as its editor. I thought at the time that

was much the same thing as selling it to Count Metternich. But I suppose it wasn't.

To some extent that undertaking had justified its existence for me. It had got together, at any rate between its covers, a great number—the majority of the distinguished writers of imaginative literature in England of that day and a great many foreign writers of distinction. It had been quite impossible to get the distinguished to come together in person. The attractions of their hilltops and attendant worshippers were too overpowering. Conrad came and stayed for several days with me on several occasions, but he always managed to be out at tea-time, in case anyone literary should come in. James always rang up on the telephone before coming to see me, so as to make sure of meeting no writers—and so it went down the list. I think that only one contributor to my first two numbers did not tell me that the *Review* was ruined by the inclusion of all the other contributors. James said: "Poor old Meredith, he writes these mysterious nonsenses and heaven alone knows what they all mean." Meredith had contributed merely a very short account of his dislike for Rossetti's breakfast manners. It was quite as comprehensible as a seedsman's catalogue.

Meredith said on looking at James' *Jolly Corner* which led off the prose of the review:

"Poor old James. He sets down on paper these mysterious rumblings in his bowels—but who could be expected to understand them?" So they went on.

With the younger writers it was different. They crowded into my office drawing-room, they quarrelled, they shouted. They attended on me like bodyguards when I took my walks abroad. I remember only one dull moment.

Most beautiful and incredibly wealthy ladies who liked to look up to those spirited young creatures and ask them to their dances used to crowd my office. It was rather a handsome large drawing-room in an old house. There were pictures by pre-Raphaelites, old furniture, a rather wonderful carpet. The

room was lit from both ends and L shaped so that if you
wanted a moment's private conversation with anyone you could
go round the corner. Miss Thomas, large, very blonde and
invariably good-tempered presided over the tea table. Ezra
looked after the cakes.

On the dull occasion nothing would go. I had a red-purple
velvet divan. It was the gift of my mother, so I had to display it. But it was a startling object. On it sat three young
men as dumb as milestones. Thomas Hardy remained for the
whole afternoon round the corner of that L talking in low
tones to the wife of the Bishop of Edinburgh.

The rest of the room was occupied by beautiful creatures
who had come specially to hear Thomas Hardy and those
young men. The young men sat side by side on that egregious
divan. Their legs were stretched out, their ankles were clothed,
as to the one pair in emerald green socks, as to the next in
vermilion and as to the next in electric blue. Merely to look
in the direction of that divan was to have a pain in the eyes.
The young men kept their hands deep in their trouser pockets
and appeared to meditate suicide. Ezra did not even eat any
cakes.

He had the toothache. Next to him was Gilbert Cannan:
he had just been served with papers in a disagreeable action.
Next to Cannan was Mr. Hugh Walpole. He had just published a particularly admirable novel called *Mr. Perrin and
Mr. Traill*. But he was suffering agonies of fear lest his charming mother, who was the wife of the Bishop of Edinburgh
and hidden round that corner, might hear something that
should shock her. I think myself that humorous lady, taking
a swallow's flight into Bohemia, would have liked to be a
little shocked.

Gilbert Cannan was in any case the most silent man
I have ever known. I used at about that time to take my
morning constitutional either with Ezra on the one side of me
and Mr. D. Z. on the other, or between Mr. Galsworthy and
Cannan. Cannan never once spoke during all those prome-

nades. Or . . . just once. We used to meet in Holland Street, cross Church Street, walk down the narrow passage going towards Kensington Palace, along the walls of the Palace, past the Round Pond, down the Row and so to the Achilles Statue, where we would part.

On one occasion when we were just parting, Cannan gave every sign of speaking. He really made a sound. We hung on his lips. We certainly both respected him as a profound thinker and were only too anxious to hear what he might have to say after so long a period of cogitation. It came. It was:

"I see Kent have beaten Sussex by four runs."

On one of those walks we perceived the blue-white beard, dark, fierce eyebrows, billy-cock hat and reefer coat of Mr. John Burns bearing down on us. He said:

"Come and have a walk with me, H . . . I feel queer." He detached me from my companions. It was certainly queer to see him in that frivolous place of cavaliers and parterres and sunlight and low laughter. He stopped dramatically and pointed at a flower bed.

"The last time I was here," he said, "walking along in a workingman's dress a policeman said to me: 'This ain't no place for the likes of you. Out you go . . .' Now . . ." and Mr. Burns with another sweep of his arm took in the whole landscape: "*I* planted them pelargoniums. . . . *I* had that statue of a naked boy put where it is . . . I had those trees re-arranged. That's a change. . . ." It was no doubt true, his Ministry having charge of His Majesty's Parks and a great many odds and ends of administration. But I could not see how he could have planned from memory of the place alone that admirable landscape.

He also—like so many other politicians—expressed unbounded admiration for my work. He once told me that he had written a book about me. I never saw it and hardly believed that he was in earnest. He had at one time the idea that I might help him write his memoirs. That was, I think, after his resignation. I should have liked to do it, for he had

taken part in a great many extraordinary affairs and his conversation was always very vivid. But the idea came to nothing.

His vitality was extraordinary. I was once huddled up in
a fur coat on top of a bus in mid-January with him. He said:
"You wear too many clothes. As for me you can see
everything that I have on and I am as warm as toast." I
could see: his billy-cock hat, his reefer coat, unbuttoned, a
waistcoat of the same material as the coat, trousers, a blue
shirt with a turned down collar, socks, shoes and a black tie.

I used to go in and see him at the Ministry in Whitehall and take him out to lunch at the *Mont Blanc* whenever
I wanted to get anybody a job that he could give or invent.
The *Mont Blanc* was a once rather famous French restaurant
—famous in literary circles. Edward Garnett used to give a
lunch there every Tuesday at which there attended quite usually Mr. Galsworthy, Edward Thomas, Conrad and Hudson,
when they were in town, Muirhead Bone, the etcher, his
brother, the master mariner, and a whole group of serious and
advanced individuals. I was regarded as too Philistine to be
very welcome but I used to go there frequently on other days
and with other guests.

One day Edward Thomas who was a writer of great delicacy and misfortunes—he died very gallantly in the War—
was sadly in need of a job. I went to find Mr. Burns and
said:

"Come out and lunch. I want you to meet somebody."

He said: "You aren't going to take me where I shall meet
any damn journalists. They overhear what I say and report it
all in their papers."

I said we would go to the *Mont Blanc*. He had lately
been perpetrating one of his indiscretions. When we got there
Edward Thomas came in and I introduced him to the President of the Board of Trade. The Customs Service looks after
our morals; the Board of Trade superintends our arts. Mr.
Burns said, with a tone of deep suspicion:

"Thomas? That's a Welsh name."

Thomas said he was Welsh. I said that I wanted Mr. Burns to give him the superintendence of the Welsh Ancient Monuments. Mr. Burns said:

"A Welshman.... Well, I suppose a Welshman ought to have that job." Then he raised his voice to a perfect roar to say: "But I hope he's not a blank blank blank of a Welshman like that blank blank blank...." Let us say Dai Bach. Meetings of His Majesty's Ministers are not love-feasts. There were not more than twenty journalists in that room.

Burns was one of the Ministers who resigned on the Asquith Cabinet's declaration of war with Germany. The last time I saw him was after that at the *Mont Blanc* where he had lunched with me. I said I supposed he had plenty of time to write his memoirs now, but I should not be able to help him because I expected to be going to France at once. We talked nevertheless about them and he told me a great deal about his childhood. We parted on the steps of the restaurant. His last words were—and for the first time his voice had a note of sadness:

"Never resign, H.... It doesn't pay."

CODA

On the twenty-eighth of June 1914 I stood on the edge of the kerb in Piccadilly Circus and looked at London. I did not know it but I was taking my last look at the city—as a Londoner. And yet perhaps I did know it.

I was feeling free and as it were without weight. It was a delicious day, the sky very high and bright above the Fountain; the flower-girls had brought with them a perfect mountain of colour. The Circus was blocked and blocked and blocked again with vehicles. The Season, with a week to run, was at its height. But I was going that night for a long stay to the birthplace of my great-great-grandfather, Dr. John Brown, at Duns in Berwickshire. I was finished with the Season. I was tired out and my private affairs in literature were all arranged for me. I had "made my effort," as racing people, say during the last six months. I had always held two things. No man should write more than one novel. No man should write that novel before he is forty. I had been forty six months before. On my birthday I had sat down to write that novel. It was done and I thought it would stand. There was to be no more writing for me—not even any dabbling in literary affairs.

The English Review seemed then profoundly to have done its work. Ezra and his gang of young lions raged through London. They were producing an organ of their own. It was to be called—prophetically—*Blast*.

One day Ezra and the young man I have called Mr. D. Z.

399

took me for a walk. In Holland Street D. Z. had grasped my arm as if he had been a police constable. Those walks were slightly tormenting. Ezra talked incessantly on one side of me in his incomprehensible Philadelphian which was already ageing. That made it all the more incomprehensible. Mr. D. Z., dark, a little less hirsute but more and more like a conspirator went on and on in a vitriolic murmur. On this occasion he raised his voice for a little, so as to be heard by me but not by Ezra. Ezra would not have stood for it.

D. Z. said:

"Tu sais, tu es foûtu! Foûtu! Finished! Exploded! Done for! Blasted in fact. Your generation has gone. What is the sense of you and Conrad and Impressionism. You stand for Impressionism. It is finished, *Foûtu*. Blasted too! This is the future. What does anyone want with your old-fashioned stuff? You try to make people believe that they are passing through an experience when they read you. You write these immense long stories, recounted by a doctor at table or a ship captain in an inn. You take ages to get these fellows in. In order to make your stuff seem convincing. Who wants to be convinced? Get a move on. Get out or get under.

"This is the day of Cubism, Futurism, Vorticism. What people want is me, not you. They want to see me. A Vortex. To liven them up. You and Conrad had the idea of concealing yourself when you wrote. I display myself all over the page. In every word. I...I...I...."

He struck his chest dramatically and repeated: "I...I... I... The Vortex. Blast all the rest." I was reminded of a young lady I once went to call on and who came running downstairs exclaiming:

"Devil, devil, devil take them all but me."

But Mr. D. Z. was perfectly right. I don't mean that I only thought then that he was right. I think it now. Impressionism *was* dead. The day of all those explosive sounds had come. Louder blasts soon drowned them out and put back the hands of the clock to somewhere a good deal the other side of mere Impressionism. But in that moment they were undoubtedly all right. It was in a sense another foreign invasion, like the one with which this book opens. There was hardly a born Londoner in it. D. Z., Ezra, H. D., the beautiful poetess, Epstein, Fletcher, Robert Frost, Eliot were all trans-Atlantically born from the point of view of London. Henri Gaudier was a Marseillaise. They had all become Londoners because London was unrivalled in its powers of assimilation—the great, easy-going, tolerant, loveable old dressing-gown of a place that it was then. It was never more to be so.

Those young people had done their best to make a man of me. They had dragged me around to conspiracies, night-clubs, lectures where Marinetti howled and made noises like machine-guns. They had even tried to involve me in their splits. Of course they split. The Ezra-D. Z. contingent blasted another contingent led by Mr. Nevinson the artist. Those continued I think to call themselves Futurists. I was, I suppose, identified with the Vorticists. At any rate for years after that every time that Mr. Nevinson met me he would say: "How fat you are!"—which was supposed to be blasting. Ezra, on the other hand—out of affection—used to call me "the pink egg." So they pranced and roared and blew blasts on their bugles and round them the monuments of London tottered.

I went home after that conversation and wrote my farewell to literature—quite formally. It was printed in a short-lived periodical called the *Thrush*. Thrushes had no chance of making themselves heard in those days. The Vorticists kindly serialised my novel—my Great Auk's Egg, they called it. The Great Auk lays one egg and bursts. That bird was no louder than a thrush in the pages of *Blast*.

So I was done with letters—and with the Left. Of what I was going to do I had little notion. But Provence still called. I had paid a prolonged visit to the neighbourhood of Tarascon just before and chosen my house. I had written a long poem about Heaven which I had placed in the Alpilles, tiny grey mountains just outside the town of Tartarin. That poem had produced remarkable reverberations in America. It was given prizes, crowned with gilt laurel leaves. Leaders were written about it in many of the newspapers of the Eastern sea-board. It was said to have put up the marriage-rate in New York. Elinor Wylie, the beautiful poetess and most beautiful woman, told me that she and her husband, William Benet, had become engaged whilst reading my poem to each other in Central Park.

In England its publication was stopped by the police. Mr. Courtney proposed to publish it in the *Fortnightly Review* but was a little afraid. Masterman took it to the Home Secretary. The Home Secretary said that if it were published he would have to authorise a prosecution. It gave a materialist picture of heaven. God appeared in it. It is against the law for God to appear in England. That poem was, during the War, published under the auspices of the Ministry of Information—as government propaganda! It might encourage young men who were about to die if they thought they would go to a nice heaven.

Masterman had a good deal of it by heart. Whilst we had been in Germany together he had driven me nearly crazy by quoting at the most inopportune moments—when I was making out a railway schedule or deciphering the bills of our party— by remarking in his solemn and unctuous parliamentary voice:

> *"But these there must be in Heaven*
> *...Even in Heaven."*

We had gone up the Rhine from the source to Bingen, crossed over the Eiffel range to Trêves, visited the battlefields of 1870. All the time I was trying to keep Masterman's nose on the grindstone. He was supposed, with my interpretation, to be interviewing German waiters as to the workings of their insurance act. At Metz he asked a waiter what nationality he considered himself. The waiter answered:

"Muss-Preussen"—"Obligatory Prussian." After that Masterman was saying on every available occasion: *"Muss-*

Preussen—We're all going to be *Muss-Preussens* before long, Ford old dear."

We drove in a horse-drawn landau to Sedan. Masterman had finally struck against waiter-interviews. He wanted to see battlefields.... He had a passion for the study of military strategy. I should never have gone to see a battlefield. Masterman knew the position of every battalion of Würtembergers or Saxons at every hour during the day of the battle.

As we drove back the coachman from his box called down about half a dozen times:

"Wollen die Excellenzen durch Frankreich fahren?" "Do the Excellencies wish to be driven through France?" It was the first time we had been called Excellencies. We were travelling incognito. Masterman said:

"What's he saying? What's he saying?"

Wherever a German had been buried in French soil along that border the Prussians had driven out a tongue of land and made it German. The direct road went all through these strips. Half the apples on a tree in that late July weather might be German, half French. Masterman said:

"Before long, Ford old dear, the taxi-men in Piccadilly will be saying: 'Do you want to be taken through England or up Oxford Strasse?' "

He had a sardonic humour, that large, sleepy, always smiling, crooked-nosed statesman.

At Metz Station the station-master—of the rank of major-general and covered with decorations—was waiting for us at the salute at the foot of the immense flight of granite steps.

He said: "Will the Excellencies deign to hurry a little? We are keeping our Constantinople-Berlin Express waiting for them."

Mrs. Masterman had a kodak. She shot it at everything she passed. It was forbidden to photograph anything in the Metz district. She snapshotted policemen, generals on horseback, troops on the march, odd-looking ditches and mounds, placarded VERBOTEN, and running as if without purpose along hill sides. On the boat before Bingen the camera had got out of order. It had been repaired in Trêves. When she developed all her films after arriving in London there was not one that shewed anything but the extreme tops of church steeples, the eagles on the tops of generals' helmets, or the tops of the heads of storks standing over their nests on gables. They used to manage things quite well in old Germany. They did not want to interfere with the innocent amusements of a British Cabinet Minister's wife but they had had her camera lens elevated by the repairer.

When we got back to Trêves I went up a hill with Mrs. Masterman so that she might photograph the great view, going into France. There was on top of the hill a column and on top of the column a colossal virgin. The view from the top of the column was so immense and impressive that she said Charlie *must* see it. Charlie did not much like climbing.

So I took him up there that afternoon. He refused to climb the column but the view from the base was sufficient. We lay sleepily on the turf in the hot afternoon.

Seven hundred feet below us a great, beautiful white bird, with the tips of its wings turned back, glided noiselessly along above a green field and dipped with supreme grace to rest. I had never seen an aeroplane before. So the first I ever saw was a German war-plane and I saw it from above. We were looking over the Trêves aerodrome.

I was studying my map. I said:

"There's Longwy...."

Masterman, whose eyes had been closed, sat bolt upright and said:

"Where?... Where's Longwy?"

The *Daily Mail* that we received with the other papers from England had been very pointedly and with great satisfaction calling attention to Longwy. The French had been making enormous fortifications and massing troops out there in the grey district over which the heat shimmered. That was why I had said: "There's Longwy."

Masterman looked at the small, dark patch in that plain for a very long time. Suddenly he said:

"By this date next year we shall be at war with Germany." It was the second of August 1913. He was two days out.

As for me I screamed with laughter. It was almost too good a joke. I knew Germany as well as it was possible to know a country; I had lived there for long periods; I had connections with her from innumerable angles. I had even at one time contemplated settling in Germany for good. I had found that impossible because life there was too bitter and hard and the poverty too great. If I had two settled convictions they were those of pity for the distress of the German people and absolute belief in their love of peace. I still retain my absolute belief in their love of peace. Just before that date I had made a speech at a dinner of one of the great city companies—the Cordwainers, I think—. I had declared my conviction that nothing in the world would ever make the German people go to war. The authorities might wish it, but the people would refuse. It was mostly among members of the Left that I had lived in Germany. Substantially that was what happened. German Authority did not win the War because the heart of the people would not stay the distance. Of that I am convinced.

I went on jeering and jeering at Masterman. I said: "You Liberals are all mad. I suppose your friend Dai Bach wants to prevent German pheasants from eating German mangold wurzels. Why should Germany go to war?"

He said grimly: "The roar of foreign guns has not been heard in London since 1662. And then only that once. You'll have that experience in 1914. Germany will go to war next August because by then she will be on the verge of bankruptcy."

We never mentioned the subject again till the third of August 1914. On that day Masterman told me that a majority of the Cabinet, of which majority he was one, had delivered an ultimatum to Germany which meant certain war ... if the German troops crossed the Belgian frontier.

I said—it was in the hall of the Foreign Office in Whitehall:

"The German troops will never cross the Belgian frontier.... Never ... Never ... Never ..."

Next morning about eleven his secretary rang me up and said:

"Mr. Masterman asks me to tell you that the Germans crossed the Belgian frontier near a place called Gemmenich at four o'clock this morning."

I could not believe it. Gemmenich is near Spa. I knew Spa as well as it was possible to know a small town that one visits frequently and whose Spa doctor attended to one's family's complaints.

I shall say nothing more about the War. But at Spa on the day after Masterman had made that prophecy there happened one of the great tragedies of my life. We had bought a good deal of wine from the landlord of the *Hotel zur Post* in Trêves. I had been there often and knew him well. As a reward for having brought him a British Excellency he gave me a bottle of 1813. In the Mosel there is a stone that is only uncovered in years of great drought—which are years of glorious vintages. On such years they chain a barrel of brandy to that stone. When it is again uncovered they remove the old barrel and chain on a new one. That stone had not been uncovered since 1813. The bottle that the host gave me had been filled from the 1813 barrel.

I told him that the host had given it to him. I liked to see him look pleased; his face lit up so cherubically.

He was *immensely* pleased. He said:

"Hurray. We will give it to George when he comes to lunch. He's a connoisseur of liqueurs." Only a little later he would have wished to fill his liqueur glasses on such occasions with prussic acid. Or perhaps castor oil. In the night at Spa Masterman had toothache. He used up the entire contents of that bottle, pouring it into his mouth and spitting it out. He could have got a bottle as strong for one franc fifty by signing his bill.

So I stood on the kerb in the Circus and felt adrift.

The day before I had attended the congress of German professors of history that had assembled in London. Professor Delbrück had been immensely interested in the scorpion that I carried in my cigarette case. It came from the Château d'Amour in the Alpilles. It died next day. From there I had taken some Americans to see the House of Commons. Mr. Burns had kindly shewed them around. As we stood in Westminster Hall he pointed to the arch at the end of the building and said:

"The first time I went through there was on my head. I was being thrown out." He explained that he had been with some deputation visiting some minister when he had been a workingman and his remarks had given offence.

I said: "Well, John, the next time you distinguish yourself here it will be by throwing Christabel out through the arch."

Christabel Pankhurst was the leader of the W.S.P.U.— the Militant Suffragettes. Burns exclaimed: "My God! is there a raid coming?" He turned white as chalk; his features expressed panic. He dashed up to the nearest policeman and I could hear him telling the man to telephone to Scotland Yard for reinforcements. That was what happened when you merely mentioned those ladies in the precincts of the House of Commons in those days.

We were sitting at tea on the terrace with one of the other ministers when Mr. Justice Darling became visible at a distance. The minister said: "There's old Darling. He's trying the Suffragettes. We've promised him an earldom if he gives it to them hot."

I took it that he was joking. But perhaps he wasn't. That is why I do not mention his name. I said:

"Why *don't* you give women the vote?" He answered:

"I'll tell you. My election agent tells me that if women

had the vote in my constituency they would vote two to one against me and I should lose my seat. What price my seat?"

I was supposed by those gentlemen to be in the inner councils of the Suffragettes and to arrange outrages for them. I wasn't, though I had the most intense admiration for those noble and beautiful-souled women. But I gave them all the help I could both in writing and with suggestions. I wrote for them a pamphlet called *This Monstrous Regiment of Women*. It is the only work of mine that I care to mention by name in these pages ... and proud of it still!

I will give in twenty-three words the reason for my conviction. In England of those days the only people who were refused citizenship were children, criminals, lunatics—and the mothers of our children.

That seems to be a sufficient reason. It is not a good thing for children that their mothers should be branded as one with criminals and lunatics. I think that the only reason I had in my mind for returning to London was my determination to aid those women in attaining what they wanted, and anxiety as to the future. The militant agitation had reached such extreme lengths and the government's opposition was so stubborn. I was filled with real dread. I knew of thousands—but thousands and thousands of women who were ready and would for certain sacrifice their lives to their cause in the coming autumn. The House was shortly to rise and there would be peace on the whole till September. I did not see how the country could possibly go on.

And the thought of the sufferings, mental or physical, of those women tormented me. They were the best women in the country. In the world or ever, perhaps. They shrank unspeakably from publicity and from physical suffering. Yet they confronted both as unshrinkingly.

I had stopped to dinner in the house with Mr. Hugh Law, Nationalist Member for, I think, a division of Dublin. I was warmly friendly with many Irish M.P.s and their supporters. I used to give a small tennis party every Thursday after-

noon and the most frequent players—apart from Ezra who
plays tennis like a galvanised, agile gibbon—had been Irish
members of whatever complexion. Mr. Law, the Nationalist,
would play side by side with Mr. Moore the Ulster Unionist.
They would crack Irish provincial jokes one with the other
all through the afternoon with Ezra standing on his head
on the other side of the net. In the evening from opposite
sides of the House of Commons they would call down the
curse of God one upon the other with unmistakable passion
and sincerity. I knew quite well the two gentlemen I have
mentioned, Mr. Stephen Gwynn, Professor Kettle, a number
of Ulster gun-runners and a number of violent Sinn Feiners.
So that obviously I could know nothing about the Irish
question. I once tried from the lips of several Nationalists
of differing shades of opinion to give some account in an
editorial in *The English Review* of an outrage that excited
them all equally. But when Mr. Law and Mr. Gwynn and
Mr. Kettle and several others had had their say I could
not tell, as it were, whether the member of the Royal Irish
Constabulary had murdered the widow woman and stolen her
goose or whether the widow's goose had bitten the policeman's leg off. And it was all inextricably mixed up with the
fact that Dublin Castle would pay no attention to the dis-
graceful condition of the door to the telephone bureau in
Rathmines sub-post office.

So after dinner that night I had finally said to Mr. Law:
"What do you want? How would you propose to settle
the Irish question?" He said: "Do you want to know?
People don't really want to know."

I said that I wanted it passionately. A dreamy look came
into his poetic eyes. He said:

"Och. Just give me the Connaught Rangers and let me
go through the Three Counties with them."

It would no doubt have settled the question. The Connaught Rangers were the toughest Catholic Irish troops in

His Majesty's Army. The three counties were the Loyal and Protestant North.

Two years ago I happened to find in New York my engagement book for 1914. As I had made up my mind to make that city my headquarters from then on I had taken a number of old papers over there in order to sort them out and store them. The engagement book was by chance among them. It was tied up with the soiled, soaked translation into French of my one novel. I had begun to make it in Bécourt-Bécordel Wood in July 1916.

The engagement book was an amazing, packed affair. From the middle of May to the end of June, except for the week-ends which I had spent either at Selsey, where I lived next to Masterman and the editor of the *Outlook,* or at other people's country houses—there were only six days on which I did not have at least three dinner and after-dinner dates. There would be a dinner, a theatre or a party, a dance. Usually a breakfast at four after that. Or Ezra and his gang carried me off to their night club which was kept by Mme. Strindberg, decorated by Epstein and situated underground.

London was adorable then at four in the morning after a good dance. You walked along the south side of the park in the lovely pearl grey coolness of the dawn. A sparrow would chirp with a great volume of distinct sound in the silence. Another sparrow, another—a dozen, a hundred, ten thousand. They would be like the violins of an orchestra. Then the blackbirds awakened, then the thrushes, then the chaffinches. It became the sound of an immense choir with the fuller notes of the merle family making obbligatos over the chattering counterpoint of the sparrows. Then, as like as not, you turned into the house of someone who had gone before you from the dance to grill sausages and make coffee. Then you breakfasted—usually on the lead roof above a smoking-room, giving onto a deep garden. There would be birds there too. Those who cannot remember London then do not know what life could hold. Alas. . . .

I had behind me other activities. I wrote a shadow play for Mme. Strindberg and had to act it myself in place of the lovely actress who should have done it. A too ardent admirer of Mme. Strindberg had stolen the manuscript because he could not bear to let my play be produced.

One night I came home rather earlier than usual and found Lady Gregory camped on my doorstep. She said:

"You have got to finance and manage the Irish Players."

I said:

"Delighted! But why?"

Miss Maire O'Neill the adorable Pegeen Mike of *The Playboy of the Western World* had attended a public meeting of Suffragettes. Miss Horniman, the guarantor of the company in England, had telegraphed from Liverpool that she would withdraw the subsidy if she did not receive an unconditional apology from every member of the company. The company had refused.

Lady Gregory said: "You will have to do it. You are responsible for the Suffragettes. It was reading you made Maire O'Neill go to that meeting."

I said: "How much do you want?" She said: "Two thousand pounds." I said: "All right. I will get it for you," and we drove to the theatre where W. B. Yeats was rehearsing *The Well of the Saints*.

Their publicity had not been very well managed and we put on the *Playboy* for the first time to a perfectly empty house. Very few of the critics had cared to come. The Irish Players played that play as if it had been the direst tragedy ever written. For the second performance I had bought all the reserved seats in the house and had sent them to all London. All London came. You never saw such a house. There was over half the Cabinet and more than half of the Opposition Front Bench. Mr. Balfour and Mr. Burns sat together in the middle of the front row of the stalls; there were ambassadors; shoals of titles. We just missed having royalty because there was something going on at the other Court. Ours was the Court Theatre.

The Players played the *Playboy* as if it had been a roaring farce. The night before it might have been *Œdipus Tyrannus*. It is susceptible of both treatments.

Ellen Terry said a pretty thing. At the supper that we gave on the stage she lost a great paste star that she had been wearing. When it was given back to her she held it over Maire O'Neill's head. She said:

"My dear, 'a star danced and underneath it you were born.' This is the star. Take it." It had been said to her before that. She meant that she was resigning her place to that young thing. She had the most graceful gestures and kindnesses of any woman that ever lived.

Four—or perhaps three—Christmas days ago I saw those same Irish players playing *Juno and the Paycock* in New York to five people, including two that I had brought. They came home with me after the play and I gave them grilled sausages and Dublin stout. It must have been Mr. Allen Tate, the beautiful poet, who found those not too easily found comestibles in New York on Christmas day at one in the morning. They were as gay as on the second night of the *Playboy* at the Court.

The money for the subsidy did not at first seem difficult to obtain. But an unforeseen difficulty arose. I had organised one or two drawing-room meetings at the houses of people like Governors of the Bank of England who lent them kindly enough. We needed a relatively small sum, for the company was doing pretty well. The *Playboy* at least played to bumper houses. There was by then a committee of which Mr. Shaw was the president.

We organised a really swell meeting in the studio of Mr. Jacob Epstein at Chelsea. There must have been an enormous sum of money represented in that room. I had to make my appeal for funds first because I was going on somewhere else. I made the silly sort of speech that you make on such occasions. I said that if you wanted to keep Ireland quiet the best thing you could do would be to give the Irish good theatres. Before I had finished speaking the Monds, Wertheimers, Speyers and the usual subscribers to things of the sort had sent me up notes saying that they would subscribe between them a good deal more than was needed. I hurried away rejoicing.

When I went home to dress, Lady Gregory was again occupying my doorstep. She said:

"What are we to do now?" I asked about what? She said:

"To raise that money."

Mr. Bernard Shaw had spoken after me. He had said:

"You idle rich. You are the last sort of people who should come to a meeting like this. Catch you subscribing a penny. All you think of is..." I don't remember what it was but his words were to that effect. All those subscribers had withdrawn their promises of subscriptions. We had to begin all over again.

A little earlier in the season London had been startled by an invitation running: YOU ARE INVITED TO DINNER AT THE PALL MALL RESTAURANT TO CELEBRATE ONE OF THE WEDDINGS OF MARY QUEEN OF SCOTS. No one knew who had issued the invitation. But a great many people went and we met every one that we knew and a great many people that we were glad to know. The dinner was admirable, the wines exceedingly well selected. Still we had no idea who were our hosts and hostesses. Suddenly a delightfully dainty little blonde lady escorted by an extraordinarily humorous looking red-headed Scotsman was on a little dais making a little speech with a strong Chicagoan intonation. She said:

"Friends. Today is my birthday. I was in London and lonely. I wanted you all to dine with me. But I knew you would none of you dine with me if I said 'Please come and dine with Mary Borden Turner on her birthday.' So I looked in the calendar and found it was the wedding anniversary of another Mary."

The gentleman who had escorted her burst into laughter. He was the husband of that delightful person. Mrs. Turner immediately became an extremely popular London hostess. Now she had taken the manor house in the village of my great-great-grandfather's birth. That ancestor of mine was a remarkable person. He was the first anti-lancet doctor. The Scots doctors expelled him from the Scottish faculty of medicine; their English confrères put him into prison, where he died. Napoleon always had any of John Brown's pupils whom his forces took prisoner released as benefactors to humanity.

It was with the consciousness at the back of my head that I was going to visit the birthplace and be sheltered by the roof of the Turners that I stood on the kerb in the Circus and looked up at the sky. I was not to look up at that sky again until it was dark indeed. As a matter of fact one looks very seldom at the skies in great cities. But on that night all London was blacker than the grave. She had attained to a gravity and augustness that she had never had before. She had come into line with all the great capitals of the world. She had heard the roar of foreign guns and had suffered.

I went home to pack my things. Next morning I was on the high platform of Berwick station. Berwick town is in Berwickshire and Berwickshire in Scotland. But Berwick town is neither English nor Scottish. It is "juist Berwick." The King's proclamations are ordered to be affixed to the church doors of England, Scotland, Wales and Ireland and the town of Berwick on Tweed. I once had a cousin who was Mayoress of Berwick.

The air was very clear. The North Sea very blue. London was far away. I bought a newspaper—a Liberal sheet of the more grandmotherly kind. It told me that the Suffragettes were naughty, naughty girls and that they must be stopped. It was very angry with the King over several pages. The King was acting almost—oh but only just almost—unconstitutionally. He had asked all the leaders of all the Irish parties to meet in a Round Table conference at Buckingham Palace under his own Presidency. The *Daily News* said it was a really very naughty King.

I imagined I knew all about that. I had seen Masterman a month before really angry for the first time in my life. He said that the King was impossible to get on with. He was as determined that the Irish Question should be settled to the satisfaction of all his Irish subjects, as his father had been to have the Entente Cordiale with France. The Cabinet was unanimously against the Buckingham Palace conference. They wanted to do nothing that could enhance royal prestige. The matter had come to an absolute impasse.

Finally, according to Masterman—and I made a note of his words immediately afterwards. It was the only note I ever made, but the occasion seemed very extraordinary—the King had said:

"Very well, gentlemen. I am the richest commoner in England. If you wish me to abdicate I will abdicate, supposing that to be the wish of the country. But before that we will have a general election and I have not much doubt as to the results as between you and me." So he had his conference.

I was immensely glad. All my life I had been a passionate Home Ruler. I hate, I hate, I hate—three times—the idea of people of one race and religion being ruled over by people of alien race and another religion. But the Irish Question was a nightmare—a worse nightmare than the case of the Suffragettes. Here was a majority of one island with a minority of another religion and at intense enmity one with the other. The thought of the Connaught Rangers or the King's Royal Rifles going through the Three Counties was unspeakable. And then ... inside the territory of that Protestant minority was a tiny Catholic minority, as inside the Catholic territory of the majority was a small Protestant minority. Not even an Abbey Theatre in every village in Ireland could stop bloodshed in that sorrowful country. So I was glad the King was determined to have that question settled to the satisfaction of all parties of his Irish subjects. There had been a mutiny of English officers in the camp at Curragh outside Dublin. ...

I was putting down the paper with its large anti-Royal and anti-feminine headings. I had a sudden sinking at the heart—most sinister feeling. There was a three-line paragraph —such is editorial prescience—tucked away at the bottom of a page and headed minutely:

AUSTRIAN HEIR MURDERED IN SERAJEVO

It was London's news of the 28th June, 1914, reaching me there in a border town.

I said to myself:

"Oh, the Socialists and Labour will stop a war. They are the tail that wags the Liberal dog all the world over." And I really believed it and got into the branch train for Duns with a serene heart.

Duns Manor was delightful. The hospitable Turners had allowed me to suggest some of the guests. So Mr. D. Z. was there and Ezra was to have come, and the turf of the Scottish lawns was like close, fine carpeting and the soft Scottish sunshine and the soft Scottish showers did the heart good. And my grandfather's birthplace was a pretty old cottage and I played golf on Morpeth Town links with a cobbler, a descendant of my great-great-grandfather's great uncle. He was a wonderful player. He carried a cleek with him and a couple of balls on his morning walk across the links from his cottage in the outskirts to his cobbler's stall in the town. Before every difficult shot he said:

"Aye, this will take some heid wark," and took from his pocket, whilst he surveyed the line his ball was to take, an immense flask that he called a half mutchkin. He drank slowly and long. Then his ball lay dead.

We sat on the lawns in the sunlight and people read aloud —which I like very much. D. Z. had brought the proofs from

Blast of my one novel. I read that. Mrs. Turner who has become a novelist of really great gifts and authenticity read from some magazine the instalments of the work of a writer of whom I had never heard. His name was James Joyce. I thought the magazine was the *Little Review* and the story *Ulysses*, but I have been reminded that it could not have been. It must then have been *The Portrait of the Artist as a Young Man.* So for me Armageddon was bridged.

On the fourth of August the Northern Edition of *The Daily Mail* appeared with, on its placards:

NORTHERN BOXING COMPETITION
MORPETH CHAMPIONSHIP